The Greville Memoirs

The Greville Memoirs

—————————⊙—————————

Edited by
ROGER FULFORD

The Macmillan Company
NEW YORK

*For copyright reasons, paperback copies of this
book may not be issued to the public, on loan or otherwise,
except in their original soft covers*

Library of Congress Catalog Card Number: 63-15933

FIRST PUBLISHED 1875–87
REVISED EDITION © ROGER FULFORD 1963

FIRST PUBLISHED IN THE UNITED STATES OF AMERICA
BY THE MACMILLAN COMPANY, 1963

Made and printed in Great Britain
by William Clowes and Sons, Limited, London and Beccles

Contents

LIST OF ILLUSTRATIONS   vii

ACKNOWLEDGMENT   ix

INTRODUCTION   xi

The Memoirs

1821	1
1822	7
1823	17
1824	26
1830	27
1831	61
1832	86
1833	100
1837	102
1838	137
1839	149
1841	176
1842	177
1845	203

Contents

1847   231

1848   241

1851   265

1854   273

1857   280

1860   287

INDEX   289

List of Illustrations

facing page

'The Bad Hat': Grey removes William IV's crown while
Brougham makes off with the King's conscience   64
     From a print of April 1831

Lord Melbourne   65
     Detail of the portrait by Sir Edwin Landseer

The Duke of York   65
     Detail of a portrait after John Jackson

Princess Lieven   80
     From a lithograph after a drawing by John Lucas

Lord George Bentinck   80
     Detail of the portrait by Samuel Lane, 1836

The Ranton Shooting Party   81
     Detail of the painting by Sir Francis Grant

The Coalition Ministry, 1854   256
     From a pencil-and-wash drawing by Sir John Gilbert, 1855

Lord Palmerston   257
     From the portrait by John Partridge, 1846

Charles Spurgeon   257
     Detail of the portrait by Alexander Melville

List of Illustrations

facing page

Lord John Russell 272
 From a pencil-and-watercolour drawing by G. F. Watts

Lord Clarendon 272
 Detail of the drawing by George Richmond

Charles Greville 273
 From a portrait, about 1855, in the Goodwood Collection

Acknowledgment

The Publishers wish to thank the following for permission to reproduce illustrations appearing in this book:

The Trustees of the British Museum for the illustrations facing pages 64 and 80 (top); the Earl of Clarendon for page 272 (bottom); the Trustees of the Goodwood Collection for page 273; the Earl of Lichfield for page 81; and the National Portrait Gallery for pages 65 (both), 80 (bottom), 256, 257 (both) and 272 (top).

The jacket is reproduced, by courtesy of the Trustees of the British Museum, from the entry for 2nd May 1821 in the manuscript of *The Greville Memoirs* (Add. MSS. 41097).

Introduction

The Greville Memoirs are the outstanding authority for the political history of this country from 1827 to 1860. They are also extremely valuable for what they tell us about foreign affairs within those years, and they are important for the vivid picture they give of official and social life under George IV and William IV and during the first two decades of Queen Victoria's reign.

They have rather unaccountably been called 'Memoirs' whereas the more graphic and more correct description would be the Greville 'Diaries' or the Greville 'Journal'. 'Memoirs' are generally a biography or history, compiled later from notes or diaries kept at the time by the writer. The Greville Memoirs are on the contrary a journal, written at the time of the events which the writer is chronicling. They are a day by day record, though not kept every day, which has come down to us virtually unaltered from the days on which it was written. Their writer read them through, especially as he grew older, but he did not tamper with the text, though he occasionally commented on their accuracy or interest and very occasionally deleted a passage which he thought unfair or which recalled some transitory scandal best forgotten. These adjustments of the text are really an indication of the writer's anxiety to be fair and accurate: they affect only a fragment of the million and more words which he wrote and do not dull the contemporary freshness of the diary.

Charles Cavendish Fulke Greville can best be described as a broad-minded and intelligent product of the Whig aristocracy, with very powerful connexions but slender private means, and therefore driven to an active life by lack of wealth. He was a member of the distinguished family of which Lord Warwick is now the head, and his grandfather, Fulke Greville, was a man of some note in the eighteenth century who appears in Fanny Burney's diary and Boswell's *Life of Johnson*. Charles Greville's mother was Lady Charlotte Bentinck, daughter of the Prime Minister, Duke of Portland. This family connexion explains why Charles Greville was able to write the vivid obituary of Lord George Bentinck which begins on page 251. Lady Charlotte was the intimate friend of the Duke of Wellington, and the diarist's younger brother, Algernon, was the Duke's private secretary. His only sister married Lord Ellesmere. These family connexions gave him an assured position in society, and an opportunity of mixing in circles which were well-informed.

Charles Greville was born in 1794, and he was educated at Eton and Christ Church. He left Oxford, without taking a degree, on being appointed private secretary to the Secretary of State for War. His duties in this office were not arduous, and he became a popular young man in London society. As was the habit in Regency days he conducted some well-publicised love affairs: his correspondence with a baronet's wife about their child was intercepted by the husband and somewhat shamelessly read by him to his cronies in White's Club. He never married.

Through the influence of his grandfather, the Duke of Portland, he was made, when he was ten, Clerk-Extraordinary to the Privy Council. This ensured him the reversion to the joint-clerkship, which in fact fell vacant in 1821. This Government office prevented him from leading a political life, for which he was by nature suited, but it was a vantage point from which he could observe the working of the machinery of government. Also through his grandfather he was given a sinecure appointment as Secretary of the Island of Jamaica. The emoluments of the two offices—the Privy Council where he worked and the Jamaica secretaryship in which he paid someone else to do the work—brought him in a spending income of between £3,000 and £4,000 a year. He always lived far in excess of this income.

No doubt the reason for this was horse-racing. He describes in the diary some of his successes on the turf, but he must also have lost large sums of money. He never won the Derby, though one of his best-known horses, Orlando, had won that race before he bought it. That was in the celebrated Running Rein Derby, when Running Rein was disqualified, and the race given to Orlando. He also owned Alarm, and his horse Mango won the St. Leger in 1837. As a young man he had been in charge of the Duke of York's racing stable, and he was an old and respected member of the Jockey Club. But he could never be called a gay addition to a company of racing men for he was always despondent. Lord Winchilsea, who wrote an amusing poem about the misfortunes of one of Greville's horses, called him Gruncher Gruel Esq. (Among his intimates he was known as Punch or Gruncher.) He gives us no very detailed accounts of his experiences on the turf, but he was assailed by an almost morbid loathing of the time he wasted there and particularly of the company he encountered. Part of the explanation for his animadversions on Lord George Bentinck and on Lord Derby (the Prime Minister) was that they were among the few prominent politicians whom he met racing. Charles Greville was a serious-minded man, enjoying intelligent company and conspicuously well-read. He had great influence with *The Times*, constantly provided that paper with inside information, contributed letters under the pseudonym 'C', and on one occasion wrote a leading article. He was devoted to his brothers and sisters, though deafness cut him off in middle-life from society. He retired from the Privy Council in 1860, and died in 1865.

The reader will recall these experiences and characteristics of Charles Greville because they are essential to an understanding of what he wrote. Although he never says this, it is safe to assert that he would have greatly enjoyed an active public life, and would have excelled in it. He therefore views public men as his rivals, with a little of that inevitable jealousy which gives an edge to his writing. Although he was a paid servant of the Government he never felt, as it could be argued that Pepys felt, in a subordinate capacity to ministers of the Crown. He was the friend of most of them, and often put his experience, advice and knowledge at their service. Till deafness clouded his usefulness he was always a force behind the scenes. One example may illustrate this. He was a close friend of Princess Lieven ever since her husband had been the Russian Ambassador in London in the 1820's. His excellent obituary of her will be found on page 280. He sent her long accounts of affairs in England, and she told a friend that she always sent them on for the Emperor to see, though Greville's handwriting, notoriously difficult to master, bothered the imperial eyes. The truth about Greville is that he was a far more important man than was implied by his achievements.

Certainly his comments on his fellows are severe. But if he hits hard at George IV, at William IV, at Queen Victoria, at the Duke of Wellington and a host of others he hits himself with all the zest of a penitent. His constant lamentations over his wasted life, wasted on the race-course, the card-table and drawing-room company will make an immediate impression on the reader. It was just because he minded passionately about causes that he cared perhaps too little for individuals. He always felt the contrast between the ideals of public life and the sordid entanglements of stable and paddock. His diary in consequence is no mere political treatise, but a picture of the struggles of the day seen by a man of sense and sensibility.

In one respect Greville has been singularly unlucky. He kept his diary in London and at the end of his life he lent some volumes of it to his colleague in the Privy Council office—Henry Reeve. Greville died very suddenly when some of the volumes were still with Reeve. What exactly was said or arranged between them will never be known but Reeve regarded himself as the custodian and appointed editor of the journals. Within nine years of Greville's death he launched the first volumes on the public. Their reception was noisy. A morning newspaper called the book 'a legacy of malice, ill-will and perfidy.' Lord Winchilsea—a sharp-tongued, fashionable lord, compared the diaries with 'lives of the Apostles written by Judas Iscariot.' Queen Victoria spoke of Greville's 'indiscretion, indelicacy, ingratitude towards friends, betrayal of confidence, and shameful disloyalty towards his sovereign.' Disraeli called the publication 'a social outrage.' Lord Winchilsea composed some lines, which have been often quoted—

> *For fifty years he listened at the door,*
> *He heard some secrets and invented more.*
> *These he wrote down, and women, statesmen, kings*
> *Became degraded into common things.*

Some of this startled horror still hangs over the diaries to this day. But the culprit was not the writer but the editor who published them far too soon, while a few of those criticised were still living and while friends and relations of the victims abounded. It was extremely unfortunate for Greville's reputation since the people who chat about a book, invariably a larger company than those who read it, pictured this serious-minded diarist as—to use the description of him in a newspaper—'this white-vested old *chroniquer scandaleux.*' Now that the prejudices and susceptibilities of those times have vanished into history, the general reader has the chance to meet Charles Greville as he really was—not only a faithful chronicler but a thoughtful and meditative product of his boisterous age.

Some quarter of a century ago I was engaged, with Mr. and Mrs. Ralph Partridge, in editing a definitive edition of the diaries (work started by Mr. Lytton Strachey) and in restoring the alterations and omissions made by the first editor. It has not been easy to remove anything from a book which, in its entirety, has given immense enjoyment and pleasure. I have viewed my task as one of extracting rather than expunging passages; the latter would be a task I could not enjoy; in fact only one-tenth of the original could be included in this book. I have therefore tried to keep a coherent account of one political struggle—the Reform Bill—and intelligible versions of some of the later ones. But I have tried to give plenty of those passages on more general matters which reveal something of the man himself, his circle of friends, and the London and country-house life of his generation.

This edition is taken from the definitive edition—seven volumes and an index volume—published by Messrs. Macmillan in 1938. Unhappily this is now an expensive book, and if the reader feels inclined for a deeper incursion into the diary than can be offered in this paper-back and cannot secure the 1938 edition he is recommended to the Silver Library edition published by Messrs. Longmans in 1903. In order to save space I have removed virtually all the notes, identifying persons and places by two or three words in the index. My aim has been to give as far as possible an uninterrupted narrative from the original diary.

ROGER FULFORD

1821

This extract from the diary begins when George IV has been king for a year; a few weeks earlier he had been obliged to drop the proceedings against the Queen, whose conduct when travelling abroad had given rise to much scandal.

February 7th 1821—The King went to the play last night (Drury Lane) for the first time, the Dukes of York and Clarence and a great suite with him. He was received with immense acclamations, the whole pit standing up, hurrahing and waving their hats. The boxes were very empty at first, for the mob occupied the avenues to the theatre, and those who had engaged boxes could not get to them. The crowd on the outside was very great. Lord Hertford dropped one of the candles as he was lighting him in, and made a great confusion in the box. He sat in Lady Bessborough's box, which was fitted up for him. He goes to Covent Garden to-night. A few people called out 'The Queen,' but very few. A man in the gallery called out, 'Where's your wife, Georgy?'

At Cov. Garden when it was announced that he was going to the play they hissed and made a great noise, and when God save the King was called for they made them sing God save the Queen.

(I have scratched out the above because it is not true.)

February 11th 1821—I came to town from Euston the end of last month. The debates were expected to be very stormy, and the minorities very large, not that anybody expected Ministers to go out. It has all ended as such anticipations usually do, in everything going off very quietly and the Government obtaining large majorities. Their Parliamentary successes and the King's reception have greatly elated them, and they think (and with reason probably) that they are likely to enjoy their places for the term of their natural lives, not that they care about the King's popularity except inasmuch as it may add strength to their administration. They do not conceal their contempt or dislike of him, and it is one of the phenomena of the present times that the King should have Ministers whom he abuses and hates, and who entertain corresponding sentiments of aversion to him; yet they defend all his errors and follies, and he affords them constant countenance and protection. As to the speeches, it is useless to mention them; each party insists upon the excellence of the speakers on its own side, and invariably decries those of the other. Peel seems to have made a pretty good speech, and Lambton spoke well. Burdett's sentence has excited the indignation of the Tories, who wanted him to be imprisoned for a year or two. He was miserably dejected before his sentence, and horrified at the prospect of going to prison. He had persuaded himself that he should die there. The King was delighted by his reception at the theatres, and told Lady Bessborough, as he came downstairs, he never was more gratified.

Gibbs and Howard[1] smashed last Thursday. They have robbed everybody they could, and are said to have broke for £180,000. The confusion in people's affairs is immense.

Lord Norbury when somebody said they wondered how the Queen had amused herself at Algiers, replied she was as happy as the Dey was long.

Somebody said they wondered which of the newspapers the Queen read. Ld. N. said she took in the Courier.

February 23 1821—Yesterday the Duke of York proposed to me to take his horses, which I accepted. Nothing could be more kind than the manner in which he proposed it.

Monday, March 5th 1821—Lord Chetwynd died on Wednesday morning last. I came that day from Newmarket and was informed of the event on getting out of the carriage. Thus if I do not lose any money at play my difficulties are at an end. I have experienced a great proof of the vanity of human wishes. In the course of three weeks I have attained the three things which I have most desired in the world for years past, and upon the whole I do not feel that my happiness is at all increased; perhaps if it was not for one cause it might be, but untill that ceases to exist it is in vain that I acquire every other advantage or possess the means of amusement. I will not despair altho' hope hardly lingers in my mind.

March 22nd 1821—I was sworn in the day before yesterday, and kissed hands at a Council at Carlton House yesterday morning.

March 25th—Lord Fife has been dismissed from his place of Lord of the Bedchamber for voting against the Malt Tax, and Lord Lovaine has been appointed instead.

April 15th 1821—This town has been occupied with Ball's marriage and Petersham's affairs for this last ten days.[2] I have every reason to believe

---

[1] A firm of moneylenders.
[2] Uxbridge's sister had been engaged to a rich Mr. Ball: Lord Petersham had involved himself with a married lady.

that some pecuniary concerns of Uxbridge's are mixed up with the former, and have caused all the apparent inconsistencies which have seemed so mysterious. With regard to the latter I know that P. was cudgelled for two of the D. of Y.s servants were on the spot, and saw what took place.

April 19th 1821—The night before last Hobhouse made his furious attack upon Canning. Last night everybody expected that Canning would speak, and was extremely anxious to hear what notice he would take of Hobhouse. The army estimates came on first in the evening, and almost all the members went away, intending to return to the Reform debate, but when Reform came on there were only 100 members in the House. 'Le combat finit faute de combattants,' and when everybody came crowding down at nine o'clock the House had been up half an hour, having divided 53 to 41.

May 2nd 1821—When the Canonry of Windsor became vacant Lady C.[1] asked the King to give it to Mr. Sumner, who had been Mount Charles's Tutor. The King agreed: the man was sent for, and kissed hands at Brighton. A letter was written to Lord Liverpool to announce the appointment. In the meantime Lord L. had sent a list of persons, one of whom he should recommend to succeed to the vacancy, and the letters crossed. As soon as Ld. L. received the letter from Brighton he got into his carriage and went down to the King, and stated that unless he was allowed to have the distribution of this patronage without any interference, he could not carry on the Government, and would resign his office if Sumner was appointed. The man was only a Curate, and had never held a living at all. The King 'chanta palinodie', and a sort of compromise was made, by which Lady C.'s friend was withdrawn, and the King begged it might be given to Dr. Clarke, to which appointment Lord L. consented, altho he did not approve of him; he did not, however, wish to appear too difficult. Told me by Lady Harrowby.

Lady C. lives in one of the houses in Marlbro Row. All the members of her family are continually there, and are supplied with horses, carriages, etc., from the King's stables. She rides out with her daughter, but never with the King, who always rides with one of his gentlemen. They never appear in public together. She dines there every day; before the King comes into the room she and Lady Elizabeth join him in another room, and he always walks in with one on each arm. She comports herself entirely as Mistress of the House, but never suffers her daughters to leave her. She has received magnificent presents, and Lady Elizabeth the same; particularly the mother has strings of pearls of enormous value. Madame de Lieven

[1] Lady Conyngham.

said she had seen the pearls of the Grand Duchesses and the Prussian Princesses, but had never seen any nearly so fine as Lady C.'s. The other night Lady Bath was coming to the Pavilion. After dinner Lady C. called to Sir William Keppel and said, 'Sir William, do desire them to light up the Saloon' (this Saloon is lit by hundreds of candles). When the King came in she said to him, 'Sir, I told them to light the Saloon, as Lady Bath is coming this evening.' The King seized her arm and said with the greatest tenderness, 'Thank you, thank you, My Dear; you always do what is right; you cannot please me so much as by doing everything you please, everything to show that you are Mistress here.' Madame de L. was sitting by her when this scene took place and repeated it to Ly Harrowby who told it to me.

May 12th 1821—I have suffered the severest blow I ever had in my life by the death of Lady Worcester. I loved her like a sister, and I have lost one of the few persons in the world who cared for me, and whose affection and friendship served to make life valuable to me. She has been cut off in the prime of her life and in the bloom of her beauty, and so suddenly too. Seven days ago she was at a ball at Court, and she is now no more. She died like a heroine, full of cheerfulness and courage to the last. She has been snatched from life at a time when she was becoming every day more fit to live, for her mind, her temper, and her understanding were gradually and rapidly improving; she had faults, but her mind was not vicious, and her defects may be ascribed to her education and to the actual state of the society in which she lived. Her virtues were inherent in her character; every day developed them more and more, and they were such as to make the happiness of all who lived with her and to captivate the affection of all who really knew her. I have never lost anyone I loved before, and though I know the grief I now feel will soon subside (for so the laws of nature have ordained), long, long will it be before I forget her, or before my mind loses the lively impression of her virtues and of our mutual friendship.

This is one of those melancholy events in life to which the mind cannot for a long time reconcile or accustom itself. I saw her so short a time ago 'glittering like the morning star, full of life and splendour and joy'; the accents of her voice still so vibrate in my ear that I cannot believe I shall never see her again. What a subject for contemplation and for moralising! What reflections crowd into the mind!

Hume told me once that he had witnessed many deathbeds, but he had never seen anything like the fortitude and resignation displayed by her. She died in his arms, and without pain. As life ebbed away her countenance changed, and when at length she ceased to breathe, a beautiful and tranquil smile settled upon her face.

4

Call round her tomb each object of desire,
Each purer frame informed by purer fire;
Let her be all that cheers or softens life,
The tender sister, daughter, friend, and wife:
Bid her be all that makes mankind adore,
Then view this marble, and be vain no more.

June 24th 1821—The King dined at Devonshire House last Thursday se'nnight. Lady C. had on her head a sapphire which belonged to the Stuarts, and was given by the Cardinal of York to the King. He gave it to the Princess Charlotte, and when she died he desired to have it back, Leopold being informed it was a crown jewel. This crown jewel sparkled in the headdress of the Marchioness at the ball. I ascertained the Duke's[1] sentiments upon this subject the other day. He was not particularly anxious to discuss it, but he said enough to show that he has no good opinion of her. The other day, as we were going to the races from Oatlands, he gave me the history of the D. of Wellington's life. His prejudice against him is excessively strong, and I think if ever he becomes King that the other will not be Commander-in-Chief. He does not deny his military talents, but he thinks that he is false and ungrateful, that he never gave sufficient credit to his officers, and that he was unwilling to put forward men of talent who might be in a situation to claim some share of credit, the whole of which he was desirous of engrossing himself. He says that at Waterloo he got into a scrape and allowed himself to be surprised, and he attributes in great measure the success of that day to Lord Anglesea, who, he says, was hardly mentioned, and that in the coldest terms, in the Duke's despatch.

August 6th 1821—For ever be this day accursed which has been to me the bitterest of my existence. The particulars will remain too deeply engraved on my memory to need being written down here.

(The devil take me if I have any idea to what this alludes. *Feby. 1836.*)

December 18th 1821—Have not written anything for months. 'Quante cose mi sono accadute!' My progress was as follows, not very interesting:—To Newmarket, Whersted, Riddlesworth, Caversham, Euston, Elveden, Welbeck, Sprotborough, Nun Appleton, Welbeck, Burghley, and London. Nothing worth mentioning occurred at any of these places. George Anson had ... (*about 8 letters expunged*) at Newmarket and Henry has had her since. Sprotborough was agreeable enough. The Granvilles, Montagu, Wilmot, and the Wortleys were there. Lady Caroline[2] spoke to me about talking to Coppy, and gave me to understand that she was falling in love

[1] Of York.   [2] Wortley.

5

with me. C'était le dernier de mes soucis. I came to town to meet her and for a week we have met almost every day in delightful security but she is gone and she vexes me to death with letters and with her more than ridiculous jealousy of Marion. I am enraged, annoyed and bored to death with it. I went to Brighton yesterday se'nnight for a Council. I was lodged in the Pavilion and dined with the King. The gaudy splendour of the place amused me for a little and then bored me. The dinner was cold and the evening dull beyond all dulness. They say the King is anxious that form and ceremony should be banished, and if so it only proves how impossible it is that form and ceremony should not always inhabit a palace. The rooms are not furnished for society, and, in fact, society cannot flourish without ease; and who can feel at ease who is under the eternal constraint which etiquette and respect impose? The King was in good looks and good spirits, and after dinner cut his jokes with all the coarse merriment which is his characteristic. Lord Wellesley did not seem to like it, but of course he bowed and smiled like the rest. I saw nothing very particular in the King's manner to Lady Conyngham. He sat by her on the couch almost the whole evening, playing at patience, and he took her in to dinner; but Madame de Lieven and Lady Cowper were there, and he seemed equally civil to all of them. I was curious to see the Pavilion and the life they lead there, and I now only hope I may never go there again, for the novelty is past, and I should be exposed to the whole weight of the bore of it without the stimulus of curiosity. I have read very little except scraps.

December 19th—I dined with Gwydir yesterday, and sat next to Lieven. He told me that Bloomfield is no longer in favour, that he has been supplanted by Francis Conyngham, who now performs almost all the functions which formerly appertained to Bloomfield. He is quite aware of his decline, and submits himself to it in a manly way. He is no longer so necessary to the King as he was, for a short time ago he could not bear that Bloomfield should be absent, and *now* his absence is unfelt. Francis goes to the King every morning, usually breakfasts with him, and receives all his orders. He was invited to go to Panshanger for two days, and was very anxious to go, but he could not obtain leave from the King to absent himself. Bloomfield does not put himself forward, 'même il se retire'. He said, and it is understood that he has made up his mind to resign his situation and leave the Court. The King is still perfectly civil and good-humoured to him, but has withdrawn his confidence from him, and B. is no longer his first Servant.

I asked Lieven whether Francis Conyngham, in performing the other duties which had been hitherto allotted to Bloomfield, also exercised the functions of Private Secretary, because this involved a much more serious question. He said that he did not know; all he knew was that whilst he was at Brighton Bloomfield was absent for five days, and that during that time the other had ostensibly occupied the place which Bloomfield used to hold about the King's person. The commencement of this revolution in the King's sentiments is to be dated from the journey to Hanover. Now Bloomfield sits amongst the guests at dinner at the Pavilion.

1822

July 16 1822—C' è un secolo dopo che abbia scritto qualche cosa in questo libro. Mi seca tanto di notare tutti gli avvenimenti che fanno un rumore per alcuni giorni e poi andano dalla memoria. Since I wrote last I have been continually in town. I have won the Derby,[1] my sister is married, and I have done nothing but make love to Georgiana Lennox. At the Priory I went into her room at night but was fool enough to go away without doing anything. I shall not be such a fool again. How habit and practice change our feelings, our opinions; and what an influence they have upon our thoughts and actions! Objects which I used to contemplate at an immeasurable distance, and to attain which I thought would be the summit of felicity, I have found worth very little in comparison to the value my imagination used to set upon them.

We have the Catholick question—Canning's speech—the Marriage bill— Lady Glengall's dragging every body down, and canvassing with unparalleled activity and effrontery—the Chancellor's rage—the Duke's carriage seized—his horses made over to me.

London is nearly over, has been tolerably agreeable; but I have been very often bored to death by the necessity of paying some attention to keep up an interest with G.L. Having had so much trouble, I don't choose to drop it without bringing the thing to a conclusion.

July 30th—Madame de Lieven is ill with the King, and is miserable in consequence. Lady Cowper is her confidante, and the D. of Wellington; but this latter pretends to know nothing of it, and asked me the other day what it was, I am sure in order to discover what people say. When the Duke was at Brighton in the winter, he and the King had a dispute about the army. It began (it was at dinner) by the King's saying that the Russians

---

[1] With the Duke of York's colt Moses.

7

or the Prussians (I forget which) were the best infantry in the world. The Duke said, 'Except your Majesty's.' The King then said the English cavalry were the best, which the Duke denied, said that an inferior number of French regiments would always beat a superior number of English, and, in short, that they were not half so effective. The King was very angry; the dispute waxed warm, and ended by his Majesty rising from the table and saying, 'Well, it is not for me to dispute on such a subject with your Grace.' The King does not like the Duke, nor does the Duke of York. This I know from himself.

The affair of the Bishop[1] has made a great noise. The people of the public house have made a good deal of money by showing the place. Lord Sefton went to see the Soldier in prison. He says he is a fine soldierlike man and has not the air which these wretches usually have. The Bishop took no precautions, and it was next to impossible he should not have been caught. He made a desperate resistance when taken, and if his breeches had not been down they think he would have got away. It seems that the Soldier will be proceeded against with the greatest vigour, and the Magistrate is much blamed for having taken such small bail as that which he required. The Duke will not spare the Soldier. Lord Lauderdale said the other day that the greatest dissatisfaction would pervade the publick mind at the escape of the Bishop and the punishment of the Soldier, and the people, who cannot discriminate, or enter into nice points of law, will only see in such apparent injustice a disposition to shield an offender in the higher classes of society from the consequences of his crime, while the law is allowed to take its course with the more humble culprit. He said that he would have exacted the greatest bail of the Bishop that ever had been taken; this was £20,000 which was taken of Sir Thomas Picton.

August 13th—I went to Cirencester on Friday and came back yesterday. At Hounslow I heard of the death of Lord Londonderry. When I got to town I met several people who had all assumed an air of melancholy, a visage de circonstance, which provoked me inexpressibly, because it was certain that they did not care; indeed, if they felt at all, it was probably rather satisfaction at an event happening than sorrow for the death of the person. It seems Lord Londonderry has been unwell for some time, but not seriously, and a few days before this catastrophe he became much worse, and particularly was very much dejected. He told Ld. Granville some time ago that he was worn out with fatigue, and he told Count Münster the other day that he was very ill indeed. The D. of Wellington saw him on Friday, and was so struck by the appearance of illness about him that he

[1] Bishop of Clogher.

8

sent Bankhead to him. He was cupped on Saturday in London, and was better, and went to Cray. On Sunday he was worse, and the state of dejection in which he appeared induced his attendants to take certain precautions, which unfortunately, however, proved fruitless. They removed his pistols and his razors, but he got hold of a penknife which was in the room next his, and on Sunday night or early on Monday morning he cut his throat with it. There is not a Minister in Town but Lord Liverpool, Vansittart, and the Chancellor. Lord Bathurst is at Cirencester, the D. of Wellington in Holland, Ld. Sidmouth in Yorkshire, Peel and Ld. Melville in Scotland with the King. No event ever gave rise to more speculation with the few people there are left to speculate, and the general opinion seems to be that Canning will not go to India, but will be appointed in his room. It certainly opens a door to his ambition as well as to that of Peel, who, unless Canning comes into office, must of necessity lead the House of Commons. Another speculation is that Lord Liverpool will take this opportunity of resigning, and that the King will form a Whig Ministry. I do not believe Lord L. wishes to resign, and my opinion is that Canning will come into office.

I had hardly any acquaintance with Lord Londonderry, and therefore am not in the slightest degree affected by his death. As a Minister he is a great loss to his party, and still greater to his friends and Dependents, to whom he was the best of Patrons; to the Country I think he is none. Nobody can deny that his talents were great, and perhaps he owed his influence and authority as much to his character as to his abilities. His appearance was dignified and imposing; he was affable in his manners and agreeable in society. The great feature was a cool and determined courage, which commanded universal respect and which gave an appearance of resolution and confidence to all his actions, inspired his friends with admiration and excessive devotion to him, and caused him to be respected by his most violent opponents. As a speaker he was prolix, monotonous, and never eloquent, except, perhaps, for a few minutes when provoked into a passion by something which had fallen in debate. But, notwithstanding these defects, and still more the ridicule which his extraordinary phraseology had drawn upon him, he was always heard with attention. He never spoke ill; his speeches were continually replete with good sense and strong argument, and though they seldom offered much to admire, they generally contained a great deal to be answered. I believe he was considered one of the best Managers of the H. of Commons who ever sat in it, and he was eminently possessed of the good taste, good humour, and agreeable manners which are more requisite to make a good Leader than eloquence, however brilliant. With these qualities, it may be asked why he was not a better

Minister, and who can answer that question? or who can aver that he did not pursue the policy which he conscientiously believed to be most advantageous to his country? Nay, more, who can say but from surmise and upon speculation that it was not the best? I believe that he was seduced by his vanity, that his head was turned by emperors, kings, and congresses, and that he was resolved that the country which he represented should play as conspicuous a part as any other in the political Dramas which were acted on the Continent. The result of his policy is this, that we are mixed up in the affairs of the Continent in a manner we have never been before, and which entails upon us endless negotiations and enormous expenses. We have associated ourselves with the Members of the Holy Alliance, and countenanced their acts of ambition and despotism in such a manner as to have drawn upon us the detestation of the nations of the Continent; and our conduct towards them at the close of the war has brought a stain upon our character for bad faith and desertion which no time will wipe away, and the recollection of which will never be effaced from their minds.

August 14th—Since I wrote the above I have read a biographical sketch of Lord Londonderry in the Times newspaper.

August 19th—I went to Brighton on Saturday to see the Duke of York; returned to-day. The Pavilion is finished. The King has had a subterranean passage made from the house to the stable, which is said to have cost £3000 or £5000; I forget which. There is also a bath in his apartment, with pipes to conduct water from the sea; these pipes cost £600. The King has not taken a sea bath for sixteen years.

The Marquess of Londonderry is to be buried to-morrow in Westminster Abbey. It is thought injudicious to have anything like an ostentatious funeral, considering the circumstances under which he died, but it is the particular wish of Lady L. She seems to consider the respect which is paid to his remains as a sort of testimony to his character, and nothing will pacify her feelings or satisfy her affection but seeing him interred with all imaginable honors. It seems that he gave several indications of a perturbed mind a short time previous to his death. For some time past he had been dejected, and his mind was haunted with various apprehensions, particularly with a notion that he was in great personal danger. On the day (the 3rd of August) he gave a great dinner at Cray to his political friends, some of them finding the wine very good, wished to compliment him upon it, and Arbuthnot called out, 'Lord Londonderry!' He instantly jumped up with great vivacity, and stood as if in expectation of something serious that was to follow. When he was told that it was about the wine they wished to speak to him, he sat down; but his manner was so extraordinary that Huskisson remarked it to Wilmot as they came home. In the last interview which the Duke of Wellington had with him he said he never heard him converse upon affairs with more clearness and strength of mind than that day. In the middle of the conversation, however, he said, 'To prove to you what danger I am in, my own servants think so, and that I ought to go off directly, that I have no time to lose, and they keep my horses saddled that I may get away quickly; they think I should not have time to go away in a carriage.' Then ringing the bell violently, he said to the servant, 'Tell me, sir, instantly who ordered my horses here; who sent them up to Town?' The man answered that the horses were at Cray, and had never been in town. The Duke desired the man to go, and in consequence of this strange behaviour wrote the letter to Bankhead which has since been published.

August 20th—Knighton went with the King to Scotland, and slept in one of H.M.'s own cabins, that next to him. He is supposed to have been appointed Privy Purse. Bloomfield has got the mission to Stockholm. When Bloomfield was dismissed a disposition was shown to treat him in a very unceremonious manner; but he would not stand this, and displayed a spirit which he was probably enabled to assume in consequence of what he knows. When they found he was not to be bullied they treated with him, and gave him every honour and emolument he could desire.

September 22nd 1822—I went to Sprotboro on the 15th and on the 16th I won 5700 on the St. Ledger. There was all kind of roguery with regard to the trials of the horses in Croft's stables and they laid 100 to 1 against the winner. I did not know he was to start until I saw him come in first.

I saw Lady Bathurst on the 13th. Canning had not then sent his answer, and greatly surprised were the Ministers at the delay. Lord Liverpool's proposal to him was simple and unclogged with conditions—the Foreign Office and the lead in the H. of Commons. The King's repugnance to his coming into office was extreme, and it required all the efforts of his Ministers to surmount it. The D. of Wellington and Peel have all the credit of having persuaded the King to consent, but Lord Bathurst's arguments influenced him as much as those of any person, and he told Lady C. that he was more satisfied by what Lord B. had said to him on the subject than by any of the Ministers. I know that with the Canning party Lord Bathurst is supposed to have joined with the Chancellor in opposing his appointment. The danger in which the D. of Wellington was sensibly affected the King, because at this moment the Duke is in high favour with him, and when he heard he was so ill he sent Knighton to him to comfort him with a promise that he would reconsider the proposal of receiving Canning, and the next day he signified his consent. I saw a note from Lady C. to Lady Bathurst, in which she gave an account of the uneasiness and agitation in which the King had been in consequence of the Duke's illness, saying how much she had suffered in consequence, and how great had been *their* relief, when Knighton brought word that he was better. 'The Dear King,' she said, was more composed. She added that she (Lady B.) would hear that evening what would give her pleasure, and this was that the King had agreed to take Canning. In a conversation also Lady C. said that she did hope, now the King had yielded his own inclination to the wishes and advice of his Ministers, that they would behave to him better than they had done. Canning was sworn in on Monday. His friends say that he was very well received. The King told Madame de Lieven that having consented to receive him, he had behaved to him, *as he always did*, in the most gentlemanlike manner he could, and that on delivering to him the seals, he said to him that he had been advised by his Ministers that his abilities and eloquence rendered him the only fit man to succeed to the vacancy which Lord Londonderry's death had made, and that, in appointing him to the situation, he had only to desire that he would follow the steps of his predecessor. This Madame de Lieven told to Lady Jersey, and she to me. It seems that the King was so struck with Lord Londonderry's manner (for he said to the King nearly what he said to the Duke of Wellington), and so persuaded that some fatal catastrophe would take place, that when Peel came to inform him of what had happened, he said to him before he spoke, 'I know you are come to tell me that Londonderry is dead.' Peel had just left him, and upon receiving the despatches immediately returned; and when Lady Conyngham was told by Lord Mount Charles that there was a report that he was dead, she said, 'Good God! then he has destroyed himself.' She knew what had passed with the King.

September 23rd—George Bentinck, who thinks there never existed such a man as Canning, and who probably has heard from him some circumstances connected with his resignation at the time of the Queen's trial, told Henry[1] that it was in consequence of a dispute between the King and his Ministers concerning the payment of the expence of the Milan Commission. The Ministers wished the King to pay the expences himself, and he wished them to be defrayed by Government. Lord Londonderry promised the King (without the concurrence of the other Ministers) that the expenses should be paid by Government, but with money ostensibly appropriated to

[1] The diarist's brother.

other purposes. This Canning could not endure, and resigned. Such is his story, which probably is partly true and partly false.

November 5th—I have been to Newmarket, Euston, Riddlesworth, Rendlesham, Whersted, besides going to Town several times and to Brighton. Since I left London for the Doncaster races I have travelled near 1200 miles. I lost 4000 at play between the 1st and 2nd and the 2nd and 3rd meetings and during the Houghton. The first two meetings I did not play at all. At Riddlesworth the Duke of York told me a great deal about the Queen and Brougham, but he was so unintelligible that part I could not make out and part I do not remember. What I can recollect amounts to this, that the Emperor of Austria was the first person who informed the King of the Queen's conduct in Italy, that after the enquiry was set on foot a negotiation was entered into with the Queen, the basis of which was that she should abdicate the title of Queen, and that to this she had consented. He said that Brougham had acted a most infamous part, for that he had acquiesced in the propriety of her acceding to these terms, and had promised that he would go over to her and confirm her in her resolution to agree to them; that he had not only not gone, but that whilst he was making these promises to Government he had written to the Queen desiring her to come over. The Duke told me that a man (whose name he did not mention) came to him and said, 'So the Queen comes over?' He said, 'No, she does not.' The man said, 'I know she does, for Brougham has written to her to come; I saw the letter.' If Lord Liverpool and Lord Londonderry had thought proper to publish what had been done on the part of Brougham, he would have been covered with infamy; but they would not do it, and he thinks they were wrong. The rest I cannot remember.

Welbeck, November 16th 1822—I have had a great deal of conversation with Titchfield, particularly about Canning, and he told me this curious fact about his coming into office:—When the K. had consented to receive him he wrote a letter nearly in these words to Lord Liverpool: 'The K. thinks that the brightest jewel in his crown is to extend his forgiveness (I am not sure that this was the word) to a subject who has offended him, and he therefore informs Lord L. that he consents to Mr. Canning forming a part of the Cabinet. This letter was communicated by Lord Liverpool to Canning, and upon reading it he was indignant, as were his wife and his daughter. The consequence was that he wrote a most violent and indignant reply, addressed to the same person to whom the other letter had been addressed, and which was intended in like manner to have been shown to the King, as the K.'s letter was to him. Upon hearing what had passed, however, down came Lord Granville and Mr. Ellis in a great hurry, and used every argument to dissuade him from sending the letter, urging that he had entirely misunderstood the purport of the letter which had offended him; that it was intended as an invitation to reconciliation, and contained nothing which could have been meant as offensive; that the country would be so dissatisfied (which ardently desired and expected that he should come into office) if he rejected this overture that he would not be justified in refusing his services to the public who so anxiously wished for them. These arguments, vehemently urged and put in every possible shape, prevailed, and the angry reply was put in the fire, and another written full of gratitude, duty, and acquiescence.

November 24 1822, London—The morning I left Welbeck I had a long conversation with Titchfield upon various matters connected with politics and his family, particularly about Lord William's correspondence with Lord Liverpool about the Government of India. He showed me this correspondence, in which, as I anticipated, Lord William had the worst of it. Lord Liverpool's answer was unanswerable. He showed me also a very long letter which he had received from Lord William, together with the copies of the correspondence, which was written the evening before he went abroad. In this letter (which I only read once, and which was so long that I cannot recollect it) he gave a detailed account of his sentiments upon the Indian matter, with the reasons for his having acted as he did, also his feelings with regard to the manner in which Canning had behaved upon the occasion and a conversation which he had with Mrs. Canning. This latter I think exceedingly curious, because it serves to show what the object and the pretensions of Canning are in taking office, and exhibits that ambition the whole extent of which he dares not avow. It seems that the Directors were anxious that Lord William should be appointed Governor-General, and this he knew through Friends of his in the Court. Government, however, having signified their dissent to his nomination, Lord Amherst was nominated by the Court and accepted. Lord William's displeasure with Canning arises from an idea that Canning was backward in supporting his interests in this matter, and that he kept aloof from Lord William, and acquiesced in his rejection without ever communicating with him on the subject. Had Canning stated to him the difficulties under which he laboured, from his anxiety to serve him on the one hand and his obligation of coinciding with his colleagues on the other, Ld. William would not have hesitated to *desire* him to abandon his interests rather than involve himself in any embarrassment on his account. He wrote to Lord Liverpool to complain that the Court of Directors being inclined to nominate him, Lord L. had interposed his influence to prevent that nomination; that he did not ask Lord L. to consent to his appointment, but he did ask him not to interpose his influence to prevent his nomination, because that nomination was essential to his character, as proving that the Court of Directors were satisfied of the injustice with which he had been treated in the affair of the Vellore Mutiny. Lord Liverpool's answer was short and civil, assuring him that he had neither directly nor indirectly exerted any influence at all, maintaining his right to give his opinion to the Directors in case it had been asked, and stating that Lord Amherst had been proposed by the Court and accepted by Government. Whilst this matter was still pending, and before Ld. Amherst's appointment had been made known, Lord William went to Gloucester Lodge. He saw Mrs. Canning, and being anxious to acquire information concerning the Indian appointment, he told her that she had an opportunity of obliging him by telling him anything she knew concerning it. She answered very quickly and in a very bad humour, 'Oh, it is all settled; Ld. Amherst is appointed.' She then put into his hand a letter which Canning had received that morning from the Duke of Portland, declining his offer of the Private Secretaryship for John and George, alleging as a reason the hostile politics of Lord William and Titchfield. Mrs. C. said that she had no idea that they would not have supported Canning, that she was aware they differed on some matters of minor importance, but that she had imagined their general opinions to be similar; that she had conceived Ld. William's opposition to have been directed against Lord Londonderry, and that it would have ceased with his death; that *the present must be considered as a new administration, and that Canning must be virtually Minister of the Country.'* Ld. William replied that he could not view it in that light, that he thought it likely the introduction of Canning into the Cabinet might effect a beneficial influence on the measures of Government, and more particularly that a system of foreign policy might be adopted more congenial to his sentiments upon that subject; that it would give him the greatest pleasure to see such a change of measures as would enable him to give his support to a Government of which Canning was so conspicuous a member, but that he could not think that to be a new Administration which was composed (with the sole exception of Canning) of precisely the same persons of which it consisted before he joined them.

George,[1] after having refused the Private Secretaryship, was talked over by Canning and accepted it. He tried to gain over John,[2] but he refused.

Canning wished that Manners Sutton should be appointed Governor-General, in order that Wynn might be made Speaker, and room made for Huskisson in the Cabinet; but Wynn would not have given up his situation,

[1] Lord George Bentinck.   [2] 4th Duke of Portland.

and it is very much suspected that if he had, the strength of Government would have been insufficient to procure his election as Speaker, so unpopular is he in the House.

(This about Huskisson I believe now was not true—I know not where I got the information. *Feby. 1836.*)

December 24th—The other day I went to Bushey with the Duke of York, and as we passed over Wimbledon Common he showed me the spot where he fought his duel with the D. of Richmond. He then told me the whole story and all the circumstances which led to it, most of which are in print. That which I had never heard before was that at a masquerade three masks insulted the Prince of Wales, when the Duke interfered, desired the one who was the most prominent to address himself to him, and added that he suspected him to be an officer in his Regiment (meaning Col. Lennox), and if that was so he was a coward and a disgrace to his profession; if he was not the person he took him for, he desired him to unmask, and he would beg his pardon. The three masks were supposed to be Colonel Lennox, the Dss. of Gordon, and Ly. Charlotte. This did not lead to any immediate consequences, but perhaps indirectly contributed to what followed. The Duke never found out whether the masks were the people he suspected.

The last time I was with him he told me a variety of particulars about the D. of Wellington's conduct at the siege of Seringapatam, of Lord Harris's reluctance to entrust the command of a storming party to him, of his not arriving at the place of rendezvous the first night, of Lord Harris's anger and the difficulty with which he was brought to consent to his being employed the second night, when he distinguished himself so signally. Amongst various other matters, of which it is impossible to bring away a perfect recollection, from his confused manner of narrating, and particularly his inaccuracy as to dates, he told me (with many recommendations to secrecy) that which immediately explained to me the dislike which he certainly bears to the Duke and (which I did not know before) to Lord Londonderry. He said that after the retreat of our army under Sir J. Moore from Spain (he was not quite certain himself as to the exact period, though a reference to the history of that period will probably elucidate the matter) Lord L. sent for him, and communicated to him that it was the intention of Government to send out an expedition to Portugal, and to confer the command of it upon him. He replied that if called upon he should consider it his duty to serve, but he should never solicit any command. Nothing more passed at that time, but the newspapers by some means immediately got hold of this project and violently attacked the Government for thinking of sending him out. He does not appear to have known what intermediate deliberations led to a change in the determination of the Ministers with regard to him. He says that Lord Chatham, who was much attached to him, and was then a Cabinet Minister, came to him one day and told him he was betrayed, and that he was sacrificed to make way for Sir A. Wellesley; that soon after this Lord Londonderry sent for him, and said that he was extremely sorry that public opinion was so strongly against his appointment to the command of the army that it was impossible for Government to confer it upon him. Soon after this the expedition was formed, and Sir A. W. was appointed to the command. This was the Duke's own version of the transaction.

1823

Some particulars concerning the late King's will told me by the Duke of York as we were going to Oatlands to shoot on Wednesday, the 8th of January, 1823.

The King was empowered by Act of Parliament to make a will about the year 1766. In 1770 he made a will, by which he left all he had to the Queen for her life, Buckingham House to the Duke of Clarence, some property to the Duke of Kent, and to the Duke of York his second best George and some other trifling remembrance. He considered the Duke of York provided for by the Bishopric of Osnaburgh. Of this will three copies were made; one was deposited in the German *chancellerie* in England, one in Hanover, and the other it was believed the King kept himself. He afterwards resolved to cancel this will, and two of the copies of it were destroyed, the third still existing (I could not make out by what means—if he told me I have forgotten—or which copy it was that survived). In 1810 the King made another will, but for various reasons he always put off signing it, once or twice, because he wished to make alterations in it; at length he appointed a day to sign it, but when the Chancellor brought it one of the witnesses was absent, and the signature was again postponed. Other days were afterwards fixed for this purpose, but before the signature was affixed the King was taken ill, and consequently the will never was signed. After the death of the King, the only good will, therefore, was his original will of 1770, which was produced and read in the presence of the King, the

Chancellor, Vice-Chancellor, Lord Liverpool, the D. of York, Adair, the King's solicitor (I forget his name), and one or two others whom he mentioned. Buckingham House, which had been left to the D. of Clarence, had been since sold; the Queen and the D. of Kent were dead; the only legatee, therefore, was the D. of York. Now arose a difficulty—whether the property of the late King demised to the King or to the Crown. The Chancellor said that the only person who had anything to say to the will was the D. of York; but the Duke and the King differed with regard to the right of inheritance, and the Duke, wishing to avoid any dispute or discussion on the subject, begged to wash his hands of the whole matter. The King conceives that the whole of the late King's property devolves upon him personally, and not upon the Crown, and he has consequently appropriated to himself the whole of the money and jewels. The money did not amount to more than £120,000. So touchy is he about pecuniary matters that his Ministers have never dared to remonstrate with him, nor to tell him that he has no right so to act. The consequence is that he has spent the money, and has taken to himself the jewels as his own private property. The Duke thinks that he has no right thus to appropriate their Father's property, but that it belongs to the Crown. The King has acted in a like manner with regard to the Queen's (Charlotte's) jewels. She possessed a great quantity, some of which had been given her by the late King on her marriage, and the rest she had received in presents at different times. Those which the late King had given her she conceived to belong to the Crown, and left them back to the present King; the rest she left to her daughters. The King has also appropriated the Queen's (Caroline's) jewels to himself, and conceives that they are his undoubted private property. The Duke thinks that the Ministers ought to have taken the opportunity of the coronation, when a new crown was to be provided, to state to him the truth with regard to the jewels, and to suggest that they should be converted to that purpose. This, however, they dared not do, and so the matter remains. The King had even a design of selling the library collected by the late King, but this he was obliged to abandon, for the Ministers and the Royal Family must have interfered to oppose so scandalous a transaction.

Saturday, January 25th 1823—I came from Gorhambury with the Duke of Wellington last Wednesday, and he was very communicative. He gave me a detailed history of the late Congress, and told me many other things which I should be glad to recollect.

After the two treaties of Paris and Vienna the Allied Powers agreed to meet in Congress from time to time to arrange together any matters of general interest which might arise, and to settle and discuss any differences which might occur between any two Powers, a rule being laid down that the affairs of no Power should be discussed without that Power being invited to the deliberation. The affairs of Naples were the first which attracted their attention. Austria complained that the ramifications of the secret political societies which had sprung up at Naples tended to disturb and revolutionise the Italian possessions, and demanded the consent of the Allied Powers that she should abate the nuisance. The cause was deemed sufficient to justify her interference, and the events followed which are known. The Congress at Verona was assembled for the purpose of taking into consideration the affairs of Italy, and for discussing the propriety of relieving Naples from the burden of their military force which had been maintained there for the purpose of extinguishing the revolutionary spirit. At this Congress France came forward and complained that the revolution which had taken place in Spain menaced her internal tranquillity, and demanded the advice of Congress as to the measures she should adopt. In this it will be observed that the rule of every Power being called upon to attend a deliberation in which its affairs were to be discussed was dispensed with. Austria, Russia, and Prussia immediately replied that if she considered the Spanish revolution to be dangerous to her repose, she would be justified in stifling that revolution by force of arms, and offered to cooperate with her in the attempt. England refused to give any answer to the demands of France, and demanded in return what was her case against Spain. To this no answer was given. The part then taken by the Duke was to deprecate hostilities, both publicly as Plenipotentiary of England and privately in the various conversations which he had with the Emperor of Russia, who seems to have been the strongest advocate for making war upon Spain. It seems that the imprudence of the Spaniards has afforded some colour to the right assumed by their enemies of interfering with their affairs, for they have upon several occasions attempted to foment the troubles which either existed or threatened to appear both in Naples and Piedmont; and the Emperor of Russia told the Duke that he had detected the Spanish Minister at St. Petersburg in an attempt to corrupt his soldiers at the time of the mutiny of the Previnsky Guards, and that he had consequently sent him out of the country. The Duke replied that if the Emperor of Russia had reasonable grounds of complaint against Spain, he would be fully justified in declaring war against her, and that he would advise him to do so if he could march 150,000 men into Spain; but in suffering three years to elapse without making any complaint he had virtually renounced his right to complain, and that it was unfair to rake up a forgotten grievance against Spain at a time when she was menaced by another Power upon other grounds. The Duke said that the Emperor of Russia once talked to him of the practicability of marching an army into Spain; and seemed to think he might do so. The Duke said that the French Government would never allow it, when he said he could send them by sea. The Duke told him it would take 20,000 ships. One of the arguments of the Emperor of Russia was this: that constituted as their Governments were (military Governments) it was impossible for them to tolerate consistently with their own security any revolution which originated in military insubordination.

After the Congress the Duke returned to Paris, and found that not only Monsieur de Villèle was averse to war, but that the King, Monsieur, and the Duke and Duchess d'Angoulême were equally disinclined to commence hostilities. His endeavours have been incessantly directed to confirm their pacific dispositions, and to induce the Spanish Government to display moderation in their language and conduct. I asked him if such were the sentiments of the ruling Powers in France upon what the question now turned, and why all idea of war was not abandoned, since both parties were pacifically inclined. He said that France had been led into a dilemma by a series of erroneous measures, that hers was a false position, that having made the demands she had done to the Allied Powers, having held such lofty language, and having made such a show of military preparation, her difficulty was how to retract and retrace her steps with honor and credit to herself; that she was a nation whose character depended in great measure upon her military renown, and that it would reflect disgrace upon her to have made such mighty preparations and assumed so peremptory a tone without performing any action commensurate with the expectations she had raised. He said that appearances certainly became more warlike, but that he still hoped peace would be maintained; that if war ensued it would be entered into contrary to the interests and inclinations of all the parties concerned, and that it would have been brought about by a succession of circumstances over which they had no controul; that it was impossible for two armies to remain for a length of time so near each other without mutual incursions being made, insults and injuries exchanged, which must inevitably end in a state of warfare and hostility; that the recall of the French Minister from Madrid would contribute to this result, for both in the Cortes and the Andalusian Society expressions would be uttered offensive to the French Government, and misrepresentations would be made which would have the effect of exasperating the parties and of widening the breach; and that there being no agent of France at Madrid to furnish explanations and destroy the effect of the misrepresentations, there would be a constant correspondence between Madrid and Paris, in which vent would be given to all the angry feelings that ever existed. The Duke advised that no answer should be given to the notes of the three Powers, nor to that of the French Minister. Had the Spanish Government declined to take notice of the notes, they would have imposed upon them the difficulty of taking the next steps. However, he admitted that the answer to the French note was very moderate. There is no statesman in Spain. There are some eloquent men in the Cortes, particularly Torreno and Arguelles. Torreno is the ablest man, but he has injured his character by peculation. The state of Spain is such that the most violent and turbulent possess the greatest share of influence. Portugal is in a state of greater intellectual improvement, and amongst the Portuguese there are some men of ability—Palmella, and another whose name I have forgotten. But Spain is not only deficient in men of education and talent to direct her councils, but she has no army, and not one officer of capacity. Not one was formed by the late war, for such were their vanity and ignorance that they would learn nothing from the English.

Upon one occasion only the Spaniards gained a victory; the day on which St. Sebastian was stormed. Soult attacked a Spanish corps commanded by General Freyre. When the Duke was informed of the attack he hastened to the scene of action and placed two British Divisions in reserve, to support the Spaniards, but did not allow them to come into action. He found the Spaniards running away as fast as they could. He asked them where they were going. They said they were taking off the wounded. He immediately sent and ordered the gates of Irun, to which they were flying, to be shut against them, and sent to Freyre to desire he would rally his men. This was done, and they sustained the attack of the French; but General Freyre sent to the Duke to beg he would let his Divisions support him, as he could not maintain himself much longer. The Duke said to Freyre's aide-de-camp, 'If I let a single man fire, the English will swear they gained the victory, and he had much better do it all himself; besides, look through my glass, and you will see the French are retreating.' This was the case, for a violent storm of rain had occurred, and the French, who had crossed a river, finding that it began to swell, and that their bridges were in danger of being carried away, had begun to retreat. The Spaniards maintained their position, but the Duke said he believed they owed it to the storm more than to their own resolution.

The Duke wrote to Alava some time ago (three years, I think) and desired him to advise the King from him, now that he had accepted the Constitution, to throw himself upon his Ministers. He has not written to Alava, nor Alava to him, for three years, because he knows that all letters are opened and read. He says the King of Spain is not clever, but cunning, that his manners are good. He is in correspondence with the Allied Sovereigns, and is playing false. He has the means of corresponding, because, although his household is composed of men friendly to the revolution, there is no restraint upon his person, and he sees whomever he pleases. In case of war the French would obtain complete success. He conceives their object would be to obtain possession of the person of the King, to overthrow the Constitution, establish the King upon the throne with a Constitution perhaps similar to the French Charte, and to establish an army of occupation to maintain such an order of things till he should be able to form an army of his own.

He saw the King of France twice. He was much broke, but talked of living twelve or fourteen years. The second time he was in better health and spirits than the first time. Madame du Cayla sent to the Duke to ask him to call upon her; he went twice and she was not at home. At his Levee the King said, 'Il y a une personne qui regrette beaucoup de n'avoir pas eu le plaisir de vous voir.' The courtiers told him the King meant Madame du C. He went the same evening and saw her. She is a fine woman, about forty, and agreeable. She sees the King every Wednesday; he writes notes and verses to her, and he has given her a great deal of money. He has built a house for her, and given her a _terre_ near St. Denis which is valued at 1,500,000 francs. The King likes M. de Villèle exceedingly. He has occasionally talked to the Duke of Bonaparte. One day, when they were standing together at the window which looks upon the garden of the Tuileries, he said, 'One day Bonaparte was standing here with ——, and he said, pointing to the Chamber of Deputies, "Vous voyez ce bâtiment-là: si je les démuselerais, je serais détrôné." "I," said the King, "have given them freedom of debate, and I think I go on very well with it."'

The Duke said he had been struck down by a musket shot whilst reconnoitring the enemy as they were retreating in the Pyrenees. The people round him thought he was killed, but he got up directly. Alva was wounded a few minutes before him, and Major Brooke nearly at the same time. He is of opinion that Massena was the best French general to whom he was ever opposed.

He said that Bonaparte had not the patience requisite for defensive operations. His last campaign (before the capture of Paris) was very brilliant, probably the ablest of all his performances. The Duke is of opinion that if he had possessed greater patience he would have succeeded in compelling the Allies to retreat; but they had adopted so judicious a system of defence that he was foiled in the impetuous attacks he made upon them, and after a partial failure which he met with, when he attacked Blücher at Laon and Craon, he got tired of pursuing a course which afforded no great results, and leaving a strong body under Marmont to watch Blücher, he threw himself into the rear of the Grand Army. The march upon Paris entirely disconcerted him and finished the war. The Allies could not have maintained themselves much longer, and had he continued to keep his force concentrated, and to carry it as occasion required against one or other of the two armies, the D. thinks he must eventually have forced them to retreat, and that their retreat would have been a difficult operation. His army could not have reached the scene of operations for two months. The Allies did not dare attack Napoleon. If he had himself come up he should certainly have attacked him, for his army was the best that ever existed.

I remember that the Duke told me that he traced back the present politicks of France to their chagrin at the dissolution of the Family Compact.[1] At the general pacification the Duke, on the part of the English Government, insisted upon this treaty not being renewed, and made a journey to Madrid for the purpose of determining the Spanish Government. Talleyrand and the King of France made great efforts to induce the Duke to desist from his opposition to the renewal of the treaty, and both were exceedingly mortified at being unable to shake the determination of our Government on this point.

September 17th—Near seven months since I have written any thing. What concerns myself is principally winning and losing and getting H. with child.[2] I neither won nor lost in the spring. I had won a large sum in the course of the year at play. I broke my arm, in two months I lost the whole of my winnings and much more. I won near 3000 on the Derby, lost 400 on the Oaks, and did not get paid 500—lost 1300 on the St Ledger, and am now a very considerable loser by the year.

I have been constantly in London for the last seven months doing nothing. Events there have been none. The question of peace or war excited extra-

---

[1] The 'Family Compact' was based on three separate treaties between France and Spain of 1733, 1743 and 1761. Their essence was a combination against England by the Bourbon kings of France and Spain. A clause of the Anglo-Spanish treaty of 1814 forbade any such union in future. This clause, though secret, was published by Canning in April 1823.

[2] Harriet, third daughter of George Clark of West Hatch, Essex; married Sir Bellingham Reginald Graham, seventh baronet, 1810; died in Paris, October 9th, 1830. The birth of the child here referred to was unknown to Sir Bellingham Graham until June 1824, when he became aware of it through an intercepted correspondence between Lady Graham and Greville (*The Creevey Papers*, 1904. Vol. II. pp. 77–8).

ordinary interest, but from the moment the war began, almost all interest ceased, and the approaching termination of the struggle is contemplated with perfect indifference. Lord Maryborough has been politely pushed out of the cabinet and the mint. The King wrote him a letter desiring his acceptance of the Buck hounds upon Ld. Cornwallis's death, and though he was at first mightily tickled with the compliment, he soon found it was a bad joke to exchange the solid pudding for the empty praise and he is very peevish—dissatisfied with the Ministers who caused this to be done without intimating it to him, and with the D. of W. who he thinks might have prevented it.

The D. of Wellington told me that Knighton managed the King's affairs very well, that he was getting him out of debt very quickly, and that the Ministers were well satisfied with him. When he was appointed to the situation he now holds, he called at Apsley House to announce it to the Duke, and expressed his hopes that the appointment would not displease him. The Duke said that he could have no objection, but he would give him a piece of advice which he trusted he would take in good part: this was, that he would confine himself to the discharge of the functions belonging to his own situation, and that he would not in any way interfere with the Government; that as long as he should so conduct himself he would go on very well, but that if ever he should meddle with the concerns of the Ministers he would give them such offence that they would not suffer him to remain in a situation which he should thus abuse. Knighton thanked him very much for his advice, and promised to conform himself to it. It seems that he told this to the King, for the next time the Duke saw him the King said he had heard the advice which he had given to a person, and that he might depend upon that person's following it entirely.

November 29th—In the various conversations which I have with the Duke of York he continually tells me a variety of facts more or less curious, sometimes relating to politicks, but more frequently concerning the affairs of the Royal Family, that I have neglected to note down at the time, and I generally forget them afterwards. I must acknowledge, however, that they do not interest me so much as they would many other people. I have not much taste for Court gossip. Another reason, too, is the difficulty of making a clear narrative out of his confused communications. The principal anecdotes he has told me have been, as well as I recollect, relative to the Duchess of Gloster's marriage, to the Duke of Cumberland's marriage and all the dissensions to which that event gave rise in the Royal Family, the differences between the King and Prince Leopold, and other trifling matters which I have now forgotten. In all of these histories the King acted a part, in which

his bad temper, bad judgment, falseness, and duplicity were equally conspicuous. I think it is not possible for any man to have a worse opinion of
another than the Duke has of the King. From various instances of eccentricity I am persuaded that the King is subject to occasional impressions
which produce effects so like insanity that if they continue to increase he
will end by being decidedly mad. The last thing which I have heard was at
Euston the other day. I went into the Duke's room and found him writing;
he got up and told me that he was thrown into a great dilemma by the conduct of the King, who had behaved extremely ill to him. The matter which
I could collect was this:—Upon the disturbance breaking out in the West
Indies it became necessary to send off some troops as quickly as possible. In
order to make the necessary arrangements without delay, the Duke made
various dispositions, a part of which consisted in the removal of the regiment on guard at Windsor and the substitution of another in its place.
Orders were expedited to carry this arrangement into effect, and at the same
time he communicated to the King what he had done and desired his
sanction to ... (Resumed) *March 6th 1824* ... the arrangement. The Duke's
orders were already in operation, when he received a letter from the King to
say that he liked the regiment which was at Windsor, and that it should not
move; and in consequence of this fancy the whole business was at a stand-
still. Thus he thought proper to trifle with the interests of the country to
gratify his own childish caprice. He gave, too, great offence to the Duke, in
hindering his dispositions from being carried into effect.

At the same time the Duke told me another thing which he thought was
indirectly connected with the first. It seems one of the people about the
Court had ordered some furniture to be removed from Cumberland Lodge
to Windsor (something for the Chapel). Stephenson, as head of the Board
of Works, on being informed this was done, wrote to the man to know by
what orders he had done it. The man showed the letter to the King, who
was exceedingly incensed, and wrote to Lord Liverpool to say that Stephenson's letter was insulting to him, and desired he might be turned out. After
some correspondence on the subject Lord Liverpool persuaded the King to
reinstate him; but he was obliged to make all sorts of apologies and excuses
for having done what it was his duty to do. Stephenson is a friend and servant of the Duke's, and in his ill-humour he tried to revenge himself upon
the Duke as well as on Stephenson, and he thwarted the Duke in his military arrangements. What made his conduct the less excusable was that it was
important that these things should be done quickly, and as the Duke was
out of town a correspondence became necessary, by which great delay would
be caused.

1824

Saturday, March 6th—Poor Titchfield died last night at eight o'clock, having lingered for some days in a state which gave to his family alternate hopes and fears. He was better till yesterday afternoon, when he was removed into another room; soon after this he grew weaker, and at eight o'clock he expired. He is a great loss to his family, of which he was by much the cleverest member, and he was well calculated to fill the situation in which fortune had placed him. His talents were certainly of a superior description, but their efficacy was counteracted by the eccentricity of his habits, the indolence of his mind, and his vacillating and uncertain disposition. He was, however, occasionally capable of intense application, and competent to make himself master of any subject he thought fit to grapple with; his mind was reflecting, combining, and argumentative, but he had no imagination, and to passion, 'the sanguine credulity of youth, and the fervent glow of enthusiasm' he was an entire stranger. He never had any taste for society, and attached himself early to politicks. He started in life with an enthusiastick admiration for Mr. Canning, but after two or three years, being thrown into the society of many of his political opponents, he began to entertain opinions very different from those of Mr. C. He never, however, enlisted under any political banner, and his great object seemed to be to prove to the world that he belonged to no party. After Mr. Canning came into office he took the earliest opportunity of informing his constituents that he was unfettered by any political connexion with him. Titchfield was never at a public school, but was educated at home. Such an education—the most injudicious which can be given to a young man destined to fill a great situation—was not without its effect upon his mind. The superior indulgences and early habits of authority and power in which he was brought up, without receiving correction from any of those levelling circumstances which are incidental to public schools, threw a shade of selfishness and reserve over his character, which time, the commerce of the world, and a naturally kind disposition had latterly done much to correct. The subject to which he had principally devoted his attention was political economy, and in the discussions in the H. of C. upon currency he had particularly distinguished himself. Whatever he attempted he had done so well that great expectations were entertained of his future success, and the indications he had given of talent will ensure to his memory a lasting reputation. He has died at a moment the most fortunate, perhaps, for his fame as a public man; but his loss to his family is very great, and by them will be long felt and deeply lamented.

1830

London, July 16th 1830—Returned here on the 6th of this month, and have waited these ten days to look about me and see and hear what is passing. The present King and his proceedings occupy all attention, and nobody thinks any more of the late King than if he had been dead fifty years, unless it be to abuse him and to rake up all his vices and misdeeds. Never was elevation like that of King William the 4th. His life has been hitherto passed in obscurity and neglect, in miserable poverty, surrounded by a numerous progeny of bastards, without consideration or friends, and he was ridiculous from his grotesque ways and little meddling curiosity. Nobody ever invited him into their house, or thought it necessary to honor him with any mark of attention or respect; and so he went on for above forty years, till Canning brought him into notice by making him High Admiral at the time of his grand Ministerial schism. In that post he distinguished himself by making ridiculous speeches, by a morbid official activity, and a general wildness which was thought to indicate incipient insanity, till shortly after Canning's death and the Duke's accession (as is well known), the latter dismissed him. He then dropped back into obscurity, but had become by this time some-what more of a personage than he was before. His brief administration of the Navy, the death of the Duke of York, which made him Heir to the throne, his increased wealth and regular habits, had procured him more con-sideration, though not a great deal. Such was his position when George IV broke all at once, and after three months of expectation William finds him-self King.

July 18th—King George had not been dead three days before everybody discovered that He was no loss, and King William a great gain. Certainly nobody ever was less regretted than the late King, and the breath was hardly out of his body before the press burst forth in full cry against him, and raked up all his vices, follies, and misdeeds, which were numerous and glaring enough.

The new King began very well. Everybody expected he would keep the Ministers in office, but he threw himself into the arms of the Duke of Wel-lington with the strongest expressions of confidence and esteem. He proposed to all the Household, as well as to the members of Government, to keep their places, and they all did except Ld. Conyngham and the Duke of Mon-trose. He soon after, however, dismissed most of the Equerries, that he might fill their places with the members of his own family. Of course such

27

a King wanted not due praise, and everybody was quick to find out that we had gained infinitely by the change and plenty of anecdotes were raked up of his former generosities, kindnesses, etc. etc. His first speech to the Council was well enough given, but his burlesque character began even then to show itself. Nobody expected from him much real grief, and he does not seem to know how to act it consistently; he spoke of his brother with all the semblance of feeling, and in a tone of voice properly softened and subdued, but just after, when they gave him the pen to sign the declaration, he said, in his usual tone, 'This is a damned bad pen you have given me.' My worthy colleague Mr. James Buller (the best but stupidest of men) began to swear Privy Councillors in the name of 'King George IV.—William I mean,' to the great diversion of the Council.

A few days after my return I was sworn in, all the Ministers and some others present. His Majesty presided very decently, and looked like a respectable old Admiral. The Duke told me he was delighted with him—'If I had been able to deal with my late master as I do with my present, I should have got on much better'—that he was so reasonable and tractable, and that he had done more business with him in ten minutes than with the other in as many days.

I met George Fitzclarence, the same day, and told him what the Duke said, and he told me how delighted his Father was with the Duke, his entire confidence in him, and how the Duke might as entirely depend upon the King; that he had told H.M., when he was at Paris, that Polignac and the D. of Orleans had both asked him whether the D. of Clarence, when he became King, would keep the Duke of Wellington as his Minister, and the King said, 'What did you reply?' 'I replied you certainly would; did not I do right?' 'Certainly, you did quite right.'

He began immediately to do good-natured things, to provide for old friends and professional adherents, and he bestowed a pension upon Tierney's widow. The great offices of Chamberlain and Steward he abandoned to the Duke of Wellington. There never was anything like the enthusiasm with which he was greeted by all ranks; though he has trotted about both town and country for sixty-four years, and nobody ever turned round to look at him, he cannot stir now without a mob, patrician as well as Plebeian, at his heels. All the Park congregated round the gate to see him drive into town the day before yesterday. But in the midst of all this success and good conduct certain indications of strangeness and wildness peep out which are not a little alarming, and he promises to realise the fears of his Ministers that he will do and say too much, though they flatter themselves that they have muzzled him in his approaching progress by reminding him

28

that his words will be taken as his Ministers' and he must, therefore, be chary of them; but at the late King's funeral he behaved with great indecency. That ceremony was very well managed, and a fine sight, the military part particularly, and the Guards magnificent. The attendance was not very numerous, and when they had all got together in St. George's Hall a gayer company I never beheld; with the exception of Mt. Charles, who was deeply affected, they were all as merry as griggs. (Qu. what is a Grigg?) The King was chief Mourner, and, to my astonishment, as he entered the chapel directly behind the body, in a situation in which he should have been apparently, if not really, absorbed in the melancholy duty he was performing, he darted up to Strathaven, who was ranged on one side below the Dean's stall, shook him heartily by the hand, and then went on nodding to the right and left. He had previously gone as Chief Mourner to sit for an hour at the head of the body as it lay in state, and he walked in procession with his household to the apartment. I saw him pass from behind the screen. Lord Jersey had been in the morning to Bushey to kiss hands on being made Chamberlain, when he had received him very graciously, told him it was the Duke and not himself who had made him, but that he was delighted to have him, etc. At Windsor, when he arrived, he gave Jersey the white wand, or rather took one from him he had provided for himself, and gave it him again with a little speech. When he went to sit in state, Jersey preceded him, and he said when all was ready, 'Go on to the body, Jersey; you will get your dressed Coat as soon as you can.' The morning after the funeral (having slept at Frogmore), he went all over the Castle (into every room in the house), which he had never seen before except a few of them when he came there as a guest; after which he received an address from the ecclesiastical bodies of Windsor and Eton, and returned an answer quite unpremeditated which they told me was excellent.

He is very well with all his family, particularly the Duke of Sussex, but he dislikes and seems to know the Duke of Cumberland, who is furious at his own discredit. The King has taken from him the Gold Stick, by means of which he had usurped the functions of all the other Colonels of the Regiments of the Guards, and put himself always about the late King. He says that the Duke's rank is too high to perform these functions, and has put an end to his services. He has only put the Gold Sticks on their former footing, and they are all to take the duty in turn—so Arbuthnot told me.

In the meantime the Duke of Cumberland has shown his teeth in another way. His horses have hitherto stood in the stables which are appropriated to the Queen, and the other day Errol, her new Master of the Horse, went to H.M. and asked her where she chose her horses should be; she said, of course, she knew nothing about it but in the proper place. Errol then said the D. of Cumberland's horses were in her stables, and could not be got out without an order from the King. The King was spoken to, and he commanded the Duke of Leeds to order them out. The Duke of Leeds took the order to the Duke of Cumberland, who said 'he would be damned if they should go,' when the Duke of Leeds said that he trusted he would have them taken out the following day, as unless he did so he should be under the necessity of ordering them to be removed by the King's Grooms, when the Duke was obliged sulkily to give way. When the King gave the order to the D. of Leeds, he sent for Taylor that he might be present, and said at the same time that he had a very bad opinion of the Duke of Cumberland, and he wished he would live out of the Country.

His good-nature, simplicity, and affability to all about him are certainly very striking, and in his elevation he does not forget any of his old friends and companions. He was in no hurry to take upon himself the dignity of King, nor to throw off the habits and manners of a country gentleman. When Chesterfield went to Bushey to kiss his hand and be presented to the Queen, he found Sir John and Lady Gore there lunching, and when they went away he called for their carriage, handed Lady Gore into it, and stood at the door to see them off. When Howe came over from Twickenham to see him, he said the Queen was going out driving, and should 'drop him' at his own house. The Queen, they say, is by no means delighted at her elevation. She likes quiet and retirement and Bushey (of which he has made her Ranger), and does not want to be a Queen. However, 'l'appétit viendra en mangeant.' He says he does not want luxury and magnificence, has slept in a cot, and he has dismissed the King's cooks, 'renversé la marmite.' He keeps the stud (which is to be diminished) because he thinks he ought to support the turf. He has made Mt. Chas. a Lord of the Bedchamber, and given the Robes to Sir C. Pole, an admiral. Altogether he seems a kind-hearted, well-meaning, not stupid, burlesque, bustling old fellow, and if he doesn't go mad may make a very decent King, but he exhibits oddities. He would not have his servants in mourning—i.e. not those of his own family and household—but he sent the D. of Sussex to Mrs. Fitzherbert to desire she would put hers in mourning, and consequently so they are. The King and she have always been friends, as she has, in fact, been with all the Royal Family, but it was very strange. Yesterday morning he sent for the officer on guard, and ordered him to take all the muffles off the drums, all the scarfs, etc. off the regimentals, and so to appear on Parade, where he went himself. The Colonel would have put the officer under arrest for doing this without his orders, but the King said he was Commanding Officer of his own Guard, and forbad him. All odd, and people are frightened, but his wits will at least last till the new Parliament meets. I sent him a very respectful request through Taylor that he would pay £300, all that remained due of the Duke of York's debts at Newmarket, & to his Jockey which he assented to directly, as soon as the Privy Purse should be settled— very good-natured. In the meantime it is said that the Bastards are dissatisfied that more is not done for them, but he cannot do much for them at once, and he must have time. He has done all he can: he has made Errol Master of the Horse, Sidney a Guelph Knight and Equerry, George Fitzclarence ditto Adjutant-General, and doubtless they will all have their turn.

Of course the stories about the rapacity of the Conynghams have been innumerable. The King's will excited much astonishment, but as yet nothing is for certain known about the money, or what became of it, or what he gave away, and to whom, in his lifetime.

July 20th—Yesterday was a very busy day with H. Majesty, who is going much too fast, and begins to alarm his Ministers and astonish the world. In the morning he inspected the Coldstreams, dressed (for the first time in his life) in a military uniform and with a great pair of gold spurs half-way up his leg like a game-cock, although he was not to ride, for having chalkstones in his hands he can't hold the reins. The Queen came to Lady Bathurst's to see the review and hold a sort of drawing-room, when the Ministers' wives were presented to her, and official men, to which were added Lady Bathurst's relations; everybody was undressed except the Officers. She is very ugly, with a horrid complexion, but has good manners, and did all this (which she hated) very well. She said the part as if she was acting and wished the green curtain to drop. After the review the King, with the Dukes of Cumberland, Sussex, and Gloster, and Prince George and the Prince of Prussia, and the Duchess of Cumberland's son, came in through the garden gate; the Duchess of Gloster and Princess Augusta were already there; they breakfasted and then went away, the Duke of Gloster bowing to the company while nobody was taking any notice of him or thinking about him. Nature must have been merry when she made this Prince, and in the sort of mood that certain great Artists used to exhibit in their comical caricatures; I never saw a countenance which that line in M'Flecknoe would so well describe—

And lambent dullness plays around his face.

At one there was to be a Council, to swear in Privy Councillors and Lord-Lieutenants, and receive Oxford and Cambridge Addresses. The review made it an hour later, and the Lieutenants, who had been summoned at one, and who are great, selfish, pampered aristocrats, were furious at being kept waiting, particularly Lord Grosvenor and the Duke of Newcastle, the former very peevish, the latter better humoured. I was glad to see them put to inconvenience. I never saw so full a Court, so much nobility with Academical Tag rag and bobtail. After considerable delay the King received the Oxford and Cambridge Addresses on the Throne, which (having only one throne between them) he then abdicated for the Queen to seat herself on and receive them too. She sat it very well, surrounded by the Princesses and her Ladies and household. When this mob could be got rid of the table was brought in and the Council held. The Duke was twice sworn as Constable of the Tower and Lieutenant of Hants; then Jersey and the new Privy Councillors; and then the host of Lieutenants six or seven at a time, or as many as could hold a bit of the bible. I begged the King would, to expedite the business, dispense with their kneeling, which he did, and so we got on rapidly enough; and I whispered to Jersey, who stood by me behind the King with his white wand, 'The pace is good, isn't it?' As they each kissed his hand, I told him their name or County, or both, and he had a civil word to say to everybody, inviting some to dinner, promising to visit others, reminding them of former visits, or something good-humoured; he asked Lord Egremont's *permission* to go and live in his County, at Brighton.

All this was very well; no great harm in it; more affable, less dignified than the late King; but when this was over, and after so much fatigue, when he might very well have sat himself quietly down and rested, he must needs put on his plain cloathes and start on a ramble about the Streets, all alone too. In Pall Mall he met Watson Taylor, and took his arm and went up St. James's Street. There he was soon followed by a mob making an uproar, and when he got near White's a whore came up and kissed him. Belfast (who had been sworn in Privy Councillor in the morning), who saw this from White's, and Clinton thought it time to interfere, and came out to attend upon him. The mob increased, and always holding W. Taylor's arm, and flanked by Clinton and Belfast, who got shoved and kicked about to their inexpressible wrath, he got back to the Palace amid shouting and bawling and applause. When he got home he asked them to go in and take a quiet walk in the garden, and said, 'Oh, never mind all this; when I have walked about a few times they will get used to it, and will take no notice.' There are other stories, but I will put down nothing I do not see or hear, or hear from eye witnesses. Belfast told me this in the Park, fresh from the scene and smarting from the buffeting he had got. All the Park was ringing with it, and I told Lady Bathurst, who thought it so serious she would get Ld. B. to write to the Duke directly about it. Lord Combermere wanted to be made a Privy Councillor yesterday, but the Duke would not; he is in a sort of half-disgrace, and is not to be made yet, but will be by-and-by.

21st, Grove Road—Came and established myself here last night after the Duchess of Bedford's ball. Lady Bathurst told me that the Queen spoke to her yesterday morning about the King's walk and being followed, and said that for the future he must walk early in the morning, or in some less publick place, so there are hopes that his activity may be tamed. He sent G. Fitzclarence off from dinner in his silk stockings and cocked hat to Boulogne to invite the K. of Würtemberg to come here; he was back in fifty-six hours, and might have been in less. He employs him in everything, and I heard him yesterday ask the D. of Leeds for two of his father's horses to ride about on his jobs and relieve his own, which the Duke agreed to, but made a wry face. Mount Charles has refused to be Lord of the Bedchamber; his wife can't bear it, and he don't like it nor to go to Windsor under such altered circumstances.

I hardly ever record the scandalous stories of the day, unless they relate to character or events, but what relates to publick men is different from the loves and friendships of the idiots of society. Since I have been away the Chancellor[1] has had a touch of love, and for a person not less immaculate than Lady Fitzroy Somerset. I met her (Lady Chancellor) at the Review breakfast the other day and she told me all about it, Lord Worcester having previously given me an account. He seems to have been fou—tout à fait perdu la tête—for he wrote her note after note, and some from the Bench telling her he was sitting to lawyers to whom he could not listen for his thoughts were all occupied with her. Pleasant for the Suitors this, and would make a pretty paragraph for a speech on Chancery abuses, at least as an argumentum ad Cancellarium. The other told me it was all true, that he had exhibited himself very ridiculously, that she had remonstrated with him strongly, had told him she did not care what he did, so that he abstained from being ridiculous. He swore he had not succeeded, to which she replied so much the worse, as success would have been the best excuse for his folly that he was so in her powers that he dares not be angry with what she says or what she does. I don't know in what her power consists but she says she can certainly unfrock him if she chuses. The fact is she is a whore and he is a knave. La belle would have nothing to say to him so he has been obliged to quitter la partie.

July 24th. Went to St. James's the day before yesterday for a Council for the dissolution, but there was none. Yesterday morning there was an idea of having one, but it is to-day instead, and early in the morning, that the

[1] Lord Lyndhurst.

Ministers may be able to go to their fish dinner at Greenwich. I called on the Duke yesterday morning to know about a Council, but he could not tell me. Then came a Mr. Moss (or his card) while I was there. 'Who is he?' I said. 'Oh, a man who wants to see me about a canal. I can't see him. Everybody will see me, and how the Devil they think I am to see everybody, to be the whole morning with the King, and to do the whole business of the country, I don't know. I am quite worn out with it.' I longed to tell him that it is this latter part they would willing relieve him from.

I met Vesey Fitzgerald, just come from Paris, and had a long conversation with him about the state of the Government; he seems aware of the difficulties and the necessity of acquiring some strength, of the universal persuasion that the Duke will be all in all, and says that in the Cabinet nobody can be more reasonable and yielding and deferential to the opinions of his colleagues. But Murray's appointment, he says, was a mistake, and Aberdeen's (Qu. does he do so ill?). Goulburn has been hardly treated he thinks, and that the Duke cannot whistle off these people as others would have him do. As to Murray it is ridiculous and no personal consideration should induce the Duke to sacrifice the interests of the country by keeping him; it may be disagreeable to dismiss him, but he must do it. Hay told me that for the many years he had been in office he had never met with any public officer so totally inefficient as he, not even Warrender at the Admiralty Board.

In the meantime the King has had his Levee, which was crowded beyond all precedent. He was very civil to the people, particularly to Sefton, who had quarrelled with the late King.

Yesterday he went to the H. of Lords, and was admirably received. I can fancy nothing like his delight at finding himself in the state coach surrounded by all his pomp. He delivered the Speech very well (they say, for I did not go to hear him). He did not wear the crown, which was carried by Lord Hastings. Etiquette is a thing he cannot comprehend. He wanted to take the King of Würtemberg with him in his coach, till he was told it was out of the question. In his private carriage he continues to sit backwards, and when he goes with men makes one sit by him and not opposite to him. Yesterday, after the H. of Lords, he drove all over the town in an open calèche with the Queen, Princess Augusta and the King of Würtemberg, and coming home he set down the K. (dropt him, as he calls it) at Grillon's Hotel. The K. of England dropping another King at a Tavern!! It is impossible not to be struck with his extreme good-nature and simplicity, which he cannot or will not exchange for the dignity of his new situation and the trammels of etiquette; but he ought to be made to understand that his simplicity degenerates into vulgarity, and that without departing from his natural urbanity he may conduct himself so as not to lower the character with which he is invested, and which belongs not to him, but to the country.

At his dinner at St. James's the other day more people were invited than there was room for, and some half-dozen were forced to sit at a side table. He said to Lord Brownlow, 'Well, when you are flooded (he thinks Lincolnshire is all fen) you will come to us at Windsor.' To the Freemasons he was rather good. The D. of Sussex wanted him to receive their address in a solemn audience, which he refused; and when they did come he said, 'Gentlemen, if my love for you equalled my ignorance of everything concerning you, it would be unbounded,' and then he added something good-humoured. The consequence of his trotting about, and saying the odd things he does, is that there are all sorts of stories about him which are not true, and he is always expected everywhere. In the meantime I believe that politically he relies implicitly on the Duke, who can make him do anything. Agar Ellis (who is bustling and active, always wishing to play a part, and gets mixed up with the politicks of this and that party through his various connexions) told me the other day that he knew the Duke was knocking at every door, hitherto without success, and that he must be contented to take a *party,* and not expected to strengthen himself by picking out individuals. I think this too, but why not open his doors to all comers? There are no questions now to stand in his way; his Government must be remodelled, and he may last for ever personally.

July 25th—Yesterday at Court at eleven; a Council for the dissolution. This King and these Councils are very unlike the last—few people present, frequent, punctual, less ceremony observed. Though these Ministers have been in office all their lives, nobody knew how many days must elapse before Parliament was summoned; some said sixty, some seventy days, but not one knew, nor had they settled the matter previously; so Lord Rosslyn and I were obliged to go to Bridgewater House, which was near, and consult the journals. It has always been fifty-two days of late.

In the afternoon another embarrassment. We sent the proclamations to the Chancellor (one for England and one for Ireland), to have the Great Seal affixed to them; he would only affix the Seal to the English, and sent back the Irish unsealed. The Secretary of State would not send it to Ireland without the Great Seal, and all the Ministers were gone to the fish dinner at Greenwich, so that there was no getting at anybody. At last we got it done at Lincoln's Inn and sent it off. The fact is, nobody knows his business, and the Chancellor least of all. The King continues very active; he went after the Council to Buckingham House, then to the Thames Tunnel, has immense dinners every day, and the same people two or three days running. He has dismissed the late King's band, and employs the bands of the Guards every night, who are ready to die for it, for they get no pay and are prevented earning money elsewhere. The other night the K. had a party, and at eleven he dismissed them thus: 'Now, Ladies and Gentlemen, I wish you a good night. I will not detain you any longer from your amusements, and shall go to my own, which is to go to bed; so come along, my Queen.' The other day he was very angry because the Guard did not know him in his plain cloathes and turn out for him—the first appearance of jealousy of his greatness he has shown—and ordered them to be more on the alert for the future.

July 26th—Still the King; his adventures (for they are nothing else) furnish matter of continual amusement and astonishment to his loving subjects. Yesterday morning, or the evening before, he announced to the Duke of Wellington that he should dine with him yesterday; accordingly the Duke was obliged, in the middle of his preparations for his breakfast, to get a dinner ready for him. In the morning he took the K. of Würtemberg to Windsor, and just at the hour when the Duke expected him to dinner he was driving through Hyde Park back from Windsor—three barouches-and-four, the horses dead knocked up, in the front the two Kings, Jersey, and somebody else, all covered with dust. The whole mob of carriages and horsemen assembled near Apsley House to see him pass and to wait till he returned. The Duke, on hearing he was there, rushed down without his hat and stood in his gate in the middle of servants, mob, etc., to see him pass. He drove to Grillon's 'to drop' the K. of W., and at a quarter past eight he arrived at Apsley House. There were about forty-five men, no women, half the Ministers, most of the foreign Ministers, and a mixture rather indiscriminate. In the evening I was at Lady Salisbury's, when arrived the Duke of Sussex, who gave a short account to Sefton of what had passed, and of the King's speech to the company. 'You and I,' he said, 'are old Whigs, my Lord, and I confess I was somewhat astonished to hear his Majesty's speech.' I went afterwards to Crockford's, where I found Matuscewitz, who gave me a whole account of the dinner. The two Kings went out to dinner arm-in-arm, the Duke followed; the King sat between the K. of W. and the Duke. After dinner his health was drunk, to which he returned thanks, sitting, but briefly, and promised to say more by-and-by when he should give a toast. In process of time he desired Douro to go and tell the band to play the merriest waltz they could for the toast he was about to give. He then gave 'The Queen of Würtemberg,' with many eulogiums on

36

her and on the connubial felicity of her and the K.; not a very agreeable theme for his host, for conjugal fidellity is not his forte. At length he desired Douro to go again to the band and order them to play 'See the conquering hero comes,' and then he rose. All the company rose with him, when he ordered everybody to sit down. Still standing, he said that he had been so short a time on the throne that he did not know whether etiquette required that he should speak sitting or standing, but, however this might be, he had been long used to speak on his legs, and should do so now; he then proposed the Duke's health, but prefaced it with a long speech—instituted a comparison between him and the D. of Marlboro; went back to the reign of Queen Anne, and talked of the great support the D. of Marlborough had received from the Crown, and the little support the D. of Wellington had had in the outset of his career, though after the battle of Vimiera he had been backed by all the energies of the country; that, notwithstanding his difficulties, his career had been one continued course of victory over the armies of France; and then, recollecting the presence of Laval, the French Ambassador, he said, 'Remember, Duc de Laval, when I talk of victories over the French Armies, they were not the Armies of my ally and friend the K. of France, but of him who had usurped his throne, and against whom you yourself were combating'; then going back to the Duke's career, and again referring to the comparison between him and Marlboro, and finishing by adverting to his political position, that he had on mounting the throne found the Duke Minister, and that he had retained him because he thought his Administration had been and would be highly beneficial to the country; that he gave to him his fullest and most cordial confidence, and that he announced to all whom he saw around him, to all the Ambassadors and Ministers of foreign Powers, and to all the Noblemen and Gentlemen present, that as long as he should sit upon the throne he should continue to give him the same confidence. The Duke returned thanks in a short speech, thanking the King for his confidence and support, and declaring that all his endeavours would be used to keep this country in relations of harmony with other nations. The whole company stood aghast at the King's extra-ordinary speech and declaration. Matuscewitz told me he never was so astonished, that for the world he would not have missed it, and that he would never have believed it if he had not heard it.

Falck gave me a delightful account of the speech and of Laval. He thought (not understanding one word), that all the King was saying was complimentary to the King of France and the French nation, and he kept darting from his seat to make his acknowledgments, while Esterhazy held him down by the tail of his coat, and the King stopt him with his hand outstretched, all with great difficulty. He said it was very comical.

July 27th—Review in the morning (yesterday), breakfast at Apsley House, Chapter of the Garter, dinner at St. James's, party in the evening, and ball at Apsley House. I don't hear of anything remarkable, and it was so hot I could not go to anything, except the breakfast, which I just looked in to for a minute, and found everybody sweating and stuffing, and the royalties just going away. That Ass the D. of Gloster keeps up his quarrel with the Duke; the D. of Cumberland won't go to Apsley House, but sent the Duchess and his Boy. The Queen said at dinner the other day to the D. of C., 'I am very much pleased with you for sending the Duchess to Apsley House,' and then turned to the D. of Gloucester and said, 'but I am not pleased with you for not letting the Duchess go there.' The fool answered that the Duchess should never go there; he would not be reconciled, forgetting that it matters not twopence to the D. of Wellington and a great deal to himself. There are 40 stories about the King's sayings and doings.

I have been employed in settling half-a-dozen disputes of different sorts, but generally without success, trifling matters, foolish or violent people, not worth remembering any of them. The Chancellor, who does not know his business, has made an attack on my office about the proclamations, but I have vindicated it in a letter to Lord Bathurst—it don't signify however.

July 28th—Yesterday Charles Wynne and I settled the dispute between Clive and Charlton about the Ludlow matters. Charlton agrees to retire from the contest both in the Borough and Corporation, and Clive agrees to pay him £1125 towards his expenses, and not to oppose the reception of any petition that may be presented to the H. of Commons for the purpose of re-opening the question of the right of voting. Both parties are very well satisfied with this termination of their disputes. Met the Chancellor at Ly. Ravensworth's breakfast yesterday, who told me he had sent a rejoinder to my letter to Ld. Bathurst about the proclamations.

July 29th—Yesterday a standing Council at the Levee, to swear in Ld. Hereford and Vesey Fitzgerald, and declare Ld. Bathurst and the D. of Northumberland President and Lord-President. Previously the King received the address of the departing Ministers, and then that of the Quakers, presented by William Allen; they were very prim and respectable persons; their hats were taken off by each other in the room before the Throne Room, and they did not bow, though they seemed half-inclined; they made a very loyal address, but without 'Majesty,' and said 'O King.' There was a question after his answer what they should do. I thought it was whether they should kiss hands, for the K. said something to Peel, who went and asked them, and I heard the King say, 'Oh, just as they like; they needn't if they don't like; it's all one.'

But the great event of the day was the reception of the King of France's two decrees, and the address of his Ministers, who produced them; nothing could surpass the universal astonishment and consternation. Falck told me he was reading the newspaper at his breakfast regularly through, and when he came to this the teacup almost dropt from his hands, and he rubbed his eyes to see whether he saw correctly. Such was the secrecy with which this measure was conceived and acted on, that Pozzo, who is quicker and has better intelligence than anybody, had not a notion of it, as Matuscewitz told me. Aberdeen learnt it through the 'Times,' and had not a line from Stuart. That, however, is nothing extraordinary. I suspect somebody had it, for Raikes wrote me a note the day before, to ask me if there was not *something bad* from France. Matuscewitz told me that Russia would not afford Charles X the smallest support in his new crusade against the Constitution of France, and this he pronounced openly *à qui voulait l'entendre*. I suspect the Duke will be desperately annoyed. The only Minister I had a word with about it was Ld. Bathurst, whose Tory blood bubbled a little quicker at such a despotic act, and while owning the folly of the deed he could not help adding 'he should have repressed the press when he dissolved the Chambers, then he might have done it.' Anyhow we have enlivening times coming.

July 30th—Everybody anxious for news from France. A few hope, and still fewer think, the King of France will succeed, and that the French will submit, but the press here joins in grand chorus against the suppression of the liberty of that over the water. Matuscewitz told me he had a conference with the Duke, who was excessively annoyed; but what seems to have struck him more than anything is the extraordinary secrecy of the business, and neither Pozzo nor Stuart having known one word of it. Up to the last Polignac has deceived everybody, and put such words into the King's mouth that nobody could expect such a *coup*. The King assured Pozzo di Borgo the day before that nothing of the sort was in contemplation. This, like everything else, will be judged by the event—desperate fatuity if it fails, splendid energies and accurate calculation of opposite moral force if it succeeds. I judge that it will fail, because I can see no marks of wisdom in the style of execution, and the State paper is singularly puerile and weak in argument. It is passionate and not dexterous, not even plausible. All this is wonderfully interesting, and will give us a lively autumn.

The King has been to Woolwich, inspecting the Artillery, to whom he gave a dinner, with toasts and hip, hip, hurraing and three times three, himself giving the time. I tremble for him; at present he is only a mountebank, but he bids fair to be a maniac.

Brougham will come in for Yorkshire without a contest; his address was very eloquent. He is rather mad without a doubt; his speeches this year have been sometimes more brilliant than ever they were; but who with such stupendous talents was ever so little considered? We admire him as we do a fine actor, and nobody ever possessed such immense means, and displayed a mind so versatile, fertile, and comprehensive, and yet had such little efficacy and influence. He told me just before he left town that Yorkshire had been proposed to him, but that he had written word he would not stand, nor spend a guinea, nor go there, not even take the least trouble about the concerns of any one of his constituents, if they elected him; but he soon changed his note.

July 31st—Yesterday morning I met Matuscewitz in St. James's Street, who said, 'You have heard the news?' But I had not, so I got into his cabriolet, and he told me that Bülow had just been with him with an account of Rothschild's estafette, who had brought intelligence of a desperate conflict at Paris between the people and the Royal Guard, in which 1000 men had been killed of the former, and of the eventual revolt of two Regiments, which decided the business; that the Swiss had refused to fire on the people; the King gone to Compiègne, the Ministers missing, and the Deputies who were at Paris had assembled in the Chambers, and declared their sittings permanent. No confirmation came of this which was believed. At night Lord Fitzharris (who has married Ly. Tankerville's daughter and niece to Polignac) told me that he had seen Vaudreuil at her house, who had received one of two Couriers who had been sent to him, and that he had brought news to this effect. The Regiment of Chasseurs à cheval which refused to act and had been dismounted and disarmed, was commanded by Vaudreuil's Brother. He is provoked to death with Laval for marching off at this crisis. Nothing can exceed the interest and excitement that all these proceedings create here, and unless there is a reaction, which does not seem probable, the game is up with the Bourbons. They richly deserve their fate. It remains to be seen what part Bourmont and the Algerian army will take; the latter will probably side with the nation, and the former will be guided by his own interest, and is not unlikely to endeavour to direct a spirit which he could not expect to controul. He may reconcile himself to the country by a double treachery.

At night—To-day at one o'clock Stuart's messenger arrived with a meagre account, having left Paris on the night of the 29th. The tri-coloured flag had been raised; the National Guard was up, commanded by Old Lafayette (their chief forty years ago), who ruled in Paris with Gérard, the D. de Choiseul, Odier, Casimir Périer, Lafitte, and one or two more. The Tuileries and the Louvre had been pillaged; the King was at St. Cloud, where Marshal Marmont had retired, and had with him a large force. Nobody, however, believed they would fight against the people. The Deputies and the Peers had met, and the latter separated without doing anything; the former had a stormy discussion, but came to no resolution. Some were for a republic, some for the D. d'Orlèans, some for the D. de Bordeaux with the D. d'Orlèans as Regent. Rothschild had another Courier with later intelligence. The King had desired to treat, and that proposals might be made to him; all the Ministers escaped from Paris by a subterraneous passage which led from the Tuileries to the river, and were at St. Cloud. The Duke told Matuscewitz that 'Marmont had taken up a good military position,' as if it was a military and not a moral question. Strange he should think of such a thing, but they are all terrified to death at the national flag and colours, because they see in its train revolutions, invasions, and a thousand alarms. I own I would rather have seen an easy transfer of the Crown to some other head under the white flag. There was Ly Tankerville going about to-day enquiring of everybody for news, trembling for her brother 'and his Brigade.' Late in the day she got Ly. Jersey to go with her to Rothschild, whom she saw, and Madame Rothschild, who showed her all their letters. Tankerville, who is a sour, malignant little Whig, loudly declares Polignac ought to be hung. The elections are going against Government, and no candidate will avow that he stands on Government interest, or with the intention of supporting the Duke's Ministry, which looks as if it had lost all its popularity.

August 2nd—Yesterday Sunday—no news and no reports, except one that Marmont was killed. I never believe reports. The elections still go against Government. G. Dawson returned from Dublin; all the Peels lost their seats. Fordwich beat Baring at Canterbury by 370 votes. It is said the King was in a state of great excitement at Woolwich the other day, when it was very hot, and he drank a good deal of wine.

Evening—This morning, on going into town, I read in the 'Times' the news of the day—the proclamation of the Provisional Government, the invitation to the D. of Orleans and his proclamation, the account of the conversation between Lafitte and Marmont, etc. It is in vain to look for private or official information, for the 'Times' always has the latest and the best; Stuart sends next to nothing. Soon after I got to George Street the Duke of Wellington came in, in excellent spirits, and talked over the whole matter. He said he could not comprehend how the Royal Guard had been defeated by the mob, and particularly how they had been forced to evacuate the Tuileries; that he had seen English and French troops hold houses whole days not ¼ so strong. I said that there could not be a shadow of doubt that it was because they *would* not fight, that if they *would* have fought they must have beat the mob, and reminded him of the French at Madrid, and asked him if he did not think his Regiment would beat all the populace of London, which he said it would. He described the whole affair as it has taken place, and said that there can be no doubt that the moneyed men of Paris (who are all against the Government) and the Liberals had foreseen a violent measure on the part of the King, and had organised the resistance; that on the appearance of the edicts the Bankers simultaneously refused to discount any bills, on which the great manufacturers and merchants dismissed their workmen, to the number of many thousands, who inflamed the public discontent, and united to oppose the military and the execution of the decrees. He said positively that we should not take any part, and that no other Government ought or could. He does not like the D. of Orleans, and thinks his proclamation mean and shabby, but owned that under all circumstances his election to the Crown would probably be the best thing that could happen. The D. de Chartres he had known here, and thought he was intelligent. The Duke considered the thing as settled, but did not feel at all sure they would offer the Crown to the D. of Orleans. He said he could not guess or form an opinion as to their ulterior proceedings.

After discussing the whole business with his usual simplicity, he began talking of the D. of Cumberland and his resignation of the command of the Blues. Formerly the Colonels of the two Regiments of Life Guards held alternately the Gold Stick, and these two Regiments were under the immediate orders of the King, and not of the Commander-in-Chief. When the Duke of Wellington returned from Spain and had the command of the Blues, the King insisted upon his taking the duty also; so it was divided into three, but the Blues still continued under the Commander-in-Chief. But when the D. of Cumberland wanted to be continually about the late King, he got him to give him the command of his Household troops; this was at the period of the death of the D. of York and the D. of Wellington's becoming Commander-in-Chief. The D. of Cumberland told the D. of Wellington that he had received the King's verbal commands to that effect, and from that time he alone kept the Gold Stick, and the Blues were withdrawn from the authority of the Horse Guards. The Duke of Wellington made no opposition; but last year, during the uproar of the Catholic question, he perceived the inconvenience of the arrangement, and intended to have spoken to the King about it, for the D. of Cumberland was concerned in organising mobs to go down to Windsor to frighten Lady Conyngham and the King, and the Horse Guards, who would naturally have been called in to suppress any tumult, would not have been disposable without the Duke of C.'s concurrence, so much so that on one particular occasion, when the Kentish men were to have gone (20,000 strong) to Windsor, the Duke of Wn. detained a Regiment of light cavalry who were marching elsewhere, that he might not be destitute of military aid. Before, however, he did anything about this with the King ('I always,' he said, 'do one thing at a time') H.M. was taken ill and died.

On the accession of the present King the Duke of Cumberland wished to continue the same system, which H.M. was resolved he should not, and he ordered that the Colonels of the Regiments should take the Stick in rotation. He also ordered (through Sir R. Peel) that Ld. Combermere should command the Troops at the funeral as Gold Stick. This the Duke of C. resisted, and sent down orders to Ld. Cathcart to assume the command. The Duke of W., however, represented to Ld. Cathcart that he had better do no such thing, as nobody could disobey the King's orders given through the Secretary of State, and accordingly he did nothing. But the King was determined to put an end to the pretensions of the D. of Cd., and spoke to the Duke on the subject, and said that he would have all the Regiments placed under the orders of the Commander-in-Chief. The Duke recommended him to replace the matter in the state in which it stood before the D. of Cd.'s pretensions had altered it, but he would not do this, and chose to abide by his original intention; so the three regiments were placed under the orders of the Horse Guards like the rest, and the D. of Cd. in consequence resigned the command of the Blues.

August 3rd—Had a party here last night, cold and rainy. Notwithstanding the above story, the King dined with the D. of C. at Kew yesterday. I went yesterday to the sale of the late King's wardrobe, which was numerous enough to fill Monmouth Street, and sufficiently various and splendid for the wardrobe of Drury Lane. He hardly ever gave away anything except his linen, which was distributed every year. These cloathes are the perquisite of his Pages, and will fetch a pretty sum. There are all the coats, etc. he has ever had for fifty years, 300 whips, canes without number, every sort of uniform, the costumes of all the orders in Europe, splendid furs, pelisses, etc., hunting-coats and breeches, and among other things a dozen pair of conduroy breeches he had made to hunt in when Don Miguel was here. His profusion in these articles was unbounded, because he never paid for them, and his memory so accurate that one of his Pages told me he recollected every article of dress, no matter how old, and that they were always liable to be called on to produce some particular coat or other part of apparel of years gone by. It is difficult to say whether in great or little things that man was most odious and contemptible.

Nothing from France yesterday but the most absurd reports.

August 5th—Yesterday morning at Council; all the Ministers and the Duke of Rutland, Ld. Somers, Rosslyn, and Gower to be sworn Lieutenants. Talked about France with Sir G. Murray, who was silly enough to express his disappointment that things promised to be soon and quietly settled, and hoped the King would have assembled an army and fought for it. Afterwards a Levee. While the Queen was in the closet they brought her word that Charles X was at Cherbourg, and had sent for leave to come here; but nobody knew yesterday if this was true or not. In the afternoon met Vaudreuil, and had a long conversation with him on the things. He said, 'My family has been twice ruined by these cursed Bourbons, and I will be damned if they shall a third time!' that he had long foreseen the inevitable tendency of Polignac's determination, ever since he was here, when he had surrounded himself with low agents and would admit no gentleman into his confidence; one of his *affidés* was a man of the name of Carrier, a relation of the famous Carrier de Nantes. His Father-in-law had consulted him many months ago what to do with £400,000 which he had put in the French funds, and he advised him to sell it out and put it in his drawer, which he did, sacrificing the interest for that time. He had hitherto done nothing, been near none of the Ministers, feeling that he could say nothing to them; no communication had been made to him, but whenever any should be he intended to reply to it. Laval ran away just in time, and Vaudreuil was so provoked at his evasion that he sent after him to say that in such important circumstances he could not take upon himself to act without his Ambassador's instructions. No answer of course. He thinks that if this had not taken place a few years must have terminated the reign of the Bourbons, and that it is only the difference between sudden and lingering death; that when he was at Paris he had seen the dissatisfaction of the young officers in the Guards, who were all Liberal; and knowing these sentiments, what a condition they must have been in when called upon to charge and fire on the people while secretly approving of their conduct, 'entre leurs devoirs de Citoyens et de Militaires!'

I had a conversation with Fitzgerald (Vesey) the other day about the Government and its prospects. They want him greatly to return to office, but he is going abroad again for his health, and I suspect is not very anxious to come in just now, when things look gloomily. He thinks they have acted very injudiciously in sending down candidates to turn out their opponents, which attempts have generally failed, and only served to exasperate the people interested more and more against them—such men as the Grants (as he said), who cannot be kept out of Parliament. But they manage everything ill, and it is impossible to look at the present Ministry and watch its acts, and not marvel that the Duke should think of going on with it. If he does not take care he will be dragged down by it, whereas if he would, while it is yet time, remodel it altogether, and open his doors to all who are capable of serving under him (for all are ready to take him as Chief), he might secure to himself a long and honorable possession of power. Then it is said he can't whistle off these men merely because it is convenient, but he had better do that than keep them on bungling through all the business of the country. Besides, I have some doubts of his tenderheartedness in this respect.

10th, Goodwood—Saturday, the 7th, the King and Queen breakfasted at Osterley on their way to Windsor. They had about sixty or seventy people to meet them, and it all went off very well, without anything remarkable. I went to Stoke after, where there was the usual sort of party.

The King entered Windsor so privately that few people knew him, though he made the horses walk all the way from Frogmore, that he might be seen. On Saturday and Sunday the Terrace was thrown open, and the latter day crowded by multitudes and a very gay sight; there were sentinels on each side of the east front to prevent people walking under the windows of the living-rooms, but they might go where else they liked. The King went to Bagshot and did not appear. All the late King's private drives through the Park are also thrown open, but not to carriages. We went, however, a long string of four carriages, to explore, and got through the whole drive round by Virginia Water, the famous fishing-pagoda, and saw all the penetralia of the late King, whose ghost must have been indignant at seeing us (Sefton particularly) scampering all about his most secret recesses. It is an exceedingly enjoyable spot, and pretty, but has not so much beauty as I expected.

Came here yesterday, and found thirty-two people assembled. (*The next five lines of MS. have been cut out.*) I rode over the downs three or four miles (from Petworth), and never saw so delightful a country to live in. There is an elasticity in the air and turf which communicates itself to the spirits.

In the meantime the French Revolution has been proceeding rapidly to its consummation, and the Duke of Orleans is King. Montrond, who was at Stoke, thinks that France will gravitate towards a Republic, and principally for this reason, that there is an unusual love of equality, and no disposition to profit by the power of making *majorats*, therefore that there never can be

45

anything like an aristocracy. We are so accustomed to see the regular working of our constitutional system, with all its parts depending upon each
other, and so closely interwoven, that we have difficulty in believing that
any monarchical government can exist which is founded on a basis so different. This is the great political problem which is now to be solved. I
think, however, that in the present settlement it is not difficult to see the
elements of future contention and the working of a strong democratical
spirit. The Crown has been conferred on the D. of Orleans by the Chamber
of Deputies alone, which, so far from inviting the Chamber of Peers to
discuss the question of succession, has at the same time decreed a material
alteration in that Chamber itself. It has at a blow cut off all the Peers of
Villèle's great promotion, which is an enormous act of authority, although
the measure may be advisable. There is also a question raised of the hereditary quality of the peerage, and I dare say that for the future at least Peerages will not be hereditary; not that I think this signifies as to the existence
of an aristocracy, for the constant subdivision of property must deprive the
Chamber of all the qualities belonging to an English House of Lords, and
it would perhaps be better to establish another principle, such as that of
promoting to the Chamber of Peers men (for life) of great wealth, influence,
and ability, who would constitute an aristocracy of a different kind indeed,
but more respectable and efficient, than a host of Poor hereditary Senators.
What great men are Lord Lonsdale, the D. of Rutland, Ld. Cleveland, etc.
but strip them of their wealth and power, what would they be? Among the
most insignificant of mankind; but they all acquire a factitious consideration by the influence they possess to do good and evil, the extension of it over
multitudes of dependants. The French can have no aristocracy but a personal one; ours is in the institution; theirs must be individually respectable,
as ours is collectively looked up to. In the meantime it will be deemed a
great step gained to have a monarchy established in France at all, even for
the moment, but some people are alarmed at the excessive admiration which
the French Revolution has excited in England, and there is a very general
conviction that Spain will speedily follow the example of France, and probably Belgium also. Italy I don't believe will throw off the yoke; they have
neither spirit nor unanimity, and the Austrian military force is too great
to be resisted. But Austria will tremble and see that the great victory which
Liberalism has gained has decided the question as to which principle, that
of light or darkness, shall prevail for the future in the world.

August 14th, London—Staid at Goodwood till the 12th; went to Brighton,
riding over the Downs from Goodwood to Arundel, a delightful ride. How
much I prefer England to Italy! There we have mountains and sky; here

vegetation and verdure, fine trees and soft turf; and in the long run the latter are the most enjoyable. Yesterday came to London from Brighton; found things much as they were, but almost everybody gone out of town. The French are proceeding steadily in the reconstruction of their Government, but they have evinced a great democratical spirit. The new King, too, conducts himself in a way that gives me a bad opinion of him; he is too complaisant to the rage for equality, and stoops more than he need do— overdoes it. It is a piece of abominable bad taste (to say no worse) to have conferred a pension on the author of the Marseillaise hymn; for what can be worse than to rake up the old ashes of Jacobinism, and what more necessary than to distinguish as much as possible this Revolution from that of 1789? Then he need not be more familiar as King than he ever was as Duke of Orleans, and affect the manners of a Citizen and a plainness of dress and demeanour very suitable to an American President, but unbecoming a descendant of Louis XIV.

The new Charter is certainly drawn up with great moderation, the few alterations which have been made approximating it to the spirit of the English constitution, and in the whole of the proceedings the analogies of our Revolution have been closely followed. But there has been a remarkable deviation, which I think ominous, and I can't imagine how it has escaped with so little animadversion here. That is the cavalier manner in which the Chamber of Peers has been treated, for the Deputies not only assumed all the functions of Government and legislation, and disposed by their authority of the crown without inviting the concurrence of the other Chamber, but at the same time they exercised an enormous act of authority over the Chamber of Peers itself in striking off the whole of that great promotion of Charles X, which, however wise and perhaps unconstitutional, was perfectly legal, and those Peers had, in fact, as good a right to their Peerages as any of their colleagues. They have reconstructed the Chamber of Peers, and conferred upon it certain rights and Privileges; but the Power which can create can also destroy, and it must be pretty obvious after this that that Chamber will be for the future nothing better than a superior Court of Judicature, depending for its existence upon the will of the popular branch. There are some articles of the old Charter which I am astonished at their keeping, but which they may possibly alter at the revision which is to take place next year, those particularly which limit the entrance to the Chamber of Deputies to men of forty, and which give the initiation of laws to the King. But on the whole it is a good sign that they should alter so little, and looks like extreme caution and a dislike to rapid and violent changes.

In the meantime we hear nothing of the old King, who marches slowly on with his family. It has been reported in London that Polignac is here, and also that he is taken. Nobody knows the truth. I have heard of his behaviour, however, which was worthy of his former imbecility. He remained in the same presumptuous confidence up to the last moment, telling those who implored him to retract while it was still time that they did not know France, that he did, that it was essentially Royalist, and all resistance would be over in a day or two, till the whole ruin burst on him at once, when he became like a man awakened from a dream, utterly confounded with the magnitude of the calamity and as pusillanimous and miserable as he had before been blind and confident. It must be owned that their end has been worthy of the rest, for not one of them has evinced good feeling, or magnanimity, or courage in their fall, nor excited the least sympathy or commiseration. The Duc of Fitzjames made a good speech in the Chamber of Peers, and Chateaubriand a very fine one a few days before, full of eloquence in support of the claim of the Duc de Bordeaux against that of Louis Philippe I.

In the meantime our Elections here are still going against Government, and the signs of the times are all for reform and retrenchment, and against slavery. It is astonishing the interest the people generally take in the slavery question, which is the work of the Methodists, and shows the enormous influence they have in the country. The Duke (for I have not seen him) is said to be very easy about the next Parliament, whereas, as far as one can judge, it promises to be quite as unmanageable as the last, and is besides very ill-composed—full of Boys and all sorts of strange men.

August 20th, Friday—On Monday to Stoke; Alvanley, Fitzroy Somerset, Matuscewitz, Stanislas Potocki, Glengall, Mornay, etc. were there. Lady Sefton (who had dined at the Castle a few days before) asked the King to allow her to take Stanislas to see Virginia Water in a carriage (which is not allowed), but which he agreed to. Accordingly we started, and, going through the private drives, went up to the door of the tent opposite the fishing-house. They thought it was the Queen coming, or at any rate a party from the Castle, for the man on board the little frigate hoisted all the colours, and the boatmen on the other side got ready the royal barge to take us across. We went all over the place on both sides, and were delighted with the luxury and beauty of the whole concern. On one side are a number of tents, communicating together in separate apartments and forming a very good house, a dining-room, drawing-room, and several other small rooms, very well furnished; across the water is the fishing-cottage, beautifully ornamented, with one large room and a dressing-room on each side; kitchen, offices, etc. are in a garden full of flowers, shut out from everything.

Opposite the windows is moored a large boat, in which the band used to play during dinner, and in summer the late King used to dine every day either in the house or in the tents. We had scarcely seen anything when Mr. Turner, the head-keeper, arrived in great haste, having seen us from the opposite side, and very angry at our carriages having come there, which is a thing forbidden and he did not know of our leave.

The next day I called on Batchelor (he was *Valet de chambre* to the Duke of York, afterwards to George IV), who has an excellent apartment in the Lodge,[1] and which (he said) had been occupied by Nell Gwynne, though I did not know the Lodge was built at that time. I was there a couple of hours, and heard all the details of the late King's illness, and other things. For many months before his death those who were about him were aware of his danger, but nobody dared to say a word. The King liked to cheat people with making them think he was well, and when he had been at Council he would return to his apartments and tell his *Valets de chambre* how he had deceived them. During his illness he was generally cheerful, but occasionally dejected, and constantly thought of his Brother the Duke of York, and of the similarity of their symptoms, and was always comparing them. He had been latterly more civil to Knighton than he used to be, and Knighton's attentions to him were incessant; whenever he thought himself worse than usual, and in immediate danger, he always sent for Sir William. Lady Conyngham and her family always went into his room once a day; till his illness she never went into his room but he always used to go and sit in hers. It was true that last year, when she was so ill, she was very anxious to leave the Castle, and that it was Sir William Knighton who with great difficulty induced her to stay there. At that time She was in wretched spirits, and did nothing but pray from morning till night. However her conscience does not seem ever to have interfered with her ruling passion, avarice, and She went on accumulating. During the last illness wagons were loaded every night and sent away from the Castle, but what their contents were was not known, at least he did not say. All Windsor knew this. Those servants of the King who were about his person had opportunities of hearing a great deal, for he used to talk of everybody before them, and without reserve or measure. He said that a year ago when Mt. Charles was sent away with his family from Cumberland Lodge (and which he was so indignant at at the time), it was in consequence of some indiscretion of which he had been guilty, in talking either of what passed in the house or in letting out some political matter of which he had come to the knowledge, and that it was the Duke of Wellington who had given the information to the King

[1] The Lower Lodge in Windsor Castle now part of the Royal Mews.

in consequence of which he was expelled. Batchelor did not know precisely what the thing was, but it must have been political if the Duke took it up; nor did he know to whom he had talked, only that this was the cause.

This man had become a great favourite with the King. The first of his Pages, William Holmes, had for some time been prevented by ill health from attending him. He had been with him from a boy, and was also a great favourite; by appointments and perquisites he had as much as £12,000 or £14,000 a year, but had spent so much in all sorts of debauchery and living like a gentleman that he was nearly ruined. There seems to have been no end to the *tracasseries* between these men, their anxiety to get what they could out of his wardrobe in the last weeks, and their dishonesty in the matter, all of which he told me in great detail but which don't much matter. He told me he was sure that it was Jack Radford who had said something to the King against me which had prevented his putting his horses under my care when the D. of York died. The King was more than anybody the slave of habit and open to impressions, and even when he did not like people he continued to keep them about him rather than change. He told me a vast number of particulars but most of them trifling.

While I was at Stoke news came that Charles X had arrived off Portsmouth. He has asked for an asylum in Austria, but when once he has landed here he will not move again, I dare say. The enthusiasm which the French Revolution produced is beginning to give way to some alarm, and not a little disgust at the Duc of Orleans' conduct, who seems anxious to assume the character of a Jacobin King, affecting such simplicity and laying aside all the pomp of royalty. I don't think it can do, and there is certainly enough to cause serious disquietude for the future.

Sefton in the meantime told me that Brougham and Lord Grey were prepared for a violent opposition, and that they had formed a formal junction with Huskisson, being convinced that no Government could now be formed without him. I asked him if Palmerston was a party to this junction, and he said he was, and the first thing I heard when I got to town was that there is a negotiation going on between Palmerston and the Duke, and that the former takes every opportunity of declaring his goodwill to the latter, and how unshackled he is. Both these things can't be true, and time will show which is. It seems odd that Palmerston should abandon his party on the eve of a strong coalition, which is not unlikely to turn out the present Administration, but it is quite impossible to place any dependence upon publick men nowadays. There is Lord Grey with his furious opposition, having a little while ago supported the Duke (in a sort of way), having advised Rosslyn to take office, and now, because his own vanity is hurt at

not being invited to take office, or more consulted, upon the slight pretext
of the Galway Bill in the last Parliament he rushes into rancorous opposition, and is determined to give no quarter and listen to no compromise.
Brougham is to lead this Opposition in the H. of C., and Ld. Grey in the
Lords, and nothing is to be done but as the result of general deliberation
and agreement. Brougham in the meantime has finished his triumph at
York in a miserable way, having insulted Martin Stapylton on the hustings,
who called him to account, and then he forgot what he had said, and slunk
away with a disclaimer of intentional offence, as usual beginning with intemperance and ending with submission. His speeches were never good, but
at his own dinner he stated so many untruths about the Duke of Wellington
that his own partisans bawled out 'No, no,' and it was a complete failure.
His whole spirit there was as bad as possible, paltry, lying and commonplace. That man, with all his talents, never can or will *do* in any situation;
he is base, cowardly, and unprincipled, and with all the execrable judgement
which, I believe, often flows from the perversion of moral sentiment.
Nobody can admire his genius, eloquence, variety and extent of information, and the charm of his society more than I do; but his faults are glaring,
and the effects of them manifest to anybody who will compare his means
and their results.

August 23rd—General Baudron is come over with a letter from K. L.
Philip to K. William. He saw the Duke and Aberdeen yesterday. There is
nothing new. Charles X goes to Lulworth Castle, and is by way of going
to Austria, but I think he will not move again. He has got some money.
What are called moderate people are greatly alarmed at the aspect of affairs
in France, but I think the law (which will be carried) of abolishing capital
punishment in political cases is calculated to tranquillise men's minds everywhere, for it draws such a line between the old and the new Revolution.
The Ministers will be tried and banished, but no blood spilt. Lord Anglesey
went to see Charles X, and told him openly his opinion of his conduct. The
King laid it all upon Polignac. The people of Paris wanted to send over a
deputation to thank the English for their sympathy and assistance—a sort
of fraternising affair—but the King would not permit it, which was wisely
done, and it is a good thing to see that he can curb in some degree that
spirit; this Vaudreuil told me last night. It would have given great offence
and caused great alarm here.

August 24th—Alvanley had a letter from Montrond yesterday from Paris.
He was with M. de Molé when a letter was brought him from Polignac,
beginning, 'Mon cher Collègue,' and saying that he wrote to him to ask his
advice what he had better do, that he should have liked to retire to his own

estate, but it was too near Paris; that he should like to go into Alsace, and that he begged he would arrange it for him, and in the meantime send him some boots, and shirts, and breeches.

The King continues off Cowes, many people visiting him. They came off without cloaths or preparation of any kind, so much so that Lady Grantham has been obliged to furnish Mesdames de Berri and d'Angoulême with everything; it seems they have plenty of money. The King says he and his Son have retired from publick life; and as to his Grandson, he must wait the progress of events; that his conscience reproaches him with nothing.

The dinner in St. George's Hall on the King's birthday was the finest thing possible—all good and hot, and served on the late King's gold plate. There were one hundred people at table. After dinner the King gave the D. of W.'s health, as it was the anniversary of Vimiera; the Dukes of Cumberland and Gloster turned their glasses down. I can't agree with Charles X that it would be better to '*travailler pour son pain*' than be K. of England.'

I went yesterday all over Lambeth Palace, which has been nearly rebuilt by Blore, and admirably done; one of the best houses I ever saw. Archbishop Juxon's Hall has been converted into the library of the Palace, and is also amazingly well done and a fine thing in its way. It is not to cost above £40,000. The Lollards' Tower, which is very curious, with its iron rings, and the names of the Lollards written on the walls, is not to be touched.

At night—Went to Lady Glengall's to meet Marmont. He likes talking of his adventures, but he had done his Park talk before I got there; however, he said a great deal about old campaigning, Buonaparte, etc., which, as well as I recollect, I will put down.

About the battle of Salamanca, that, without meaning to detract from the glory of the English arms, he was inferior in force; our army provided with everything, well paid, and the country favourable, his 'dénuée de tout,' without pay, in a hostile country; that all his provisions came from a great distance and under great escorts, and his communications were kept up in the same way. Of Russia, that Buonaparte's army was destroyed by the time he got to Moscow, destroyed by famine; that there were two ways of making war, by slow degrees with magazines, etc. or by rapid movements and reaching places where abundant means of supply and reorganisation were found, as he had done at Vienna and elsewhere, but in Russia supplies were not to be had. He had pushed on with this rapidity and destroyed his army: that Marshal (Davoust I think, but am not sure) had done a *corps d'armée* of 80,000 men, and reached Moscow with 15,000; the cavalry were 50,000 sabres, at Moscow they were 6000. Somebody asked him if his Generals had not dissuaded him from going to Russia. He said no; they liked it; but he ought

to have stopt at Smolensk, made Poland independent, and levied 50,000
Cossacks, the Polish Cossacks being better than the Russian, who would
have kept all his communications clear, and allowed the French army to
repose, and then he would have done in two campaigns what he wished to
accomplish in one; instead of which he never would deal with Poland liberally, but held back with ulterior views, and never got the Poles cordially
with him. Of the campaign of '13 that it was ill-conducted by Napoleon and
full of faults; his creation of the army wonderful, and the battle of Dresden
would have been a great movement if he had not suddenly abandoned Vandamme after pushing him on to cut off the retreat of the Allies. It was an
immense fault to leave all the garrisons in the Prussian and Saxon Fortresses.
The campaign of '14 was one of his most brilliant. He (Marmont) commanded a *corps d'armée*, and fought most of the celebrated actions, and he
never had 4000 men; at Paris, which he said was 'the most honourable part
of his whole career,' he had 7500. Napoleon committed a great fault in
throwing himself into the rear as he did; should have fallen back upon
Paris, where his own presence would have been of vast importance, and
sent Marmont into the rear with what Troops he could collect. I told him
what the Duke of Wellington had once told me, that if the Emperor had
continued the same plan, and fallen back on Paris, he would have obliged
the Allies to retreat; and asked him what he thought. He rather thought so
too, but said the Emperor had conceived one of the most splendid pieces of
strategy that ever had been devised, and which failed by the disobedience
of Eugene. He sent orders to Eugene to assemble his army, in which he had
35,000 French Troops, to amuse the Austrians by a negotiation for the
evacuation of Italy; to throw the Italian Troops into Alessandria and
Mantua (I think); to destroy the other fortresses, and going by forced
marches with his French Troops, force the passage of the Mt. Cenis, collect
the scattered *corps d'armée* of Augureau (who was near Lyons) and another
French General (whose name I forget), which would make his force amount
to above 60,000 men, and burst upon the rear of the Allies, so as to cut off
all their communications. These orders he sent to Eugene, but Eugene
'rêvait d'être roi d'Italie après sa chute,' and he sent his A.D.C. Tascher to
excuse himself. The movement was not made, and the game was up. Lady
Dudley Stewart was there, Lucien's daughter and Bonaparte's niece. Marmont was presented to her, and She heard him narrate all this; there is
something very simple, striking, and soldierlike in his manner and appearance. He is going to Russia. Yesterday I was invited to meet him at dinner
but could not go.

He was very communicative about events at Paris, lamented his own ill-luck, involved in the business against his wishes and feelings; he disapproved of Polignac and his measures, had no notion the *ordonnance* was thought of. In the morning was going to St. Germain for the day, when his A.D.C. brought him the newspaper with the *ordonnances*. *Il tomba de son haut.* Soon after the Dauphin sent to him to desire that, as there might be some 'vitres cassées,' that he would take the command of the Troops. Directly after the thing began. He had 7000 or 8000 men; not a preparation had been made of any sort; they had never thought of resistance, had not consulted Marmont or any military man; he soon found how hopeless the case was, and sent eight estafettes to the K. one after another during the action to tell him so and implore him to stop while it was time. They never sent any answer. He then escaped to St. Cloud, where he implored the King to yield. It was not till after seven hours' pressing that he consented to name M. de Mortemar Minister, but would not withdraw the edicts. He says that up to Wednesday night they would have compromised and accepted M. de Mortemar and the suppression of the edicts, but the King still demurred. On Wednesday night he yielded, but the communications were interrupted. That night the meeting at the Palais Royal took place, at which his fate was determined; and on Thursday morning, when his offers arrived, it was too late, and they would no longer treat. He had been treated with the greatest ingratitude by the Court, and had taken leave of them for ever—coldly of the King and Dauphin; and the Duchesse de Berri alone shook hands with him and thanked him for his services and fidelity. He says never man was so unlucky, that he was *Maréchal de quartier* and could not refuse to serve, —only acted on the defensive; that 2000 of the Troops and 1500 of the populace were killed. The Swiss did not behave well, but the Lanciers de la Garde beautifully, and all the Troops were acting against their feelings and opinions. Marmont said that Stuart had sent Cradock to Charles X to desire he would go as slowly as he could to give time for a reaction which he expected would take place. Cradock did go to the King, but I rather doubt this story.

August 27th—At Court the day before yesterday; Parliament prorogued and summoned. General Baudrand came afterwards and delivered his letter, also a private letter 'from the D. of Orleans to the D. of Clarence'—as the French King called it, 'anciens amis.' He was well received and well satisfied. I never knew such a burst of indignation and contempt as Polignac's letter has caused—letter to the President of the Chamber of Peers. As Dudley says, it has saved history the trouble of disreputing that man, and speaks volumes about the recent events. Such a man to have been Prime Minister of France for a year!!

August 29th—Dined with Dudley the day before yesterday to meet Marmont, who is made very much of here by the few people who are left. He had been to Woolwich in the morning, when the Duke of Wellington had given orders that everything should be shown to him, and the honors handsomely done. He was very much gratified, and he found the man who had pointed the gun which wounded him at Salamanca, and who had since lost his own arm at Waterloo. Marmont shook hands with him and said, 'Ah, mon ami, chacun a son tour.' Lady Aldboro came in the evening, and flew up to him with 'Ah, mon cher Maréchal, embrassez-moi'; and so after escaping the cannon's mouth at Paris, he was obliged to face Ly. Aldboro's mouth here. This was my first dinner at Dudley's, brought about *malgré lui* by Lady Glengall. He has always disliked and never invited me, but now (to all appearance) we are friends. He said he had been to see an old man who lives near the World's End—Chelsea—who is 110 years old; he has a good head of hair, with no grey hairs in it; his health, faculties, and memory perfect; is Irish, and has not lived with greater temperance than other people. I sat next to Palmerston, and had a great deal of conversation with him, and from the tenour of his language infer that he has no idea of joining Government. Agar Ellis assured me the other day that there was not a word of truth in the reported junction between Ld. Grey and Huskisson. The Duke has got two months to make his arrangements, but I am afraid he is not prepared for all the sacrifices his position requires. It is now said that the exasperation against the late Ministers (particularly Polignac) is so great in France that it is doubtful whether they will be able to save their lives.

November 25th[1]—The accounts from the country on the 23rd were so bad that a Cabinet sat all the morning, and concerted a proclamation offering large rewards for the discovery of offenders, rioters, or burners. Half the Cabinet walked to St. James's, where I went with the proclamation in my pocket, and we held a Council in the King's room to approve it. I remember the last Council of this sort we held was on Queen Caroline's business. She had demanded to be heard by counsel in support of her asserted right to be crowned, and the King ordered in Council that she should be heard. We held the Council in his dressing-room at Carlton House; he was in his bedgown, and we in our boots.

Yesterday the accounts were better. There was a Levee and Council, all the Ministers present but Palmerston and Holland. The King made a dis-

---

[1] The Conservative Government under Wellington had fallen a few days earlier, and the King had asked Lord Grey to form a Government on 19 November.

course, and took occasion (about some Admiralty order) to introduce the whole history of his early naval life, his first going to sea and the instructions which George III gave Admiral Digby as to his treatment. All the old Ministers came to the levee except the Duke of Wellington, who went into Hants to try his influence as Lord-Lieutenant in putting down riots. Anson as Master of the Buckhounds was made a Privy Councillor, not usually a Privy Councillor's place, but the King said he rather liked increasing the number than not. Clanricarde has a Gold Stick, so there is Canning's son-in-law in office under Lord Grey. There has been a difficulty about the Master-General of the Ordnance, and a little difference between Lord Grey and Ld. Hill: when Richmond was withdrawn, he determined to appoint Sir W. Gordon, but as he would have to give up a permanent for a temporary office, he bargained that he should have a Govt. and Grand Cross of the Bath. Lord Grey at the same time promised his Brother Sir Charles Grey a Grand Cross, but Lord Hill (who as Commander-in-Chief has all the Crosses at his disposal) was offended at what he considered a slight to him, and went to the King to complain. It is probable that Lord Grey knew nothing of the matter, and fancied they were all recommended by himself. As the matter stands now, Gordon's appointment is suspended. The only other difficulty is to find a Secretary at War. Sandon is to have it, if they can make no better arrangement. I had a long conversation with the D. of Richmond yesterday about refusing the salary of his office, and entreated him to take it, for most people think it great nonsense his declining to take it. He alleged a great many bad reasons for declining, but promised to reconsider the matter.

November 28th. The Duke of Wellington, who as soon as he was out of office repaired to Hants, and exerted himself as Lord-Lieutenant to suppress the disorders, returned yesterday, having done much good, and communicated largely with the Secretary of State. The Government are full of compliments and respects to him, and the Chancellor wrote him a letter entreating he would name any gentleman to be added to the Special Commission which was going down to the County over which he 'so happily presided.' He named three.

There has been nothing new within these three days, but the alarm is still very great, and the general agitation which pervades men's minds unlike what I have seen. Reform, economy, echoed backwards and forwards, the doubts, the hopes, and the fears of those who have anything to lose, the uncertainty of everybody's future condition, the immense interests at stake, the magnitude and imminence of the danger, all contribute to produce a nervous excitement, which extends to all classes and to almost every individual. Until the Ministers are re-elected nobody can tell what will be done in Parliament, and Lord Grey himself has no idea what sort of strength the Government will have in either House; but there is a prevailing opinion that they ought to be supported at this moment, although the Duke of Wellington and Peel mean to keep their party together. Lyndhurst's resignation with his Colleagues (added to his not being invited to join this Government) has restored him to the good graces of his party, for Ld. Bathurst told me he had behaved very honourably. He means now to set to work to gain character, and as he is about the ablest public man going, and nearly the best speaker, he will yet bustle himself into consideration and play a part once more. Peel, Lyndhurst, and Harding are three capital men for the foundation of a party—as men of business superior to any three in this Cabinet. But I doubt if the Duke will ever be in a civil office again, nor do I think the Country would like to see him at the head of a Government, unless it was one conducted in a very different manner from the last. For the present deplorable state of things, and for the effervescence of public opinion, which threatens the overthrow of the constitution in trying to amend it, Peel and the Duke are entirely responsible; and the former is the less excusable because he might have known better, and if he had gone long ago to the Duke, and laid before him the state of public opinion, told him how irresistible it was, and had refused to carry on the Government in the H. of C. with such a crew as he had, the Duke must have given way. Notwithstanding the great measures which have distinguished his Government, such as Catholic Emancipation, and the repeal of the Test Acts, a continual series of systematic blunders, and utter ignorance of, and indifference to, public opinion, have rendered the first of these great measures almost useless. Ireland is on the point of becoming in a worse state than before the Catholic question was settled; and why? Because, first of all, the settlement was put off too long, and the fever of agitation would not subside, and because it was accompanied by an insult to O'Connel, which he has been resolved to revenge, and which he knows he can. Then instead of depriving him of half the means by paying the Priests, and so getting them under the influence of Government, they neglected this, and followed up the omission by taxing Ireland, and thus uniting the whole nation against us. What is this but egregious presumption, blindness, ignorance, and want of all political calculation and foresight? What remains now to be done? Perhaps nothing, for the anti-Union question is spreading far and wide with a velocity that is irresistible, and it is the more dangerous then, that the desire for the repeal of the Union is rather the offspring of imagination than of reason, and arises from vague, excited hopes, not, like the former agitation, from real wrongs, long and deeply felt. But common shifts and expedients, partial measures, will not do now, and in the state of the game a deep stake must be played or all will be lost. To buy O'Connel at any price, pay the Catholic Church, establish poor laws, encourage emigration, and repeal the obnoxious taxes and obnoxious laws, are the only expedients which have a chance of restoring order. It is easy to write these things, but perhaps difficult to carry them into execution, but what we want is a head to conceive and a heart to execute such measures as the enormous difficulties of the times demand.

December 1st—The last two or three days have produced no remarkable outrages, and though the state of the country is still dreadful, it is rather better on the whole than it was; but London is like the capital of a country desolated by civil war or foreign invasion, and we are always looking for reports of battles, burnings, and other disorders. Wherever there has been anything like fighting, the mob has always been beat, and has shown the greatest cowardice. They do not, however, seem to have been actuated by a very ferocious spirit; and, considering the disorders of the times, it is remarkable that they have not been more violent and rapacious. Lord Craven, who is just of age, with three or four more young Lords, his friends, defeated and dispersed them in Hampshire. They broke into the D. of Beaufort's house at Heythrop, but he and his Sons got them out without mischief, and afterwards took some of them; and on Monday, as the field which had been out with the King's hounds were returning to town, they were summoned to assist in quelling a riot at Woburn, which they did; and the gentlemen charged and broke the people, and took some of them, and fortunately some troops came up to secure the Prisoners. The alarm, however, still continues, and a feverish anxiety about the future universally prevails, for no man can foresee what course events will take, nor how his own individual circumstances may be affected by them.

The Government in the meantime promises fair, and they begin by a display of activity, in early attendance at their offices, and unusual recommendations of diligence and economy. But Lord Grey's Government is already carped at, and not without apparent reason. The distribution of Offices is in many instances bad; many of the appointments bad, and the number of his own family provided for severely criticised. There are of Lord Grey's family: Howick, Under-Secretary; Ellice, Secretary of the Treasury; Barrington, Lord of the Admiralty; Durham, Privy Seal; Wood, Private Secretary (though he has no salary); Lambton's Brother in the Household. Melbourne at the Home Office is considered an inefficient successor to Peel, Graham too young and not enough distinguished for the Admiralty;

Poulett Thomson, an ultra political communist, and himself in trade, with a very bad character in the City; he is by way of having left his house, but with an understanding that he is to be taken back whenever he leaves office, so his going out of it is a farce. Althorp put him in. There never was a more sudden rise than this; a young merchant, after two or three years of Parliament and two or three speeches, is made Vice-President of the Board of Trade, Treasurer of the Navy, and a Privy Councillor. Chas. Grenfell told me yesterday that he heard at a meeting of the Bank Directors somebody say that if Thomson and Ellice were 2 years in office they would make half a million apiece. Then Althorp as Chancellor of the Exchequer may be a good one, but nobody expects much from anything that is already known about him. This constitution of the Government has already done harm, and has stamped a character of rapacity upon Lord Grey, which he will hear of in proper time; but at this moment he has got all the press on his side, and people are resolved to give him credit for good intentions. Brougham has captivated the Archbishop of Canterbury by offering to give livings to any deserving Clergymen he would recommend to him. I met him at dinner yesterday in the greatest spirits, elated and not altered by his new dignity. He is full of projects of reform in the administration of Justice, and talks of remodelling the Privy Council as a Court of Appeal, which would be of great use.

December 2nd—The Liverpool Election is just over—considering the present state of things, a remarkable contest. It is said to have cost near £100,000 to the two parties, and to have exhibited a scene of bribery and corruption perfectly unparalleled; no concealment or even semblance of decency were observed; the price of tallies and of votes rose, like stock, as the demand increased, and single votes fetched from £15 to £100 apiece. They voted by tallies; as each tally voted for one or the other candidate they were furnished with a receipt for their votes, with which they went to the committee, when through a hole in the wall the receipt was handed in, and through another the stipulated sum handed out; and this scene of iniquity has been exhibited at a period when the cry for Reform is echoed from one end of the country to the other, and in the case of a man (Denison) who stood on the principle of Reform, and is what is called a virtuous character. Nobody yet knows whence the money for Denison comes (the Ewarts are enormously rich), but it will be still more remarkable if he should pay it himself, when he is poor, careful of money, and was going to India the other day in order to save £12,000 or £15,000. If anybody had gone down at the eleventh hour and polled one good vote, he would have beat both candidates and disfranchised the borough. As it is, it is probable the matter will be taken up and the borough disfranchised. The right of voting is as bad as possible in the freemen, who are the lowest rabble of the town and, as it appears, a parcel of venal wretches. Here comes the difficulty of Reform, for how is it possible to reform the Electors?

December 5th—The country is getting quieter, but though the immediate panic is passing away, men's minds are not the less disquieted as to our future prospects. Not a soul knows what plan of Reform the Ministers will propose, nor how far they are disposed to go. The Duke of Devonshire has begun in his own person by announcing to the Knaresboro people that he will never again interfere with that borough. Then the Black Book, as it is called, in which all places and pensions are exhibited, has struck terror into all who are named and virtuous indignation into all who are not. Nothing can be more *mal à propos* than the appearance of this book at such a season, when there is such discontent about our institutions and such unceasing endeavours to bring them into contempt. The history of the book is this:— Graham moved last year for a return of all Privy Councillors who had more than £1000 a year, and Goulburn chose to give him a return of *all persons* who had more than £1000 a year, because he thought the former return would be invidious to Privy Councillors; so he caused that to be published, which will remove no obloquy from those he meant to save, but draw down a great deal on hundreds of others, and on the Government under which such things exist. I speak feelingly, for 'quorum pars magna' sum.

In the meantime the Government is going on what is called well—that is, there is a great disposition to give them a fair trial. All they have done and promise to do about economy gives satisfaction, and Reform (the awful question) is still at a distance. There has been, however, some sharp skirmishing in the course of the week, and there is no want of bitterness and watchfulness on the part of the Old Government. In the Committee which has been named to enquire into the salaries of the Parliamentary Offices they mean to leave the question in the hands of the Country Gentlemen; but they do not think any great reductions will be practicable, and as Baring is chairman it is not probable that much will be done. They think Brougham speaks too often in the H. of Lords, but he has done very well there; and on Friday he made a reply to Lord Stanhope, which was the most beautiful piece of sarcasm and complete cutting-up (though with very good humour) that ever was heard, and an exhibition to the like of which the Lords have not been accustomed. The Duke of Wellington made another imprudent speech, in which (in answer to Lord Radnor, who attributed the state of the country to the late Government) he said that it was attributable to the events of July and August in other countries, and spoke of them in a way which showed clearly his real opinion and feelings on the subject.

1831

January 2nd 1831—Came up to town yesterday to dine with the Villiers at a dinner of clever men, got up at the the Athenæum, and was extremely bored. The original party was broken up by various excuses, and the vacancies supplied by men none of whom I knew. There were Poulett Thomson, three Villiers, Taylor, Young, whom I knew; the rest I never saw before— Buller, Romilly, Senior, Maule, a man whose name I forget, and Walker, a police magistrate, all men of more or less talent and information, and altogether producing anything but an agreeable party. Maule was Senior Wrangler and Senior Medallist at Cambridge, and is a lawyer. He was Nephew to the man with whom I was at school thirty years ago, and I have never seen him since; he was then a very clever boy, and assisted to teach the boys, being admirably well taught himself by his Uncle, who was an excellent Scholar and a great Brute. I have young Maule now in my mind's eye suspended by the hair of his head while being well caned, and recollect as if it was yesterday his doggedly drumming a lesson of Terence into my dull and reluctant brain as we walked up and down the garden-walk before the house. When I was introduced to him I had no recollection of him, but when I found out who he was I went up to him with the blandest manner as he sat reading a newspaper, and said that 'I believed we had once been well acquainted, though we had not met for twenty-seven years.' He looked up and said, 'Oh, it is too long to talk about,' and then turned back to his paper. So I set him down for a brute like his Uncle and troubled him no further. I am very sure that dinners of all fools have as good a chance of being agreeable as dinners of all clever people; at least the former are often gay, and the latter are frequently heavy. Nonsense and folly gilded over with good breeding and *les usages du monde* produce more agreeable results than a collection of rude, awkward intellectual powers.

February 6th—Parliament met again on the 3rd, and the House of Commons exhibited a great array on the Opposition benches; nothing was done the first day but the announcement of the Reform measure for the 2nd of March, to be brought in by John Russell in the H. of C., though not a Cabinet Minister. The fact is that if a Cabinet Minister had introduced it, it must have been Althorp, and he is wholly unequal to it; he cannot speak at all, so that though the pretence is to pay a compliment to John because he had on former occasions brought forward plans of Reform, it is really an expedient to take the burthen off the Leader of the Government. The next night came on the Civil List, and as the last Government was turned out on this question, there had existed a general but vague expectation that some wonderful reductions were to be proposed by the new Chancellor of the Exchequer. Great, then, was the exultation of the Opposition when it was found that no reductions would be made, and that the measure of this Government only differed from that of the last in the separation of the King's personal expenses from the other charges and a *prospective* reduction in the Pension List. There was not much of a debate. Althorp *did it,* ill by all accounts; Graham spoke pretty well; and Calcraft, who could do nothing while in office, found all his energies when he got back to the Opposition benches, and made (everybody says) a capital speech. There is certainly great disappointment that the Civil List does not produce some economical novelty, and to a certain degree the popularity of the Government will be affected by it. But they have taken the manliest course, and the truth is the Duke of Wellington had already made all possible reductions, unless the King and the Government were at once to hang out the flag of poverty and change their whole system. After what Sefton had told me of the intentions of Government about the Pension List, and my reply to him, it was a satisfaction to me to see that they found they could not act on such a principle; and accordingly Lord Althorp at once declared the opinion and intentions of Government about the Pensions, instead of abandoning them to the rage of the House of Commons. There is not even a surmise as to the intended measure of Reform, the secret of which is well kept, but I suspect the confidence of the Reformers will be shaken by their disappointment about the Civil List. It is by no means clear, be what it may, that the Government will be able to carry it, for the Opposition promises to be very formidable in point of numbers; and in speaking, the two parties are, as to the first class, pretty evenly divided—Palmerston, the Grants, Graham, Stanley, J. Russell, on one side; Peel, Calcraft, Harding, Dawson, on the other; fewer in numbers, but Peel immeasurably the best on either side—but in the second line, and among the younger ones, the Opposition are far superior.

March 2nd—The great day at length arrived, and yesterday John Russell moved for leave to bring in his Reform Bill. To describe the curiosity, the intensity of the expectation and excitement, would be impossible, and the secret had been so well kept that not a soul knew what the measure was (though most people guessed pretty well) till they heard it. He rose at six o'clock, and spoke for two hours and a quarter—a sweeping measure indeed! much more so than anyone had imagined, because the Ministers had said it was one which would give *general* satisfaction, whereas this must dissatisfy all the moderate and will probably just stop short enough not to satisfy the Radicals. They say it was ludicrous to see the faces of the members for those places which are to be disfranchised as they were severally announced, and Wetherell, who began to take notes, as the plan was gradually developed, after sundry contortions and grimaces and flinging about his arms and legs, threw down his notes with a mixture of despair and ridicule and horror. Not many people spoke last night: Inglis followed J. Russell, and F. Leveson closed the debate in the best speech he has ever made, but as usual too flowery. Everything is easy in these days, otherwise how Palmerston, Goderich, Grant, etc. can have joined in a measure of this sweeping, violent, and speculative character it is difficult to conceive, they who were the disciples of Castlereagh and the adherents of Canning; but after the Duke of Wellington and Peel carrying the Catholic question, Canning's friends advocating Radical Reform, and Eldon living to see Brougham on the Woolsack, what may one not expect?

What everybody enquires is what line Peel will take, and though each party is confident of success in this question, it is thought to depend mainly upon the course he adopts and the sentiments he expresses. Hitherto he has cautiously abstained from committing himself in any way, and he is free to act as he thinks best, but he certainly occupies a grand position when he has *omnium oculos in se conversos*, and the whole House of Commons looking with unutterable anxiety to his opinions and conduct. Such have the course of events and circumstances made this man, who is probably yet destined to play a great part, and it may be a very useful one. God knows how this plan may be received in the country, and what may be its fate in Parliament. The Duke of Wellington, however, is right enough when he says that the great present danger is lest people should be too much afraid, for anything like the panic that prevails I never saw, the apprehension that enough will not be done to satiate the demon of popular opinion, and the disposition to submit implicitly to the universal bellow that pervades this country for what they call Reform without knowing what it is. As to this question, the greatest evil of it is that it is a pure speculation, and may be productive of the best consequences, or the worst, or even of none at all, for all that its authors and abettors can explain to us or themselves.

March 3rd—Last night the debate went on, nobody remarkable speaking but Macaulay and Wetherell; the former very brilliant, the latter long, rambling, and amusing, and he sat down with such loud and long cheering as everybody agreed they had never heard before in the H. of Commons, and which was taken not so much as a test of the merits of the speech as of an indication of the disposition of the majority of the House. Wetherell was very good fun in a conversation he imagined at Cockermouth between Sir James Graham and one of his constituents. It is thought very strange that none of the Ministers have spoken, except Althorp the first night. The general opinion is that it will be lost in the H. of C., and that then Parliament will be dissolved, unless the King should take fright and prefer to change his Ministers.

5th, Saturday—Thursday night the great speeches were those of Hobhouse on one side and Peel on the other, which last was received with the greatest enthusiasm, and some say it was the finest oration they had ever heard within the walls of Parliament; it seems by the report of it to have been very able and very eloquent. The people come into the 'Travellers' after the debate, and bring their different accounts all tinctured by their particular opinions and prejudices, so that the exact truth of the relative merits of the speakers is only attainable by the newspaper reports, imperfect as they are, the next day. The excitement is beyond anything I ever saw. Last night Stanley answered Peel in an excellent speech and one which is likely to raise his reputation very high. He is evidently desirous of pitting himself against Peel, whom he dislikes; and it is probable that they are destined to be the rival Leaders of two great Parliamentary Parties, if things settle down into the ancient practices of Parliamentary warfare. The other events of last night were the resignation of Charles Wynne and his opposition to the Bill, and the unexpected defection from Government of Lord Seymour, the D. of Somerset's son, and Jeffrey's speech, which was very able, but somewhat tedious.

March 7th 1831—Nothing talked of, thought of, dreamt of, but Reform. Every creature one meets asks, What is said now? How will it go? What is the last news? What do *you* think? and so it is from morning till night, in the streets, in the clubs, and in private houses. Yesterday morning met Hobhouse; told him how well I heard he had spoken, and asked him what he thought of Peel's speech; said it was brilliant, imposing, but not much in it. Everybody cries up (more than usual) the speeches on their own side, and despises those on the other, which is peculiarly absurd, because the speaking has been very good, and there is much to be said on both sides that the speech of an adversary may be applauded without any admission of his being in the right. Hobhouse told me he had at first been afraid that his constituents would disapprove this measure, as so many of them would

'The Bad Hat'
A satire on the Reform Bill as leading inevitably to a republic
While William IV watches the illuminations celebrating his dissolution of Parliament,
Grey removes the Crown; Brougham makes off with the King's conscience; O'Connell
looks on approvingly

From a print of April 1831

Lord Melbourne

Detail of the portrait by Sir Edwin Landseer

The Duke of York

Detail of a portrait after John Jackson

be disfranchised, but that they had behaved nobly and were quite content and ready to make any sacrifices for such an object. I asked him if he thought it would be carried; he said he did not like to think it would not, for he was desirous of keeping what he had, and he was persuaded he should lose if the Bill was rejected. I said it was an unlucky dilemma when one half of the world thought like him and the other half were equally convinced that if it be carried they shall lose all that they have.

March 10th—The debate has gone on, and is to be over to-night; everybody heartily sick of it, but the excitement as great as ever. Last night O'Connel very good, and vehemently cheered by the Government, Stanley, Duncannon, and all, all differences giving way to their zeal; Attwood, the other way, good; Graham, a total failure, got into nautical terms and a simile about a ship, in which he floundered and sunk. Sir J. York quizzed him with great effect. Praed some say a failure, others good, but I believe more of the latter. Graham's failure I predicted. To-day the City went up with their address, to which the King gave a very general answer. There was great curiosity to know what his answer would be. I rather think this address was got up by Government. Brougham had written to Liverpool *to encourage the Reformers there*, and he owned it to G. Villiers last night; and Pearson was with Ellice at the Treasury for an hour the day before this address was moved in the City. They have gone so far that they certainly wish for agitation here. The Duke of Wellington is alarmed; nobody guesses how the question will go. I have written a pamphlet and sent it to be printed, but I don't know if it will take; it is a declamatory tirade against Reform. Went to Lady Jersey the day before yesterday to read her correspondence with Brougham, who flummeried her over with notes full of affection and praise, to which she responded in the same strain, and so they are friends again. While I was reading her reply the D. of Wellington came in, on which She huddled it up, and I conclude he has not seen her effusion. News arrived that the Poles have been beat and have submitted. There is a great fall in the French funds, as they are expected not to pay their dividends. Europe is in a nice mess. The events of a quarter of a century would hardly be food for a week nowadays.

March 11th—It is curious to see the change of opinion as to the passing this Bill. The other day nobody would hear of the possibility of it, now everybody is beginning to think it will. The tactics of Opposition have been very bad, for they ought to have come to a division immediately, when I think Government would have been beat, but it was pretty certain that if they gave time to the country to declare itself the meetings and addresses would fix the wavering and decide the doubtful. There certainly never was anything like the unanimity which pervades the country on the subject; and though I do not think they will break out into rebellion if it is lost, it is impossible not to see that the feeling for it (kept alive as it will be by every sort of excitement) must prevail, and that if this particular Bill is not carried some other must very like it, and which, if it is much short of this, will only leave a peg to hang fresh discussions upon. The Government is desperate and sees no chance of safety but from their success in this measure, but I have my doubts whether they will render themselves immortal by it. It is quite impossible to guess at its effects at present upon the H. of Commons in the first return which may be made under it, but if a vast difference is not made, and if it shall still leave to property and personal influence any great extent of power, the Tory party, which is sure to be revived, will in all probability be too strong for the Reforming Whigs. The Duke of Wellington expected to gain strength by passing the Catholic question, whereas he was ruined by it.

March 15th—It is universally believed that this Bill will pass, except by some of the ultras against it, or by the fools. But what next? That nobody can tell, though to see the exultation of the Government one would imagine they saw their way clearly to a result of wonderful good. I have little doubt that it will be read a second time, and be a good deal battled in Committee. Though they are determined to carry it through the Committee with a high hand, and not to suffer any alterations, probably some sort of compromise in matters of inferior moments will be made. But when it comes into operation how disappointed everybody will be, and first of all the people! Their imaginations are raised to the highest pitch, but they will open their eyes very wide when they find no sort of advantage accruing to them, when they are deprived of much of the expence and more of the excitement of elections, and see a House of Commons constructed after their own hearts, which will probably be an assembly in all respects inferior to the present. Then they will not be satisfied, and as it will be impossible to go back, there will be plenty of agitators who will preach that we have not gone far enough; and if a Reformed Parliament does not do all that popular clamour shall demand, it will be treated with very little ceremony. If, however, it be true that the tendency of this Bill will be to throw power into the hands of the landed interest, we shall have a great Tory party, which will be selfish, bigoted, and ignorant, and a Radical party, and the Whig party, who will have carried the measure, will sink into insignificance. Such present themselves to my mind as possible alternatives, as far as it is practicable to take anything like a view of probabilities in the chaos and confusion that mighty alterations like these produce.

I dined with Lord Grey on Sunday; they are all in high spirits. Howick told his Father that he had received a letter from some merchant in the North praising the Bill, and saying he approved of the whole Government except of P. Thomson. In the evening Brougham, J. Russell, etc. arrived. I hear of Brougham from Sefton, with whom he passes most of his spare time, to relieve his mind by small talk, *persiflage*, and the gossip of the day. He tells Sefton 'that he likes his office, but that it is a mere plaything, and there is nothing to do; his life is too idle, and when he has cleared off the arrears, which he shall do forthwith, that he really does not know how he shall get rid of his time'; that 'he does not suffer the prolixity of the Counsel, and when they wander from the point he brings them back and says, "You need not say anything on that point; what I want to be informed upon is so and so."' He is a wonderful man, the most extraordinary I ever saw, but there is more of mountebankery than of greatness in all this. It may do well enough for Sefton, who is as ignorant as he is sharp and shrewd, and captivated with this congenial offhandism, but it requires something more than Brougham's flippant *ipse dixit* to convince me that the office of Chancellor is such a sinecure and bagatelle. He had a Levee the other night, which was brilliantly attended—the Archbishops, D. of Wellington, Ld. Grey, and a host of people. Sefton goes and sits in his private room and sees his receptions of people, and gives very amusing accounts of his extreme politeness to the Lord Mayor and his cool *insouciance* with the Archbishop of Canterbury. The stories of him as told by Sefton would be invaluable to his future Biographer, and never was a life more sure to be written hereafter.

March 17th—The Reform Bill is just printed, and already are there various objections raised against different parts of it sufficient to show that it will be pulled to pieces in Committee. Both parties confident of success on the second reading, but the country *will* have it; there is a determination upon the subject, and a unanimity perfectly marvellous, and no demonstration of the unfitness of any of its parts will be of any avail; some of its details may be corrected and amended, but substantially it must pass pretty much as it is.

I still think the second reading will pass, and, all things considered, that it would be the best thing that could happen; it is better to capitulate than to be taken by storm. The people are unanimous, good-humoured, and determined; if the Bill is thrown out, their good humour will disappear, the country will be a scene of violence and uproar, and a most ferocious Parliament will be returned, which will not only carry the question of Reform, but possibly do so in a very different form. We should see the *iræ leonum vincla recusantum*, and this proposition is so evident, this state of things is so indisputable, that it is marvellous to me how anybody can triumph and exult in the anticipation of a victory the consequences of which would be more unfortunate than a defeat. If indeed a victory could set the matter at rest, confirm our present institutions, and pacify the people, it would be very well; but Reform the people will have, and no human power, moral or physical, can now arrest its career. It would be better, then, to concede with a good grace, and to modify the measure in Committee, which may still be practicable, than to oppose it point-blank without a prospect of success.

22nd—The debate began again last night, and was adjourned. It was dull, and the House impatient. To-night they will divide, and after a thousand fluctuations of opinion it is thought the Bill will be thrown out by a small majority. Then will come the question of a dissolution, which one side affirms will take place directly, and the other that the King will not consent to it, knowing, as 'the man in the street' (as we call him at Newmarket) always does, the greatest secrets of Kings, and being the confidant of their most hidden thoughts. As for me, I see nothing but a choice of difficulties either way, and victory or defeat would be equally bad. It is odd enough, but I believe Lord Lansdowne thinks just the same, for He asked me yesterday morning what I thought would be the result, and I told him my opinion on the whole question, and he replied, 'I can add nothing to what you have said; that is exactly my own opinion,' and I have very little doubt that more than half the Cabinet in their hearts abhor the measure. Knatchbull was taken ill in the morning, and could not go to the House at all.

March 23rd—The House divided at three o'clock this morning, and the second reading was carried by a majority of *one* in the fullest House that ever was known—303 to 302—both parties confident up to the moment of division; but the Opposition most so, and at last the Government expected to be beat. Denman told somebody as they were going to divide that the question would be lost; Calcraft and the Wynnes going over at the eleventh hour did the business. I believe that this division is the best thing that could happen, and so I told the Duke in the morning, and that I had wished it to be carried by a small majority; I met him walking with Arbuthnot in the Park. He said, 'I could not take such a course' (that was in answer to my saying I wished it to be read a second time, to be lost in the Committee). I said, 'But you would have nothing to do with it personally.' 'No; but as belonging to the party I could not recommend such a course,' which seemed as if he did not altogether disagree with my view of it. I stopt at the

'Travellers' till past three, when a man came in and told me the news. I walked home, and found the streets swarming with members of Parliament coming from the House. My belief is (if they manage well and are active and determined) that the Bill will be lost in Committee, and then this will be the best thing that could have occurred.

March 24th—The agitation the other night on the division was prodigious. The Government (who staid in the House) thought they had lost it by ten, and the Opposition, who were crowded into the lobby, fancied from their numbers that they were sure of winning. There was betting going on all night long, and large sums have been won and lost. The people in the lobby were miscounted, and they thought they had 303. At the levee yesterday and Council; the Government are by way of being satisfied, but hardly can be. I met the Duke of Wellington afterwards, who owned to me that he thought this small majority for the Bill was on the whole the best thing that could have occurred, and that seems to be the opinion generally of its opponents.

Nothing particular at the levee; Brougham was very good fun. The King, who had put off going to the Opera on account of the death of his Son-in-law Kennedy, appeared in mourning (crape, that is), which is reckoned bad taste; the public allow natural feeling to supersede law and etiquette, but it is too much to extend that courtesy to a bastard 'Son-in-law,' and his daughter not in England. Somebody said that 'it was the first time a King of England had ever appeared in mourning that his subjects did not wear.' In the evening to the Ancient Concert, where the Queen was, and by-the-bye in mourning, and the Margravine and Duchess of Gloster too, but they (the two latter) could hardly be mourning for Ld. Cassilis's Son. Horace Seymour, Meynell, and Calvert were all turned out of their places in the Lord Chamberlain's department on account of their votes the other night.

A sort of repose from the cursed Bill for a moment, but it is said that many who opposed it before are going to support it in Committee; nobody knows. There were great sums betted on it. The Opposition when they divided were sure they had a majority. When the Speaker put the question, each party roared 'Aye' and 'No' *totis viribus*. He said he did not know, and put it again. After that he said, 'I am not sure, but I think the ayes have it.' Then the noes went out into the lobby, and the others thought they never would have done filing out, and the House looked so empty when they were gone that the Government was in despair. They say the excitement was beyond anything. I never heard anything like the complaints of Peel—of his coldness, incommunicativeness, and deficiency in all the qualities requisite for a leader, particularly at such a time. There is nobody else, or he would be deserted for any man who had talents enough to take a prominent part, so much does he disgust his adherents. Nobody knows what are his opinions, feelings, wishes, or intentions; he will not go *en avant*, and nobody feels any dependence upon him. There is no help for it and the man's nature can't be altered. I said all this to Ross yesterday, his devoted adherent, and he was obliged to own it, with all kinds of regrets and endeavours to soften the picture.

April 14th—The Reform campaign has reopened with a violent speech from Hunt denouncing the whole thing as a delusion; that the people begin to find out how they are humbugged, and that as it will make nothing cheaper they don't care about it. The man's drift is not very clear whether the bill is really unpalatable at Preston or whether he wants to go further directly. At the same time J. Russell announced some alterations in the Bill, not, as he asserted, trenching upon its principle, but, as the Opposition declares, altering it altogether. On the whole, these things have inspired its opponents, and, as they must delay, are in so far bad for the Reform cause. Besides, though the opinion of the country is universally in its favor, they do not seem to care very much about it and people are beginning to think that it may be rejected without any apprehension of such dreadful consequences ensuing as have been predicted. Then the state of Ireland is such that it is thought Ministers cannot encounter a dissolution; not that I feel any security on that head, for I believe the Cabinet is ruled by two or three men reckless of everything provided they can prolong their own power.

April 24th—At Newmarket all last week, and returned to town last night to hear from those who saw it the extraordinary scenes in both Houses of Parliament (the day before) which closed the eventful week. The Reform battle began again on Monday last. The night before I went out of town I met Duncannon, and walked with him up Regent Street, where he told me that he did not believe Ministers would be beat, but if they were they should certainly dissolve instantly; that *he* should have liked to dissolve long ago, but they owed it to their friends not to have recourse to a dissolution if they could help it. On Monday General Gascoyne moved that the Committee should be instructed not to reduce the members of the H. of C., and this was carried after two nights' debate by eight. The dissolution was then decided upon. Meanwhile Ld. Wharncliffe gave notice of a motion to address the King not to dissolve Parliament, and this was to have come on Friday. On Thursday Ministers were again beat in the H. of Commons on a question of adjournment, and on Friday morning they got the King to go down and prorogue Parliament in person the same day. This *coup d'état* was so sudden that nobody was aware of it till within two or three hours of the time, and many not at all. They told him that the cream-colored horses could not be got ready, when he said, 'Then I will go with anybody else's horses.' Mash went off in a carriage to the Tower, to fetch the Crown, and they collected such attendants as they could find to go with him. The Houses met at one or two o'clock. In the H. of Commons Sir R. Vyvyan made a furious speech, attacking the Government on every point, and (excited as he was) it was very well done. The Ministers made no reply, but Sir F. Burdett and Tennyson endeavoured to interrupt with calls to order, and when the Speaker decided that Vyvyan was not out of order Tennyson disputed his opinion, which enraged the Speaker, and soon after he called up Peel, for whom He was resolved to procure a hearing. The scene then resembled that which took place on Lord North's resignation in '82, for Althorp (I think) moved that Burdett should be heard, and the Speaker said that 'Peel was in possession of the House to speak on that motion.' He made a very violent speech, attacking the Government for their incompetence, folly, and recklessness, and treated them with the utmost asperity and contempt. In the midst of his speech the guns announced the arrival of the King, and at each explosion the Government gave a loud cheer, and Peel was still speaking in the midst of every sort of noise and tumult when the Usher of the Black Rod knocked at the door to summon the Commons to the House of Peers. There the proceedings were if possible still more violent and outrageous; those who were present tell me it resembled nothing but what we read of the 'Serment du jeu de Paume,' and the whole scene was as much like the preparatory days of a revolution as can well be imagined. Wharncliffe was to have moved an address to the Crown against dissolving Parliament, and this motion the Ministers were resolved should not come on, but he contrived to bring it on so far as to get it put upon the Journals. The Duke of Richmond endeavoured to prevent any speaking by raising points of order, and moving that the Lords should take their regular places (in separate ranks), which, however, is impossible at a royal sitting, because the cross benches are removed; this put Lord Londonderry in such a fury that he rose, roared, gesticulated, held up his whip, and four or five Lords held him down by the tail of his coat to prevent his flying on somebody. Lord Lyndhurst was equally furious, and some sharp words passed which were not distinctly heard. In the midst of all the din Lord Mansfield rose and obtained a hearing. Wharncliffe said to him, 'For God's sake, Mansfield, take care what you are about, and don't disgrace us more in the state we are in.' 'Don't be afraid,' he said; 'I will say nothing that will alarm you'; and accordingly he pronounced a trimming philippic on the Government, which, delivered as it was in an imposing manner,

attired in his robes, and with the greatest energy and excitation, was prodigiously effective. While he was still speaking, the King arrived, but he did
not desist even while H.M. was entering the H. of Lords, nor till he
approached the throne; and while the King was ascending the steps the
hoarse voice of Ld. Londonderry was heard crying 'Hear, hear, hear!' The
King from the robing-room heard the noise, and asked what it all meant.
The conduct of the Chancellor was most extraordinary, skipping in and out
of the House and making the most extraordinary speech. In the midst of
the uproar he went out of the House, when Lord Shaftesbury was moved
into the chair. In the middle of the debate Brougham came in and said, 'it
was most extraordinary that the King's undoubted right to dissolve Parliament should be questioned at a moment when the H. of C. had taken the
unprecedented course of stopping the supplies,' and having so said (which
was a lie) he flounced out of the House; he was by way of going to receive
the King on his arrival. The King ought not properly to have worn the
crown, never having been crowned; but when he was in the robing-room he
said to Lord Hastings, 'Lord Hastings, I wear the crown; where is it?' It
was brought to him, and when Lord Hastings was going to put it on his
head he said, 'Nobody shall put the crown on my head but myself.' He put
it on, and then turned to Lord Grey and said, 'Now, my Lord, the coronation is over.' George Villiers said that in his life he never saw such a scene,
and as he looked at the King upon the throne with the crown loose upon
his head, and the tall, grim figure of Ld. Grey close beside him, with the
sword of state in his hand, it was as if the King had got his Executioner
by his side, and the whole picture was strikingly typical of his and our
future destinies.

Such has been the termination of this Parliament and of the first act of
the new Ministerial drama; there never was a Government ousted with
more ignominy than the last, nor a Ministry that came in with higher pretensions, greater professions, and better prospects than the present, but
nothing ever corresponded less than their performances with their pretensions. The composition of the Government was radically defective, and with
a good deal of loose talent here was much of passion, folly, violence, and
knavery, together with inexperience and ignorance mixed up with it, that
from the very beginning they cut the sorriest possible figure. Such men as
Richmond, Durham, Althorp, and Graham, in their different ways, were
enough to spoil any Cabinet, and consequently their course has been marked
by a series of blunders and defeats. Up to the moment of the dissolution
few people expected it would happen, some thinking the King would not
consent, others that the Government would never venture upon it, but the

King is weak and the Ministry reckless. That disposition (which at first appeared so laudable) of putting himself implicitly into the hands of his Ministers, and which seemed the more so from the contrast it afforded to the conduct of the late King, who was always thwarting his Ministers, throwing difficulties in their way, and playing a double part, becomes vicious when carried to the extent of paralysing all free action and free opinion on his part, and suffering himself to be made the instrument of any measures, however violent. It may be said, indeed, that he cordially agrees with these men, and has opinions coincident with theirs, but this is not probable; and when we remember his unlimited confidence in the Duke up to the moment of his resignation, it is impossible to believe that he can have so rapidly imbibed principles the very reverse of those which the Duke maintained. It is more likely that he has no opinions, and is really a mere puppet in the hands into which he may happen to fall. Lord Mansfield had an audience, and gave him his sentiments upon the state of affairs. He will not say what passed between them, but it is clear that it was of no use.

The Queen and the Royal Family are extremely unhappy at all these things, but the former has no influence whatever with the King. In the meantime there are very different opinions as to the result of the elections, some thinking the Government will not gain much by the dissolution, others that they (or at least Reform) will gain everything. It seems to me quite impossible that they should not gain everything, but time is gained to the other side. The census of 1831 will be out and the chapter of accidents may and must make much difference; still I see no possibility of arresting the progress of Reform, and whether this Bill or another like it passes is much the same thing. The Government have made it up with O'Connel, which is one mouthful of the dirty pudding they have had to swallow, as one of their own friends said of them.

May 7th—At Newmarket all last week. Nothing could go on worse than the elections—Reformers returned everywhere, so much so that the contest is over, and we have only to wait the event and see what the H. of Lords will do. In the H. of C. the Bill is already carried. It is supposed that Ministers themselves begin to be alarmed at the devil they have let loose, and well they may; but he is out, and stop him who can. The King has put off his visit to the City because he is ill, as the Government would have it believed, but really because he is furious with the Lord Mayor at all the riots and uproar the night of the illumination. That night the Queen went to the Ancient Concert, and on her return the mob surrounded the carriage; she had no guards, and the footmen were obliged to beat them off with their canes to prevent their thrusting their heads into the coach. She was frightened and the King very much annoyed. He heard the noise and tumult, and paced backwards and forwards in his room waiting for her return. When She came back Howe, her Chamberlain, as usual preceded her, when the King said, 'How is the Queen?' and went down to meet her. Howe, who is an eager anti-Reformer, said, 'Very much frightened, sir,' and made the worst of it. She was in fact terrified, and as She detests the whole of these proceedings, the more distressed and disgusted. The King was very angry, and immediately declared he would not go to the City at all. It is supposed that Government will make a large batch of Peers to secure the Bill in the House of Lords, but the press have already begun to attack that House, declaring that if they pass the Bill it will be from compulsion, and if they do not that they are the enemies of the people.

May 11th—The elections are going on universally in favor of Reform; the great interests in the Counties are everywhere broken, and old connexions dispersed. In Worcestershire Captain Spencer, who has nothing to do with the county, and was brought there by his Brother-in-law, Ld. Lyttelton, has beat Lygon, backed by all the wealth of his family; the Manners have withdrawn from Leicestershire and Cambridgeshire, and Ld. E. Somerset from Glostershire; Worcester too is beat at Monmouth. Everywhere the tide is irresistible; all considerations are sacrificed to the success of the measure. At the last Essex election Colonel Tyrrell saved Western, who would have been beat by Long Wellesley, and now Western has coalesced with Wellesley against Tyrrell, and will throw him out. In Northamptonshire Althorp had pledged himself to Cartwright not to bring forward another Candidate on his side, and Milton joins him and stands. The state of excitement, doubt, and apprehension which prevails will not quickly subside, for the battle is only beginning; when the Bill is carried we must prepare for the second act.

May 14th—The elections still going on for Reform. They count upon a majority of 140 in the H. of C., but the Tories meditate resistance in the H. of L., which it is to be hoped will be fruitless, and it is probable the Peers will trot round as they did about the Catholic question when it comes to the point. There is great hubbub at Northampton about a pledge which Althorp is supposed to have given not to bring forward another Candidate against Cartwright, which the anti-Reformers say he has violated in putting up Milton, and moreover that such conduct is very dishonest; and as his honesty was his principal recommendation, if he should have forfeited that what would remain to him? On the contrary, his friends say that he gave no such pledge, that he expressed a hope there might be no contest, but the people would have Milton; and though Althorp regretted his standing, as he did stand they were obliged to join for their common safety. So much for this electioneering squabble, of which time will elicit the truth.

In the meantime the elections have been going languidly on, and are now nearly over; contrary to the prognostications of the Tories, they have gone off very quietly, even in Ireland not many contests, the anti-Reformers being unable to make any fight at all; except in Shropshire they are dead-beat everywhere. Northamptonshire the sharpest contest, and the one which has made the most ill blood. Althorp and Milton who joined against Cartwright have been greatly abused, in consequence of the former having in a manner pledged himself not to get up a contest; but thought on the first blush of the thing he appeared to have behaved shabbily, he wrote an account of his share of the transaction in which he cleared himself pretty well, and proved that he certainly had not been instrumental to Milton's standing, and that he in fact had much rather there had been no contest at all. What he ought to have done was to decline joining with Milton after what had passed. He might have endeavoured to dissuade him from standing, and if he was determined have told him that after what had passed between Cartwright and himself he would not join against C. with anybody. Milton however comes by no means so well out of it. He has been writing anonymous letters in the newspapers and getting up by every means this contest, with full knowledge of Althorp's pledge, and now he has got it up will contribute neither his purse nor his person to carry it on, for he sends his Son to the hustings, and leaves Althorp to pay all the expences. This election has produced a good deal of violence; elsewhere the Reformers have it hollow, and no matter what the characters of the Candidates, if they are only for the Bill. Calcraft and Wellesley, the former not respected, the later covered with disgrace, have beat Bankes and Tyrrell. Lowther had not a chance in Cumberland, where Sir James Graham got into another scrape, for in an impertinent speech he made an attack upon Scarlett, which drew upon him a message and from him an apology. Formerly, when a man made use of offensive expressions and was called to account, he thought it right to go out and stand a shot before he eat up his words, but nowadays that piece of chivalry is dispensed with, and politicians make nothing of being scurrilous one day and humble the next. Hyde Villiers has been appointed to succeed Sandon at the Board of Controul as a Whig and Reformer. He was in a hundred minds what line he should take, and had written a pamphlet to prove the necessity of giving Ministers seats in both Houses (as in France), which he has probably put in the fire. I am very glad he has got the place; and though his opinions were not very decided before, he has always been anti-Tory, and has done nothing discreditable to get it, and it was offered to him in a very flattering manner.

June 5th—All last week at Fern Hill for the Ascot races; the Chesterfields, Tavistocks, Belfasts, G. Ansons, Montagu, Stradbroke, B. Greville, etc. etc. The Royal Family came to the course the first day with a great *cortège*— eight coaches-and-four, two Phaetons, pony sociables, led horses, etc.— Munster riding on horseback behind the King's carriage, Augustus (the parson) and Frederick driving Phaetons. The D. of Richmond was in the King's *calèche* and Lord Grey in one of the coaches. The reception was strikingly cold and indifferent, not half so good as that which the late King used to receive. He was bored to death with the races, and his own horse broke down. On Wednesday he did not come; on Thursday they came again. Beautiful weather and unprecedented multitudes. The King was much more cheered than the first day, or the greater number of people made a greater noise. A few cheers were given to Lord Grey as he returned, which he just acknowledged and no more. On Friday we dined at the Castle; each day he asked a crowd of people from the neighbourhood. We arrived at a little before seven; the Queen was only just come in from riding, so we had to wait till near eight. Above forty people at dinner, for which the room is not nearly large enough—very handsome; the dinner not bad, but the room insufferably hot. The Queen was taken out by the D. of Richmond, and the King followed with the Duchess of Saxe Weimar, the Queen's Sister. He drinks wine with everybody, asking seven or eight at a time. After dinner he drops asleep. We sat for a short time. Directly after coffee the band began to play; a good band, not numerous, and principally of violins and string instruments. The Queen and the whole party sat there all the evening, so that it was, in fact, a concert of instrumental music. The King took Lady Tavistock to St. George's Hall and the ball-room, where we walked about, with two or three Servants carrying lamps to show the proportions, for it was not lit up. The whole thing is exceedingly magnificent, and the manner of life does not appear to be very formal, and need not be disagreeable but for the bore of never dining without twenty strangers. The Castle holds very few people, and with the King and Queen's immediate suite and *toute la bâtardise* it was quite full. The King's four Sons were there, *signoreggiandi tutti*, and the whole thing 'donnait à penser' to those who looked back a little and had seen other days. We sat in that room in which Lyndhurst has often talked to me of their famous five hours' discussion with the late King, when the Catholic Bill hung upon his caprice. Palmerston told me he had never been in the Castle since the eventful day of Herries' appointment and non-appointment; and how many things have happened since! What a *changement de décoration*; no longer George the 4th, capricious, luxurious, and misanthropic, liking nothing but the society of listeners and flatterers, with the Conyngham tribe and one or two Tory Ministers and Foreign Ambassadors; but a plain, vulgar, hospitable gentleman, opening his doors to all the world, with a numerous family and suite (with a frightful Queen and a posse of bastards *originally*), a Whig Minister, and no foreigners, and no Toad-eaters at all. Nothing more different, and looking at him one sees how soon this act will be finished, and the scene be changed for another probably not less dissimilar. Queen, bastards, Whigs, all will disappear, and God knows what replace them.

June 19th—The last few days I have been completely taken up with Quarantine, and taking means to prevent the cholera coming here. That disease made great ravages in Russia last year, and in the winter the attention of Government was called to it, and the question was raised whether we should have to purify goods coming here in case it broke out again, and if so how it was to be done. Government was thinking of Reform and other matters, and would not bestow much attention upon this subject, and accordingly neither regulations nor preparations were made. All that was done was to commission a Dr. Walker, a Physician residing at St. Petersburg, to go to Moscow and elsewhere and make enquiries into the nature and progress of the disease, and report the result of his investigation to us. He turned out, however, to be a very useless and inefficient agent. In the meantime as the warm weather returned the cholera again appeared in Russia, but still we took no further measures until intelligence arrived that it had reached Riga, at which place 700 or 800 sail of English Vessels, loaded principally with hemp and flax, were waiting to come to this country. This report soon diffused a general alarm, and for many days past the newspapers have been full of letters and full of lies, and every sort of representation is made to Government or through the press, as fear or interest happen to dictate. The Consuls and Ministers abroad had been for some time supplying us with such information as they could obtain, so that we were in possession of a great deal of documentary evidence regarding the nature, character, and progress of the disease. The first thing we did was to issue two successive Orders in Council placing all Vessels coming from the Baltick in quarantine, and we sent for Sir Henry Halford and placed all the papers we had in his hands, desiring that he would associate with himself some other Practitioners, and report their opinion as speedily as possible whether the disease was contagious and whether it could be conveyed by goods. They reported the next day *yes* to the first questions, *no* to the second. In 1804, on the occasion of the yellow fever at Gibraltar, Government formed a

Board of Health, and took the opinion of the College of Physicians, and it was intended to pursue the same course in this instance, but Ld. Lansdowne and Auckland chose to take Halford's preliminary opinion, contrary to my advice, for I foresaw that there would be a great embarrassment if He and the College did not agree. Just so it turned out, for when the case was submitted, with all the papers, to the College, they would not adopt his opinion, much to his annoyance, and, as I believe, because they did not like to be merely called on to confirm what he had already said, and that they thought their independence required a show of dissent. The report they sent was very short and very unsatisfactory, and entirely against all the evidence they had before them; they advised precautionary measures. I immediately wrote back an answer saying that their report was not satisfactory, and desiring a more detailed opinion, and the reasons which had dictated their conclusion; but in the meantime we set to work in earnest to adopt measures against any emergency. The only way of performing quarantine (with goods), it was found, would be by the employment of men-of-war, and we accordingly applied to the Admiralty to supply ships for the purpose. This Lord Grey, Graham, and Sir Byam Martin objected to, but Sir Thomas Hardy and Captain Elliot did not. We proved that the ships would sustain no injury, so after a battle they agreed to give them. We made a variety of regulations, and gave strict orders for the due performance of quarantine, and tomorrow a proclamation is to be issued for constituting a Board of Health and enjoining obedience to the Quarantine laws, so that everything has been done that can be done, and if the cholera comes here it is not our fault. Most of the authorities think it will come, but I doubt it. If indeed it is wafted through the air it may, but I don't think it will if it is only to be communicated by contact. All the evidence proves that goods cannot convey it; nevertheless we have placed merchandise under a discretionary quarantine, and though we have not promulgated any general regulations, we release no vessels that come from infected places, or that have got enumerated goods on board. Poulett Thomson, who is a Trader as well as Privy Councillor, is very much disgusted in his former capacity at the measures he is obliged to concur in in his latter. This topic has now occupied for some days a good deal of the attention even of the fine fools of this town, and the Tories would even make it a matter of party accusation against the Government, only they don't know exactly how. It is always safe to deal in generalities, so they say that 'Government ought to be impeached if the disease comes here.'

There was a meeting of Peers to the amount of nearly seventy at Lord Mansfield's the other day, which went off greatly to their satisfaction. They unanimously agreed to determine upon nothing in the way of amendment until they had seen the King's Speech, to which, however, they will consider themselves bound to move an amendment, provided it contains anything laudatory of the Reform Bill. The Duke of Wellington was not at the meeting, having been taken ill. I met him the day before at dinner, and had a good deal of conversation with him. He is in pretty good spirits, and thinks they may make a good fight of it yet; told me that Lyndhurst would certainly go thoroughly with them, praised him largely, said he was the best Colleague that any man ever had, and that he should be very sorry ever to go into any Cabinet of which he was not a member. The King dined with the Duke yesterday, and was to give him a very fine sword. Lord Lansdowne told me that Leopold is inconceivably anxious to be King of Belgium, that short of going in direct opposition to the wishes and advice of all the Royal Family and of the Government he would do anything to be be-King'd, and, what is equally absurd, that the others cannot bear that he should be thus elevated. It is difficult to decide which are the greatest fools. Breakfasted yesterday with John Russell—Luttrell, Rogers, Sydney Smith, Allen, Moore and Lady Hardy—very agreeable.

July 8th—Second reading carried at five in the morning by 136 majority, somewhat greater than the Opposition had reckoned on. Peel made a powerful speech, but not so good as either of his others on Reform. Goulburn told me that the speech in answer to the Lord Advocate on the Irish Bill, when not 100 people were in the House, was his best. Coronation fixed for the 23rd, and to be short and cheap. Breakfasted with Rogers; went afterwards to the Duchess of Bedford's, where I heard from Lady Lyndhurst rigmaroles about her tracasseries with Lord Grey, who is however in love with her, and She can always make it up with him when She pleases. I desired her to tell Lyndhurst all the Duke had said to me about him, for in these times it is as well they should draw together. He will be a match for Brougham in the H. of Lords, for he can be concise, which the other cannot, and the Lords in the long run will prefer brevity to wit, sarcasm, and anything else.

22nd—At court yesterday. The night before last Croker and Macaulay made two fine speeches on Reform; the former spoke for 2½ hours, and in a way he had never done before. Macaulay very brilliant. There was a meeting at Ebrington's yesterday, called by him, Littelton, Lawley, etc., of members of the H. of C. only, and they (without coming to any resolution) were all agreed to prevail on the Government not to resign in the event of the Reform Bill being rejected in the H. of Lds. I have no doubt, therefore, in spite of what Ld. Grey said, and the other circumstances I have mentioned above, that they will not resign; but I doubt whether there will be any occasion.

There was a dinner (of eight I understand) at Apsley H. yesterday; the Cabinet of Opposition, to discuss matters before having a general meeting. (At the Duke's dinner there were sixteen or seventeen, all the Chief anti-Reformers of the Peers.) They agreed to oppose the second reading. Dudley, who was there, told me it was tragedy first and farce afterwards; for Eldon and Kenyon, who had dined with the D. of Cumberland, came in after dinner. Chairs were placed for them on each side of the Duke, and after he had explained to them what they had been discussing, and what had been agreed upon, Kenyon made a long speech on the first reading of the Bill, in which it was soon apparent that he was very drunk, for he talked exceeding nonsense, wandered from one topick to another, and repeated the same things over and over again. When he had done Eldon made a speech on the second reading, and appeared to be equally drunk, only (Ld. Bathurst told me) Kenyon in his drunkenness talked nonsense, but Eldon sense. Dudley said it was not that they were drunk as Lords and Gentlemen sometimes are, but they were drunk like Porters.) Lyndhurst was not there, tho invited. He dined at Holland House. It is pretty clear, however, that he will vote for the second reading, for his wife is determined he shall. I saw her yester-day, and She is full of pique and resentment against the Opposition and the Duke, half real and half pretended, and chatters away about Lyndhurst's not being their cat's-paw, and that if they chuse to abandon him, they must not expect him to sacrifice himself for them, etc. etc. The pretexts She takes are, that they would not go to the H. of Lds. on Tuesday and support him against Brougham on the Bankruptcy Bill, and that the D. of Wellington wrote to her and *dared* her to influence her husband in the matter of Re-form. The first is a joke, the second there may be a little in, for vanity is always uppermost, but they have both some notion of interest, which they pursue in whatever way they best can. The truth is that I am by no means sure *now* that it is safe or prudent to oppose the second reading; and though I think it very doubtful if any practicable alteration will be made in Com-mittee, it will be better to take that chance, and the chance of an accom-modation and compromise between the two parties and the two Houses, than to attack it in front. It is clear that the Government are resolved to carry the Bill, and equally clear that no means they can adopt would be un-popular. They are averse to making more Peers if they can help it, and would rather go quietly on, without any fresh changes, and I believe they are conscientiously persuaded that this Bill is the least democratical Bill it is possible to get the country to accept, and that if offered in time this one

Princess Lieven

*From a lithograph
after a drawing by
John Lucas*

Lord George Bentinck

*Detail of the portrait by
Samuel Lane, 1836*

The Ranton Shooting Party

Mounted, Lord Lichfield; standing on his right, Lord Melbourne; boy sitting on the ground, Lord Anson

Detail of the painting by Sir Francis Grant

will be accepted. I had heard before that the country is not enamoured of this Bill, but I fear that it is true that they are only indifferent to the conservative (aristocratick *originally*) clauses of it (if I may so term them), and for that reason it may be doubtful whether there would not be such a clamour raised in the event of the rejection of this as would compel Ministers to make a new Bill, more objectionable than the old. If its passing clearly appears to be inevitable, why, the sooner it is done the better, for at least one immense object will be gained in putting an end to agitation, and restoring the country to good-humour, and it is desirable that the H. of Lords shall stand as well with the people as it can. It is better, as Burke says, 'to do early, and from foresight, that which we may be obliged to do from necessity at last.' I am not more delighted with Reform than I have ever been, but it is the part of prudence to take into consideration the present and the future, and not to harp upon the past. It matters not how the country has been worked up to its present state, if a calm observation convinces us that the spirit that has been raised cannot be allayed, and that is very clear to me now.

24th—Peel closed the debate on Thursday night with a very fine speech, the best (one of his opponents told me, and it is no use asking the opinions of friends if a candid opponent is to be found) he had ever made, not only on that subject, but on any other; he cut Macaulay to ribbands. Macaulay is very brilliant, but his speeches are harangues and never replies; whereas Peel's long experience and real talent for debate give him a great advantage in the power of reply, which he very eminently possesses. Macaulay, however, will probably be a very distinguished man. These debates have elicited a vast deal of talent, and have served as touchstones to try real merit and powers. As a proof of what practice and a pretty good understanding can do, there is Althorp, who appears to be an excellent Leader, and contrives to speak decently upon all subjects, quite as much as a Leader need do; for I have always thought that it should not be his business to furnish rhetorick, and flowers of eloquence, but good-humour, judgement, firmness, discretion, businesslike talents, and gentlemanlike virtues.

Dined at Richmond on Friday with Lyndhursts; the *mari* talks against the Bill, the woman for it. They are like the old divisions of families in the Civil Wars.

Oct. 12th—The Reformers appear to have rallied their spirits. Lord Grey went to Windsor, was graciously received by the King, and obtained the dismissal of Lord Howe, which will serve to show the King's entire goodwill to his present Ministers. Ebrington's resolution of confidence was carried by a great majority in the H. of C. after some violent speeches from Macaulay,

Shiel, and O'Connel, and very moderate ones and in a low tone on the other side. Macaulay's speech was as usual very eloquent, but as inflammatory as possible. Such men as these three can care nothing into what state of confusion the country is thrown, for all they want is a market to which they may bring their talents; but how the Miltons, Tavistocks, Althorps, and all who have a great stake in the country can run the same course is more than I can conceive or comprehend. Party is indeed, as Swift says, 'the madness of many,' when carried to its present pitch. In the meantime, the Conservative party are as usual committing blunders, which will be fatal to them. Lord Harrowby was to have moved yesterday or the day before, in the H. of Lords, a resolution pledging the House to take into consideration early in the next session the acknowledged defects in the representation, with a view to make such ameliorations in it as might be consistent with the Constitution, or something to this effect. This has not been done because the Duke of Wellington objects. He will not concur because he thinks the proposition should come from Government; as if this was a time to stand upon such punctilios, and that it was not of paramount importance to show the country that the Peers are obstinately bent upon opposing all Reform. I had hoped that he had profited by experience, and that at least his past (enormous *originally*) errors in politics might have taught him a little modesty, and that he would not have thwarted measures which were proposed by the wisest and most disinterested of his own party. I can conceive no greater misfortune at this moment than such a disunion of that party, and to have its deliberations ruled by the obstinacy and prejudices of the Duke. He is a great man in little things, but a little man in great matters— I mean in civil affairs; in those mighty questions which embrace enormous and various interests and considerations, and to comprehend which great knowledge of human nature, great sagacity, coolness, and impartiality are required, he is not fit to govern and direct. His mind has not been sufficiently disciplined, nor saturated with knowledge and matured by reflection and communication with other minds, to enable him to be a safe and efficient leader in such times as these.

(In reading over these remarks upon the Duke of Wellington, and comparing them with the opinions I now entertain of his present conduct, and of the nature and quality of his mind, I am compelled to ask myself whether I did not then do him injustice. On the whole I think not. He is not, nor ever was, a little man in anything, great or small; but I am satisfied that he has committed great political blunders, though with the best and most patriotic intentions, and that his conduct throughout the Reform contest was one of the greatest and most unfortunate of them.—*July 1838*.)

15th—The Dorsetshire election promises to end in favor of Ashley; there will probably be a contest for Cambridgeshire, which may also end in favor of the anti-Reform Candidate. These victories I really believe to be unfortunate, for they are taken (I am arguing as if they were won, though, with regard to the first, it is the same thing by contrast with the last election) by the Tories and anti-Reform champions as undoubted proofs of the reaction of public opinion, and they are thereby encouraged to persevere in opposition under the false notion that this supposed reaction will every day gain ground. I wish it were so with all my soul, but believe it is no such thing, and that although there may be fewer friends to *the Bill* than there were, particularly among the Agriculturists, Reform is not a whit less popular with the mass of the people in the manufacturing districts, throughout the Unions, and generally amongst all classes and in all parts of the country. When I see men, and those in very great numbers, of the highest birth, of immense fortunes, of undoubted integrity and acknowledged talents, zealously and conscientiously supporting this measure, I own I am lost in astonishment and even in doubt; for I can't help asking myself whether it it is possible that such men would be the advocates of measures fraught with all the peril we ascribe to these, whether we are not in reality mistaken and labouring under groundless alarm generated by habitual prejudices and erroneous calculations. But often as this doubt comes across my mind, it is always dispelled by a reference to and comparison of the arguments on both sides, and by the lessons which all that I have ever read and all the conclusions I have been able to draw from the study of history have impressed on my mind. I believe these measures to be full of danger, but that the manner in which they have been introduced, discussed, defended, and supported is more dangerous still. The total unsettlement of men's minds, the bringing into contempt all the institutions which have been hitherto venerated, the aggrandisement of the power of the people, the embodying and recognition of popular authority, the use and abuse of the King's name, the truckling to the press, are things so subversive of government, so prejudicial to order and tranquillity, so encouraging to sedition and disaffection, that I do not see the possibility of the country settling down into that calm and undisturbed state in which it was before this question was mooted, and without which there can be no happiness or security to the community. A thousand mushroom orators and politicians have sprung up all over the country, each big with his own ephemeral importance, and every one of whom fancies himself fit to govern the nation. Amongst them are some men of active and powerful minds, and nothing is less probable than that these spirits of mischief and misrule will be content to subside into their original nothingness, and retire after the victory has been gained into the obscurity from which they emerged.

Lord Wharncliffe, a member of the Conservative Opposition, had been in negotiation with the Government over the possibility of a more moderate Bill.

December 3rd—Wharncliffe showed me his correspondence with the Duke of Wellington on this negotiation. They differed greatly, but amicably enough, though I take it he was not very well pleased with Wharncliffe's last letter, in which he distinctly told him that his speech on the Address, and declaration against any Reform, was what overthrew his Government. This he never will admit, and, passing over the proximate cause, always refers his fall to (what was certainly the remote cause) the Catholic question —that is, to the breaking up of the Tory party which followed it, and the union of the old Tories with the Whigs and Radicals on purpose to turn him out. In this correspondence Wharncliffe has much the best of it, and I was surprised to find with what tenacity the Duke clings to his cherished prejudices, and how he shuts his eyes to the signs of the times and of the real state of the country. With the point at issue he never would grapple. Wharncliffe argued for concession, *because* they have not the means of resistance, and that they are in fact at the mercy of their opponents. The Duke admitted the force against them, but thought it would be possible to govern the country without Reform 'if the King was not against them'—an important increment of his conditions; there is no doubt that 'the King's name is a tower of strength, which they upon the adverse faction want'— and he continued through all his letters arguing the question on its abstract merits, and repeating the topic that had been over and over again urged, but without reference to the actual state of things and the means of resistance. It seems, however, pretty clear that he will oppose this Bill just as he did the last, and he will probably have a great many followers; but the Party is broken up, for Wharncliffe and Harrowby will vote for the second reading; the Bishops will generally go with them, and probably a sufficient number of Peers. If Lord Grey can see a reasonable chance of carrying the Bill without making Peers, there can be very little doubt he will put off that resource till the last moment.

11th—Yesterday Harrowby had an interview with Ld. Grey, the result of which I do not know. Walked with Stuart (de Rothesay) in the morning, who had seen the Duke of Wellington the day before. I said I was afraid he was very obstinate. He said, 'No, he thought not, but that the Duke fancied Wharncliffe had gone too far.'

The cholera which for some days appeared to be subsiding at Sunderland, has resumed fresh vigour, and yesterday 19 new cases were reported—the greatest number since the beginning (in any one day)—besides two others at Newcastle.

To-morrow Reform comes on. Some say that it will be as hotly disputed as ever, and that Peel's speeches indicate a bitterness undiminished, but this will not happen. It is clear that the general tone and temper of parties is softened, and thought a great deal of management and discretion is necessary to accomplish anything like a decent compromise, the majority of both parties are earnestly desirous of bringing the business to an end by any means. What has already taken place between the Government and Wharncliffe and Harrowby has certainly smoothed the way, and removed much of that feeling of asperity which before existed. The press, too, is less violent, the 'Morning Herald' openly preaching a compromise, and the 'Times' taking that sort of sweep which, if it does not indicate a change, shows a disposition to take such a position as may enable it to adopt any course.

13th—John Russell brought on his Bill last night in a very feeble speech. A great change is apparent since the last Bill; the House was less full, and a softened and subdued state of temper and feeling were evinced. Peel made an able and a bitter speech, though perhaps not a very judicious one. There are various alterations in the Bill; enough to prove that it was at least wise to throw out the last. Althorp, who answered Peel, acknowledged that if the old Bill had been opposed in its earliest stage it never could have been brought forward again, or made an avowal to that effect. In fact, Peel is now aware (as everybody else is) of the enormous fault that was committed in not throwing it out at once, before the Press had time to operate, and rouse the country to the pitch of madness it did. On what trifles turn the destinies of nations! William Bankes told me last night that Peel owned this to him; said that he had earnestly desired to do so, but had been turned from his purpose by Granville Somerset!! And why? Because he (in the expectation of a dissolution) must have voted against him, he said, in order to save his popularity in his own county.

14th—People generally are mightily satisfied at the tone of the discussion the other night, and, what is of vast importance, the Press has adopted a moderate and conciliatory tone, even the 'Times,' which is now all for compromise. It is clear as daylight that the Government will consent to anything which leaves untouched the great principles of the Bill, and the country desires to see the question settled, and, if possible, rest from this eternal excitement.

20th—The second reading of the Reform Bill was carried at one o'clock on Saturday night by a majority of two to one, and ended very triumphantly for Ministers, who are proportionally elated, and their opponents equally depressed. Croker had made a very clever speech on Friday, with quotations from Hume, and much reasoning upon them. Hobhouse detected several inaccuracies, and gave his discovery to Stanley, who worked it up in a crushing attack upon Croker. It is by far the best speech Stanley ever made, and so good as to raise him immeasurably in the House. Lord Grey said it placed him at the very top of the H. of C., without a rival, which perhaps is jumping to rather too hasty a conclusion. He shone the more from Peel's making a very poor exhibition. He had been so nettled by Macaulay's sarcasms the night before on his tergiversation, that he went into the whole history of the Catholic question and his conduct on that occasion, which, besides savouring of that egotism with which he is so much and justly reproached, was uncalled for and out of place. The rest of his speech was not so good as usual, and he did not attempt to answer Stanley.

1832

Mar. 28—There appear to have been as many different opinions as of people on the discussion in the H. of L. when the Bill was brought up, and it seems paradoxical, but is true, that though it was on the whole satisfactory, nobody was satisfied. Lord Grey complained to me that Ld. Harrowby was too stiff; Ld. Harrowby complained that Ld. Grey was always beating about the bush of compromise, but never would commit himself fairly to concession. Melbourne complained last night that what was done was done in such an ungracious manner, so niggardly, that he hated the man (Harrowby), etc. The ultra-Tories are outrageous 'that He gave up everything without reason or cause'; the ultra-Whigs equally furious 'that he had shown how little way he was disposed to go in Committee; his object was to turn out the Government,' etc.; and what is comical, neither party will believe that Harrowby really is so obnoxious to the other as he is said to be. Each is convinced that he is acting in the interests of the other. What a position, what injustice, blindness, folly, obstinacy, brought together and exhibited! If ever there was a man whose conduct was exempt from the ordinary motives of ambition, and who made personal sacrifices in what he is doing, it is Lord Harrowby, and yet there is no reproach that is not cast upon him, no term of abuse that is not applied to him, no motive that is not ascribed to him.

No wonder a man who has seen much of them is sick of politics and public life. Nothing now is thought of but the *lists*, and of course everybody has got one. The Tories still pretend to a majority of seven; the Govt. and Harrowby think they have one of from ten to twenty, and I suspect fifteen will be found about the mark. The unfortunate thing is that neither of our cocks are good for fighting, not from want of courage, but Harrowby is peevish, ungracious and unpopular, and Wharncliffe carries no weight, and on the whole perhaps is rather ridiculous. To be sure neither of them pretend to make a party, but then their opponents insist upon it that they do, and men shrink from enlisting (or being supposed to enlist) under Wharncliffe's banner. However, notwithstanding the violence of the noisy fools of the party, and of the women, there is a more rational disposition on the part of practical men, for Wharncliffe spoke to Ellenborough yesterday, and told him that though he knew he and Harrowby were regarded as traitors by all of them, he did hope that when the Bill came into Committee they would agree to consult together, and try and come to some understanding as to the best mode of dealing with the question, that it was absurd to be standing aloof, etc.; to which Ellenboro replied that he perfectly agreed with him, was anxious to do so, and intended to advise his friends to take that course.

April 1st—Wharncliffe got Lord Grey to put off the second reading for a few days on account of the Quarter Sessions, which drew down a furious attack from Londonderry, and was in fact very foolish and unnecessary, as it looks like a concert between them, of which it is very desirable to avoid any appearance, as in fact none exists. The violence of the Tories continues unabated, and there is no effort they do not make to secure a majority, and they expect either to succeed or to bring it to a near thing. In the meantime the tone of the other party is changed. Dover, who makes lists, manages proxies, and does all the little jobbing, whipping-in, busy work of the party, makes out a clear majority, and told me he now thought the Bill would get through without Peers. The Government, however, are all agreed to make the Peers if it turns out to be necessary; and especially if the Bill should be thrown out, it seems clear that they would by no means go out, but make the Peers and bring it in again; so I gather from Richmond, and He who is the most violently opposed of the whole Cabinet to Peer-making, is now ready to make any number if necessary. There is, however, I hope, a disposition to concession, which, if matters are tolerably well managed, may lead to an arrangement. Still Wharncliffe, who must have a great deal to do in Committee, is neither prudent nor popular. The Tories are obstinate sulky, and indisposed to agree to anything reasonable. It is the unity of object and the compactness of the party which gives the Government

strength. Charles Wood told me the other day that they were well disposed
to a compromise on two especial points, one the exclusion of Town voters
from the right of voting for Counties, the other the metropolitan members.
On the first he proposed that no man voting for a town in right of a £10
house should have a vote for the County in right of any freehold in that
town. That would be half-way between Wharncliffe's plan and the present.
The second, that Marylebone should return two members, and Middlesex
two more—very like Grey's proposition which Harrowby rejected—but I
suggested keeping the whole and raising the qualification, to which he
thought no objection would lie.

At the Dss. de Dino's ball the night before last I had a very curious conversation with Melbourne about it all. He said that 'he really believed there
was no strong feeling in the country for the measure.' We talked of the
violence of the Tories, and their notion that they could get rid of the whole
thing. I said the notion was absurd *now*, but that I fully agreed with him
about the general feeling. 'Why, then,' said he, 'might it not be thrown
out?'—a consummation I really believe he would rejoice at, if it could be
done. I said because there was a great party which would not let it, which
would agitate again, and that the country wished ardently to have it settled;
that if it could be disposed of for good and all, it would be a good thing
indeed, but that this was now become impossible. I asked him if his colleagues were impressed as he was with this truth, and he said, 'No.' I told
him he ought to do everything possible to enforce it, and make them moderate, and induce them to concede, to which he replied, 'What difficulty can
they have in swallowing the rest after they have given up the rotten
boroughs? That is, in fact, the essential part of the Bill, and the truth is
I do not see how the Government is to be carried on without them. Some
means may be found; a remedy may possibly present itself, and it may work
in practice better than we now know of, but I am not aware of any, and I
do not see how any Government can be carried on when these are swept
away.' These were, if not his exact words, the exact sense, and a pretty
avowal for a man to make at the eleventh hour who has been a party concerned in this Bill during the other ten. I told him I agreed in every respect,
but that it was too late to discuss this now, and that the rotten boroughs
were past saving, that as to the minor points, they (the Waverers) thought
them of importance, looked upon them as securities, compensations, and
moreover as what would save their own honor, and that the less their real
importance was the more easily might they be conceded. We had a great
deal more talk, but then it is all talk, and *à quoi bon* with a man who holds
these opinions and acts as he does? Let it end as it may, the history of the

Bill, and the means by which it has been imagined, brought forward, supported, and opposed, will be most curious and instructive. The division in the Lords must be very close indeed.

I heard yesterday, however, from Keate, who is attending me (and who is the King's Surgeon, and sees him when he is in town), that he saw H.M. after the Levee on Wednesday, and that he was ill, out of sorts, and in considerable agitation; that he enquired of him about his health, when the K. said he had much to annoy him, and that 'many things passed there (pointing to the Cabinet, out of which he had just come) which were by no means agreeable, and that he had had more than usual to occupy him that morning.' Keate said he was very sure from his manner that something unpleasant had occurred. This was, I have since discovered, the question of a creation of Peers again brought forward, and to which the King's aversion has returned, so much so that it is doubtful if he will after all consent to a large one. It seems that unless the Peers are made (in the event of the necessity arising) Brougham and Althorp will resign; at least so they threaten. I have seen enough of threats, and doubts, and scruples, to be satisfied that there is no certainty that any of them will produce the anticipated effects, but I am resolved I will try, out of these various elements, if I cannot work out something which may be serviceable to the cause itself, though the materials I have to work with are scanty. The Ministers were all day yesterday settling who the new Peers shall be, so seriously are they preparing for the *coup*. They had already fixed upon Lds. Molyneux, Blandford, Kennedy, Ebrington, Cavendish, Brabazon, and Charles Fox, Littleton, Portman, Francis, Lawley, Western, and many others, and this would be what Lord Holland calls assimilating the House of Lords to the spirit of the other House, and making it harmonise with the prevailing sense of the people.

14th—The Reform Bill (second reading) was carried this morning at seven o'clock in the House of Lords by a majority of nine. The House did not sit yesterday. The night before Phillpotts, the Bishop of Exeter, made a grand speech against the Bill, full of fire and venom, very able. It would be an injury to compare this man with Laud; he more resembles Gardiner; had he lived in those days he would have been just such another, boiling with ambition, an ardent temperament, and great talents. He has a desperate and a dreadful countenance, and looks like the man he is. The last two days gave plenty of reports of changes either way, but the majority has always looked like from seven to ten. The House will adjourn on Wednesday, and go into Committee after Easter; and in the meantime what negotiations! and what difficulties to get over! The Duke of Wellington and Lord Harrowby have had some good-humoured talk, and the former seems well disposed to join in amending the Bill, but the difficulty will be to bring these extreme and irritated parties to any agreement as to terms. I am very glad this second reading is over, and the majority is very decent. The debate in the Lords, though not so good as last year, has been, as usual, much better than that in the Commons.

15th—The debate in the H. of Lords was closed by a remarkable reply from Lord Grey, full of moderation, and such as to hold out the best hopes of an adjustment of the question—not that it pacified the ultra-Tories, who were furious. The speech was so ill-reported at that late hour that it is not generally known what he did say, and many of those who heard it almost doubt their own accuracy, or suspect that he went further than he intended, so unlike was it to his former violent and unyielding language. He said, with regard to a creation of Peers, that nothing could justify him in recommending the exercise of that prerogative but a collision between the two Houses of Parliament, and that in such a case (he is reported to have said) he should deem it his duty first to recommend a dissolution, and to ascertain whether the feeling of the country was with the other House (there were not the words, but to this effect). If this be at all correct, it is clear that he cannot make the Peers to carry the clauses, for, in fact, the collision between the two Houses will not have arrived unless the Commons should reject any amendments which may be made by the Lords. The tone, however, of the violent supporters of Government is totally changed; at Lord Holland's last night they were singing in a very different note, and, now, if the counsels of the Lords are guided by moderation and firmness, they may deal with the Bill *almost* as they please; but they must swallow Schedule A.[1] The difficulties, however, are great; the High Tories are exasperated and vindictive, and will fiercely fight against any union with the seceders. The Duke is moderate in his tone, ready to act cordially with all parties, but he owes the seceders a grudge, is anxious to preserve his influence with the Tories, and will probably insist upon mutilating the Bill more than will be prudent and feasible. The Harrowby and Wharncliffe party, now that the second reading is over, ceases to be a party. It was a patched-up, miscellaneous concern at best, of men who were half-reasoned and half-frightened over, who could not bear separating from the Duke, long to return to him, and, besides, are ashamed of Wharncliffe as a Chief. There never was such a 'Chef de circonstance.' He is a very honest man, with a right view of things and a fair and unprejudiced understanding, vain and imprudent, without authority, commanding no respect, and in a false position as the

[1] Schedule A listed certain parliamentary boroughs which were to be disfranchised.

ephemeral leader he is, marching in that capacity *pari passu* with Harrowby, who is infinitely more looked up to, but whose bilious complexion prevents his mixing with society and engaging and persuading others to follow his opinions; nor has he (Ld. Harrowby) any plan or design beyond the object of the moment. He has no thought of mixing again in public life, he does not propose to communicate with anybody on anything further than the middle course to be adopted now, and few people are disposed to sever the ties on which their future political existence depend for the sake of culti-vating this short-lived connexion. If the Government, therefore, look to the seceders who have carried the question for them to carry other points, they will find it won't do, for their followers will melt into the mass of the anti-Reformers, who, though they will still frown upon the chiefs, will gladly take back the rank and file. A fortnight will elapse, in the course of which opportunities will be found of ascertaining the disposition of the great party and the probability of an arrangement.

The debate was good on Friday, but very inferior to the last. Phillpotts got a terrific dressing from Lord Grey, and was handled not very delicately by Goderich and Durham, though the latter was too coarse. He had laid him-self very open, and, able as he is, he has adopted a tone and style inconsistent with his lawn sleeves, and unusual on the Episcopal Bench. He is carried away by his ambition and his alarm, and horrifies his Brethren, who feel all the danger (in these times) of such a colleague. The episode of which he was the object was, of course, the most amusing part of the whole.

Newmarket, 22nd—Ill and laid up with the gout for this week past. Came here on Friday, 20th. The carrying of the second reading of the Bill seems to have produced no effect. Everybody is gone out of town, the Tories in high dudgeon. The Duke of Wellington has entered a protest with all the usual objections, which has been signed by a whole rabble of Peers, but not by Lyndhurst, Ellenboro, or Carnarvon, who monopolise the brains of the party; they declined. In the meantime things look better. Wharncliffe, Har-rowby, and Haddington have had two interviews with Lyndhurst and Ellenboro, and though they did not go into particulars the result was satis-factory, and a strong disposition evinced to co-operation and moderation. It was agreed they should meet again next week, and see what could be arranged. On Friday Palmerston sent to Wharncliffe and desired to see him. They met, and Palmerston told him that he came from Lord Grey, who was desirous of having an interview with him, adding that Lord Grey had now become convinced that he might make much more extensive concessions than he had ever yet contemplated. He added that Lord G. would rather see Wharncliffe alone, without Harrowby, whose manner was so snappish and unpleasant that he could not talk so much at his ease as he would to Wharncliffe alone. Wharncliffe replied that he could have no objection to see Lord Grey, but that he must fairly tell him his situation was no longer the same, having put himself in amicable communication with Lyndhurst and Ellenboro; that the concurrence of the Tories was indispensable to him and his friends to effect the alterations they contemplated, and he could not do anything which might have to them the appearance of underhand dealing; that he would tell L. and E., and if they made no objection he would see Ld. G. Ellenboro was gone out of town, but he went to Lyndhurst, who immediately advised him to see Lord Grey, and said it was most desirable that they should be made acquainted with the views and disposition of Government, and he undertook to write word to the Duke of Wellington of all that had passed. Ld. Grey was unable to leave Sheen yesterday, so it was arranged that the meeting should be delayed till Wharncliffe's return to London. Richmond has, however, got a letter of four sides from Grey, empowering him to treat here with Wharncliffe, and Stanley and Graham being expected, it is very likely some progress may be made. Nothing can promise better, and if the Chiefs of the Tories can be brought to moderation the stupid obstinacy of the mass will not matter, and I do not think they will dare hold out, for when a negotiation on such a conciliatory basis is proposed, a terrible case would be made hereafter against those who should refuse to listen to it. The advantages are so clear that nothing would make them persist in the line of uncompromising opposition but an unconquerable repugnance to afford a triumph to the Waverers, which a successful termination would do; not that they would profit by it, for they are so few, and those who will have been wrong so many, that clamour will silence justice, and a thousand excuses and pretences will be found to deprive them of their rightful credit. It is a long time—not probably since the days of Charles II—that this place (Newmarket) has been the Theatre of a political negotiation, and, conceding the importance of the subject, the actors are amusing—Richmond, Graham, Wharncliffe, and myself. By-and-bye it is perfectly true that (if I have not mentioned it before) the Royal carriages were all ready the morning of the decision of the second reading to take the King to the H. of Lords to prorogue Parliament, and on Tuesday the Peers would have appeared in the 'Gazette.'

May 12—The day after the debate Grey and Brougham went to Windsor and proposed to the King to make fifty Peers. They took with them a minute of Cabinet signed by all the members except the Duke of Richmond. Palmerston proposed it in Cabinet, and Melbourne made no objection. H.M. took till the next day to consider, when he accepted their resignations, which was the alternative they gave him. At the Levee the same day nothing occurred; the King hardly spoke to the Duke, but he afterwards saw Lyndhurst (having sent for him). This was not well done, for besides the character of the man which makes him the least fit to form an administration, it was a sort of insult to his ex-Ministers to send at once for the person who had been the immediate instrument in turning them out. I do not know what passed between them, but the Duke of Wellington was soon sent for. The Duke and Lyndhurst endeavoured to prevail on Peel to take the Government upon himself, and the former offered to act in any capacity in which he could be useful, but Peel would not. Some communication also took place between Lyndhurst and Harrowby, but the latter declared at once he would support the new Government, but not take office. When Peel finally declined, the Duke accepted. The King saw Peel and the Speaker. Nothing is known of the formation of the Cabinet, but the reports were first that Alexander Baring was to be Chancellor of the Exchequer, and since that he has refused on account of his health, and that Lyndhurst is to go to the King's Bench, Tenterden to retire, and the Great Seal to be put in commission.

The first act of the Duke was to advise the King to reject the address of the Birmingham Union, which he did, said he knew of no such body. All very proper. In the morning I called upon Wood at the Treasury, to explain to him that I had never been cognisant of the late proceeding in the H. of Lords, and that I was far from approving the conduct of my old associates. He said he had never believed that I was any party to it, and regretted that I had not been in town, when it was just possible I might have persuaded them of the unworthiness of the course they were taking. He said that I did not know how bad it was, for that Wharncliffe had distinctly said that if such a thing was proposed he should oppose it, and that Palmerston was present when he said so. This Wharncliffe positively denies, and yesterday he went to Palmerston to endeavour to explain, taking with him a minute which he said he had drawn up at the time of all that passed, but which he had never before shown or submitted for correction, and which Palmerston told him was incorrect, inasmuch as it omitted that engagement. They are at issue as to the fact. The position of the respective parties is curious. The Waverers undertook a task of great difficulty with slender means, and they accomplished it with complete success. All turned out as they expected and desired, but, after having been in confidential communication with both parties, they have contrived mortally to offend both, and to expose themselves to odium from every quarter, and to an universal imputation of insincerity and double-dealing, and this without any other fault than mismanagement and the false position in which they found themselves, without influence or power, between two mighty parties. The Tories, who have exhibited nothing but obstinacy and unreasonableness, and who thwarted the Waverers by every means they could devise, have reaped all the benefit of their efforts, and that without admitting that they were right or thanking them for bringing matters to this pass. They are triumphant, in spite of all they did to prevent their own triumph, and have had all the spiteful pleasure of abuse and obloquy, all the glory of consistency, and the satisfaction of pertinacity, with all the advantages that an opposite line of conduct promised to give them.

The King took leave of his Ministers with a great effusion of tenderness, particularly to Richmond, whom he entreated to remain in office; but I take it that he easily consoles himself, and does not care much more for one Minister than another.

The debate in the H. of C. was not so violent as might have been expected, and the Tories were greatly elated with the divisions on Ebrington's motion, because there was a majority less by fifty-six than on a similar motion when the Bill was rejected in October. The circumstances were, however, different, and some would not vote because they disapprove of creating Peers, which this vote would have committed them to approve of. There is so much of wonder, and curiosity, and expectation in the town that there is less of abuse and exasperation than might have been expected, but it will all burst forth. The Town is perfectly quiet. What is odd enough is that the King was hissed as he left London the other day, and the Duke cheered as he came out of the Palace. There have been some meetings, with resolutions to support the Bill, approbation of Ministers, and against the payment of taxes, and there will probably be a good deal of bustle and bluster here and elsewhere; but I do not believe in real tumults, particularly when the rabble and the unions know that there is a Government which will not stand such things, and that they will not be able to bandy compliments with the Duke as they did with Althorp and Johnny, not but what much dissatisfaction and much disquietude must prevail. The funds have not fallen, which is a sign that there is no alarm in the City. At this early period of the business it is difficult to form any opinion of what will happen; the present Government in opposition will again be formidable, but I am disposed to think things will go on and right themselves: we shall avoid a creation of Peers, but we must have a Reform Bill of some sort, and perhaps a harmless one after all, and if the elements of disorder can be resolved into tranquillity and order again, we must not quarrel with the means that have been employed, nor the quantum of moral injustice that has been perpetrated.

The Tories are very indignant with Peel for not taking office, and if, as it is supposed, he is to support Government and the Bill out of office, and when all is over come in, it is hardly worth while for such a farce to deprive the King and the country of his services in the way that they could be most useful, but he is still smarting under Catholic question reminiscences, while the Duke is more thick-skinned. After he had carried the Catholic question the world was prepared for a good deal of versatility on his part, but it was in mere derision that (after his speech on Reform in 1830) it used to be said that he would very likely be found proposing a Bill of Reform, and here he is coming into office for the express purpose of carrying on this very Bill against which the other day he entered a protest which must stare him in the face through the whole progress of it, or, if not, to bring in another of the same character, and probably nearly of the same dimensions. Pretexts are, however, not wanting, and the necessity of supporting the King is made paramount to every other consideration. The Duke's worshippers (a numerous class) call this the finest action of his life, though it is difficult to perceive in what the grandeur of it consists, or the magnitude of the sacrifice. However, it is fair to wait a little, and hear from his own lips his exposition of the mode in which he intends to deal with this measure, and how he will reconcile what he has hitherto said with what he is now about to do.

14th, Monday—Nothing more was known yesterday, but everybody congregated at the clubs, asking, discussing, and wondering. There was a great meeting at Apsley House, when it was supposed everything was settled. The Household went yesterday to St. James's to resign their sticks, etc.; amongst the rest Lord Foley. The King was very civil to him; made him sit down and said, 'Ld. Foley, you are a young man.' 'Sir, I am afraid I cannot flatter myself that I have any right to that appellation.' 'Oh, yes; you are a young man—at all events in comparison with me—and you will probably come into office again; but I am an old man, and I am afraid I shall not have the pleasure of seeing you there.' It is supposed that this *coup* has been preparing for some time. All the Royal Family, bastards and all, have been incessantly *at* the King, and he has probably had more difficulty in the long run in resisting the constant importunity of his *entourage*, and of his womankind particularly, than the dictates of his Ministers; and between this gradual but powerful impression, and his real opinion and fears, he was not sorry to seize the first good opportunity of shaking off the Whigs. When Lord Anglesey went to take leave of him at Windsor he was struck with the change in his sentiments, and told Ly. Anglesey so, who told my Brother.

It is gratifying to find that those with whom I used to dispute, and who would hear of nothing but rejecting the second reading, now admit that my view was the correct one, and Vesey Fitzgerald, with whom I had more than one discussion, complimented me very handsomely upon the justification of my view of the question which the event had afforded. The High Tories, of course, will never admit that they could have been wrong, and have no other resource but to insist boldly that the King never would have made Peers at all.

London, May 17th, Thursday—The events of the last few days have passed with a rapidity which hardly left time to think upon them—such sudden changes and transitions from rage to triumph on one side, and from foolish exultation to mortification and despair on the other. The first impression was that the Duke of Wellington would succeed in forming a Government with or without Peel. The first thing he did was to try and prevail upon Peel to be Prime Minister, but he was inexorable. He then turned to Baring, who, after much hesitation, agreed to be Chancellor of the Exchequer. The work went on, but with difficulty, for neither Peel, Goulburn, nor Croker would take office. They then tried the Speaker, who was mightily tempted to become Secretary of State, but still doubting and fearing, and requiring time to make up his mind. At an interview with the Duke and Lyndhurst at Apsley House he delivered his sentiments on the existing state of affairs in a speech of three hours, to the unutterable disgust of Lyndhurst, who returned home, flung himself into a chair and said that 'he could not endure to have anything to do with such a *damned tiresome old Bitch*.' After these three hours of oratory Manners Sutton desired to have till the next morning (Monday) to make up his mind, which he again begged might be extended till the evening. On that evening (Monday) ensued the memorable night in the H. of Commons, which everybody agrees was such a scene of violence and excitement as never had been exhibited within those walls. Tavistock told me he had never heard anything at all like it, and to his dying day should not forget it. The House was crammed to suffocation; every violent sentiment and vituperative expression was received with shouts of approbation, yet the violent speakers were listened to with the greatest attention. Tom Duncombe made one of his blustering Radical harangues, full of every sort of impertinence, which was received with immense applause, but which contrasted with an admirable speech, full of dignity, but also of sarcasm and severity, from John Russell—the best he ever made. The conduct of the Duke of Wellington in taking office *to carry the Bill,* which was not denied, but which his friends feebly attempted to justify, was assailed with the most merciless severity, and (what made the greatest impression) was condemned, though in more measured terms, by moderate men and Tories, such as Inglis and Davies Gilbert. Baring, who spoke four times, at last proposed that there should be a compromise, and that the ex-Ministers should resume their seats and carry the Bill. This extraordinary proposition was drawn from him by the state of the House, and the impossibility he at once saw of forming a new Government, and without any previous concert with the Duke, who, however, entirely approved of what he said. After the debate Baring and Sutton went to Apsley House, and related to the Duke what had taken place, the former saying He would face a thousand devils rather than such a House of Commons. From that moment the whole thing was at an end, and the next morning (Tuesday) the Duke repaired to the King, and told him that he could not form an Administration. This communication, for which the debate of the previous night had prepared everybody, was speedily known, and the joy and triumph of the Whigs were complete.

The King desired the Duke and Lyndhurst (for they went together) to advise him what he should do. They advised him to write to Lord Grey (which he did), informing him that the Duke had given up the commission to form a Government, that he had heard of what had fallen from Mr. Baring in the House of Commons the night before on the subject of a compromise, and that he wished Lord Grey to return and resume the Government upon that principle. Lord Grey sent an answer full of the usual expressions of zeal, respect, etc., but that he could give no answer till he had consulted his colleagues. He assembled his Cabinet, and at five o'clock the answer was sent.

Yesterday morning Lord Grey saw the King; but up to last night nothing was finally settled, everything turning upon the terms to be exacted, some of the violent of the Party desiring they should avail themselves of this opportunity to make Peers, both to show their power and increase their strength; the more moderate, including Lord Grey himself and many of the old Peer-makers, were for sparing the King's feelings and using their victory with moderation, all, however, agreeing that the only terms on which they could return were the certainty of carrying the Reform Bill unaltered, either by a creation of Peers or by the secession of its opponents. Up to the present moment the matter stands thus: the King at the mercy of the Whigs, just as averse as ever to make Peers, the violent wishing to press him, the moderate wishing to spare him, all parties railing at each other, the Tories broken and discomfited, and meditating no further resistance to the Reform Bill. The Duke is to make his *exposé* to-night.

Peel, who has kept himself out of the scrape, is strongly suspected of being anything but sorry for the dilemma into which the Duke has got himself, and they think that he secretly encouraged him to persevere, with promises of present support and future co-operation, with a shrewd anticipation of the fate that awaited him. I am by no means indisposed to give credit for this, for I well remember the wrath of Peel when the Duke's Government was broken up in 1830, and the various instances of secret dislike and want of real cordiality which have peeped from under a decent appearance of union and friendship. Nothing can be more certain than that he is in high spirits in the midst of it all, and talks with great complacency of its being very well as it is, and that the salvation of character is everything. This from him, who fancies he has saved his own, and addressed to those who have forfeited theirs, is amusing.

The joy of the King at what he thought was to be his deliverance from the Whigs was unbounded. He lost no time in putting the Duke of Wellington in possession of everything that had taken place between him and them upon the subject of Reform, and with regard to the creation of Peers, admitting that he had consented, but saying he had been subjected to every species of persecution. His ignorance, weakness, and levity put him in a miserable light, and prove him to be one of the silliest old gentlemen in his dominions; but I believe he is mad, for yesterday he gave a great dinner to the Jockey Club, at which (notwithstanding his cares) he seemed in excellent spirits; and after dinner he made a number of speeches, ridiculous and nonsensical, beyond all belief but to those who heard them, rambling from one subject to another, repeating the same thing over and over again, and altogether such a mass of confusion, trash, and inbecillity as made one laugh and blush at the same time.

As soon as the Duke had agreed to try and form a Government he applied to the Tories, who nearly all agreed to support him, and were prepared to go all lengths, even to that of swallowing the whole Bill if necessary; the Duke of Newcastle particularly would do anything. These were the men who were so squeamish that they could not be brought to support amendments even, unless they were permitted to turn the Schedules upside-down, straining at gnats out of office and swallowing camels in. (4 *lines here expunged*.) It is remarkable that after the sacrifice Wharncliffe made to reingratiate himself with the Tories, incurring the detestation and abuse of the Whigs, and their reproach of bad faith, the former have utterly neglected him, taking no notice of him whatever during the whole of their proceedings from the moment of the division, leaving him in ignorance of their plans and intentions, never inviting him to any of their meetings, and although a communication was made by Lyndhurst to Harrowby (they wanted Harrowby to be Prime Minister), the latter was not at liberty to impart it to Wharncliffe. It is not possible to be more deeply mortified than he is at the treatment he has experienced from these allies after having so committed himself. From the account of the King's levity throughout these proceedings, I strongly suspect that (if he lives) he will go mad. While the Duke and Lyndhurst were with him, at one of the most critical moments (I forget now at which) he said, 'I have been thinking that something is wanting with regard to Hanover. Duke, you are now my Minister, and I beg you will think of this; I should like to have a slice of Belgium, which would be a convenient addition to Hanover. Pray remember this,' and then resumed the subject they were upon.

19th—The night before last the Duke made his statement. It was extremely clear, but very bald, and left his case just where it was, as he did not say anything that everybody did not know before. His friends, however, extolled it as a masterpiece of eloquence and a complete vindication of himself. The Tory Lords, who spoke after him bedaubed him with praise, and vied with each other in expressions of admiration. These were Carnarvon, Winchilsea, and Haddington. There was not one word from the Duke (nor from the others) indicative of an intention to secede, which was what the Government expected. His speech contained a sort of covert attack upon Peel; in fact, he could not defend himself without attacking Peel, for if the one was in the right in taking office the other must have been in the wrong in refusing to join him. There was nothing, however, which was meant as a reproach, though out of the House the Duke's friends do not conceal their anger that Peel would not embark with him in his desperate enterprize.

Lyndhurst was exceedingly able, highly excited, very eloquent, and contrived to make his case a good one. (2½ *lines expunged*.) It was a fine display and very short. Carnarvon and Mansfield were outrageously violent, but both in their way clever, and parts of the latter's speech were eloquent. Lord Grey was excellent, short, very temperate and judicious, exactly what was requisite and nothing more. Nobody else spoke on his side, except Mulgrave at the end.

The debate, however interesting, left the whole matter in uncertainty; and the next day the old question began again. What was to be done—Peers or no Peers? A Cabinet sat nearly all day, and Lord Grey went once or twice to the King. He, poor man, was at his wits' end, and tried an experiment (not a very constitutional one) of his own by writing to a number of

Peers, entreating them to withdraw their opposition to the Bill. These letters were written (I think) before the debate. On Thursday nothing was settled, and at another meeting of the Cabinet a minute was drawn up agreeing to offer again the same advice to the King. Before this was acted upon Richmond, who had been absent, arrived, and he prevailed upon his colleagues to cancel it. In the meantime the Duke of Wellington, Lyndhurst, and other Peers had given the desired assurances to the King, which he communicated to Lord Grey. These were accepted as sufficient securities, and declarations made accordingly in both Houses of Parliament. If the Ministers had again gone to the King with this advice, it is impossible to say how it would have ended, for he had already been obstinate, and might have continued so on this point, and he told Verulam that he thought it would be contrary to his coronation oath to make Peers. Our princes have strange notions of the obligations imposed by their coronation oath.

On Thursday in the H. of Commons Peel made his statement, in which, with great civility and many expressions of esteem and admiration of the Duke, he pronounced as bitter a censure of his conduct, while apparently confining himself to the defence of his own, as it was possible to do, and as such it was taken. I have not the least doubt that he did it *con amore*, and that he is doubly rejoiced to be out of the scrape himself and to leave others in it.

The Bill was given its third reading, without particular excitement, on 4 June. The first House of Commons under the Act was elected at the beginning of 1833.

1833

Sept. 3—The Parliament is up, and not before people were sick of it, and had dropt out of town one by one till hardly any Parliament was left. It may be worth while to take a little survey of the present condition of things as compared with what it was a few months ago, and consider at this resting time what has been the practical effect of the great measure of Reform, without going very deeply into the question. The Reform Bill was carried, *in toto*, the Tories having contrived that everything that was attempted should be gained by the Reformers. No excuse, therefore, was left for the Parliament, and if 'the People' did not chuse a good one it was their own fault. It

was chosen, and when it met was found to be composed of a majority of supporters of the present Government, a certain number of Tories, not enough to be powerful, and many Radicals, who soon proved to be wholly inefficient. It speedily became manifest that in point of ability it was not only inferior to the last, but perhaps to any Parliament that has sat for many years. There were 350 new members (or some such number) but not one man among them of shining or remarkable talent; Cobbett, Buckingham, Roebuck, and such men soon found their level and sunk into insignificance. The House appeared at first to be very unruly, not under the command of Government, very talkative, noisy, and ill-constituted for the transaction of business. After a little while it got better in this respect, the majority, however, though evidently determined to support Government, would not be *commanded* by it, and even men in place often took up crochets of their own, and voted against Government measures; but whenever the Ministers seemed to be in danger they always found efficient support, and on the Malt Tax the House even stultified itself to uphold them. As the Session proceeded the men who gained reputation and established the greatest personal influence were Peel and Stanley; Macaulay rather lost than gained; Althorp lost entirely, but the weight of his blunders and unfitness could not sink him, his personal character and good humour always buoyed him up. The great measures, some of the greatest that any Parliament ever dealt with, were got through with marvellous facility. They did not for the most part come on till late in the Session, when the House had got tired, and the East India Charter Bill was carried through most of the stages in empty Houses. The measures have generally evinced a Conservative character, and the Parliament has not shown any disposition to favor subversive principles or encourage subversive language. It has been eminently liberal in point of money, granting all that Ministers asked without the slightest difficulty; twenty millions for the West Indians, a million for the Irish Clergy, were voted almost by acclamation. Hume cut no figure in this Parliament. Notwithstanding apprehensions and predictions the Government has contrived to carry on the business of the country very successfully, and great measures have been accomplished in every department of the State, which do not seem liable to any serious objections; and in the midst of many troubles, of much complaining and bickering the Country has been advancing in prosperity, and recovering rapidly from the state of sickly depression in which it lay at the end of last year. It is fair to compare the state of affairs now and then, merely reciting facts, and let the praise rest where it may, whether it be due to the wisdom of men or the result of that disposition to right itself which has always appeared inherent in the British common-wealth. Some months ago there appeared every prospect of a war in Europe; the French were in Belgium, whence many predicted they would never be got away; Ireland was in a flame, every post brought the relation of fresh horrors and atrocities; in England trade was low, alarm and uncertainty prevalent, and a general disquietude pervaded the nation, some fearing and others desiring change, some expecting, others dreading the great things which a Reformed Parliament would do. The Session is over, and a Reformed Parliament turns out to be very much like every other Parliament, except that it is rather differently and somewhat less ably composed than its predecessors. The hopes and the fears of mankind have been equally disappointed, and after all the clamour, confusion, riots, conflagrations, furies, despair, and triumphs through which we have arrived at this consummation, up to the present time, at least, matters remain pretty much as they were, except that the Whigs have got possession of the power which the Tories have lost. We continue at peace, and with every prospect of so being for some time; we are on good terms with France, and by degrees inducing the French to extend their incipient principles of free trade, to the benefit of both countries. In Ireland there never has been a period for many years when the country was so quiet; it may not last, but so it is at the present moment. In England trade flourishes, running in a deep and steady stream, there are improvement and employment in all its branches. The landed interest has suffered and suffers still, but the wages of labour have not fallen with the rents of Landlords, and the agricultural labourers were never better off. Generally there is a better spirit abroad, less discontent, greater security, and those vague apprehensions are lulled to rest which when in morbid activity, carrying themselves from one object to another, are partly the cause and partly the effect of an evil state of things. We hear nothing now of associations, unions, and public meetings, and (compared with what it was) the world seems in a state of repose.

1837

Paris, January 17th— Arrived here last night at five, having left Dover at a quarter one the day before; three hours to Boulogne, twenty-two to Paris.

*25th—24th—*walked about Paris, dined at the Embassy, and went to Court at night; above fifty English, forty Americans, and several other foreigners were presented. The Palace is very magnificent; the present King has built a new staircase, which makes the suite of rooms continuous, and the whole has been regilt and painted. We were arranged in the throne-room by nations, the English first, and at a quarter before nine the doors of the Royal apartments were opened, and the Royal Family came forth. We all stood in a long line (single file) reaching through the two rooms, beginning and ending again at the door of the King's apartment. The King walked down the line attended by Lord Granville, then the Queen with the eldest Princess under her arm, then Madame Adélaïde with the other, and then the Duke of Orleans. Aston attended the Queen, and the *attachés* the others. They all speak to each individual, and by some strange stretch of invention find something to say. The King is too civil; he has a fine head, and closely resembles the pictures of Louis XIV. The Queen is very gracious and dignified, Adélaïde very good-humoured, and the D. of Orleans extremely Princely in his manners. In the morning I went to the Tuileries by appointment, when he received me, kept me for a quarter of an hour talking about race-horses, and invited me to breakfast on Saturday, and to go with him to Meudon to see his stud.

25th—went sight-seeing; to the Invalides, the Panthéon, and the Madeleine. The former is very well worth seeing, and nothing is more remarkable than the Kitchen, which is the sweetest and the cleanest I ever saw. The Chapel is fine, with no remarkable tombs except those of Turenne and Vauban. The Panthéon is under repair; there are the tombs of Voltaire and Rousseau. The interior of the Madeleine is very rich, but it is inferior to the outside; the simple grandeur of the latter is somewhat frittered away in the minute ornaments and the numerous patches of coloured marble of the church. However, it will be with all its faults a magnificent building. Went to the Théâtre Français at night, and saw Madame Volnys and Monrose in Scribe's new play 'the Camaraderie,' which was very well acted and received with great applause.

25th—27th, Wednesday; ball at Tuileries, one of the great balls, and magnificent spectacle indeed. The long line of light gleaming through the whole length of the Palace is striking as it is approached, and the interior, with the whole suite of apartments brilliantly illuminated, and glittering from one end to the other with diamonds and feathers and uniforms, and dancing in all the several rooms, made a magnificent display. The supper in the theatre was the finest thing I ever saw of the kind; all the women sup first, and afterwards the men, the tables being renewed over and over again. There was an array of Servants in gorgeous liveries, and the apartment was lit by thousands of candles (no lamps) and as light as day. The company amounted to between 3000 and 4000, from all the great people down to national guards, and even private Soldiers. None of the Carlists were there, as they none of them chuse to go to Court. The King retired before eleven; it was said that he had received anonymous letters warning him of some intended attempt on his person, and extraordinary precautions were taken to guard against the entrance of any improper people.

26th—having seen all the high society the night before, I resolved to see all the low last night, and went to Musard's ball—a most curious scene; two large rooms in the rue St. Honoré almost thrown into one, a numerous and excellent orchestra, a prodigious crowd of people, most of them in costume, and all the women masked. There was every description of costume, but that which was the most general was the dress of a French post-boy, in which both males and females seemed to delight. It was well-regulated uproar and orderly confusion. When the music struck up they began dancing all over the rooms; the whole mass was in motion, but though with gestures the most vehement and grotesque, and a licence almost unbounded, the figure of the dance never seemed to be confused, and the dancers were both expert in their capers and perfect in their evolutions. Nothing could be more licentious than the movements of the dancers, and they only seemed to be restrained within limits of tolerable decency by the cocked hats and burnished helmets of the Police and Gendarmes which towered in the midst of them. After quadrilling and waltzing away, at a signal given they began galloping round the room; then they rushed pêle mêle, couple after couple, like Bedlamites broke loose, but not the slightest accident occurred. I amused myself with this strange and grotesque sight for an hour or more, and then came home.

27th—called on Talleyrand and sat with him for an hour. Talked of England in a very Conservative strain. Called on the D. de Broglie, Mesdames de Marescalchi and Durazzo, dined at the Embassy, then to Madame de Lieven's and Pembroke's concert. Not a profitable life, but not dull, and the day glides away.

February 2nd—Nothing worth noticing for the last three or four days. Dined the day before yesterday with the Duc de Poix, and went to Hope's ball; his house a sumptuous palace in miniature, all furnished and decorated with inconceivable luxury and *recherche*; one room hung with cachemires. Last night to a small ball at Court. Supper in the gallery de Diane—round tables, all the Ladies supping first; the whole thing as beautiful and magnicent as possible, and making all our fêtes look pitiful and mean after it.

Our King's Speech was here before seven o'clock yesterday evening, about twenty-nine hours after it was delivered; a rapidity of transmission almost incredible. Lord Granville had predicted to me in the morning that they would be very angry here at no mention being made of France, and so it was. I heard the same thing from other quarters, and He told me that he had found himself not deceived in his expectations, and the King had himself complained. The French Government had taken such pains latterly to conciliate ours, by their speeches in the Chambers, and by applying for votes of money to enable them to employ more custom-house officers for the express purpose of preventing the transmission of arms and stores to the Spanish Pretender; in short, giving us every proof of goodwill; that Lord G. was desirous of having some expressions of corresponding goodwill and civility inserted in the Speech, and said as much to Palmerston; but He refused.

I have been riding with Lord Granville the last two days, when he talked a good deal about France and French affairs. His own position here is wonderfully agreeable, because all the business of the two Countries is transacted by him here, and Sébastiani's[1] is little more than a nominal Embassy. This has long been the case, having begun in Canning's time; then the great intimacy which subsisted between the D. de Broglic and Ld. G. confirmed it during his Ministry, and the principal cause of Talleyrand's hatred to Palmerston was the refusal of the latter to alter the practice when He was in England, and his mortification at finding the part he played in London to be only secondary to that of the British Ambassador in Paris.

Lord de Ros, a personal friend of the diarist, had been accused by John Cumming of cheating at cards—playing with marked cards and 'sauter la coupe'—cutting the pack to the advantage of the person cutting. de Ros brought a libel action against Cumming which he lost.

February 19th—I was interrupted and have never found time to say to what I was going to return,[2] but I shall bring down my narrative—of De Ros's trial, for that it was—to the present time. I had received at Paris a letter from Cumming informing me that I must appear at the trial, my testimony having been rendered indispensable (in consequence of the imputations cast upon them by De Ros in order to prove their animus towards him). But he engaged that no questions should be put to me that it would be disagreeable to me to answer, and none tending to criminate him. I replied that no questions could be put to me that it would not be disagreeable to me to answer, and entreated him to let me off if possible. A few days after I received a letter from De Ros, complaining that Cumming kept him in the

[1] The French Ambassador in London.
[2] On February 7 the diarist had described a visit to Boulogne ending 'and now I must return——'

dark as to the evidence, appealing to my recollection of his engagement, at the period of his accepting the proposal of an action, to furnish him with such information as would be indispensable in order to prepare his defence, and entreating I would write to Cumming on the subject, adding that the trial would come on about the 10th. I instantly replied and said I would write to Cumming which I did. At the same time I told him how sorry I was to hear the trial really was coming on, and the more because I was called as a witness, and I sent him Cumming's letter to me. A day or two after this I received Cumming's reply to the letter I had written to him on receiving his summons, in which he said that he could not let me off, and he presumed I should have no objection to give evidence as to the marked cards which had been left at my house. I replied that I had the greatest objection to be questioned on that point, which I looked upon as a very different thing from speaking to *their* conduct, and that any evidence of the sort would be a link in the chain by which he was to be convicted; and I therefore protested against such a course, and appealed to the engagement contained in his first letter. No answer to this could have been received, and I left Paris.

On Saturday evening I was dining with Richard Greville at Boulogne, when they came and told me an English Courier had arrived with letters for me; when upon going out of the room to see this Courier, I found Ramozet, formerly a Servant of De Ros's, who had been (immediately after the receipt of my letter) despatched by him to find me at Paris or meet me on the road. For this purpose he had been furnished with duplicate letters; in the event of my not being at Calais or Boulogne he was to send another messenger with one set of letters to Paris, and to wait with the other set at Boulogne to intercept me and prevent my embarking for England. There was one letter from himself and one from Wm. De Ros entreating me not to return to England, nor to appear upon the approaching trial—the one threatening me with the loss of his friendship, and the other with the indignation of society if I did. These letters however did not turn me from my purpose. I felt that I was bound in honor to go, and the next morning I went. My answers to them announced my arrival in town. I did not see either of them, but others letters passed between Henry and myself, arising out of one which I was compelled to write informing him that I had repaid a sum of money which I had borrowed of him many years ago; but although I considered myself bound in honor to appear if summoned, I moved heaven and earth with Cumming to induce him to let me off, for I had a very great horror of going through this terrible duty. He was at length so moved by my expostulations that he resolved to let me off if he could, and on the Tuesday afternoon he came to me at White's and told me that he was in possession of a letter which De Ros had written to him about November last, in which he had given him full credit for his motives and conduct; that his Counsel pressed him to produce this letter, but that he thought he could not honorably do so, considering that it was a private communication; that it had occurred to him to propose that De Ros should give his consent to the production of the letter, and that he might then let me off. I eagerly grasped at the suggestion, but he added that he had not consulted his Counsel on the subject, and the arrangement must therefore be considered subject to their consent. I told him he had better give me a copy of the letter to send to De Ros, and he went home to make one, which I was to call for in my way to dinner. Finding myself late, I sent him a verbal message by my Servant, requesting him to send the letter and to appoint a meeting directly after dinner; to which he replied (enclosing the letter) that He was engaged, and that there was no use in our meeting again until I should have communicated with De Ros. I assumed (rather hastily) that this was a positive authority, superseding the conditional one he had given me before dinner, to make the bargain with De Ros, if he was so inclined; and accordingly I sent the copy and made the proposal to him, and he instantly accepted it. I met Cumming in the evening, and told him I had done so; he said he hoped I had not done it finally, as he had not consulted his Lawyers, and he had told me it must be subject to their consent. I replied that I was sorry if there had been any mistake, but that I had interpreted his note into a positive authority to conclude, and had accordingly done so, and now I concluded the agreement final. So we parted, and the next day I heard nothing of Cumming, whereupon I concluded that I was let off and told everybody that I was not to appear. But on Wednesday Cumming consulted his Lawyers, who told him he must not consent, and in the afternoon, meeting Alvanley at White's and the latter saying 'so I hear you have let C.G. off,' he replied 'only conditionally, if my Counsel agree.' Alvanley instantly went to De Ros and told him, and he then wrote a note to me requesting I would call on him without delay. This note, which was dated '6 o'clock,' I did not receive till ½ past 8, at which hour I repaired to Park Place, and on going into the room I found only Wm. and Lady Georgiana there. I asked 'where was H?' They said gone to a consultation.—'What did he want with me?' Wm. then said what Alvanley had told him and that he had sent for me to remonstrate, as he had conceived the bargain about the letter and my own appearance was final and unconditional. He was going on to argue the matter when I stopped him. I said that if there had been any mistake, it might be mine or Cumming's, but it was not De Ros's; that I had come over under the sense of what I considered an unavoidable obligation to Cumming, and after what had passed I thought I had contracted another obligation equally binding towards De Ros; that He and his Brother might therefore set their minds at rest, as I gave him my word of honor *I would not appear.* He said that it would be a great relief to H.; that he had suffered more from the prospect of my appearance than from anything else that had occurred; and that if He had found himself disappointed and deceived after what had just occurred, and that the bargain he had fancied was settled had been broken off, he declared he believed that the vexation *would have killed him.* I said He might tell him what my determination was, and as it appeared probable I should have to sustain a conflict with Cumming on the subject, He had better (as I could not see him) let his Brother write to me his feelings and view of the transaction, as it would assist me in the event of such a conflict. He said this should be done, as soon as He came home, and I might expect a letter at the Travellers'. An hour after, I did receive a letter, and great was my astonishment at reading a dry communication to this effect:—that after the communication which Cumming had made to Alvanley, he considered the negotiation at an end; he withdrew his consent to the production of his letter, and insisted that no use should be made of it. Of my assurance to Wm., superseding as it did what had passed between Cumming and Alvanley, he took no notice whatever. The fact was that He had replied to my proposal without consulting his Lawyers; he had gone to the consultation with the copy of his letter in his pocket, and the Attorney General had told him it must not be produced, so he seized upon the pretext which Cumming had afforded him, and withdrew his consent.

This necessarily threw again upon me the onus of appearing. I had all along protested against being asked any questions as to the marked cards, but at last they extorted from me a reluctant consent to say that a pack of cards had been left at my house, which I had delivered to Brooke—no more —but at this stage of the business another difficulty arose. They wanted me to depose as to *their animus,* and to say what had passed between me and them; to tell the story of the letter I had written to him in September, as well as of the original anonymous warning in April. They called upon him to produce this letter, but he refused, and would not admit having received it. They therefore called on me to produce his letters to me, in which the receipt of the letter was acknowledged; but this I positively refused to do. They (Cumming and Brooke) warmly remonstrated, but I would not hear of it; and as a subpoena duces tecum was out, I would not go home, but sent for the box in which the letter was contained, and put it out of my own reach and controul. The consequence of all this was, that my evidence as to the *circumstances* was not admissible, and they could only elicit one or two facts bearing upon the case, instead of a consistent narrative.

Being thus compelled as it were by the concurrent operations of the Antagonist parties to appear as a Witness, I went on the eventful morning to my office where I resolved to wait till I was sent for, and a more miserable day I never passed. A nervous horror crept over me which made me more restless and uneasy as each succeeding hour passed away. My mind was agitated with various conflicting feelings, and as I continually revolved all the points and circumstances about which I might possibly be interrogated there was no course and extent of examination and cross-examination that I did not invent and imagine as of possible adoption by Counsel on either side. These thoughts made me so restless that I could apply myself to nothing else, and every noise that I heard, every step on the staircase, each opening of the door seemed to be the signal that my name was called; and when at last about 5 o'clock the Messenger really did come to fetch me, it was almost a relief and I went with a sort of desperate satisfaction that it would soon be over. The Court however adjourned, and I was informed that I should be put into the box the first thing the next morning—but at this period it mattered very little, for the trial appeared to be virtually over. In the middle of the day they had brought me word that 'Thessiger had made a terrific speech,' and at the close of the first day's proceedings an impression universally prevailed that De Ros had little or no chance of a verdict. Brooke Greville's evidence (on which he hoped to make so powerful an assault, and whose character he had so confidently predicted that he should irretrievably damage), was boldly and successfully given, and though the Attorney General exerted all his ingenuity and poured forth all his virulence, He failed entirely in his attempts to damage it. The Court was crowded, and there appeared to be but one opinion as to the result. Alvanley sat upon the bench, and Wm. and Lady Georgiana were present all the time, all of them constantly communicating with De Ros, who had stationed himself at a house in Great George Street very near Westminster Hall.

The next morning I was put in the box, where very few questions were asked me, but to my great vexation the very first related to the cards. It was the Judge however who asked me whether they were marked, and subsequently the foreman of the Jury asked me some question about the marks. The Attorney General (Campbell) asked me only one question— as to my having received the information from Brooke; and I was surprised to find that he did not elicit from me the evidence he might have done in De Ros's favor, and which I had in fact given him (what I meant to be) a hint, to do. My evidence finished, I went away. I was told that Alvanley shed tears when I appeared, and that my own agitation and reluctance were manifest to the whole Auditory. Indeed Denman afterwards asked Brougham the cause of it, and when told by Bm. in what a painful predicament I was placed, he said that 'I need not mind it, as my evidence was only a drop of water in a vessel all ready overflowing.' The most important witnesses were Payne and Hy. Bentinck, more particularly perhaps the latter, because he was the most invulnerable, and because he had been ignorant of the suspicion which attached to De Ros's conduct. Brooke and Payne were both open to attack, from having played with him after they suspected, and of this imprudence, and something worse, the Attorney General amply availed himself both in his cross-examination and in his reply, which was very able, though brutal and abusive beyond all endurance, and such as to create immeasurable digust. Edward Villiers came into my room between 5 and 6, with the intelligence that the Jury after a few minutes' deliberation had found a verdict for the Defendant. Denman summed up with great impartiality, gave De Ros the benefit of every doubtful point and questionable testimony, but when he told the Jury that if he was not guilty the other party must stand convicted of a base and foul conspiracy, for which no motive and no evidence appeared, his charge must be considered as decisive against him. The verdict was received with the general concurrence of the Lawyers and of society. After the evidence of H. Bentinck and Payne, Alvanley gave it up, and long before the conclusion of the trial he desired De Ros to prepare himself for the worst, and made him go home. Thus ended this extraordinary, disgraceful and disastrous trial. Those who expected wonderful revelations, detailed exhibitions of villainy and folly, were disappointed, for none such were elicited; but a hideous picture of gambling was exhibited, much that appeared to betoken vicious habits, laxity of moral principle, coldness of honorable sentiment, and the disposition of the great mass of society was to visit with promiscuous censure all the actors in this odious drama, perhaps with too undistinguishing condemnation. Those who had hitherto stood up for De Ros, and who dared do so no longer were glad to find some compensation in joining in the cry against the rest, but De Ros had destroyed everything like compassion or sympathy for himself by the atrocity of the defence he had set up; and there was a general burst of indignation at the savage fidelity with which the Attorney General had obeyed the instructions he had received, and at the manner in which he had conducted the case. This in great measure recoiled upon himself and his Client, but the manner in which he worked some of the witnesses did not fail to produce a powerful effect.

The next day, Sunday, I went to Alvanley (who had sent for me). He said that under erroneous impressions he had censured my conduct together with that of others, and he was desirous of making all the reparation he could, by owning he had been wrong and saying so to all those to whom he had ever said anything to the contrary: and he then asked me to go to De Ros with him. We went and found him in a very miserable plight and very obstinate. He refused to take his name out of any of the Clubs as we advised him, and we found as it has since turned out that He is anything but aware of his situation, by no means regards it as hopeless, and thus kicked down as he is from the top to the bottom of the tree he is meditating by what means and how soon he may begin to climb up again. There however he must be left for the present; but the disposition there is among some people to pity or excuse him, the reluctance on the part of many to give him up, show clearly enough that he has been the artificer of his own ruin, and that if He would have taken the advice that was tendered him upon the first explosion and have staid for a time abroad, he would have been able eventually to return here, not indeed undamaged but still in a tolerable position. He never would listen to advice. He always fancied that by dexterity and artifice he should find means of steering through the difficulties that surrounded him, and he committed the greatest of all faults—he took a false estimate of the moral principle and moral feeling of society. It is remarkable that from the beginning to the end of the business, long before and since the trial, he has never for a moment evinced the slightest sense of shame—great grief, great mortification, despair, anger, malice, but no compunction, no remorse, no consciousness of disgrace. I am convinced that he cannot bring himself to believe that the world views his crimes (supposing them to be true) with the horror and disgust which they are calculated to inspire. The insensibility to every principle of honor to which he owes his present condition has had a deteriorating effect upon his understanding, and all his cunning has been insufficient to repair the errors which this perversion of heart and intellect has led him into. When I went to him with Alvanley I entered the room brimfull of pity, feeling ashamed for him and melted to entire softness, but before I had been there 5 minutes in spite of his agony which was apparent I felt hard as iron, for I saw that his sufferings did not proceed from a source calculated to excite compassion or tender regret.

As soon as everything was over I resolved to have an explanation with the Duke of Wellington, and I wrote to him to say that I was aware he had thought my conduct extraordinary, and I wished to explain to him why I had not answered his letter to me in October last, and to satisfy him if possible that the opinion which I was led to believe he had entertained and expressed of me was unfounded. I went to Apsley House, when he received me with the greatest cordiality. We talked over the whole thing. I did not press him with respect to his own conduct and language, and confined myself to defending mine. He did not allude to anything he had said, talked backwards and forwards, and left on my mind the impression that he had taken a strong part; probably *had* made use of the language that was attributed to him; *had* visited me and others with no small severity of censure; but was now rather ashamed of what he had done and anxious to *get out of it*—so of course as far as I was concerned I let him off very easy, and said not one word of complaint or reproach. We parted very good friends; he said he had never known a syllable of the case and was convinced that He and I should have been of the same opinion if we had communicated together. In short it all ended very well, and with this I resolved that my explanations should end. My great object now is that this miserable subject should be suffered to sink into oblivion as soon as possible, though the folly and intemperance of some of his adherents will probably not let this happen.

March 18th—Among the many Old people who have been cut off by this severe weather, one of the most remarkable is Mrs. Fitzherbert, who died at Brighton at above eighty years of age. She was not a clever woman, but of a very noble spirit, disinterested, generous, honest, and affectionate, greatly beloved by her friends and relations, popular in the world, and treated with uniform distinction and respect by the Royal Family. The late King, who was a despicable creature, grudged her the allowance he was bound to make her, and he was always afraid lest She should make use of some of the documents in her possession to annoy or injure him. This mean and selfish apprehension led him to make various efforts to obtain possession of those the appearance of which he most dreaded, and among others, one remarkable attempt was made by Knighton some years ago. Although a Stranger to Mrs. Fitzherbert, he called one day at her house, when She was ill in bed, insisted upon seeing her, and forced his way into her bedroom. She contrived (I forget how) to get rid of him without his getting anything out of her, but this domiciliary visit determined her to make a final disposition of all the papers She possessed, that in the event of her death no advantage might be taken of them either against her own memory or the interests of any other person. She accordingly selected those papers which she resolved to preserve, and which are supposed to be the documents and correspondence relating to her marriage with George 4th, and made a packet of them which was deposited at her Bankers, and all other letters and papers She condemned to the flames. For this purpose she sent for the Duke of Wellington and Lord Albemarle, told them her determination, and in their presence had these papers burnt; She assured them that everything was destroyed, and if after her death any pretended letters or documents were produced, they might give the most authoritative contradiction to their authenticity.

May 28th—My speculation at Epsom failed, but I was not much disappointed, except that my horse ran very ill which I did not expect. I won money enough however to repay me for my trouble and anxiety, and now I feel like one delivered from prison and with my shackles knocked off. I hope to be able to turn myself with undivided interest and attention to better objects and more creditable pursuits, but it requires some effort and some time to brace the mind when it has been so thoroughly relaxed as mine has been.

The King prayed that He might live till the Princess Victoria was of age, and he was very nearly dying just as the event arrived. He is better, but supposed to be in a very precarious way. There has been a fresh squabble between Windsor and Kensington about a proposed allowance to the Princess.

June 2nd—The King has been desperate ill, his pulse down at thirty; they think He will now get over it for this time. His recovery will not have been accelerated by the Duchess of Kent's answer to the City of London address, in which She went into the history of her life, and talked of her 'friendless state' on coming to this country, the gist of it being that, having been abandoned or neglected by the Royal Family, she had thrown herself on the country.

June 11th—At Buckhurst last week for Ascot; went on Monday and returned on Friday. On Tuesday the Queen came to the Course, but only staid an hour. They had an immense party at the Castle notwithstanding the King's illness. I met Adolphus Fitzclarence at the course, who gave me an account of the King's state, which was bad enough, though not for the moment alarming; no disease, but excessive weakness without power of rallying. He also gave me an account of the late Kensington quarrel. The King wrote a letter to the Princess offering her £10,000 a year (*not* out of his Privy purse), which he proposed should be at her own disposal and independent of her mother. He sent this letter by Conyngham, with orders to deliver it into the Princess's own hands. C. accordingly went to Kensington (where Conroy received him) and asked to be admitted to the Princess. Conroy asked by what authority. He said by H.M.'s orders. Conroy went away, and shortly after Conyngham was ushered into the presence of the Duchess and Princess, when he said that He had waited on H.R.H.

by the King's commands to present to her a letter with which he had been charged by H.M. The Duchess put out her hand to take it, when He said He begged H.R.H.'s pardon, but He was expressly commanded by the King to deliver the letter into the Princess's own hands. Her mother then drew back and the Princess took the letter, when Conyngham made his bow and retired. Victoria wrote to the King, thanking him and accepting his offer. He then sent to say that it was his wish to name the person who should receive this money for her, and he proposed to name Stephenson. Then began the dispute. The Duchess of Kent objected to the arrangement, and she put forth her claim, which was that she should have £6000 of the money and the Princess £4000. How the matter had ended Adolphus did not know when I saw him.

The Duchess of Northumberland had been to Windsor and resigned her office of Governess a few days before.

On Wednesday it was announced for the first time that the King was alarmingly ill, on Thursday the account was no better, and in the course of Wednesday and Thursday his immediate dissolution appeared so probable that I concerted with Errol that I should send to the Castle at nine o'clock on Thursday evening for the last report, that I might know whether to go to London directly or not. On Wednesday the Physicians wanted to issue a bulletin, but the King would not hear of it. He said as long as He was able to transact public business he would not have the public alarmed on his account; but on Friday, nevertheless, the first bulletin was issued.

It is in this state of things, with the prospect of a new reign and a dissolution, and in complete uncertainty of the direction which affairs would take under a new influence, when it is peculiarly desirable that moderate and healing counsels should prevail, that Lyndhurst comes down to the H. of Lords and fires off one of his violent speeches, and at his bidding the Irish Municipal Corporation Bill has been again postponed. All this is very disgusting to me, and I am at a loss to comprehend why such men as the Duke and Peel lend themselves to such courses. In the H. of Commons John Russell took a very different line, for he made a strong Conservative speech in answer to an omnium gatherum Radical tirade of Roebuck's; just such a speech as a Minister ought to make. Denman was persuaded to give up his design of bringing before the H. of Lords the question of privilege, on which he is at issue with the H. of C., and there seems luckily a disposition to deal with it calmly; in fact, it is no party question. The Judges are all with their Colleagues, but Peel has taken a strong part with the H. of Commons, and made a very good speech upon it the other night.

Met Melbourne in the Park, who told me he thought the King would not recover. Met Lady Harrowby who said that Lord Harrowby was very much astonished as well as annoyed at Lyndhurst's speech the other night, it having been previously agreed upon that all violence and everything offensive should be avoided. They had resolved to postpone the Committee on the Bill as before, but it was to have been done in the most conciliatory way, and they were not prepared for this outbreak of Lyndhurst's.

June 13th—Bad accounts of the King yesterday. Melbourne desired I would get everthing ready *quietly* for a Council. He has been busily occupied in examining the precedents in order to conduct the first ceremonies properly, and the first questions have been whether the Dss. of Kent could come into Council with her daughter, and whether the Duke of Cumberland (King of Hanover as he will be) should be summoned to it.

June 16th, Friday—On Wednesday the King was desperately bad, yesterday he was better, but not so as to afford any hope, though Chambers says his recovery is not impossible. Although the bulletins tell so little, everybody is now aware of H.M.'s state. He dictates these reports himself, and will not allow more to be said; he continues to do business, and his orders are taken as usual, so he is resolved to die with harness on his back. Yesterday Lord Lansdowne sent for me to beg in the first place that everything might be ready, and in the next to say that they were perplexed to know what steps, if any, they ought to take to ascertain whether the Queen is with child, and to beg me to search in our books if any precedent could be found at the accession of James II. But they had forgotten that the case had been provided for in the Regency Bill, and that in the event of the King's death without children, the Queen is to be proclaimed, but the oath of allegiance taken with a saving of the rights of any posthumous child to K. Wm. They ought to have known this, but it is odd enough that there is nobody in office who has any personal knowledge of the usual forms at the first Council, for not one of these Ministers was in office at the accession of Wm. 4th. My Colleague, Buller, who was present as Clerk of the Council, is dead, and I was abroad.

In the morning I met Peel in the Park, and talked with him about the beginning of the new reign. He said that it was very desirable that the young Queen should appear as much as possible emancipated from all restraint, and exhibit a capacity for the discharge of her high functions; that the most probable as well as the most expedient course she could adopt, would be to rely entirely upon the advice of Melbourne, and She might with great propriety say that She thought it incumbent on her to follow the example which had been set by her two Uncles, her Predecessors, Wm. 4th having retained in office the Ministers of his Brother, and George IV, although his political predilections were known to lean another way, having also declined to dismiss the Government of his father. Peel said that he concluded King Leopold would be her great adviser. If Leopold is prudent, however, he will not hurry over here at the very first moment, which would look like an impatience to establish his influence, and if he does, the first result will be every sort of jealousy and discord between him and the Duchess of Kent. The elements of intrigue do not seem wanting in this embryo Court. Besides the Duchess of Kent and Leopold, and Conroy of course, Caradoc is suspected of a design and an expectation to become a personage; and Durham is on his way home, and his return is regarded with no little curiosity, because he may endeavour to play a great political part, and materially to influence the opinions, or at least the Councils, of the Queen. What renders speculation so easy, and events so uncertain, is the absolute ignorance of everybody, without exception, of the character, disposition, and capacity of the Princess. She has been kept in such jealous seclusion by her Mother (never having slept out of her bedroom, nor been alone with anybody but herself and the Baroness Lehzen), that not one of her acquaintance, none of the Attendants at Kensington, not even the Duchess of Northumberland, her Governess, have any idea what She is, or what She promises to be. It is therefore no difficult matter to form and utter conjectures, which nobody can contradict or gainsay but by other conjectures equally uncertain and fallacious. The Tories are in great consternation at the King's approaching death, from the advantage which they foresee their opponents must derive from it as far as the extension of their term of power is concerned, and they prognosticate, according to their custom, all sorts of dismal consequences, none of which, of course, will come to pass. *Nothing* will happen, because, in this Country, *nothing* ever does. The Whigs, to do them justice, behave with great decency; whatever they may really feel, they express a very proper concern, and I have no doubt Melbourne really feels the concern he expresses. The public in general don't seem to care much, and only wonder what will happen.

June 16th—Yesterday the King was better, so as to promise a prolongation of his existence, though not his recovery. An intimation came from Windsor, that it was desired prayers should be offered up in the Churches for him; so the Privy Council assembled to order this, but in assembling the Bishop of London objected to the form which had been used upon the last and other occasions (an order made by the Lords to the Archbishop of Canterbury to prepare a form of prayer), asserting that *the Lords* had no power to make such an order, and it was even doubted by Lawyers whether the King himself had power to order alterations in the Liturgy, or the use of particular prayers; and admitting that He had, it was in virtue of his prerogative, and as Head of the Church, but that *the Lords of the Council* had no power whatever of the kind. They admitted that he was correct in this view of the case, and consequently, instead of an order to the Archbishops, his My.'s pleasure that prayers should be offered up was conveyed to the Council, and a communication to that effect was directed to be made to the Archbishop. The King's pleasure being thus conveyed, it is his duty to obey, and the Bishops have power to direct their Clergy to pray for the King. The Bishop of London would have preferred that a prayer for his recovery as for a sick person, but mentioning him by name, should have been directed, but the A.B. was prepared with his form of prayer, and it was directed to be used.

June 18th—The King lingers on; yesterday He sent for the A.B. of Canterbury to administer the Sacrament to him.

An attack (but a feeble one) was made upon Palmerston the other night, about Sir Charles Vaughan's appointment to relieve Ponsonby at Constantinople, to which he made, as usual, a feeble and inefficient answer, but the real story did not come out. The whole history of Ponsonby is a remarkable example of what a man in favor or with powerful protection may do with impunity, and it is the more striking because Palmerston is the most imperious of official despots, and yet has invariably truckled to Lord Grey's Brother-in-law. When Ponsonby was appointed Ambassador at Constantinople, the affairs of the East were in a most critical state, notwithstanding which nothing would induce him to repair to his post, and he loitered away several months at Naples, while Russia was maturing her designs upon Turkey, and when the presence of an English Ambassador was of vital importance. This was overlooked, because to Lord Grey's Brother-in-law everything was permitted. The appointment of Mr. Urquhart as Secretary of the Embassy at Constantinople greatly displeased Lord Ponsonby, who resolved to hold no communication with him, and accordingly the Chancellerie at Constantinople has presented the amusing spectacle of an Ambassador and Secretary of Embassy who do not speak to each other, and the latter of whom has no functions whatever to discharge. A short time ago Lord Ponsonby applied for leave of absence, which was given to him, and the Government here hoped that when he came home he would not think of returning, and secretly resolved that if they could help it He should not. But as Mr. Urquhart had been placed in this strange position by Lord P., and besides, since his appointment, they had found reason to doubt whether he was altogether fit for such a trust, it was impossible to leave him at Constantinople as *Chargé d'affaires* during his Chief's absence, so they got Sir Charles Vaughan to go out on what was called a special mission, though there was nothing more in it than to meet this difficulty. Sir Charles was directed to proceed to Malta, and from thence to send a Steamer to Constantinople, which was to announce his arrival and bring back to Lord P. Sir Charles, accordingly, sent his Secretary of Embassy to announce him, who, when he arrived off Constantinople, was met by an absolute prohibition from Ponsonby to land at all, and a flat refusal on his part to stir. The Secretary had nothing to do but to return to his Principal and report his reception, and he in his turn had nothing to do but report his ridiculous position to his Employers at home, and await their orders. The result has been that Sir Charles is ordered home, and Ponsonby remains, so that Palmerston has knocked under. Ponsonby has carried his point, and Vaughan has had a *giro* to Malta and back, for which the public has to pay.

June 19th—Yesterday the King was sinking fast; the Sacrament was administered to him by the Archbishop of Canterbury. He said, 'This is the 18th of June; I should like to live to see the sun of Waterloo set.' Last night I met the Duke at the Duchess of Cannizzaro's, who after dinner crowned him with a crown of laurel (in joke of course), when they all stood up and drank his health, and at night they sang a hymn in honor of the day. He asked me whether Melbourne had had any communication with the Princess Victoria. I said I did not know, but thought not. He said, 'He ought. I was in constant communication with the present King for a month before G. 4th died. G. 4th was for a month quite as bad as this King, and I sent the D. of Clarence the bulletins every day, and besides wrote to him the private accounts I received, and what is very odd, I had a quarrel with him in the course of this. He constantly wrote to me, and in one of his letters He told me He meant to make me his Minister. I felt this was a very awkward subject for me to enter upon, and that I could not (being the Minister of the King) with any propriety treat with his successor, so I resolved to take no notice whatever of this part of his letter, and I did not. He was very indignant at this, and complained to his friends (to Lord Cassilis for instance) that I had behaved very rudely to him. When I met him—for I met him constantly at Windsor, and in the King's room—he was very cold in his manner, but I took no notice, and went on as before, and he never afterwards alluded to the subject.'

June 21st—The King died at twenty minutes after two yesterday morning, and the young Queen met the Council at Kensington Palace at eleven. There never was anything like the first impression She produced, or the chorus of praise and admiration which is raised about her manner and behaviour, and certainly not without justice. It was very extraordinary, and something far beyond what was looked for. Her extreme youth and in-experience, and the ignorance of the world concerning her, naturally ex-cited intense curiosity to see how She would act on this trying occasion, and there was a considerable assemblage at the Palace, notwithstanding the short notice which was given. The first thing to be done was to teach her her lesson, which for this purpose Melbourne had himself to learn. I gave him the Council papers, and explained all that was to be done, and He went and explained all this to her. He asked her if She would enter the room accompanied by the Great Officers of State, but She said She would come in alone. When the Lords were assembled the Lord President in-formed them of the King's death, and suggested (as they were so numerous) that a few of them should repair to the presence of the Queen and inform her of the event, and that their Lordships were assembled in consequence; and accordingly the two Royal Dukes, the two Archbishops, the Chan-cellor, and Melbourne went with him. The Queen received them in the adjoining room alone. As soon as they had returned the proclamation was read and the usual order passed, when the doors were thrown open and the Queen entered, accompanied by her two Uncles, who advanced to meet her. She bowed to the Lords, took her seat, and then read her speech in a clear, distinct, and audible voice, and without any appearance of fear or embarrassment. She was quite plainly dressed, and in mourning. After She had read her speech and taken and signed the oath for the security of the Church of Scotland, the Privy Councillors were sworn, the two Royal Dukes first, by themselves; and as these two old men, her Uncles, knelt before her, swearing allegiance and kissing her hand, I saw her blush up to the eyes, as if She felt the contrast between their civil and their natural relations, and this was the only sign of emotion which She evinced. Her manner to them was very graceful and engaging; she kissed them both, and rose from her chair and moved towards the Duke of Sussex, who was farthest from her and too infirm to reach her. She seemed rather bewildered at the multitude of men who were sworn, and who came one after another to kiss her hand, but She did not speak to anybody, nor did She make the slightest difference in her manner, or show any in her countenance, to any individual or any rank, station, or party. I particularly watched her when Melbourne and the Ministers and the Duke of Wellington and Peel approached her. She went through the whole ceremony (occasionally look-ing at Melbourne for instruction when She had any doubt what to do, which hardly ever occurred) and with perfect calmness and self-possession, but at the same time with a graceful modesty and propriety particularly interesting and ingratiating. When the business was done She retired as She had entered, and I could see that nobody was in the adjoining room. Lord Lansdowne insisted upon being declared President of the Council (and I was obliged to write a declaration for her to read to that effect), though it was not usual. The speech was admired, except by Brougham, who appeared in a considerable state of excitement. He said to Peel (whom he was standing near, and with whom he is not in the habit of communicating), "*A*melioration, that is not English; you might perhaps says *me*lioration, but improvement is the proper word.' 'Oh,' said Peel, 'I see no harm in the word; it is generally used.' 'You object,' said Brougham, 'to the sentiment, I object to the grammar.' 'No,' said Peel, 'I don't object to the sentiment.' 'Well, then, She pledges herself to the policy of *our* Government,' said Brougham. Peel told me this, which passed in the room and near to the Queen. He likewise said how amazed he was at her manner and behaviour, at her apparent deep sense of her situation, her modesty, and at the same time her firmness. She appeared, in fact, to be awed, but not daunted, and afterwards the Duke of Wellington told me the same thing, and added that if She had been his own daughter he could not have desired to see her perform her part better. It was settled that She was to hold a Council at St. James's this day, and be proclaimed there at ten o'clock, and She expressed a wish to see Lord Albemarle, who went to her and told her he was come to take her orders. She said, 'I have no orders to give; you know all this so much better than I do, that I leave it all to you. I am to be at St. James's at ten to-morrow, and must beg you to find me a conveyance proper for the occasion.' Accordingly, he went and fetched her in state with a great escort. The Duchess of Kent was in the carriage with her, but I was surprised to hear so little shouting, and to see so few hats off as She went by. I rode down the Park, and saw her appear at the window when She was proclaimed. The Dss. of Kent was there, but not prominent; the Queen was surrounded by her Ministers, and curtsied repeatedly to the people, who did not, however, hurrah till Lord Lansdowne gave them the signal from the window. At twelve She held a Council, at which She presided with as much ease as if She had been doing nothing else all her life, and though Lord Lansdowne or Bathurst had contrived between them to make some confusion with the Council Papers, She was not put out by it. She looked very well, and though so small in stature, and without any pretension to beauty, the gracefulness of her manner and the good expression of her countenance give her on the whole a very agreeable appearance, and with her youth inspire an excessive interest in all who approach her, and which I can't help feeling myself. After the Council She received the Archbishops and Bishops, and after them the Judges. They all kissed her hand, but She said nothing to any of them, very different in this from her Predecessor, who used to harangue them all, and had a speech ready for everybody.

Conyngham, when He came to her with the intelligence of the King's death, brought a request from the Queen Dowager that she might be permitted to remain at Windsor till after the funeral, and She has written her a letter couched in the kindest terms, begging her to consult nothing but her own health and convenience, and to remain at Windsor just as long as She pleases. In short, She appears to act with every sort of good taste and good feeling, as well as good sense, and as far as it has gone nothing can be more favorable than the impression She has made, and nothing can promise better than her manner and conduct do, though it would be rash to count too confidently upon her judgement and discretion in more weighty matters. No contrast can be greater than that between the personal demeanour of the present and the late Sovereigns at their respective accessions. He was a man who, coming to the throne at the mature age of sixty-five, was so excited by the exaltation, that he nearly went mad, and distinguished himself by a thousand extravagances of language and conduct, to the alarm or amusement of all who witnessed his strange freaks; and though he was shortly afterwards sobered down into more becoming habits, he always continued to be something of a blackguard and something more of a buffoon. It is but fair to his memory at the same time to say that he was a good-natured, kind-hearted, and well-meaning man and he always acted an honorable and straitforward, if not always a sound and discreet, part. The two principal Ministers of his reign, the Duke of Wellington and Lord Grey (though the former was only his Minister for a few months), have both spoken of him to me with strong expressions of personal regard and esteem. The young Queen, who might well be either dazzled or confounded with the grandeur and novelty of her situation, seems neither the one nor the other, and behaves with a decorum and propriety beyond her years, and with all the sedateness and dignity the want of which was so conspicuous in her Uncle.

June 25th—I remember when George 4th died, seven years ago, having been struck by the small apparent sensation that his death created. There was, however, at that time a great deal of bustle and considerable excitement, which were caused by the activity of the new Court, and the eccentricies of the King; but in the present instance the Crown has been transferred to the head of the new Queen with a tranquillity that is curious and edifying. The first interest and curiosity to see the young Queen and observe her behaviour having passed off, there appears nothing more to do or to think about; there are no changes, and there is no talk of change. H.M. has continued quietly at Kensington, where She transacts business with her Ministers, and everything goes on as if She had been on the throne six years instead of six days. Animated panegyricks were pronounced upon the late King in both Houses of Parliament by those who had served him; and Peel repeated in the H. of Commons, in more set phrases, the expressions of his admiration of the conduct of the Queen on her first public appearance, which he uttered to me when I saw him after the Council on Tuesday. Melbourne's funeral oration over Wm. 4th was very effective because it was natural and hearty, and as warm as it could be without being exaggerated. He made the most of the virtues he undoubtedly possessed, and passed lightly over his defects.

King Wm. 4th, if He had been born in a private station, would have passed unobserved through life like millions of other men, looked upon as possessing a good-natured and affectionate disposition, but without either elevation of mind or brightness of intellect. During many years of his life the Duke of Clarence was an obscure individual, without consideration, moving in a limited circle, and altogether forgotten by the great world. He resided at Bushey with Mrs. Jordan, and brought up his numerous children with a very tender affection: with them, and for them, he seemed entirely to live. The cause of his separation from Mrs. Jordan has not been explained, but it probably arose from his desire to better his condition by a good marriage, and he wanted to marry Miss Wykeham, a half-crazy woman of large fortune, on whom he afterwards conferred a Peerage. George 4th, I believe, put a spoke in that wheel, fortunately for the Duke as well as for the country. The death of the Princess Charlotte opened to him a new prospect, and the lack of royal progeny made his marriage as desirable an event to the public as it was convenient to himself. The subsequent death of the Duke of York, which made him Heir to the Throne, at once exalted him into a personage of political importance, and when the great Tory schism took place, upon the death of Lord Liverpool, Mr. Canning thought the Duke of Clarence's appointment to the office of Lord High Admiral would strengthen his Government, and at the same time relieve him from some of the difficulties which beset him; and he accordingly prevailed upon the King to revive the office in his person. Soon after the Duke of Wellington's elevation He found it necessary to remove the Duke of C., and it is an excellent trait in the character of the latter that, notwithstanding his vexation at the time, which was very great, he harboured no resentment against the Duke of Wellington, and never seems to have hesitated about retaining him as his Minister when he came to the throne. His exaltation (for the moment) completely turned his head, but as his situation got familiar to him he became more composed and rational, if not more dignified in his behaviour. The moral and intellectual qualities of the King, however insignificant in themselves, now became, from their unavoidable influence, an object of great interest and importance, and in the early part of his reign he acquired no small share of popularity. People liked a King whose habits presented such a striking contrast to those of his Predecessor. His attention to business, his frank and good-humoured familiarity, and his general hospitality, were advantageously compared with the luxurious and selfish indolence and habits of seclusion in the society of dull and grasping favourites which characterised the former reign.

The King, though fond of *doing* as much as possible, seemed to be more occupied with the pleasing novelty of his situation, providing for his Children, and actively discharging the duties of his high function, than in giving effect to any political opinions; and he took a correct view of his constitutional obligations, for although he continued his confidence to the D. of Wellington unabated to the last, he transferred it as entirely to Lord Grey, when the Whigs came in. He went on with his second Ministry as cordially as he had done with his first, nor does it appear that He took fright at their extensive plans of reform when they were first promulgated. He was probably bit by the popularity which the Reform Bill procured him, and it was not until he had gone too far to recede with safety that he was roused from his state of measureless content and unthinking security. The roar of the mighty conflict which the Reform Bill brought on filled him with dismay, and very soon with detestation of the principles of which he had unwittingly permitted himself to be the Professor and the Promoter; and as these feelings and apprehensions were continually stimulated by almost all the members of his family, legitimate and illegitimate, they led him into those unavailing struggles which embroiled him with his Ministers, rendered him obnoxious to the Liberal party, compromised the dignity of the Crown and the tranquillity of the country, and grievously embittered the latter years of his life. But although King William was sometimes weak, sometimes obstinate, and miserably deficient in penetration and judgement, he was manly, sincere, honest, and straitforward. The most painful moment of his life, and the greatest humiliation to which a King ever submitted, must have been when He again received the Whig Ministers in 1835; but it is to the credit of Melbourne, as well as of the King, that their subsequent personal intercourse was not disagreeable to either, and greatly to the King's honor that he has never been accused or suspected of any underhand or indirect proceeding for the purpose of emancipating himself from a thraldom so galling. Of political dexterity and artifice he was altogether incapable, and although, if he had been false, able, and artful, he might have caused more perplexity to his Whig Government and have played a better party game, it is perhaps fortunate for the Country, and certainly happy for his own reputation, that his virtues thus predominated over his talents. The most remarkable foible of the late King was his passion for speechifying, and I have recorded some of his curious exhibitions in this way. He had considerable facility in expressing himself, but what he said was generally useless or improper. He never received the homage of a Bishop without giving him a lecture; and the custom he introduced of giving toasts and making speeches at all his dinners was more suitable to a tavern than to a Palace. He was totally deficient in dignity or refinement, and neither his elevation to the throne nor his association with people of the most distinguished manners could give him any tincture of the one or the other. Though a good-natured and amiable man, he was passionate and hasty, and thus he was led into those bickerings and quarrels with the Duchess of Kent and with his own children, which were a perpetual source of discomfort or disgrace to him, and all of which might have been avoided by a more consistent course of firmness and temper on his part. His Sons generally behaved to him with great insolence and ingratitude, except Adolphus. Of the daughters I know nothing.

The various political hopes, fears, and expectations which his death has raised may be very shortly summed up. Nobody can deny that it has given the Whig Government a great advantage over the Tories. Hitherto the Government has been working against the stream, inasmuch as they had the influence of the Crown running against them; the tide has now turned in their favor, and to a certain degree they will be able to convert the Tory principle to their own advantage. The object of the Whigs is to remain in office, to put down the Radicals and Radicalism, and go on gradually and safely reforming; above all to proceed as fast as the innumerable difficulties which impede their course will let them, in bringing Ireland into a state of quiet and contentment, and to pave the way for some definite settlement of the great questions which distract that country. This I believe to be the object of Melbourne and John Russell, but at the same time they have Colleagues and Supporters who have more extensive and less moderate views, and who would like to see the Government more cordially allied to the Radicals than it is, and who are so animated against the Tories that they would do *anything* to prevent their return to power.

The great body of the Tories, on the other hand, are thirsting for office: they are, or pretend to be, greatly alarmed at the Radical tendencies of the Government, but they are well aware that in the actual state of the H. of Commons they have the power of keeping the Government in check and of defeating every Radical scheme while *in opposition*, but that it would be dangerous to attempt to turn them out and take their places. So far from being satisfied with this position of exceeding strength and utility, they are chafing and fuming that they can't get in, and would encounter all the hazards of defeat for the slightest chance of victory. It is only the prudent reserve of Peel (in which Stanley and Graham probably join) that restrains the impatience of the party within moderate bounds. The Radicals are few in number, and their influence is very low; they are angry with the Government for not making greater concessions to them, but as they still think that there is a better chance of their views being promoted by the Whigs remaining in, they continue to vote with them in cases of need, though there are some of them who would prefer the dissolution of the Ministry and war with a Tory Government rather than the present imperfect alliance which subsists between themselves and the Whigs. Charles Austin told me that he would much rather that Sutton came in (for Cambridge) than Spring Rice whom they regarded as one of the most pernicious of their opponents. The Whigs then expect to gain by the new elections and to obtain an accession of strength to *their Government*. They think the popularity of a new reign, and the partial neutrality of the Tory principle, will be of material advantage to their cause. The Tories, though they maintain that they shall not lose at the elections, evidently feel that they take the field under a great disadvantage, and do not deny that the King's death has been a heavy blow to them as a party.

June 29th—All the accounts continue to report well of the young Queen, of her quickness, sense and discretion, and the remarkable facility with which she has slid into her high station and discharges its duties. The Dss. of Kent never appears at Kensington, where the Queen occupies a separate range of apartments, and her influence is very silently exercised, if at all. The town is rife with reports of changes and appointments, some very natural and others very absurd; all agree that the power vested in Melbourne's hands is unbounded, and that (as far as Court appointments are concerned) he uses it with propriety. The great topic of interest is the question of Lord Hill's removal, which the Radicals and violent Whigs have been long driving at, but to which it is believed Melbourne is himself adverse. So Lord Stanley told me the other day he believed; and when I said that, though he might be so, it was doubtful how far he would be induced to fight the battle in his own Cabinet if it was mooted there, he said that from what he heard, he thought Melbourne was Lord and Master in his own Cabinet.

The eternal question in everybody's mouth is what is Lord Durham to have, as if it was indispensable that He should have something. When Durham left England, He was the elected Chief of the Radicals, and he was paving the way to future Court favor through a strict alliance with the Duchess of Kent and Conroy. At Petersburg his language was always moderate; now that He is returned, the Radicals, still regarding him as their Chief, look anxiously to his introduction into the Cabinet. Charles Buller, whom I met the other day, said, in reply to my asking him if Government would gain at the elections, 'I think they will gain anyhow, but *if they are wise* they will gain largely.' I said, 'I wonder what you call being wise?' He said, 'Take in Lord Durham.' But they want Durham to be taken in as a pledge of the disposition of the Government to adopt their principles, whereas Melbourne will receive him upon no such terms; and if Durham takes office, he must subscribe to the moderate principles upon which both Melbourne and John Russell seem disposed to act. After all, it appears to me that a mighty fuss is made about Durham without any sufficient reason, that his political influence is small, his power less, and that it is a matter of great indifference whether he is in office or out.

July 9th—Yesterday I went to the late King's funeral, who was buried with just the same ceremonial as his Predecessor this time seven years. It is a wretched mockery after all, and if I was King, the first thing I would do should be to provide for being committed to the earth with more decency and less pomp. A host of Persons of all ranks and stations were congregated, who 'loitered through the lofty halls,' chattering and laughing, and with nothing of woe about them but the garb. I saw two men in an animated conversation, and one laughing heartily at the very foot of the coffin as it was lying in state. The chamber of death in which the body lay, all hung with black and adorned with scutcheons and every sort of funereal finery, was like a scene in a play, and as we passed through it and looked at the scaffolding and rough work behind, it was just like going behind the scenes of a theatre. A Soldier's funeral, which I met in the morning—the plain coffin slowly borne along by his comrades, with the cap and helmet and sword of the dead placed upon it—was more impressive, more decent, more affecting than all this pomp with pasteboard crowns, and Heralds scampering about, while idleness and indifference were gazing or gossiping round about the royal remains. I would rather be quietly consigned to the grave by a few who cared for me (if any such there might be) than be the object of all this parade and extravagance. The procession moving slowly through close ranks of Horse and Foot Guards holding tapers and torches in their hands, while at intervals the bands played a dead march, had a very imposing effect. The service was intolerably long and tedious, and miserably read by the Dean of Windsor. The Queen Dowager, with the King's daughters and her Ladies, were in the Royal Closet, and the Fitz-clarences in the one adjoining. At twelve o'clock She was to depart for Bushey, and a bitter moment it must have been when She quitted for ever the Castle where She had spent seven years of prosperous and happy splendour.

We continue to hear of the young Queen's admirable behaviour, but all other subjects are swallowed up in the interest of the approaching elections. There will be more contests than ever were known, and it is amusing to see both Parties endeavouring to avail themselves of the Queen's name, the Tories affecting to consider her as a Prisoner in the hands of the Whigs, and the Whigs boasting of the cordiality and warmth of her sentiments in their favor. The Whigs have the best of this, as they have some evidence to show in support of their assertions, and the probability really is that She is well enough contented with them, as they naturally take care She should be. Of the probable changes, one of the most important is the defeat of Graham in Cumberland, an event which the Whigs hail with extreme satisfaction, for they hate him rancorously. I am under personal obligations to Graham, and therefore regret that this feeling exists; but it is not un-natural, and his political conduct is certainly neither creditable nor con-sistent. He is now little better than a Tory, a very high Churchman, and one of the least liberal of the Conservative Leaders. In Lord Grey's Govern-ment he was one of the most violent, and for going to greater lengths than the majority of his colleagues. When the Reform Bill was concocted by a committee consisting of J. Russell, Duncannon, Durham, and Graham, Graham earnestly advocated the Ballot, and Durham says he has in his possession many letters of Graham's, in which he presses for a larger measure of reform than they actually brought forward. In his address he says he has not changed, and talks of 'having belonged to the Whig Govern-ment before they had made the compact by which they are now bound to O'Connel.' Tavistock said to me yesterday that this was too bad, because He knew very well that the only understanding the Government had with O'Connell was one of mutual support in the Irish Elections, the same which existed when He was in office; and, moreover, that at that time the majority of the Cabinet (Graham included) wanted to confer office upon O'Connel, and that they were only induced to forgo that design by the remonstrances of Lord Lansdowne and the Duke of Richmond, who insisted upon a further probation before they did so. O'Connel got nothing, and soon after took to agitating and making violent speeches. This exasperated Lord Grey, who, in his turn, denounced him in the King's Speech, and hence that feud between O'Connel and the Whigs, which was only terminated by the attempt of the Tories to retake office in '35. This led to the imperfect alliance between them, half denied by the Whigs, which exposed the Government to as much obloquy as if they had concluded an open and avowed alliance with him, and perhaps to greater inconvenience. It was a great blunder not securing O'Connel in the first instance, and certainly a curious thing that such men as Lansdowne, and still more Richmond, should have influenced so important a matter and have overborne the opinions of the whole Cabinet. After all this, it is not extraordinary that his old associates should be disgusted at seeing Graham become a Tory Champion, and at hearing him more bitter against them than any man on the Opposition benches. The Tories, on the other hand, rejoice in him, and his bigotry about all Church measures cancels in their minds all his former Liberalism on that and every other respect.

Knowsley, July 18th—Tired of doing nothing in London, and of hearing about the Queen and the Elections, I resolved to vary the scene and run down to see the Birmingham railroad, Liverpool, and Liverpool races. So I started at five o'clock on Sunday evening, got to Birmingham at half-past five on Monday morning, and got upon the railroad at half-past seven. Nothing can be more comfortable than the vehicle in which I was put, a sort of chariot with two places, and there is nothing disagreeable about it but the occasional whiffs of stinking air which it is impossible to exclude altogether. The first sensation is a slight degree of nervousness and a feel of being run away with, but a sense of security soon supervenes, and the velocity is delightful. Town after town, one Park and *Château* after another, are left behind with the rapid variety of a moving panorama, and the continual bustle and animation of the changes and stoppages make the journey very entertaining. The train was very long, and heads were continually popping out of the several carriages, attracted by well-known voices, and then came the greetings and exclamations of surprise, the 'Where are you going?' and 'How on earth came you here?' Considering the recency of its establishment, there is very little embarrassment, and it certainly renders all other travelling irksome and tedious by comparison. It was peculiarly gay at this time, because there is so much going on. There were all sorts of people going to Liverpool races, Barristers to the assizes, and Candidates to their several elections. It was such a wet day that I could not see the town of Liverpool.

This is a very large place, the house immense, with no good room in it but the dining room. The Country is generally flat, but there are fine trees and thriving plantations, so that it is altogether sufficiently enjoyable. It is a strange thing to see Stanley here; he is certainly the most natural character I ever saw; never seems to think of throwing a veil over any part of himself: it is the straitforward energy which is the cause of this, that makes him so comfortable as he is. In London he is one of the great political Leaders, and the second orator in the H. of Commons, and here he is a lively rattling Sportsman, apparently devoted to racing and rabbit-shooting, gay, boisterous, almost clownish in his manners, without a particle of refinement, and if one did not know what his powers are and what his position is, it would be next to impossible to believe that the Stanley of Knowsley could be the Stanley of the House of Commons.

July 25, Tuesday—I remained at Knowsley till Saturday morning, when I went to Liverpool, got on the train at half-past eleven, and at five minutes after four arrived at Birmingham with an exact punctuality which is rendered easy by the great reserved power of acceleration, the pace at which we travelled being moderate and not above one half the speed at which they do occasionally go; one Engineer went at the rate of forty-five miles an hour, but the Company turned him off for doing so. I went to Kenilworth, and saw the ruins of Leicester's Castle, and thence to Warwick to see the Castle there, with both of which I was very much delighted, and got to town on Sunday to find myself in the midst of all the interest of the Elections, and the sanguine and confident assertions and expectations of both parties. The first great trial of strength was in the City yesterday; and though Grote beat Palmer just as last, and after a severe struggle, by a very small majority, it is so far consolatory to the Conservative interest that it shows a prodigious change since the last general election, when the Conservative Candidate was 2000 behind his opponents.

July 28th—The Borough elections in England (as far as they have gone, and they are nearly over) have disappointed the Government, who expected to gain in them. The contests have been numerous, often very close, and in some instances very costly. Norwich, won with the greatest difficulty by Douro and Scarlett, is said to have cost £50,000. A compromise was offered at Yarmouth and at Norwich, but the parties could not come to terms, and the result has been the same as if it had taken place—two Tories in one place and two Whigs in the other. There have been a vast number of changes, and, as always happens, results very different from what were expected in particular places. The balance is slightly in favor of the Tories, but the best sign of the times is the defeat of the Radicals in various places.

Grote nearly beat in the City, and probably will be turned out on a scrutiny; Roebuck and Palmer at Bath, Ewart Liverpool, Wigney Brighton, Thompson Hull. It was clear enough before from the Conservative language which was put into the Queen's mouth by her Ministers, and by that which they held themselves, that it was the only tone that would be palatable to the country, and the event of the elections confirms this impression. This is, after all, the essential point, to which the gains of either party are entirely subordinate. If the Government keeps together without internal dissensions, and nothing particular occurs to produce a change, these Ministers cannot well be turned out, because, though their majority is small, they have the undoubted support of the H. of Commons, and in my opinion they will be all the stronger from the Radicals being so reduced in numbers, as those who remain must support them, and cannot expect any concessions in return. It is quite impossible to doubt that there is in the Country a strong Conservative reaction, and it is the more valuable from not being more strongly pronounced. It is great enough to prove that our institutions are safe, but not great enough to bring the Tories back into power and to turn their heads, ready as they always are to be puffed up with every returning gale of success. The Tories have made one good exchange in the article of whippers-in for they have got Planta and Holmes instead of Bonham and Ross.

Everything that could be said in praise of the Queen, of her manners, conduct, conversation, and character, having been exhausted, we now hear no more of her. It is an interesting speculation to conjecture how soon she will begin to think and act for herself upon higher matters, as She has at once done on all minor points connected with her domestic arrangements. It is generally believed that She is perfectly independent of any influence in these things, and while in all political concerns She has put herself implicitly in Melbourne's hands, in all others She is her own Mistress. From the beginning She resolved to have nothing to do with Sir John Conroy, but to reward him liberally for his services to her Mother. Whether She secretly suspects the nature of her mother's connections with him, or is only animated by that sort of instinctive aversion which is frequently engendered without any *apparent* cause, it is difficult to discover. She began however by making him a Baronet, and She has given him a pension of £3000 a year; but He has never once been invited to the Palace, or distinguished by the slightest mark of personal favor, so that nothing can be more striking than the contrast between the magnitude of the pecuniary bounty and the complete personal disregard of which he is the object. The Queen has been extremely civil and kind to the Queen Dowager, but She has taken no notice of the King's children, good, bad, or indifferent. Munster asked for an audience to deliver up the keys of the Castle which He had, and was very graciously received by her, but She did not give him back the keys. Adolphus has lost his Lordship of the Bedchamber, but then they only retained Peers, and He keeps the command of the yacht. He has had no intimation whether his pension and his Rangership of Windsor Park are to be continued to him; they probably will, but it would have been more amiable if She had exhibited some anxiety and alacrity to render all the service and kindness in her power to the King's family, knowing as She must do their (comparatively) destitute condition.

July 30th, 1837—Madame de Lieven told me yesterday that she had an audience of the Queen, who was very civil and gracious, but timid and embarrassed, and talked of nothing but commonplaces. H.M. had probably been told that She was an *intrigante*, and was afraid of committing herself. She had afterwards an interview with the Duchess of Kent, who (She told me) it was plain to see is overwhelmed with vexation and disappointment. Her daughter behaves to her with kindness and attention, but has rendered herself quite independent of the Duchess, who painfully feels her own insignificance. The almost contemptuous way in which Conroy has been dismissed must be a bitter mortification to her, and all things considered is scarcely decent. He has been amply rewarded by a pension of 3000 a year, but the contrast between this pecuniary munificence and his personal exclusion from Court has a remarkable and rather mysterious appearance. The Duchess said to Madame de Lieven, 'qu'il n'y avait plus d'avenir pour elle, qu'elle n'était plus rien'; that for eighteen years this child has been the sole object of her life, of all her thoughts and hopes, and now She was taken from her, and there was an end of all for which she had lived heretofore. Madame de Lieven said that she ought to be the happiest of human beings, to see the elevation of this child, her prodigious success, and the praise and admiration of which she was universally the object; that it was a triumph and a glory which ought to be sufficient for her—to which She only shook her head with a melancholy smile, and gave her to understand that all this would not do, and that the accomplishment of her wishes had only made her to the last degree unhappy. King William is revenged, he little anticipated how or by what instrumentality, and if his ghost is an ill-natured and vindictive shade, it may rejoice in this bitter disappointment of his enemy. In the midst of all her propriety of manner and conduct, the young Queen begins to exhibit slight signs of a peremptory disposition, and it is impossible not to suspect that, as She gains confidence, and as her character begins to develope, She will evince a strong will of her own. In all trifling matters connected with her Court and her Palace, she already enacts the part of Queen and Mistress as if it had long been familiar to her.

August 30th—All that I hear of the young Queen leads to the conclusion that She will some day play a conspicuous part, and that She has a great deal of character. It is clear enough that She had long been silently preparing herself, and had been prepared by those about her (and very properly) for the situation to which she was destined. The impressions she has made continue to be favorable, and particularly upon Melbourne, who has a thousand times greater opportunity of knowing what her disposition and her capacity are than any other person, and who is not a man to be easily captivated or dazzled by any superficial accomplishments or mere graces of manner, or even by personal favor. Melbourne thinks highly of her sense, discretion, and good feelings; but what seem to distinguish her above everything are caution and prudence, the former to a degree which is almost unnatural in one so young, and unpleasing, because it suppresses the youthful impulses which are so graceful and attractive.

On the morning of the King's death, the Archbishop of Canterbury and Conyngham arrived at Kensington at five o'clock, and immediately desired to see 'the Queen.' They were ushered into an apartment, and in a few minutes the door opened and She came in wrapped in a dressing-gown and with slippers on her naked feet. Conyngham in a few words told her their errand, and as soon as he uttered the words 'Your Majesty,' She instantly put out her hand to him, intimating that He was to kiss hands before he proceeded. He dropt on one knee, kissed her hand, then went on to tell her of the late King's death. She next presented her hand to the Archbishop, who likewise kissed it, and when he had done so, addressed to her a sort of pastoral charge, which She received graciously and then retired. She lost no time in giving notice to Conroy of her intentions with regard to him; She saw him, and desired him to name the reward he expected for his services to her Parents. He asked for the red ribband, an Irish Peerage, and a pension of £3000 a year. She replied that the two first rested with her Ministers, and She could not engage for them, but that the pension He should have. It is not easy to ascertain the exact cause of her antipathy to him, but it has probably grown with her growth, and results from divers causes. The person in the world She loves best is the Baroness Lehzen, and Lehzen and Conroy were enemies. There was formerly a Baroness Spaeth at Kensington, Lady-in-waiting to the Duchess, and Lehzen and Spaeth were intimate friends. Conroy quarrelled with the latter and got her dismissed, and this Lehzen never forgave. She may have instilled into Victoria a dislike and bad opinion of Conroy, and the evidence of these sentiments, which probably escaped neither the Duchess or him, may have influenced their conduct towards her, for strange as it is, there is good reason to believe that She has no great affection for her mother and that She thinks she has been ill-used by both of them for some years past. Her manner to the Duchess is, however, irreproachable, and they appear to be on cordial and affectionate terms, but those who have means of knowing what passes within the Palace do not think that much affection exists under these external demonstrations. She sees hardly anything of the Duchess, who never goes to her without previously asking leave, and when the Queen gets messages or notes from her mother She frequently sends verbal answers that She is engaged and cannot receive her. Madame de Lehzen is the only person who is constantly with her. When any of the Ministers come to her, the Baroness retires at one door as they enter at the other, and the audience over She returns to the Queen. It has been remarked that when applications are made to Her My., She seldom or never gives an immediate answer, but says she will consider of it, and it is supposed that She does this because she consults Melbourne about everything, and waits to have her answers suggested by him. He says, however, that such is her habit even with him, and that when he talks to her upon any subject upon which an opinion is expected from her, she tells him she will think it over, and let him know her sentiments the next day.

The day she went down to visit the Queen Dowager at Windsor, to Melbourne's great surprise she said to him that as the flag on the Round Tower was half-mast high, and they might perhaps think it necessary to elevate it upon her arrival, it would be better to send orders beforehand not to do so. *He* had never thought of the flag, or knew anything about it, but it showed her knowledge of forms and her attention to trifles. Her manner to the Queen was extremely kind and affectionate, and they were both greatly affected at meeting. The Queen Dowager said to her that the only favor she had to ask of her was to provide for the retirement, with their pensions, of the personal attendants of the late King, Whiting and Bachelor, who had likewise been the Attendants of George 4th; to which She replied that it should be attended to, but she could not give any promise on the subject.

She is upon terms of the greatest cordiality with Melbourne, and very naturally. Everything is new and delightful to her. She is surrounded with the most exciting and interesting enjoyments; her occupations, her pleasures, her business, her Court, all present an unceasing round of gratifications. With all her prudence and discretion She has great animal spirits, and enters into the magnificent novelties of her position with the zest and curiosity of a child.

No man is more formed to ingratiate himself with her than Melbourne. He treats her with unbounded consideration and respect, he consults her tastes and her wishes, and he puts her at her ease by his frank and natural manners, while He amuses her by the quaint, queer, epigrammatic turn of his mind, and his varied knowledge upon all subjects. It it not therefore surprising that She should be well content with her present Government, and that during the progress of the elections She should have testified great interest in the success of the Whig Candidates. Her reliance upon Melbourne's advice extends at present to subjects quite beside his Constitutional functions, for the other day somebody asked her permission to dedicate some novel to her, when she said she did not like to grant the permission without knowing the contents of the work, and she desired Melbourne to read the book and let her know if it was fit that She should accept the dedication. Melbourne read the first volume, but found it so dull that He would not read any more, and sent her word that She had better refuse, which she accordingly did. She seems to be liberal, but at the same time prudent with regard to money, for when the Queen Dowager proposed to take her Band into her service, She declined to incur so great an expense without further consideration, but one of the first things She spoke to Melbourne about was the payment of her Father's debts, which she is resolved to discharge.

October 23rd—Since August 30, nearly two months, I have written not a line, for I have had nothing to record of public or general interest, and have felt an invincible repugnance to write about myself and my own proceedings. Having nothing else to talk of, however, I shall write my own history of the last seven weeks, which is very interesting to me, inasmuch as it has been very profitable. Having asked G. Bentinck to try my horse Mango before Doncaster, we went down together one night to Winchester racecourse and saw him tried. He won the trial and we resolved to back him. This we accomplished more successfully than we expected, and ten days after He won the St. Leger, and I won about £9000 upon it, the first *great* piece of good fortune that ever happened to me. I was highly elated at the moment and the prospect afforded to me of being able to pay the greater part of my debts is a source of very reasonable satisfaction. Since Doncaster, I have continued (up to this time) to win at Newmarket, so that my affairs are in a flourishing condition, but, notwithstanding these successes, I am dissatisfied and disquieted in my mind, and my life is spent in the alternations of excitement from the amusement and speculation of the turf and of remorse and shame at the pursuit itself. One day I resolve to extricate myself entirely from the whole concern, to sell all my horses, and pursue other occupations and objects of interest, and then these resolutions wax faint, and I again find myself buying fresh animals, entering into fresh speculations, and just as deeply engaged as ever. It is the force of habit, a still unconquered propensity to the sport, and a nervous apprehension that if I do give it up, I may find no substitute of equal interest. It is not that there is anything disgraceful in being addicted to that which so many better men have followed and still do follow, with quite as much zest, but whether it be from the nature of the occupation, or from my nature, or partly from both, I find that it occupies my mind to the exclusion of worthier and better thoughts. I feel that it degrades and stupifies my understanding, that it renders me less agreeable in society, less useful, less respectable in the world, and that this consciousness together with the want of the cultivation and acquired knowledge, which I might and probably should otherwise have possessed, vex and harrass me. I envy those who have no such misgivings, and who are not tormented by any such self-reproaches as these; but I envy still more (if such there be) those who entertaining such scruples and sensible of the pernicious effect which is produced upon their minds, have the resolution to break the chain which binds them, and emancipate themselves at once from such a thraldom, in order to refresh their jaded and debilitated faculties at the fountains of knowledge.

November 14th—Came to town the day before yesterday, having been at Euston, Newmarket, Gunton. Finished the year well, winning a great deal of money, but what then? Success produces agreeable moments but not a happier frame of mind. It is impossible to possess *that*, and at the same time to be dissatisfied with one's own occupation. I think I have made a step towards my emancipation. I am involved in a squabble with the Sporting Magazine, in which an impertinent article has appeared about me, which I will not endure, though I am not afraid of my reputation suffering. If that is not now established it never will be.[1]

Yesterday morning I heard of the death of Lord Egremont, who died after a week's illness (of his old complaint, an inflammation in the trachea), being within a month of eighty-six years old. He was a remarkable man, and his death will be more felt within the sphere of his influence (and that extended over the whole County of Sussex) than any individual's ever was. He was immensely rich, and his munificence was equal to his wealth. No man probably ever gave away so much money in promoting charitable in-

[1] The *Sporting Magazine* published an apology for having written that Greville exaggerated the lameness of Mango before the St. Leger.

stitutions or useful undertakings, and in pensioning, assisting, and supporting his numerous relations and dependants. His understanding was excellent, his mind highly cultivated, and he retained all his faculties, even his memory, unimpaired to the last. He was remarkably acute, shrewd, and observant, and in his manner blunt without rudeness, and caustic without bitterness. Though He had for some years withdrawn himself from the world, he took an eager interest and curiosity in all that was passing in it, and though not mixed up in politics, and sedulously keeping aloof from all party conflicts, he did not fail to think deeply and express himself strongly upon the important questions and events of the times. In his political principles and opinions He was anti-Liberal, and latterly an alarmist as well as a Conservative. He had always opposed Catholic Emancipation, which it is difficult to account for in a man so sagacious and benevolent, but from the force of prejudices early instilled into a mind of tenacious grasp which was not exposed to the changeful influence of world commerce and communication. It is probable that Lord Egremont might have acted a conspicuous part in politics if He had chosen to embark on that stormy sea, and upon the rare occasions when He spoke in the House of Lords, he delivered himself with great energy and effect; but his temper, disposition, and tastes were altogether incompatible with the trammels of office or the restraints of party connexions, and He preferred to revel unshackled in all the enjoyments of private life, both physical and intellectual, which an enormous fortune, a vigorous constitution, and literary habits placed in abundant variety before him. But in the system of happiness which he marked out for himself, the happiness of others formed a large and essential ingredient; nor did old age, as it stole upon him with gradual and insensible steps, dull the brightness of his intellect or chill the warmth of his heart. His mind was always intent upon providing for the pleasure or the benefit of those around him, and there was nothing in which he so keenly delighted as the rural festivals with which he celebrated his own birthday, when thousands of the surrounding villagers were assembled in his Park to eat, drink, and be merry. He was passionately fond of children, and perpetually followed by grandchildren and dogs without number, and animals of all description found favor in his sight. Lord Egremont was a distinguished Patron of Artists, and it was rarely that Petworth was unvisited by some Painter or Sculptor, many of whom He kept in almost continual employment, and by whom his loss will be severely felt. He was extremely hospitable, and Petworth was open to all his friends, and to all their friends if they chose to bring them, provided they did not interfere with his habits or require any personal attention at his hands: from any such obligation he considered that his age and infirmities released him. He received his guests with the utmost urbanity and courtesy, did the honors of his table, and in every other respect left them free to abide as long as they pleased, but to amuse themselves how they could. Petworth was consequently like a great Inn, where there was nothing to pay, but where the guests were not very attentively served. Everybody came when they thought fit, and departed without notice or leave-taking. He liked to have people there who he was certain would not put him out of his way, especially those who, entering into his eccentric habits, were ready for the snatches of talk which his perpetual locomotion alone admitted of, and from whom he could gather information about passing events; but it was necessary to conform to his peculiarities, and these were utterly incompatible with conversation or any prolonged discussion. He never remained for five minutes in the same place, and was continually oscillating between the library and his bedroom, or wandering about the enormous house in all directions; sometimes he broke off in the middle of a conversation on some subject which appeared to interest him, and disappeared, and an hour after, on a casual meeting, would resume it just where he had left off. But this habitual restlessness, which was so fatal to conversation, served perhaps to exhibit the vivacity of his mind and its shrewd epigrammatic turn in a more remarkable manner: and few Persons visited Petworth without being struck with astonishment at the unimpaired vigour of his intellectual powers. To have lived to a great age in the practice of beneficence and the dispensation of happiness, and to die without bodily suffering or mental decay, in the enjoyment of existence up to the instant of its close, affords an example of human prosperity, both in life and in death, which has fallen to the lot of few, but which may well excite the envy and admiration of all.

November 23rd—At Court yesterday when the Queen received the Address of the Commons. She conducts herself with surprising dignity: the dignity which proceeds from self-possession and deliberation. The smallness of her stature is quite forgotten in the majesty and gracefulness of her demeanour.

1838

Burghley, January 2nd 1838—Among other changes of habit, it has occurred to me why should not I begin in the New Year by keeping a regular diary? What I do write are merely fragments of memoirs with passing events briefly alluded to, and the odds and ends collected from different sources recorded and commented on. It is not the first time I have had thoughts of keeping a more regular journal, in which not only my doings should be noted down and my goings, but also preserve some record of my thoughts and feelings, if ever indeed I really do think and feel. The reason I have never done anything of this sort is partly that I have been too idle, and the result partly of modesty and partly of vanity. A journal to be good, true, and interesting, should be written without the slightest reference to publication, but without any fear of it; it should be the transcript of a mind which can bear transcribing. I do not in sincerity believe that my mind, or thoughts, or actions, are of sufficient importance or interest to make it worth while (for the sake of others) to take this trouble. I always contemplate the possibility that hereafter (as every personal MS. is offered to a public always greedy after such things) my journal will be read, and I regard with alarm and dislike the notion of its containing a heap of twaddle and trash concerning matters appertaining to myself which nobody else will care three straws about. If therefore I discard these scruples and do what I meditate (and very likely after all I shall not, or only for a very short time), the next thing is, Why? It seems exceedingly ridiculous to say that one strong stimulus proceeds from reading Scott's Diary—which he began very late in life and in consequence of reading Byron's—not because I fancy that I can write a diary as amusing as Scott's or Byron's, but because I am struck by the excessive pleasure which Scott appeared to derive from writing his journal, and I am (and this is the principal cause) struck with the important use to which the habit may be turned. The habit of recording is first of all likely to generate a desire to have something of some interest to record; it will lead to habits of reflection and to trains of thought, the pursuit of which may be pleasing and profitable; it will exercise the memory and sharpen the understanding generally; and though the thoughts may not be very profound, nor the remarks very lively and ingenious, or the narrative of exceeding interest, still the exercise is, I think, calculated to make the writer wiser, and perhaps better. If I do this I shall read over all I write long before anyone else will have an opportunity of doing so, and I am not likely to be over-indulgent or to spare myself if I find myself a bore. So much for my ideas on this subject; now then for the fruits thereof.

Yesterday morning left town, and slept at Newmarket, saw the horses, rode out on the Warren Hill, and came here to dinner; twenty-two people —the D. of Wellington and Aberdeen, Salisburys, Wilton, and a mob of fine people; very miserable representatives of Old Burleigh, the two insignificant-looking Marquesses,[1] who are his lineal descendants, and who display no more of his brains than they do of his beard. The Duke in great force, talked last night of Canada, and said he thought the first operations had been a failure, and he judged so because the Troops could neither take the rebel chief, nor hold their ground, nor return by any other road than that by which they came; that if Colborne could hold Montreal during the winter it would all do very well, but he was not sure that he would be able to do so; that the Government ought to exhibit to the world their determination to put this revolt down, and that to do so they must seal the St. Lawrence so as to prevent the ingress of foreigners, Belgians, French, and others, who would flock to Canada for employment against us; that the Queen could not blockade her own ports, so that they must apply to Parliament for power to effect this, and they ought to bring in a Bill forthwith for the purpose. This morning he got a letter (from a man he did not know) enclosing the latest news, which he thought very good, and promising better and more decisive results. After breakfast they went shooting.

I walked out and joined the Duke, who talked to me for I dare say an hour and a half about his Spanish campaigns, and most interesting it was. I told him that the other day Allen had asked me to find somebody, a military man, to review his dispatches in the 'Edin.' and that he had suggested Murray as the fittest person if he would undertake it; that I had accordingly spoken to Fitzroy Somerset, who had undertaken to ask Murray, and, if Murray would not, to turn in his mind what officer could be found equal to such a task; and I then asked the Duke if he knew of anybody. He seemed amazingly pleased at the idea, said he knew nobody, but Murray was the fittest man. From this he began to talk, and he told me a great deal of various sorts, which I wish I could have taken down as it fell from his lips. I was amused at the simplicity with which he talked of the great interest of these despatches, just as he might have done if they had been the work of any other man; said he had read them himself with considerable astonishment and great interest, and that everybody might see that there was not one word in them that was not strictly and literally true. Of his Generals, 'that in the beginning they none of them knew anything of the matter, that he was obliged to go from division to division and look to everything himself down to the minutest details.' I said, 'What on earth would have happened if anything had befallen you?' He laughed and said, 'I really do not know. There was a great deal of correspondence about my successor at the time Sir Thos. Graham went home. I was against having any second in command, which was quite useless, as nobody could share

[1] I.e. the second Marquess of Salisbury and the second Marquess of Exeter.

the responsibility with me. However, afterwards Graham came back, and then there was Hope next to him.' He said, 'Hill had invariably done well, always exactly obeyed his orders, and executed them successfully.' The fall of Badajoz was a great blow to him, but he did not know that it was by an act of treachery. The Spanish Government perhaps did not believe that he was approaching to relieve the place, but it was a most curious fact, that whereas it was agreed that the Spanish army should march out over the breach with the honors of war, they were obliged, after the capitulation, to make a breach for them to go over, none having been made by the besiegers. The General, with whom he finds much fault (in the ninth volume) for disobeying his orders and making false movements, was Victor Alten, but he said he treated him with great leniency, and so he did his officers on all occasions, and was as forbearing and indulgent with them as it was possible to be.

All the movements and operations before the battle of Salamanca were to the last degree interesting. He was anxiously waiting for some advantageous occasion to attack Marmont, and at last it arrived; he saw it happen, and took his resolution on the spot. He was dining in a farm-yard with his officers, where (when he had done dinner) everybody else came and dined as they could. The whole French army was in sight, moving, and the Enemy firing upon the farm-yard in which he was dining. 'I got up,' he said, 'and was looking over a wall round the farm-yard, just such a wall as that' (pointing to a low stone wall bounding the covert), 'and I saw the movement of the French left through my glass. "By God," I said, "that will do, and I'll attack them directly." I had moved up the Sixth Division through Salamanca, which the French were not aware of, and I ordered them to attack, and the whole line to advance. I had got my army so completely in hand that I could do this with ease, and in forty minutes the battle was won—"quarante mille hommes battue en quarante minutes."'
I asked him if it was true that He and Marmont had subsequently talked over the event of the battle, and that Marmont had asserted that his orders had been disobeyed, or that this movement of which he took advantage would not have been made. He said He believed there had been some conversation on the subject, and that Marmont had said he was wounded before that took place; he said he did not know if this was true, but it might be, as there had been continual fighting for some time previous. I asked him why Bonaparte had not himself come to Spain to attack him; and if He had with a great force, whether he would have driven him out. He replied that He thought Napoleon had satisfied himself that it would be a work of great difficulty, and what was more, of great length, and he had no

mind to embark in it; and that he certainly would not have driven him
out: he should have taken up some position, and have been enabled to baffle
the Emperor himself just as he had done his Marshals. Thinks that
Napoleon's military system compelled him to employ his armies in war,
when they invariably lived upon the resources of the countries they occupied, and that France could not have maintained them, as She must have
done if He had made peace: peace, therefore, would have brought about
(through the Army itself) his downfall. He traces the whole military system
of France from its first organisation during the Reign of Terror; and that
there is a letter of his on that subject in the tenth volume. I asked him
how he reconciled what he had said of the extraordinary discipline of the
French Army with their unsparing and habitual plunder of the Country,
and he said that though they plundered in the most remorseless way, there
was order and discipline in their plundering, and while they took from
the inhabitants everything they could lay their hands upon, it was done in
the way of requisition, and that they plundered for the Army and not for
themselves individually, but they were reduced to great shifts for food. At
the battle of Fuentes d'Onor he saw the French Soldiers carry off horses that
were killed to be cooked and eaten in another part of the field. 'I saw particularly with my own eyes one horse put upon a cart drawn by two
bullocks (they could not afford to kill the bullocks), and drawn off; and I
desired a man to watch where the cart went, and it was taken to another
French division for the horse to be eaten. Now we never were reduced to
eat horseflesh.' I said he alluded in one of his letters to his having been once
very nearly taken, and he said it was just before the battle of Talavera in
consequence of some troops giving way. He was on a ruined tower from
which he was obliged to leap down; and if he had not been young and
active, as he was in those days, he should certainly have been taken.

Talked a great deal of the Spanish character, unchanged at this day; of
the vast difficulties he had had to contend with from both Spanish and
Portuguese Governments, the latter as bad as the former; of their punctilios
and regard to form and ceremony. 'At the time of the battle of the Pyrenees
I had occasion to send to O'Donnel to advance, and he was mightily
affronted because he did not receive the order by an officer from head-
quarters. I was living under hedges and ditches, and had not been to head-
quarters for several days, and so I told him, but that he should have an
order if he pleased in the proper form.' I asked him if it was not then that
he found the troops in full retreat. He said they were beginning to retreat
when he arrived, 'then they threw up their caps and made a most brilliant
affair of it.'

It is impossible to convey an idea of the zest, eagerness, frankness, and *abundance* with which he talked, and told of his campaigns, or how interesting it was to hear him. He expressed himself very warmly about Hill, of all his Generals, and said, 'When I gave him my memorandum about Canada the day other I said, Why it looks as if we were at our old trade again.' He added that He 'always gave his opinion when it was required on any subject.'

Belvoir Castle, January 4th—Came here yesterday, all the party (almost) migrating, and many others coming from various parts to keep the Duke of Rutland's birthday. We are nearly forty at dinner, but it is no use enumerating the people. Last night the Duke talked of Hanover, said he really did not know much of the matter; that neither Wm. 4th nor George 4th had ever talked to him on the subject or he must have made himself acquainted with it; that the Duke of Cumberland[1] had written him word that he had never had any notion of adopting the measures he has since done till he was going over in the packet with Billy Holmes. The Duke wrote him word that he knew nothing of his case, and the only advice he could give him was to let the Affair be settled as speedily as possible. When the late King had evidently only a few days to live, the Duke of Cumberland consulted the Duke as to what he should do. 'I told him the best thing he could do was to go away as fast as he could: Go instantly,' I said, 'and take care that *you don't get pelted*.' The Duke, Aberdeen, and Fitzgerald all condemned his proceedings without reference to their justice or to his legal and constitutional right as regards Hanover, but on account of the impression (no matter right or wrong) which they are calculated to produce in this country, where it ought to be a paramount interest with him to preserve or acquire as good a character as he can. They all declared that Lyndhurst was equally ignorant with themselves of his views and intentions, with which in fact the Conservatives had no concern. The Duke also advised him not to take the oaths as Privy Councillor, nor those of a Peer in the H. of Lords, because he thought it would do him an injury in the eyes of his new subjects, that he, a King, should swear fealty as her subject to the Queen as his Sovereign; but somebody else (he thought the Duke of Buckingham) overruled this advice, and he had himself a fancy to take the oaths.

To-day we went to see the house[2] Mr. Gregory is building, five miles from here. He is a gentleman of about £12,000 a year, who has a fancy to

[1] He became King of Hanover in 1837 and suspended the Hanoverian constitution.
[2] Harlaxton.

build a magnificent house in the Elizabethan style, and he is now in the middle of his work, all the shell being finished except one wing. Nothing can be more perfect than it is, both as to the architecture and the ornaments; but it stands on the slope of a hill upon a deep clay soil, with no park round it, very little wood, and scarcely any fine trees. Many years ago, when he first conceived this design, he began to amass money and lived for no other object. He travelled into all parts of Europe collecting objects of curiosity, useful or ornamental, for his projected Palace, and he did not begin to build until he had accumulated money enough to complete his design. The grandeur of it is such, and such the tardiness of its progress, that it is about as much as he will do to live till its completion; and as he is not married, has no children, and dislikes the heir on whom his property is entailed, it is the means and not the end to which he looks for gratification. He says that it is his amusement, as hunting or shooting or feasting may be the objects of other people; and as the pursuit leads him into all parts of the world, and to mix with every variety of nation and character, besides engendering tastes pregnant with instruction and curious research, it is not irrational, although he should never inhabit his house, and may be toiling and saving for the benefit of persons he cares nothing about. The cottages round Harlaxton are worth seeing. It has been his fancy to build a whole village in all sorts of strange fantastic styles. There are Dutch and Swiss cottages, every variety of old English, and heaps of nondescript things, which appear only to have been built for variety's sake. The effect is extremely pretty. Close to the village is an old manor house, the most perfect specimen I ever saw of such a building, the habitation of an English country gentleman of former times, and there were a buff Jerkin and a pair of Jack boots hanging up in the hall, which the stout old Cavalier of the seventeenth century (and one feels sure that the Owner of that house was a Cavalier) had very likely worn at Marston Moor or Naseby.

To-day (the Cook told me) nearly four hundred people will dine in the Castle. We all went into the Servants' hall, where one hundred and forty-five had just done dinner and were drinking the Duke's health, singing and speechifying with vociferous applause, shouting, and clapping of hands. I never knew before that oratory had got down into the Servants' hall, but learned that it is the custom for those to whom 'the gift of the gab' has been vouchsafed to harangue the others, the palm of eloquence being universally conceded to Mr. Tapps, the head coachman, a man of great abdominal dignity, and whose Ciceronian brows are adorned with an ample flaxen wig, which is the peculiar distinction of the Functionaries of the whip. I should like to bring the surly Radical here who scowls and snarls at 'the

selfish aristocracy who have no sympathies with the people,' and when he
has seen these hundreds feasting in the Castle, and heard their loud shouts
of joy and congratulation, and then visited the villages around, and listened
to the bells chiming all about the vale, say whether 'the greatest happiness
of the greatest number' would be promoted by the destruction of all the
feudality which belongs inseparably to this scene, and by the substitution
of some abstract political rights for all the beef and ale and music and
dancing with which they are made merry and glad even for so brief a space.
The Duke of Rutland is as selfish a man as any of his class—that is, He
never does what he does not like, and spends his whole life in a round
of such pleasures as suit his taste, but he is neither a foolish nor a bad
man, and partly from a sense of duty, partly from inclination, he devotes
time and labour to the interest and welfare of the people who live and
labour on his estate. He is a Guardian of a very large Union, and he not
only attends regularly the meetings of Poor Law Guardians every week or
fortnight, and takes an active part in their proceedings, but he visits those
paupers who receive out-of-doors relief, sits and converses with them, invites
them to complain to him if they have anything to complain of, and tells
them that he is not only their friend but their representative at the Assembly
of Guardians, and that it is his duty to see that they are nourished and
protected. To my mind there is more 'sympathy' in this than in railing at
the rich and rendering the poor discontented, weaning them from their
habitual attachments and respects, and teaching them that the political
quacks and adventurers who flatter and cajole them are their only real
friends. The conduct of the Radicals about this Canada business supplies a
valuable illustration of their principles, and much ought to be made out of
it. It is a point I should like to work, but I shall not meddle with it. The
Radical jargon on one side and the High Church and High Tory stuff on
the other equally inflame me with a desire to reply to them, and I could
with pleasure write articles in the Times and Morning Chronicle alternately.

Belvoir Castle, January 5th—I doubted if I should bring a fresh book
with me, thinking the old had space enough left to hold all I should write,
and I am in three days obliged to begin a new one—quite a cacoethes
scribendi.

We had a great ball last night, opened by the Duke of Rutland and Dss.
of Sutherland, who had to sail down at least a hundred couple of Tenants,
shopkeepers, Valets, and Abigails. The Duke of Newcastle gave the Duke's
health at dinner (instead of the D. of Wellington, who generally discharges
that office). He made a boggling business of it, but apologised in sufficiently

handsome terms for being spokesman instead of the D. of Wellington. The Duke of Rutland made a very respectable speech in reply, and it all went off swimmingly. To-day went to see the hounds throw off; but though a hunter was offered to me would not ride him, because there is no use in risking the hurt or ridicule of a fall for one day. A man who goes out in this casual way and hurts himself looks as foolish as an amateur Soldier who gets wounded in a battle in which he is tempted by curiosity to mingle. So I rode with the mob, saw a great deal of galloping about and the hounds conveniently running over hills and vales all in sight, and then came home. They said a thousand people were out, many attracted by the expectation of the Duke of Wellington's appearing, but he was rheumatic and could not come out. He is incessantly employed in writing military statements and memorandums, having been consulted by the Government (or probably by Lord Hill on behalf of the Government) both on this Canadian question, and on the general government of the Army, and he will take as much pains to give useful advice to Melbourne's Government as if He and Peel were in office. There never was a man who so entirely sank all party considerations in national objects, and he has had the glory of living to hear this universally acknowledged. Brougham said of him, 'That man's first object is to serve his Country, with his sword if necessary, or with a pick-axe.' He also said of his despatches, 'They will be remembered when I and others (mentioning some of the most eminent men) will be forgotten.' Aberdeen told the Duke this, and he replied with the greatest simplicity, 'It is very true: when I read them I was myself astonished, and I can't think how the devil I could have written them.' This is very characteristic, very curious from a man who has not one grain of conceit in his disposition; but really great men are equally free from undue vanity or affected modesty, and know very well the value of what they do. I remember Lord Holland telling me that Mr. Fox once told him Sheridan's Begum speech was the best that ever was made. When Ld. H. said 'What do you think of yours on——?' 'Well,' said Fox, 'that was a devilish good speech too.'

Last night I sat next to Lord Fitzgerald at dinner, who said that if ever his memoirs appeared (he did not say that any existed) they would contain many curious things, and among them the proofs that the events which were supposed to have been the proximate cause of the Catholic question being carried were not the real cause, and that the resolution of the Duke of Wellington is traceable to other sources which he could not reveal. I am sadly annoyed to-day having got into a scrape about Lewis's Italian Journal. I sold the copyright to Bentley for £100, and now Lushington writes me word he will not have it published. If Bentley makes any difficulty I don't know what will happen.

Melton, January 7th (Wilton's house)—Came here to-day from Belvoir. Last night the Duke narrated the battle of Toulouse and other Peninsular recollections. All the room collected around him, listening with eager curiosity, but I was playing at whist and lost it all. Fitzgerald said to me that he had a great mind to write upon Ireland, and made a statement of the conduct of England towards Ireland for ages past; that he had mentioned his idea to Peel, who had replied, 'Well, and if you do, I am not the man to object to your doing so.' This he meant as a trait of his fairness and candour; but the fact is that it is Peel's interest that all Irish questions should be settled, and he would rejoice at anything which tended to accelerate a settlement, and I am no great believer in his fairness. I was struck with a great admiration for Peel during his hundred days' struggle, when he made a gallant fight; but this has very much cooled since that time; and now I look upon him as a man who, playing first fiddle in his own time rather from the mediocrity of others than his own excellence, will live in the pages of history as a second rate character.

Fitzgerald said one thing in conversation with me of which I painfully felt the truth, that an addiction to worthless or useless pursuits did an irretrievable injury to the mental faculties. It is not only the actual time wasted which might have been turned to good account; the slender store of knowledge acquired on all subjects instead of the accumulation which there might have been; but, more than these, the relaxation of the mental powers till they become incapable of vigorous exertion or sustained effort:—

> Quoniam medio de fonte leporum
> Surgit amari aliquid, quod in ipsis floribus angat:
> Aut quum conscius ipse animus se forte remordet
> Desidiose agere ætatem, lustrisque perire.

Or, as Dryden nobly translates it—

> For in the fountain where these sweets are sought
> Some bitter bubbles up, and poisons all the draught.
> First guilty conscience does the mirror bring,
> Then sharp remorse shoots out the angry sting,
> And anxious thoughts, within themselves at strife,
> Upbraid the long misspent, luxurious life.

I feel myself a miserable example of this species of injury, both as relates to the defects and omissions of my early education and the evil of my subsequent habits. From never having studied hard at any time, no solid foundation of knowledge has ever been laid, my subsequent reading has been desultory and very nearly useless. I have attacked various subjects as I have been prompted thereto by curiosity, or vanity, or shame, but I have never mastered any of them, and the information I have obtained has been like a house built without a foundation, which the first gust of wind would blow down and scatter abroad. Really to master a subject, we should begin at the beginning, storing the memory with consecutive facts, reasoning and reflecting upon them as we go along, till the whole subject is digested, comprehended, made manageable and producible at will; but then, for this process, the mind must be disciplined, and there must be a power of attention undiverted, and of continuous application; but if the eyes travel over the pages of a book, while the mind is far away upon Newmarket Heath (or after any other vanity and folly—but 'de me fabula'—) and nothing but broken fragments of attention are bestowed upon the subject before you, whatever it may be, the result can only be useless imperfect information, crude and superficial ideas, constant shame, and frequent disappointment and mortification. Nothing on earth can make up for the valuable time which I have lost, or enable me to obtain that sort of knowledge, or give me those habits which are only to be acquired early in life, when the memory is fresh and vigorous, and the faculties are both lively and pliant; but that is no reason why I should abandon the design of improvement in despair, for it is never too late to mend, and a great deal may yet be done. I have already resolved to discard that pursuit which has been hitherto the great obstacle to my leading a more profitable life, and I will also resolve to shake off the lethargy in which I have suffered my faculties to be steeped, and endeavour at least to apply myself to occupations more respectable as well as useful in themselves, and which may eventually contribute to the comfort and pleasure of my life by supplying the materials of rational thought and creditable employment.

Beaudesert, January 12th, Friday—On Monday went to Sutton; nobody there but Mr. Hodgson, formerly my Tutor at Eton, the friend of Byron, author of a translation of Juvenal—a clever, not an agreeable man. The house at Sutton is unfinished, but handsome enough. Came here on Wednesday; a magnificent place indeed, and very comfortable house. A good many people, nobody remarkable; very idle life. Read in the newspaper that Colburn gave Lady C. Bury £1000 for the wretched catchpenny trash called 'Memoirs of the Time of George IV,' which might well set all the world what Scott calls 'gurnelising,' for nobody could by possibility compile or compose anything more vile and despicable. My trash is at least better and less *trashy* than that, but I much doubt if any future Colburn will ever give £1000 for all my MS. Since I came here, a world of fine thoughts came into my head which I intended to immortalise in these pages; but they have all evaporated like the baseless fabrics of a vision.

January 17th, Beaudesert, Wednesday—To Sandon on Monday, and returned here yesterday; go away to-morrow. It has been a dreadfully idle life all day long, *facendo niente*, incessant gossip and dawdle, poor, unprofitable talk, and no rational employment. Brougham was here a little while ago for a week. He, Lord Wellesley, and Ld. Anglesey form a discontented triumvirate, and are knit together by the common bond of a sense of ill-usage and of merit neglected. Wellesley and Anglesey are not Radicals, however, and blame Brougham's new tendency that way. Anglesey and Wellesley both hate and affect to despise the Duke of Wellington, in which Brougham does not join. They are all suffering under mortified vanity and thwarted ambition, and after playing their several parts, not without success and applause, they have not the judgement to see and feel that they forfeit irretrievably the lustre of their former fame by such a poor and discreditable termination of their career. Douro is here, *une lune bien pâle de son père*, but far from a dull man, and not deficient in information.

Badminton, January 23rd—The debate in the Lords the other night was very interesting and creditable to the assembly. Brougham delivered a tremendous philippic of three hours, well described by the Times. The Duke of Wellington made a very noble speech, just such as it befitted him to make at such a moment, and of course it bitterly mortified and provoked the Tories, who would have had him make a party question of it, and thought of nothing but abusing, vilifying, and embarrassing the Government. This was what Peel showed every disposition to do in the House of Commons, where he made a poor, paltry half-attack, which was much more to the taste of his party than the Duke's temperate and candid declaration.

Lord Eldon died last week full of years and wealth. He had for some time past quitted the political stage, but his name was still venerated by the dregs of that party to whom consistent bigotry and intolerance are dear. Like his more brilliant Brother, he was the Artificer of his own fortune, and few men ever ran a course of more unchequered prosperity. As a Politician, he appears to have been consistent throughout, and to have offered a determined and uniform opposition to every measure of a Liberal description. He knew of no principles but those (if they merit the name of principles) of the narrowest Toryism and of High Church, and as soon as more enlarged and enlightened views began to obtain, he quitted (and for ever) public life. I suppose he was a very great Lawyer, but he was certainly a contemptible Statesman. He was a very chearful, good-natured old man, loving to talk, and telling anecdotes with considerable humour and point. I remember very often during the many tedious hours the Prince Regent used to keep the Lords of the Council waiting at Carlton House, that the Chancellor used to beguile the time with amusing stories of his early professional life, and anecdotes of celebrated Lawyers, which he told extremely well. He lived long enough to see the overthrow of the system of which he had been one of the most strenuous supporters, of the triumph of all the principles which he dreaded and abhorred, and the elevation of all the men to whom, through life, he had been most adverse, both personally and politically. He little expected in 1820, when he was presiding at the Queen's trial, that he should live to see her Attorney-General on the Woolsack, and her Solicitor-General Chief Justice of England.

1839

May 10th, Friday—I left town on Monday, having in the morning seen Le Marchant (who knows better than anybody the numbers and details of divisions); and he told me that they should have a majority of twenty: little, therefore, was I prepared to hear on Tuesday morning that they had been left with only a majority of five. It was not till they were in the H. of C. that they were aware of the defections, and of the probability of a close division, if not of a defeat. About ten of the Radicals voted against them, and ten or a dozen staid away; six of the Tories voted with Government, but the balance was quite enough to reduce the old majority to an equality. On Tuesday the Cabinet met, and resolved to resign. The Queen had not been prepared for this catastrophe and was completely upset by it. Her agitation and grief were very great. In her interview with John Russell She was all the time dissolved in tears; and She dined in her own room, and never appeared on the Tuesday evening. Melbourne advised her to send for the Duke, and on Wednesday morning She sent for him. By this time She had regained her calmness and self-possession. She told him that She was very sorry for what had occurred, and for having to part with her Ministers, particularly Lord Melbourne, for whom She felt the warmest regard, and who had acted an almost parental part towards her. The Duke was excessively pleased with her behaviour and with her frankness. He told her that his age and deafness incapacitated him from serving her as efficiently as he could desire, and that the Leader of the House of Commons ought to be her Prime Minister, and he advised her to send for Peel. She said, 'Will you desire him to come to me?' He told her that he would do anything; but, he thought, under the circumstances, it would be better that She should write to him herself. She said She would, but begged him to go and announce to Peel that he might expect her letter. This the Duke did, and when Peel received it, he went to the Palace (in full dress according to etiquette), and received her commands to form a Government. She received him (though She dislikes him) extremely well, and he was perfectly satisfied.

While the Tories were rejoicing in their victory, the Whigs, greatly exasperated, were already beginning to meditate the organisation of a strong opposition, and providing the means of carrying on an effectual war against the new Government. They do not chuse to look upon their expulsion as attributable to the defection of their Allies, but as the work of the Tories upon a mere party question, and that a very unjustifiable one, and treated in a very unjustifiable manner. I met Ellice and Labouchere in the street, and found them full of menace and sinister prediction, and to my assertion that all would go well and *easily*, they shook their heads, and insisted that the conduct of their opponents entitled them to no forbearance, and that finding none, their difficulties and embarrassments would be very great; and I found in other quarters that there is a disposition to rally and marshal the party, and commence offensive warfare; but others of the Whigs entertained no such views, and looked upon the game as quite lost for the present; and in point of fact, nothing is settled, fixed, combined, or arranged as yet; and there has not been time to ascertain the disposition or intentions of the Leaders.

While, however, there was (yesterday) this uncertainty and agitation in the Whig Camp, and the Tories were waiting in perfect security for the tranquil arrangement of the new Government, a storm suddenly arose, which threatens to scatter to the winds the new combinations, and the ultimate effects of which it is impossible for anybody to foresee. The Queen insisted upon keeping the Ladies of her household, and Peel objected, but without shaking her determination. He begged her to see the Duke of Wellington, and She agreed to see the Duke and him together. He had, however, before this gone to the Palace with *Ashley*, whom he had taken with him, fancying that because he had been in the habit of seeing a great deal of her, he might have some influence with her—a notion altogether preposterous, and exhibiting the deficiency of Peel in worldly dexterity and tact, and in knowledge of character. Ashley, a man disliked by most people and probably only tolerated by the Queen on account of his wife and the Cowper connexion, made no impression on her. When the Duke and Peel saw her, and endeavoured to persuade her to yield this point, they found her firm and immoveable, and not only resolved not to give way, but prepared with answers to all they said, and arguments in support of her determination. They told her that She must consider her *Ladies* in the same light as *Lords*: She said, 'No, I have Lords besides, and these I give up to you.' And when they still pressed her, She said, 'Now suppose the case had been reversed, that you had been in office when I had come to the throne, and that Lord Melbourne was now coming to replace you—I am persuaded that Lord Melbourne would not have required this sacrifice of me.' Finding that She would not give way, Peel informed her that under these circumstances he must consult his friends; and a meeting took place at his house yesterday afternoon.

In the meantime the old Ministers were apprised of the difficulty that had occurred, and John Russell, who knew that there was a meeting at Peel's to consider what was to be done, entreated Melbourne, if the thing was broken off upon this difficulty, not to give any advice, but to call the Cabinet and have a general consultation. At nine in the evening he was summoned to a Cabinet at Melbourne's house, and from this he inferred that negotiations with Peel had closed. The Ministers were collected from all quarters: (Hobhouse from dinner at Wilton's, Morpeth from the opera), and Melbourne laid before them a letter from the Queen, written in a bitter spirit, in a strain such as Elizabeth might have used. She said, 'Do not fear that I was not calm and composed. They wanted to deprive me of my Ladies, and I suppose they would deprive me next of my dressers and my housemaids; they wished to treat me like a girl, but I will show them that I am Queen of England.' They consulted, and a suggestion was thrown out that Lady Normanby (and some other I think) should resign. This was overruled, as was a proposition of John Russell's, that the Queen should require from Peel a precise statement of the extent of his demands. The end was, that a letter was composed for her, in which She simply declined to place the Ladies of her household at Peel's discretion. This was sent yesterday morning; when Peel wrote an answer resigning his commission into H.M. hands; but recapitulating everything that had passed. When the difficulty first arose, Peel asked her to see the Duke; she acquiesced; he fetched her, and the Duke was with her alone. The Duke it was who argued *the principle* with her—Peel had touched upon its application.

It was speedily known all over the town that the whole thing was at an end, and nothing could surpass the excitement and amazement that prevailed. The indignant Tories exclaimed against intrigue and preconcerted plans, and asserted that She refused to part with *any* of her Ladies, and that it was only a pretext to break off the Tory Government; while the Whigs cried out against harshness and dictatorial demands, and complained that it was intended to make a thorough clearance, strip her of all her friends, and destroy her social comfort. The Radicals, who had for the most part been terribly alarmed at the results of their own defection, instantly made overtures to the Whigs; and I heard at Brooks's that Ward had come over from the Reform Club, and proposed a reconciliation without any concession, except that Ballot should be made an open question. There appeared no disposition to concede anything to the Radicals, who, they were convinced, would join them without any conditions.

In the meantime Melbourne and John Russell went to the Queen, who told them her whole story. I met the latter coming from her; he said, 'I have just been for an hour with the Queen; She told me her story, and ended by saying, "I have stood by you, you must now stand by me." ' They thought her case a good one, and resolved to stand by her. Such was the state of things and such the case as reported to me by Tavistock and others of the Whig party yesterday morning, and my impression was that Peel had been unreasonable in his demands and impolitic in breaking off the negotiation on such grounds. Nevertheless I had some misgivings, because I thought the Duke of Wn. unlikely to concur in any proceeding harsh towards the Queen, or ill-considered in a political sense; but the assertion was at the same time so positive, that Peel had required the dismissal of *all* the Ladies, and the Tories defended instead of denying this, that I did not doubt the fact to have been so; and moreover I was told that Peel's behaviour had created a strong sentiment of dislike towards him in the Queen, and from her representations and the language of her letter it was clear the impression of her mind was that no consideration was intended to be shown to her feelings and wishes, but, on the contrary, that they meant to abuse their power to the utmost. At the ball last night I put the question directly to Normanby and Ben Stanley, and they both declared that the Queen's understanding was that the demand for power to dismiss the Ladies was unqualified by any intimation of an intention not to exercise that power to the utmost extent; that She believed they were *all* to be taken from her, and under this impression She had sent her ultimatum by which the whole thing was terminated. But I had afterwards a conversation with Wharncliffe, who gave me an account of all that had passed, placed the matter in a very different light, and proved beyond a doubt that there was no lack of deference and consideration on the part of Peel, but, on the contrary, the clearest indication of an intention and desire to consult her wishes and feelings in every respect, and that, instead of a sweeping demand for the dismissal of *all* her Ladies, he had approached that subject with delicacy and caution, and merely suggested the expediency of some partial changes, for reasons (especially when taken with other things) by no means insufficient. So little disposition was there on the part of Peel to regard her with distrust or to fetter her social habits, that when She said, 'You must not expect me to give up the society of Lord Melbourne,' He replied that 'Nothing could be further from his thoughts than to interfere with H.M.'s society in any way, or to object to her receiving Lord Melbourne as She pleased, and that He should always feel perfectly secure in the honor of Lord Melbourne and in hers that he would not avail himself improperly of his intercourse with her.' When She said that She should like to have Ld. Liverpool about her, he immediately acquiesced, and proposed that he should be Lord Steward, and he suggested certain other persons, whom he said he proposed because he believed they were personally agreeable to her; but when he began to talk of 'some modification of the Ladies of her household,' She stopped him at once, and declared She would not part with any of them. Thenceforward this became the whole matter in dispute; but there had been some circumstances even in the first interview which Peel and the Duke regarded as ominous and indicative of her having been primed as to the part She should play. The principal of these was an intimation of her desire that there should be *no dissolution of Parliament.* This surprised Peel very much, but he only replied that it was impossible for him to come to any determination on that point, as he might be beat on one of the first divisions, in which case it would be inevitable. It was indeed the fact of his taking the Government with a *minority* in the H. of C. which was his principal argument for desiring the power of dismissing the Ladies, or rather of changing the household, that He might not, he said, give to the world the spectacle of a Court entirely hostile to him, consisting of Ladies whose husbands were his strongest political opponents, thereby creating an impression that the confidence of the Crown was bestowed on his enemies rather than on himself. In the Duke's first interview with the Queen, he had entreated her to place her whole confidence in Peel, and had then said that, though some changes might be necessary in her household, She would find him in all the arrangements anxious to meet her wishes and consult her feelings. But She had already conceived a lively aversion for Peel, and though her manner was civil her heart was full of bitterness, looking back with regret and forward with reluctance and dismay; and without foresight, judgement and reflection sufficient to embrace remote consequences, She exhibited the talent of a clever but rather thoughtless and headstrong girl; and, secretly longing to get back her Old Ministers if she could by any pretext or expedient, She boldly and stubbornly availed herself of the opening which was presented to her. Notwithstanding her assurance to Melbourne that She was calm, She was greatly excited, though still preserving a becoming dignity in her outward behaviour.

Having satisfied myself that there had been a complete misunderstanding, which I think, as it was, might have been cleared up if there had been less precipitation and more openness and further endeavours to explain what was doubtful or ambiguous, I began to turn in my mind whether something could not be done to avert the impending danger, and renew the negotiation with Peel while it was still time. Labouchere had had a conversation with Graham, who had enlightened him, much as Wharncliffe had me; we came home together, and I found what Graham had told him had made a deep impression on him, and that he was as sensible as I am of the gravity and peril of the circumstances in which affairs are placed. I accordingly sent for Tavistock and urged him to endeavour to persuade Melbourne to see the Duke of Wellington and talk it over with him; he would at all events learn the exact truth as to what had passed, which it most essentially behoves him to know before he takes upon himself the responsibility of advising the Queen and of meeting Parliament once more with all the necessary explanations how and why he is still Minister, and from the Duke likewise he would learn what really is the animus of Peel and his Party, and what the real extent of their intended demands upon the Queen. He, and He alone, can enlighten her and pacify her mind; and if He is satisfied that there has been a misapprehension, and that Peel has required nothing but what She ought to concede, it would be his duty to advise her once more to place herself in Peel's hands. This is the only solution of the difficulty now possible, and this course, if he has sufficient wisdom, firmness and virtue to adopt it, may still avert the enormous evils which are threatened by the rupture of the pending arrangements. Tavistock acquiesced in my reasoning and agreed to go to Melbourne; but he also wanted the Duke of Wn. to say something in the H. of Lords in vindication of the Ladies of the Palace in the Hastings affair, and I persuaded him to go at once to Apsley House and ask the Duke. He did go, saw the Duke, who was very kind and promised to say what he wished on Monday next. The Duke then talked (without going into details) of the other concern, spoke kindly of the Queen, and fully confirmed all I had said of their *animus* towards her. He afterwards saw Arbuthnot, who entered into more details, told him what had passed between Peel and the Queen, and said that H.M. was in fact in a great passion. He said the Duke would certainly see Melbourne, but he could not send for him, and added that my sister and 'another Lady' had already been with the Duke and had since written to Melbourne with the same object. The fact is Melbourne had talked to my sister about it last night at the ball, and had owned to her that the Queen was under the impression I have described; and this morning when She came here I said how desirous I was that a meeting should take place between him and the Duke, who I thought might together bring about a satisfactory adjustment of all the difficulties. Tavistock came back here from Apsley House to report progress, and I sent him on to Buckingham House (where he heard Melbourne was gone) to talk the matter over with him, and so it stands at this present time.

May 12th—The Cabinet met yesterday, and resolved to take the Government again; they hope to interest the people in the Queen's quarrel, and having made it up with the Radicals they think they can stand. It is a high trial of our institutions when the caprice of a girl of nineteen can overturn a great Ministerial combination, and when the most momentous matters of Government and legislation are influenced by her pleasure about her Ladies of the Bedchamber. The Whigs resigned because they had no longer that Parliamentary support for their measures which they deemed necessary, and they consent to hold the Government without the removal of any of the difficulties which compelled them to resign, for the purpose of enabling the Queen to exercise her pleasure without any controul of interference in the choice of the Ladies of her household. This is making the private gratification of the Queen paramount to the highest public considerations: somewhat strange Whig doctrine and practice! With respect to the question of unfettered choice, a good deal may be said on both sides; but although it would be wrong and inexpedient for any Minister to exercise the right, unless in a case of great necessity, I think every Minister must have the power of advising the Queen to remove a Lady of her Court, in the same way as he is admitted to have that of removing a man. Notwithstanding the transaction of 1812, and Lord Moira's protection of George 4th in the retention of his household, it is now perfectly established in practice that the royal household is at the discretion of the Minister, and it must be so because he is responsible for the appointments; in like manner he is responsible for every appointment which the Sovereign may make; and should any of the Ladies conduct herself in such a manner as to lead the public to expect or require her dismissal, and the Queen was to refuse to dismiss her, the Minister must be responsible for her remaining about the Royal person.

The pretension of the Queen was not merely personal, *pro hâc vice*, and one of arrangement, but it went to the establishment of a principle unlimited in its application, for She declared that She had felt bound to make her stand where She did, in order once for all to resist the encroachments which She anticipated, and which would lead, She supposed, at last to their insisting on taking the Baroness Lehzen herself from her. The whole affair is incomprehensible, for while the Ministers think they were bound to support the Queen they do not pretend to maintain *the principle*, and yet it was *the principle* on which She broke off with Peel. In a constitutional point of view, the case appears to me to be much stronger than in that of a Queen Consort, for the Minister has nothing to do with a Queen Consort; he is not responsible for her appointments, nor for the conduct of her officers, and she is a *feme sole* possessed of independent rights which She may exercise according to her own pleasure, provided only that She does not transgress the law. It was a great stretch of authority when Lord Grey insisted upon the dismissal of Lord Howe, the Queen's Chamberlain; but he did so upon an extraordinary occasion, and when circumstances rendered it (as he thought) absolutely necessary that he should make a public demonstration of his influence in a Court notoriously disaffected to the Reform Bill.

The origin of the present mischief may be found in the objectionable composition of the Royal household at the accession. The Queen knew nobody, and was ready to take any Ladies that Melbourne recommended to her. He ought to have taken care that the female part of her household should not have a political complexion, instead of making it exclusively Whig as (unfortunately for her) he did. The simple truth in this case is that the Queen could not endure the thought of parting with Melbourne, who is everything to her. Her feelings which are *sexual* though She does not know it, and are probably not very well defined to herself, are of a strength sufficient to bear down all prudential considerations and to predominate in her mind with irresistible force. In the course of the transaction She thought She saw the means presenting themselves of getting Melbourne back, and She eagerly grasped at, and pertinaciously retained them. Nothing else would have emboldened her to resist the advice and opinion of the Duke of Wellington and to oppose so unbendingly her will to his authority. There is something which shocks one's sense of fitness and propriety in the spectacle of this mere baby of a Queen setting herself in opposition to this

great man, the decus and testamen of her kingdom, invested with all the
authority of his experience and sagacity, of his profound loyalty, his devoted
patriotism, and to whom her Predecessors had ever been accustomed to
look up with unlimited confidence as their surest and wisest Councillor in
all times of difficulty and danger. Nor is it little matter of wonder that
Melbourne should have consented to support her in such a case, and that
He and his colleagues should have consented to act the strange, anomalous,
unconstitutional part they have done. While they really believed that She
had been ill-used, it was natural they should be disposed to vindicate and
protect her; but after the reception of Peel's letter they must have doubted
whether the impression She had conveyed to them was altogether accurate,
and they ought in prudence, and in justice to her, even against her own
feelings, to have sifted the matter to the bottom, and have cleared up every
existing doubt before they decided on their course. But to have met as a
Cabinet, and to have advised her what answer to send to the man who still
held her commission for forming a Government, upon points relating to
its formation, is utterly anomalous and unprecedented, and a course as
dangerous as unconstitutional. The danger has been sufficiently exemplified
in the present case; for, having necessarily had no cognisance of the facts
but such as they derived from her own account of verbal communications,
they incurred the risk of giving advice upon false or mistaken grounds, as
in this instance has been the case. *She* might be excused for her ignorance
of the exact limits of constitutional propriety, and for her too precipitate
recurrence to the Counsels to which She had been accustomed; but *they*
ought to have explained to her, that until Sir R. Peel had formally and
finally resigned his commission into her hands, they could tender no advice,
and that her replies to him, and her resolutions with regard to his proposals,
must emanate solely and spontaneously from herself. As it was, the Queen
was in communication with Sir R. Peel on one side, and Ld. Melbourne on
the other, at the same time; and through them with both their Cabinets;
the unanimous resolutions of the former being conveyed by her to, and
her answer being composed by, the latter. The Cabinet of Lord Melbourne
discussed the proposals of that of Sir Robert Peel, and they dictated to the
Queen the reply in which She refused to consent to the advice tendered
to her by the man who was *at that moment* her Minister, and it was this
reply which compelled him to resign the office with which She had en-
trusted him.

May 13th—Tavistock has been here to report progress. He went on Saturday to Buckingham Palace; found Melbourne was not there, so followed
him to his house, where the Cabinet was sitting. He wrote him a letter, in

which he said that he had seen the Duke, and that his impression was that there had been a misunderstanding between Peel and the Queen; and suggested to M. that he should see the Duke, who was very willing, if he pleased to talk the matter over with him. This letter was taken in to the Cabinet, and they discussed its contents. Melbourne was not indisposed to see the Duke; but, after a careful consideration of Peel's letter, they came to the conclusion that there was no difference between the Queen's statement to them and Peel's to her, and, therefore, no misconception to correct. The Chancellor accordingly gave his opinion, that there was no ground for an interview between M. and the Duke; so there ended the last hope of a readjustment. The Queen had been very explicit with John Russell and they are satisfied She did not deceive them, which is at all events consolatory, for one of the worst features of the case was the semblance of duplicity or falsehood on the part of the Queen. Of this they entirely acquit her.

The question (they say) was all along one of *principle*, and never of the *application* of the principle; but the extraordinary part of it is that they admit that the principle is not maintainable, but yet declare that they were bound *as gentlemen*, when She had recourse to them, to support her. This is strange doctrine in Whig mouths. They have, in my opinion, abandoned their duty to the country and to the Queen, and they ought to have been impressed with the paramount obligation of instructing her in the nature and scope of her constitutional obligations and duties, and the limits of her constitutional rights, and to have advised her what She ought to do, instead of upholding her in doing that which was agreeable to her taste and inclination.

In the meantime Brougham wrote a violent letter to Tavistock, imploring him, while it was still time, to arrest the perilous course on which his friends had entered, and full of professions of regard for him and his. T. went to him in the evening, found him in a state of furious excitement, abusing the Ministry generally, and many of them by name in the grossest terms, and pouring forth a torrent of invective against men and things. After a time he became more cool, and half promised that he would not speak at all; but when he learnt (what he was not aware of) that Lord Spencer was come to town and would be in the H. of Lords, he broke out again, and said that if they had brought him up to support their miserable rotten concern, he must speak. Lord Spencer was not, however, brought up by them; he knew nothing of passing events till he read them in the 'Times,' on Saturday, at Barnet, and his reflection on them was, that if he should be sent for, he should advise the Q. to send for Peel again and concede the point. He is now, however, disposed, in case of need, to defend his friends in the H. of Lords; but if they can secure Brougham's silence as the price of his, the Ministers will be glad enough to *pair* them off.

May 19th—At Mickleham (for Epsom) from Tuesday to Friday, and (of course) nothing done, written, heard, or thought of, save and except the Derby etc. The explanations went off, on the whole, very well, without acrimony, and as satisfactorily as the case allowed. Peel's speech was excellent (though Lord Grey did not approve of it, and regretted not having the power to answer it), and without any appearance of art or dexterity he contrived to steer through all the difficult points and to justify himself without saying a word offensive to the Queen—not however that this will reconcile her to him. John Russell was very nervous, and very feeble, and ineffective. In the other House, Melbourne made (as all allow) a capital speech; Clarendon, a good and fair Judge, told me that he never heard Melbourne speak so well throughout; while the Duke was painful to hear, exhibiting such undoubted marks of caducity: it did not, however, read ill. Melbourne made one admission, for which John Russell was very angry with him, and that was of the 'erroneous impression' on the Queen's mind, because his argument was that there was 'no mistake.' Lord Grey and Lord Spencer would either of them have spoken, but it was deemed better they should not, or Brougham would have been unmuzzled, and as it was he adhered to his engagement to Tavistock and held his peace. He had said, 'If you let off Althorp or Old Grey, I must speak.'

June 1st—Laid up with the gout and confined to my room for ten days, very ill and utterly disinclined to write. Nothing new of consequence, but little things kept oozing out, throwing light on the recent transaction, and all tending to the same conclusion; showing how violent and wrong headed the Queen was, and how wicked (for it merits no milder term) was the conduct of the Ministers in upholding and abetting her instead of telling her the truth, showing her how it was her duty to act, and acting themselves as it was theirs to do. Peel (reserved and prudent as he is) cannot conceal the indignation with which he is boiling over, at the personal treatment he experienced at her hands, at her peremptory and haughty demeanour; and it is a vast evil that they have imbibed sentiments of mutual dislike and alienation which nothing will ever get over. In the meantime Parliament met, but nothing has been done. John Russell began by deferring the Education question, which he will be obliged to abandon, for the Church has risen up and put forth all its strength against it, and having been joined by the Wesleyans, will, without difficulty, defeat it. The Bishop of London made a most eloquent philippic against it at Exeter Hall the other day. Government have brought in another Jamaica Bill, not very different from Peel's proposed measure, and which they will probably contrive to pass.

The Radicals have been again bestirring themselves, and trying to turn the present occasion to account and extract some concessions from the Government. Warburton has been in communication with John Russell, and they expect some declarations from him and Melbourne of their future intentions, and some indications of a disposition to give way on some of the favourite Radical measures. Melbourne's was to be elicited by certain questions of which Lord Winchilsea gave notice, and which he actually put last night, as to the principles on which the Government was to be conducted. Melbourne replied in a very guarded and somewhat didactic style, but, so far from evincing any disposition to make Radical concessions, he intimated with sufficient clearness that he was resolved to make none whatever, and that he would not sacrifice his conscientious convictions for any political or party purpose.

After this, up got Brougham, and that boiling torrent of rage, disdain, and hatred, which had been dammed up upon a former occasion when he was so unaccountably muzzled, broke forth with resistless and overwhelming force. He spoke for three hours, and delivered such an oration as no other man in existence is capable of—devilish in spirit and design, but of superhuman eloquence and masterly in execution. He assailed the Ministers with a storm of invective and ridicule; and, while he enveloped his periods in a studied phraseology of pretending loyalty and devotion, he lashed the Queen herself with unsparing severity. He went at length and in minute detail into the whole history of the recent transaction, drew it in its true colours, and exposed its origin, progress, and motives, and thus he laid bare all the arts and falsehoods by which attempts had been made to delude and agitate the country. If it were possible to treat this as a party question, his speech would be a powerful party auxiliary, most valuable to the Tories, as a vindication of them, most damning to the Whigs *and the Queen* as an exposure of their conduct, for it was the peculiar merit of this speech that it abounded in truths and in great constitutional principles of undoubted authority and unerring application. But it is impossible unfortunately to execute justice without incurring a great and important danger. The wilful obstinate child of 20 deserves the severest reprehension, but the castigation She merits cannot be administered without impairing the authority, the dignity, the sanctity of the Crown she wears, and it is necessary to spare the individual for the sake of the institution. This it is which the Duke of Wellington feels, and this feeling induced him to rise after Brougham: in a short speech, replete with moderation and dignity, he abstained from entering upon the past, but fastened upon Melbourne's declaration, and gave him to understand that as long as he adhered to such principles as he had then declared he would be governed by, he might appeal to Parliament confidently for support.

These three speeches have all in their different ways produced a great effect: Melbourne's will not satisfy the Radicals, though they catch (as dying men at straws) at a vague expression about 'progressive reforms,' and try (or pretend) to think that this promises something, though they know not what. Brougham's speech was received by the Tory Lords with enthusiastic applause, vociferous cheering throughout, and two or three rounds at the conclusion. But the Duke's assurance of support to Melbourne exasperated his own people to the greatest degree, produced a sulky article in the 'Times,' and the usual complaints at White's and the Carlton of the Duke's being in his dotage, and so forth. Even some of his real admirers thought 'he had overdone it,' and whilst at Brooks's they did not quite know what to make of it, at the Carlton they were in the same doubt how to interpret Melbourne's cautious ambiguities. Both, however, were clear enough: M. meant to say he would 'go no further,' and the Duke meant to pat him on the back, and promise him that while he adhered to that resolution he should have no vexatious opposition to fear; but his meaning was made still more clear, for he told my Brother this afternoon that 'it was of the greatest importance to nail Melbourne to his declaration, and they must do what they could to help that poor little thing out of the difficulty in which she was placed.' He looks to the Crown of England, and not to the misguided little person who wears it; he wants to uphold *it* and not to punish *her*; and he does not care to achieve a Tory triumph at the expense of the highest Tory principle; he thinks the Monarchy is in danger, and he sees that the danger may be more surely averted by still enduring the existence of the present Government, depriving them of all power to do evil, and converting them into instruments of good, than by accelerating their fall under circumstances calculated to engender violent animosities, irreconcileable enmities, wide separation of parties, and the adoption of extreme measures and dangerous principles by many who have no natural bias that way. I entirely concur with him, and if it were possible to restore matters to something like the state they were in before the Bedchamber crisis, nothing would be so desirable; nothing so desirable as that the Whigs and the Radicals should be furnished with fresh occasion to fall out and the dissolution of the Government be the final consequence of their dissensions. Also it is expedient that time should be given for the angry waters to become smooth and calm once more, albeit the smoothness is only on their surface.

Yesterday the Grand Duke Alexander went away after a stay of some three weeks, which has been distinguished by a lavish profusion—perhaps a munificence—perfectly unexampled; he is by no means remarkable in appearance one way or the other, and does not appear to have made any great impression except by the splendour and extent of his presents and benefactions: he has scattered diamond boxes and rings in all directions, subscribed largely to all the charities, to the Wellington and Nelson memorials, and most liberally (and curiously) to the Jockey Club, to whom he has sent a sum of £300, with a promise of its annual repetition.

Macaulay is gone to Edinbro to be elected in the room of Abercrombie, so he is again about to descend into the arena of politics. He made a very eloquent and, to my surprise, a very Radical speech, declaring himself for Ballot and short Parliaments. I was the more astonished at this, because I knew he had talked very moderate language, and I remembered his telling me that he considered the Radical party to be reduced to 'Grote and his wife,' after which I did not expect to see him declare himself the Advocate of Grote's favourite measure and the darling object of the Radicals.

June 7th—Macaulay's was a very able speech and a good apology for the Whig Government, and as he has always been for Ballot, he is not inconsistent. On Sir H. Fleetwood's motion the other night (for giving votes for Counties to ten-pound householders), John Russell spoke out (though in a reforming tone) and threw the Radicals into a paroxysm of chagrin and disappointment. The Tories had heard he was going to give way, and Peel, who is naturally suspicious and distrustful, believed it; but when he found he would not give way, nor held out any hopes for the future, Peel nailed him to that point and spoke with great force and effect. This debate was considered very damaging to Whigs and Radicals, and likely to lead to a dissolution—first, of Parliament, and then of Government. But the Radicals are now adopting a whining, fawning tone, have dropt that of bluster and menace, and, having before rudely insisted on a mighty slice of the loaf, are now content to put their tails between their legs and swallow such crumbs as they can get. Peel has written and published a very stout letter, in reply to a Shrewsbury declaration presented to him, in which he defends his recent conduct, and declares he will never take office on any other terms—an announcement that will be gall and wormwood to Her most gracious Majesty.

The Palace is again the scene of squabbling, of which Conroy is the cause and the Belligerents are the mother and daughter. The Duke as usual has been called in, for in desperate cases he is always the Doctor they rely on.

June 10th—They have got rid of Conroy; he has resigned his place about the Duchess of Kent and is going abroad. There is of course a dessous des cartes, but the story told is that he has voluntarily resigned. He went to Duncannon and told him he had done so, and then went to the Duke and told him, and the Duke approves.

Notwithstanding John Russell's speech on Fleetwood's motion, and Melbourne's anti-movement declaration in the other House, they have to their eternal disgrace succumbed to the Radicals, and been squeezed into making Ballot an open question. For John Russell I am sorry. I thought he would have been stouter. The Radicals are full of exultation, and the Government underlings, who care not on what terms they can retain their places, are very joyful. I rode with Howick yesterday for a long time and talked it over with him. He pretended it was no concession after Vivian's being allowed to vote last year, and he owned that he considered the question as virtually carried; and he is moderate and means still to vote against it, sees all the danger—not so much from Ballot itself as from its inevitable train of consequences—and still consents to abandon the contest. I asked him, if he was not conscious that it was only like buying off the Picts and Scots, and that fresh demands would speedily follow with redoubled confidence; and he owned he was—and these are *Statesmen*, and this is *Government* and here we have a beginning of the evils that the caprice and folly of the Queen, backed as they were by the wickedness of the Whigs, were certain to entail. It may prolong for a brief period the sickly existence of the Government, and if a dissolution comes speedily, Whigs and Radicals may act in concert at the elections; but if they attempt to go on with the present Parliament fresh demands will rapidly ensue, and then there must be fresh concessions or another breach. It is a base and disgusting truckling to allies between whom and themselves there is nothing but mutual hatred and contempt.

June 14th—At Holland House from Tuesday till Thursday—not particularly agreeable. Melbourne came one day, but was not in spirits. Much talk with Lady Cowper about the Queen, who was eloquent on her merits but admitted that She had faults and those in her position dangerous ones—obstinacy to wit, and a very high opinion of herself—which is unquestionably the truth, and accounts for the pertinacity with which She adhered to her purpose and stood out against the Duke. Lord Holland told me some stories of George Selwyn, whom he had known in his younger days, and many of whose good sayings he remembers. He describes him as a man of great gravity and deliberation in speaking, and, after exciting extraordinary mirth by his wit and drollery, gently smiling and saying, 'I am glad you are pleased.' The old Lord Foley (Father of the last) was much discontented with his Father's will, who, knowing he was in debt and a spendthrift, had strictly tied up the property: he tried to set aside the will by Act of Parliament, and had a Bill brought into the H. of Lords for the purpose. Selwyn said, 'Our old friend Foley has worked a miracle, for he has converted the Jews from the Old to the New Testament.' When Charles Fox upon the repeated protestations of the Prince of Wales, denied in the H. of C. that He had ever been married to Mrs. Fitzherbert, somebody said 'could Charles really have been authorised by the Prince to say what he did?' 'O yes,' said George Selwyn, 'no doubt he was, and I think I can tell you the very words in which the authority was given. He said, "Villain, be sure thou prove my Love a whore."'

After the death of George 2nd somebody asked if the Princess Emily, whose virtue was not thought immaculate, was to have Guards. G.S. said 'One every now and then.'

June 15 1839—The Duke of Wn. was mainly instrumental to Conroy's removal. He did not move in it at first, but Conroy of his own accord resolved to resign, because he found all the Duchess's family (the Cobourgs etc. who are here) so strongly opposed to him that he saw he could obtain no support and countenance in any quarter. Then the Dss. of Kent sent for the Duke, and he did all he could to nail the matter. After it was settled Conroy repented and wanted to stay, and then the Duke was sent for again. He spoke very strongly and at last it was all settled, but none of the Ministers knew anything of it at the time.

June 24th, Ludlow, Monday—Left London on Friday last by railroad, went to Wolverhampton (the vilest-looking town I ever saw), and in my carriage from thence to this place, where I only arrived at a quarter-past nine. This journey takes (losing no time) about eleven and a half hours— one hundred and fifty miles—of which thirty-four by land. The road from Bridgenorth to Ludlow is very striking and commands exceedingly fine views.

The day before I left town I saw Tavistock, who told me divers things. First about the vexation of Ministers at their colleague Howick's speech on the Ballot, who had contrived, after they had swallowed all the dirt of making it an open question, to do away with the merit in the eyes of the Radicals and at the same time excite the contemptuous sneer of the Tories. He said that it was of a piece with Howick's whole conduct, whose temper was so intolerable that there was no going on with him; the spirit of contradiction eternally moves him, and especially in the Cabinet, where he makes a point of contesting almost every opinion that is suggested by anybody else. It is impossible to form an idea of the difficulty which he causes to John and what he has to endure on his account; and all this is the more provoking because Howick is the only man who assists him in the way of hard work and in mastering the details of measures, such for instance as thoroughly sifting Acts of Parliament, in all of which he is as laborious, accurate and punctual as Ellenborough on the other side. I asked him what could induce John to consent to making Ballot an open question, and he replied, that nothing else could have prevented the dissolution of the Government, and that *three* of the Ministers—(he did not say which) —threatened to resign instanter if this concession was not made. Here then (as I said to him) was another example of the evils of that cursed catastrophe which broke up the embryo Government of Peel and brought them back again: unable to go on independently and as they desire to do, they are obliged to truckle, and are squeezed into compliances they abhor, and all this degradation they think themselves bound to submit to because the principle on which their Government stands, and which predominates over all others, is that of supporting the Queen. No Tory Government ever ventured to dissociate its support of the Crown from its measures and principles as a party, in the way these people do. Macaulay made his first reappearance in the Ballot debate in a speech of unequal merit, but Peel and Graham complimented him on his return amongst them.

The continuation of the violent and libellous articles in the 'Morning Post' about Lady Flora Hastings, and the unappeased wrath of Hastings, again stirred the question of explanations and apologies; and now Brougham mixed himself up in it as the Adviser of Hastings with whom he has struck up a mighty friendship, and he has been wonderfully zealous and active in the business. Lady Hastings, it seems, has never got over the letter which Melbourne wrote to her, and her Son is indignant both at that letter and at the unredressed wrong to his sister. However Brougham thought he would be satisfied if Melbourne would make some apology to Lady Hastings, and to affect this he began to work. After conferring with Duncannon about it He went to the Duke, and the Duke agreed with him that M. might and ought to do this, and he undertook to speak to him about it. Accordingly M. went to Apsley House by appointment where they talked it over, but M. convinced the Duke that it would be better not to write an apology or explanation to Lady H., though what his arguments were I do not know. So the matter stands, and in the meantime they are in a great fright lest Lady Flora should die; because She is very ill, and if She should die the public will certainly hold an inquest on her body and bring in a verdict of wilful murder against Buckingham Palace. As if one scandal of this sort was not enough there has been another, not so serious but unbecoming and disreputable, concerning the Duchess of Montrose and Lady Sarah Ingestre, who were said to have hissed the Queen from Erroll's stand at Ascot as H.M. drove up the course. This story was rife in London, and the Duchess, when She found it was so, insisted upon vindicating herself; and besides appealing to Lady Lichfield who was in the stand, went to Buckingham House and sent for Uxbridge to complain, and through him to ask for an audience of the Queen. The Q. declined seeing her, and the Duke of M. applied (through Melbourne) for one for himself; but this affair has ended by a gracious reception of the Ladies at the drawing-room, and an assurance from Melbourne that the Q. never had believed a word of the story, and he hoped therefore that the Duke of M. would not press for an audience. The fact however, in spite of the indignant denial of the Ladies, is true. These two foolish vulgar women (for such they are) at a moment of great excitement (for it was shortly after the grand scompiglio), did by some not decorous or feminine noises testify their dislike or contempt, not probably of the Queen particularly but of the general contents of the procession, and this was so openly even ostentatiously done that it could not escape the notice of the other women in the stand, more than one of whom —and one (the Dss. of Beaufort) a Tory—told me. It is a miserable matter, but it does harm. The Queen is to blame to listen to such tales, and to allow anybody to tell her them, whether true or false. It would be more dignified to treat such tittle-tattle with contempt, and discourage its being told to her at all.

I am greatly delighted with this country, which is of surpassing beauty, and the old Castle of Ludlow, a noble ruin, and in 'ruinous perfection.' On Saturday I explored the Castle and walked to Oakley Park, Robert Clive's, who is also the owner of the Castle, which he bought of the Crown for £1500. The gardens at Oakley Park are very pretty and admirably laid out and kept, and the Park is full of fine Oaks. Yesterday I walked and rode over the hills above Ludlow, commanding a panoramic prospect of the Country round, and anything more grand and picturesque I never beheld. But above all, the hills and woods of Downton Castle, with the mountains of Radnorshire in the distance, present a scene of matchless beauty well worth coming from London to see.

Delbury, Wednesday 26th—Rode to Downton Castle on Monday, a gimcrack castle, and bad house, built by Payne Knight, an Epicurean Philosopher, who after building the Castle went and lived in a lodge or cottage in the Park: there he died, not without suspicion of having put an end to himself, which would have been fully conformable with his notions. He was a sensualist in all ways and devoid of religion, but a great and self-educated scholar. His property is now in Chancery, because he chose to make his own will. The prospect from the windows is beautiful, and the walk through the wood, overhanging the river Teme, surpasses anything I have ever seen of the kind. It is as wild as the walk over the hill at Chatsworth, and much more beautiful, because the distant prospect resembles the chearful hills of Sussex instead of the brown and sombre Derbyshire muirs. Then the path now creeps along the margin, and now rises above the clear and murmuring stream, and immediately opposite is another hill as lofty and wild, and both are covered with the finest trees—Oaks, Ash, and chestnut—which push out their gnarled roots in a thousand fantastic shapes, and grow out of base masses of rock in the most luxuriant and picturesque manner. Yesterday I came here, a tolerable place with no pretension, but very well kept, not without handsome trees, and surrounded by a very pretty country.

Malvern, June 28th—Returned to Ludford yesterday; came here to-day: stopped at Hampton Court and saw the new house, which promises to be very fine, built by Lord Sudely (Mr. Hanbury Tracy); the road from Ledbury to Malvern wonderfully fine, and nothing grander than the view of Eastnor Castle.

Troy House, July 3rd—Staid at Malvern two days, clambering to the top of the hills which overhang the place (for town it is not), from which the views are very fine over a rich but generally flat country; the prospect is grand from its great extent. There is a curious and interesting Church there, formerly of some Priory, with a handsome gateway. I came through Eastnor Park in the way to Ledbury, exceedingly fine, and the Castle something like Belvoir apparently, but I was not permitted to approach it. Nothing particular in the road till Ross, a very pretty town, where I first met the Wye, but, alas, in its muddiest state: this was the abode of 'The Man of Ross.' Very pretty road from Ross to Monmouth, through which latter place I walked, and passed by a very old house, which (as I afterwards heard) is said to have been the abode of Geoffrey of Monmouth, and they show his study. Troy, a plain, good-looking house, imperfectly kept and poorly furnished, as a house is likely to be whose owners never inhabit it. It was built by the Duke of Beaufort in 1689, who came to sulk here on the expulsion of the last of the Stuarts, having a deeply rooted sentiment of hereditary loyalty. *Multa fecerunt* and *multa tulerunt*, certainly, for that unhappy race. Here they show a chair 'in which *a plot* was contrived against Charles I—that is, in which the President of the Conspirators is said to have sat.' The story was obscure, but I did not think it advisable to press the narrator for explanations. Likewise a cradle, which tradition assigns to Henry V (Harry of Monmouth), which is evidently old enough and was splendid enough in a rude style to justify any such tradition; the only unfortunate thing is, that there is a rival cradle somewhere else with the same claim. Mr. Wyatt, the Duke's Agent, received me with great civility and hospitality, having been enjoined by the Duke to make me his guest and himself my Cicerone. Accordingly we set forth on Monday morning and went to Usk Castle, a ruin of which not much is left besides a picturesque round tower; neither the Castle nor the Country very remarkable, but we brought home a crimped salmon, for which Usk is famous— and where the crimping is said to be a secret unattainable even to the vendors of Wye and Severn Salmon,—which was, without exception, the most dainty fish I ever ate. From Usk we returned to Raglan Castle, a most noble and beautiful ruin and in a state of 'ruinous perfection.' There has often been a notion of restoring it, and an estimate was made of the probable expense, which was calculated at £30,000; but the idea and the estimate are equally preposterous: it would be reconstructing a very unmanageable house and destroying the finest ruin in England, and the cost would infallibly be three times £30,000. As there had been a question of its restoration, I expected to find greater and more perfect remains, but, though some of the apartments may be made out, it is a vast wreck. The strange thing is that the second Marquis of Worcester, when his possessions were restored to him, and when the damage done to the Castle might easily have been repaired, should not have done it, nor any of his immediate descendants. Great pains are now taken to develop the beauties of this majestick fabrick and to arrest the further progress of decay. Yesterday I rode to Goodrich Castle, stopping to see some remarkable views of the Wye, particularly one called Simmons Rock, which is very beautiful (and must be much more when the river is clear and transparent); and a curious rock called the Buckstone, which was probably a Druidical place of worship, but of which nothing is positively known, though conjecture is busy. Goodrich Castle, which was partly battered down by the Cromwellians like Raglan, is more ancient, and was much stronger than the latter; but, though not so beautiful and splendid, it is an equally curious and interesting ruin, with many of its parts still more perfect than anything at Raglan. I was exceedingly delighted with Goodrich, and there was a female Custos, zealous and intelligent, and whose husband, She told us, was continually occupied in clearing away rubbish and exposing the remains of the old Castle. We then went to Goodrich Court, a strange kind of bastard Castle built by Blore, and which the possessor, Sir Samuel Meyrick, has devoted to the exhibition of his collection of armour. There are only a few acres of ground belonging to him, on which he has built this house, but it is admirably situated, overhanging the Wye and facing the Castle, of which it commands a charming view. After being hurried through the Armoury, which was all we were invited to inspect, we embarked in a boat we had sent up, and returned to Monmouth down the Wye through some beautiful scenery, but which it was too cold to enjoy.

July 3rd (4th), Clifton—Came here last night, the wind having changed to S.W., and summer having come with it. Left Troy in the morning and went to Tintern Abbey: most glorious, which I could not describe if I would, but which produced on me an impression similar in kind and equal in amount to that which I felt at the sight of St. Peter's. No description nor any representation of it can do justice, or anything like justice, to this majestic and beautiful ruin, such is its wonderful perfection viewed in every direction, from every spot, and in the minutest detail. That the remains should be so extensive and so uninjured is marvellous, for there can be no doubt that this Abbey might be restored to its former grandeur. Much has been done by Mr. Wyatt, the Duke's Agent, both to preserve the Abbey and to develope its beauties by cutting away the trees and ivy, and clearing away the accumulation of earth; by the latter means several tombs and many detached fragments of beautiful design and workmanship have been found, and I did my best to encourage him to pursue his researches.

Casting many lingering looks behind, I left Tintern and went to Windcliffe, from the summit of which there is a very fine view; but the Wye, instead of being an embellishment, is an eyesore in the midst of such scenery: it looks like a long, slimy snake dragging its foul length through the hills and woods which environ its muddy stream. We dined in a moss-cottage at the foot of Windcliffe, and then proceeded to Chepstow, a very curious and striking ruin, and which I should have seen with much greater interest and admiration if Tintern had not so occupied my thoughts and filled my mind that I had not eyes to do justice to Chepstow. I went all over the ruins, however, and examined them very accurately; for it is one of the great merits of these different Castles, Raglan, Goodrich, and Chepstow, that they are wholly dissimilar, and each is therefore a fresh object of curiosity. Crossed the Old Passage, as it is called, in a ferry, and came on to Clifton.

Bath (evening)—After taking a cursory view of Clifton from the Roman Camp, and part of Bristol, came to Bath, where I have not been these thirty years and more. Walked about the town, and greatly struck with its handsomeness; thought of all the vicissitudes of custom and fashion which it has seen and undergone, and of the various characters, great and small, who have figured here. Here the great Lord Chatham used to repair devoured by gout, resentment, and disappointment, and leave the Government to its fate, while his Colleagues waited his pleasure submissively or caballed against his power, according as circumstances obliged them to do the first or enabled them to do the second. Here my Uncle, Harry Greville, the handsomest man of his day, used to dance minuets while all the company got on chairs and benches to look at him, and a few years since he died in poverty at the Mauritius, where he had gone to end his days, after many unfortunate speculations, upon a place obtained from the compassion of Lord Bathurst. *Sic transit gloria mundi,* and thus its frivolities flourish for their brief hour, and then decay and are forgotten. An old woman showed me the pump-room and the baths, all unchanged except in the habits and characters of their frequenters; and my mind's eye peopled them with Tabitha Bramble, Win Jenkins, and Lismahago, and with all the inimitable family of Anstey's creation, the Ringbones, Cormorants, and Bumfidgets—Tabby and Roger.

Salisbury, July 5th—Saw the Abbey Church at Bath this morning, which is handsome enough, but not very remarkable, unless for the vast crowd of its tombstones in every part; it has been completely repaired by the corporation at a great expense. Went to Stonehenge of which no description is necessary; thence to Wilton; very fine place; hurried through the gallery of marbles, but looked longer at the pictures, which I understand and taste better; saw the gardens and the stud, and then came here; went directly to the Cathedral, with which I was exceedingly delighted, having seen nothing like it for extent, lightness, and elegance. There is one modern tomb by Chantrey which is very fine, that of Lord Malmesbury, erected by his sister; but, however skilfully executed or admirably designed, I do not like such monuments so well, nor think them so appropriate to our Cathedrals, as the rude effigies of Knights and Warriors in complete armour, with their feet on couchant hounds, or those stately though sometimes gaudy and fantastic monuments, in which, among crowds of emblematical devices and armorial bearings, the Husband and the wife lie side by side in the richest costume of the day, while their children are kneeling around them; these, with the venerable figures of Abbots and Bishops, however rudely sculptured, give me greater pleasure to look upon than the choicest productions of Roubillac, Nollekens, or Chantrey, which, however fine they may be, seem to have no business there, and to intrude irreverently among the mighty dead of olden time. This Cathedral is in perfect repair within and without; the colour of the stone is singularly beautiful, and it is not blocked up with buildings, Bishop Barrington having caused all that were adjacent to be removed. The Chapter House and Cloisters are exceedingly fine, but the effect is spoilt in the former by great bars of iron which radiate in all directions from a ring attached to the supporting pillar, and which have been put there (probably without any necessity) to relieve it of a portion of the superincumbent weight. It is remarkable that wherever I have gone in my travels, I have found the same complaints of the mischievous propensities of that silly, vulgar, vicious animal, called the public. Amongst the beauties of nature or of art, rocks, caves, or mountains, in ruined Castles and Abbeys, or ancient but still flourishing Cathedrals, the same invariable love of pilfering and mutilating is to be found: some knock off a nose or a finger, other deface a frieze or a mullion from sheer love of havoc; others chip off some unmeaning fragment as a relique or object of curiosity; but the most general taste seems to be that of carving names or initials, and some of the ancient figures are completely tattooed with these barbarous engravings: this propensity I believe to be peculiar to our nation, and not to be found in any part of the Continent, where, indeed, it would probably not be permitted, and where detection and punishment would speedily overtake the offender. It is quite disgusting to see the venerable form of a Knight Templar or a mitred Abbot scarred all over with the base patronymics of Jones and Tomkins, or with a whole alphabet of their initials.

July 7th—Came to town yesterday from Basingstoke by railroad; found that Lady Flora Hastings was dead. Lady Flora said to have died of dropsy in the womb, which also accounts for her appearance of pregnancy. She suffered dreadfully in mind and body, the latter from the exertions She was compelled to make in going about, and the former from being such an object of attention and curiosity, and still more because every sort of excitement was kept up in and around her by the faction who made an instrument of her. The libels in the 'Morning Post,' so far from being stopped, have only been more venomous since her death, and this soi-disant conservative paper daily writes against the Queen with the most revolting virulence and indecency. There is no doubt that an effect very prejudicial to H.M. has been produced, and the public, the women particularly, have taken up the Cause of Lady Flora with a vehemence which is not the less active because it is so senseless. It is just the same sort of feeling which prevailed in the time of Queen Caroline, originating partly in a love of meddling with high matters, and partly from virtuous resentment (virtue that costs nothing and is easily displayed) at what is believed to be the perpetration of a wrong. The world, foolish, meddling, and ignorant, always like to have an object to run up or run down, and here they have both.

July 14th—Nothing new; proceedings in Parliament very languid. The Morning Post going on blowing the coals about Lady Flora Hastings usque ad nauseam, but which of course takes with its readers and is profitable. Scandal and malignity always go down; it is the food the public love to batten on. The Duke of Beaufort was to have asked Melbourne if Government would not prosecute these libels, and this was to have given the D. of Wn. an opportunity of defending the Ladies; but both the Duke and Melbourne objected so the project fell to the ground. Lady Breadalbane having resigned the Bedchamber the Queen has appointed Lady Sandwich very dexterously, for She gets one of the favored Paget race and the wife of a Tory Peer, thereby putting an end to the exclusively Whig composition of the Household. This is a concession with regard to *the principle*.

July 19th—There have been angry debates in the Lords about the Birmingham riots, chiefly remarkable for the excitement (so unlike his usual manner) exhibited by the Duke of Wellington, who assailed the Government with a fierceness which betrayed him into much exaggeration and some injustice. Tavistock, who, although a partisan, is a fair one, and who has a great esteem and respect for the Duke, told me that he had seen and heard him with great pain, and that his whole tone was alarmingly indicative of a decay of mental power. This is not the first time that such a suspicion has been excited. George Villiers told me, soon after he came over, how much struck he had been with the change he observed in him, and from whatever cause, he is become in speaking much more indistinct and embarrassed, continually repeating and not always intelligible, but his speeches when reported, present much the same appearance, and the sense and soundness (when the reporters have lopped off the redundancies and trimmed them according to their fashion) seemed to be unimpaired. It is, however, a serious and melancholy thing to contemplate the possibly approaching decay of that great mind, and I find he always contemplates it himself, his mother's mind having failed some years before her death. It will be sad, if after exploits as brilliant as Marlborough's, and a career far more important, useful, and honorable, he should be destined for an end like Marlborough's, and it is devoutly to be hoped that his eyes may be closed in death before 'streams of dotage' shall begin to flow from them. The Tories, with whom nothing goes down but violence, were delighted with his angry vein, and see proofs of vigour in what his opponents consider as evidence of decay; his bodily health is wonderfully good, which is perhaps rather alarming than reassuring as to the safety of his mind.

July 22nd—I met the Duke yesterday at dinner and had much talk with him. He is very desponding about the state of the country and the condition in which the Government have placed it; complains of its defenceless situation from their carrying on a war (Canada) with a peace establishment; consequently that the few Troops we have are harassed to death with duty, and in case of a serious outbreak that there is no disposable force to quell it; that the Government are ruled by factions, political and religious. On Saturday they had been beat on a question relating to the Poor Laws of great importance; and He said that they must be supported in this, and extricated from the difficulty. I was glad to meet him and see (for it is some time since I have talked to him) whether there was any perceptible change in his manner of any symptom indicative of decay. Without there being anything tangible or very remarkable, I received the impression that there was not exactly the same vigour of mind which I have been used to admire in him, and what he said did not appear to me indicative of the strong sense and acuteness which characterise him. If He has no attack, I dare say he will be able to continue to act his part with efficacy for a long time to come. I asked him in what manner Government would prosecute the inquiry they had promised into the conduct of the Birmingham Magistrates. He said what they ought to do was to order the Attorney-General to prosecute them for a corrupt neglect of their duty, a thing they would as soon put their hands in the fire as do. Such is their position, so dependent upon bad men, that they are compelled to treat with the utmost tenderness all the Enemies of the Constitution. There can be no doubt that the appointments to the Magistracy have been fraught with danger, and made on a very monstrous principle. When J. R. resolved and avowed his resolution to neutralise the provision of the Act which gave the appointment of Magistrates to the Crown instead of to the Town Council (as they had proposed) by taking the recommendations of the Council, he incurred the deepest responsibility that any Minister ever did, for he took on himself to adopt a course practically inconsistent with the law, for the express purpose of placing political power in particular hands, to which the law intended it should not be confided; and on him, therefore, rested all the responsibility of such power being wisely and safely exercised by the hands to which he determined to entrust it; and when he appoints such a man as Muntz, ex-Chartist and ex-Delegate, what must be the impression produced on all denominations of men as to his bias, and of what use is it to make professions, and deliver speeches condemnatory of the principles and conduct of Chartists and associators, if his acts and appointments are not in conformity with those professions? Mr. Muntz, He says, has abandoned

Chartism, and is no longer the man he was: but who knows that? For one man who knows what Muntz is, a hundred know what he was, and in the insertion of his name in the list the bulk of the world will and can only see, if not approbation of, at least indifference to the doctrines such men have professed, and the conduct they have exhibited to the world. It is the frightful anomaly of having a Government divesting itself of all conservative character, which constitutes the danger of our day. As the 'Times,' in one of its spirited articles, says (this very morning) 'that care not to see the Monarchy broken into pieces so that they may hurl its fragments at the heads of their opponents.'

July 25th—Lord Clarendon made his first appearance in the H. of Lords the night before last in reply to Londonderry on Spanish affairs, with great success and excellent effect, and has completely landed himself as a Parliamentary Speaker, in which, as He is certain to improve with time and practice, he will eventually acquire considerable eminence; and nothing can prevent his arriving at the highest posts. He is already marked out by the public voice for the Foreign Office, for which he is peculiarly well fitted, and there is no reason why he should not look forward to being Prime Minister in some future combination of parties, a post which he would fill better than any of the Statesmen who now play the principal parts in the political drama (*3 lines of MS. here cut out.*) The Government have at last taken fright, and have proposed Troops and Police to afford the country some sort of security during the recess and the winter. They have sent down Maule to Birmingham to investigate the evidence adducible against the Magistrates, but I don't expect they will proceed to any extremities against them. It is too probable that 'silebitur toto judicio de maximis et notissimis injuriis,' for 'non potest in accusando socios verè defendere is, qui cum reo criminum societate conjunctus est.'

August 9th, Friday—Brougham brought on his motion on Tuesday,[1] in spite of various attempts to dissuade him; but he could not resist the temptation of making a speech, which he said He expected would be the best he had ever delivered. He spoke for three hours in opening, and a hour and a quarter in reply, and a great performance by all accounts it was. The Duke of Wellington said it was the finest speech he had ever heard in Parliament. Normanby was miserably feeble in reply, and exhibited, by common consent, a sad failure, both on this occasion and on that of the Canada Bill. He is quite unequal to the office which has been thrust upon him, and he

---

[1] Lord Brougham moved on the 6th August five resolutions censuring the Irish policy of the Government: they were carried in the House of Lords by 86 votes to 52.

can't speak upon great subjects, having no oratorical art or power of dealing skilfully and forcibly with a question. It was a very damaging night to the Government as far as reputation is concerned, but in no other way, for they are perfectly callous, and the public entirely apathetic. Melbourne was very smart in reply to Brougham, but did not attempt to deal with the question. The case, after all, is not a very strong one, and, though Normanby was much to blame in releasing prisoners and commuting sentences in the manner and to the extent he did, the principle on which he acted was sound, and it has proved beneficial. Had he known how, and been equal to the task, He might have made a fine defence by taking a high instead of a deprecatory line, and by a confident appeal to results; but it required more of an Orator and a Statesman than He is to handle his case with sufficient effect, and to stand up against such a master of his art as Brougham, backed by a favourable audience. This curious and versatile creature is in the highest spirits, and finds in the admiration which his eloquence, and the delight which his mischievousness excite on the Tory benches and in Tory society, a compensation for old mortifications and disappointments. After acting Jupiter one day in the H. of Lords, He is ready to act Scapin anywhere else the next; and the day after this great display he went to dine at Greenwich with the Duchess of Cambridge and a great party, where He danced with Lady Jersey, while Lyndhurst capered also with the Dowager Lady Cowper. After dinner they drank, among other toasts, Lady Jersey's health, and when She said She could not return thanks, Brougham undertook to do it for her, speaking in her person. He said, that 'She was very sorry to return thanks in such a dress, but unfortunately She had quarrelled in the morning with her maid, who was a very cross, crabbed person, and consequently had not been able to put on the attire She would have wished, and in the difficulty She had had recourse to her old friend Lord Brougham, who had kindly lent her his best wig and the coat which he wore upon state occasions.' After more nonsense of this kind, that 'She was very sorry She could not say more, but that in the peculiar situation She then was in, She could not venture to remain any longer on her legs.'

August 10th—Went to Norwood yesterday to see Dr. Kay's Poor Law School, supposed to be very well managed, and very successful. As I looked at the class to whom a lesson was then being read, all urchins from eight to eleven or twelve years old, I thought I had never seen a congregation of more uncompromising and ungainly heads, and accordingly they are the worst and lowest specimens of humanity; starved, ill-used children of poor and vicious parents, generally arriving at the school weak and squalid, with a tendency to every vice, and without having received any moral or intellectual cultivation whatever; but the system, under able and zealous teachers, acts with rapid and beneficial effect on these rude materials, and soon elicits manifestations of intelligence, and improves and developes the moral faculties. When one sees what is done by such small means, it is impossible not to reflect with shame and sorrow upon the little or rather the nothingness, that is accomplished when the material is of the best description, and the means are unlimited,—upon the total absence of any system throughout places of education, either public or private, and consequently at the imperfect and defective education which is given to the highest and richest class of society, who are brought up thus stupidly at an enormous expense, acquiring little knowledge, and what they do acquire, so loosely and incompletely as to be of the smallest possible use. When one sees what is done here, it makes one think what ought to be done elsewhere, and then contrast the possible with the actual state of the case.

1841

May 2nd—The approach of the Newmarket meetings usually absorbs my thoughts, oppresses me with its complicated interests, and destroys all my journalising energies. After a month's interval, I take up my pen to note down the events that have occurred in it. I went to Newmarket on Saturday before the Craven Meeting, and on Sunday morning received a letter informing me of the sudden death of my sister-in-law which obliged me to return to town. This grievous affliction, so heavy and irreparable to those whom it immediately concerns, matters but little to the mass of society, who for the most part good-naturedly sympathised with the sufferers; but the object, so precious to the narrow circle of her own family, was too obscure and unimportant to the world at large to be entitled to anything more than a passing expression of regret. (2 *sheets of MS. here excised.*) I went down to the funeral, and was unutterably disgusted with the ceremony, with the bustling business of the Undertaker, mixing so irreverently with the profound grief of the Brothers and other relations who attended, the decking us out in the paraphernalia of woe, and then dragging us in mourning coaches through crowds of curious people, by a circuitous route, that as much of us as possible might be exhibited to vulgar curiosity. These are things monstrous in themselves, but to which all-reconciling custom makes us submit.

This is not the only misfortune which has fallen upon individual heads; but of all occurrences that which has excited the greatest interest has been the loss (as it must now be concluded) of the 'President' Steamer, with among others, the D. of Richmond's young Son on board. Day after day people have watched and enquired with the most intense interest for the arrival or for news of this vessel, and are only now slowly and reluctantly abandoning all hope, while the wretched Parents have been for weeks past agitated with all the alternations of hope and despair, and suffering a protracted torture worse than any certainty. So much for private woes.

1842

Broadlands, September 17th—Came here on the 14th; Rogers and Baron Rolfe. Palmerston complains that our Foreign affairs are all mismanaged from first to last, and that *we give up everything*; universal concession the rule of action, and that there can be no difficulty in settling questions if we yield all that is in dispute. He is particularly dissatisfied with the Boundary Treaty, in which he says we have been overreached by the Americans; that Lord Ashburton was a very unfit man to send there, having an American bias, besides a want of firmness in his character. Thinks the territorial concessions we have made very objectionable and quite unnecessary, and that we had already *proved* our right to the disputed land; that since the King of Holland's award, evidence (which was then wanting) has been adduced, which clearly establishes our rights. It is evident that he means to fall foul of this arrangement upon the first suitable occasion. He also complains of the treaty with the K. of Hanover, and says we have allowed him to levy duties twice as high as he has any right to. She talked to me for a long time about the old disputes on the Syrian question, and lauded his wonderful equanimity and good humour during those stormy and difficult times. She said Lord Holland's death was in great measure attributable to the vexation and excitement he underwent, and the recollection of the opposition Palmerston met with still rankles deeply in her mind. She declares that he is very happy out of office, and in no want of occupation; on the contrary, has his hands full of business, private and public. There is a very beautiful specimen of Old Saxon architecture in the church at Romsey, in very good preservation and of great antiquity.

September 24th—From Broadlands I went to Cranford through the New Forest, which I never saw before. There I staid two nights, having had some curiosity to see a place the creation of which has caused violent family quarrels, which I have been engaged in making up. On Monday I came to London, which contains a good sprinkling of people for this time of year, who congregate generally at Lady Holland's.

The 'Morning Chronicle' opened a fire upon the American Treaty in the beginning of last week, which has been well sustained in a succession of articles of very unequal merit. To these the 'Times' has responded, and in my opinion successfully. It was amusing to me to read in the columns of the 'Chronicle' all that I had been hearing Palmerston say *totidem verbis*; his articles were merely a repetition of his talk, and that as exactly as if the latter had been taken down in shorthand. As far as I can judge, he will, however, fail to carry public opinion with him; he will not be entirely supported by the writers on his own side, nor by his political adherents. Sir James Kemp, an excellent authority, both civil and military, approves of the Treaty and attaches no importance to the objections that are urged against it. The 'Examiner' writes in its favor. The Ministers think they stand on very strong grounds, and the fact is that Palmerston's determination to find fault with everything that is done in the Foreign Office, and the indiscriminate abuse which he heaps upon every part of our foreign policy, deprives his opinion of the weight which it would be entitled to, if he was only tolerably impartial. I never saw so much political bitterness as that which rankles in the hearts of himself and his wife. He abuses the acts of the Government, but he always does so with an air of gaiety and good humour, and, to do him justice, he never expresses himself with any coarseness or asperity, never so as to make social intercourse impossible, or even disagreeable, between him and his opponents, but under this gay and gallant exterior there burns a fierce hostility, and a resolution to attack them upon every point, and a more unscrupulous assailant never took the field. She talks a great deal more than he does, and it is easy to see, through her graceful, easy manner and habitual urbanity, how impatient they are of exclusion from office, and how intolerant of any dissent from or opposition to his policy and opinions. They have never forgiven Lord Holland and Clarendon for having thwarted him on the Syrian question. She alluded (at Broadlands) to the supposed desire of the latter to supplant him at the Foreign Office, which she said she did not believe, though She evidently does, and She said that Clarendon had done himself an injury which he would never get over. She talked of their opposition as if they had been the only dissentients in the Cabinet, and then, forgetting this, she discussed the conduct of others, particularly of Melbourne and John Russell, both of whom she described as alarmists, and the former as all along disinclined to the bold course which Palmerston was pursuing.

Besides the American Treaty, Palmerston is venting his indignation on the Stade Treaty with Hanover, and his conduct with reference to that matter is very illustrative of the manner in which he carries on the war. He told me at Broadlands that the K. of H. had not a shadow of right to the duties which he levied, though he had to much smaller duties, the amount of which was regulated by an Old treaty with Denmark, and that, instead of formally conceding to him what he had no right to require, we ought to resist his claim, and compel him by force (if remonstrance failed) to abandon it. The case is this. Hanover has no right to the tolls she takes, but She has levied them for above 100 years, and has thus acquired a prescriptive or *quasi* right. Complaints were formally made, but George III refused to give them up, so did George IV. Wm. IV was the first King who was disposed to make any sacrifice. He died before anything was settled, and K. Ernest succeeded. Fresh discussions arose, and the Whig Government were willing to purchase of him the abandonment or modification of his claims, and Palmerston made a formal proposal to Ompteda to that effect. But when He found he was going out of office, a very little while before their resignation, he put forth a protest against the K. of Hanover's claims, and this he did (as I am told and as seems highly probable) for the express purpose of embarrassing the question, and rendering its settlement more difficult to his successor, besides providing himself with materials for attacking such an arrangement as he foresaw would probably be made, and which he would have made had he remained in office.

The other topic on which they are most eloquent and indignant is Ellenborough's order to retreat from Cabul, of the real truth of which very little is at present known. Fitzgerald, however, told me the other day, He did think Ellenborough had not acted *discreetly* in the outset of his administration. He avers, however, distinctly, that it was Auckland's intention to withdraw the Troops after the massacre at Cabul, which was what Peel alluded to in his speech. Auckland apparently does not admit this, and both parties are anxious to enlist his opinions and intentions on their side.

We had a Council at Windsor yesterday, where I met Peel for the first time since his return from Scotland. We now go to the Council and return to town after it, instead of being invited to remain there, which is a very great improvement. This custom has gradually superseded the other without the appearance of anything offensive or uncivil, and is no doubt much more agreeable to the Queen, who has no mind to have more of the society of her present Ministers than She can help. Peel described the Scotch tour as very nervous, inasmuch as they went through all the disturbed districts, but that loyalty and interest in seeing her triumphed over every other feeling and consideration, and all went off as well as possible. He seems not to be at ease with her from all I hear, nor is it likely he ever will.

Adolphus Fitzclarence told me nothing could be more agreeable and amiable than She was (and the Prince too) on board the yacht, conversing all the time with perfect ease and good humour, and on all subjects, taking great interest and very curious about everything in the ship, dining on deck in the midst of the Sailors, making them dance, talking to the boatswain, and, in short, doing everything that was popular and ingratiating. Her chief fault (in little things and in great) seems to be impatience; in Sea phrase, She always wants to *go ahead*; she can't bear contradiction nor to be thwarted. She was put out because she could not get quicker to the end of her voyage, and land so soon as she wished. She insisted on landing as soon as it was possible, and would not wait till the authorities were ready and the people assembled to receive her. An hour or two of delay would have satisfied everybody, and though it might be unreasonable to expect this (as Peel said it was) it would have been wise to have conceded it. Adolphus says there was very alarming excitement in the town for a little while, and much discontent among the crowds who had come from distant parts, and who paid large sums for seats and windows to see her go by.

October 4th—There has been a continual discussion of the Boundary Treaty, kept up by Palmerston's articles in the 'Morning Chronicle,' which have been well replied to in the 'Times,' 'Standard,' and still more the 'Spectator' and 'Examiner.' Palmerston has certainly not acted wisely as one of the Leaders of his party. He ought to have felt the public pulse, and ascertained how his own friends would be likely to view the question, before he plunged into such violent opposition to it. It is now evident that he will not carry the public nor even his own party with him. John Russell is satisfied; he thought at first that we had conceded too much, but on further examination he changed his opinion, and he now thinks the settlement on the whole a good one, and this will in all probability be the general opinion. Everybody was alive to the inconvenience of having this question left open, and there was an universal desire to settle our various differences with America upon such terms as would conduce to the restoration of good humour and good will.

October 5th—There was a very clever letter in the 'Morning Chronicle' yesterday from some Whig, attacking the paper for the line it has taken, which produced a furious defence and retort. This morning I have got a letter from the D. of Bedford informing me that his Brother John has gone back to his original opinion about the Treaty. First, he thought we had made too great concessions, then that we had not, and now he thinks again that we have. It is probable that Palmerston has been at him, and he thinks it better to sacrifice his own opinion than to have a difference with his colleague.

I have been at Woburn for a couple of days. The D. told me there that all the people he had conversed or communicated with agreed in rejoicing that the question was settled, and were not disposed to cavil at the terms. The Duke is well and wisely administering his estate and improving his magnificent place in every way. I never saw such an abode of luxury and enjoyment, one so full of resources for all tastes. The management of his estates is like the administration of a little Kingdom. He has 450 people in his employment on the Bedfordshire property alone, not counting domestic servants. His pensions amount to £2000 a year. There is order, economy, grandeur, comfort, and general content.

The Baroness Lehzen has left Windsor Castle, and is gone abroad for her health (as she says), to stay five or six months, but it is supposed never to return. This woman, who is much beloved by the women and much esteemed and liked by all who frequent the Court, who is very intelligent, and has been a faithful and devoted servant to the Queen from her birth, has for some time been supposed to be obnoxious to the Prince, and as he is now all-powerful her retirement was not unexpected. I do not know the reason of it, nor how it has been brought about; Melbourne told me long ago that the Prince would acquire unbounded influence.

Yesterday I met Lord Ponsonby and sat next to him at dinner at Palmerston's, for although I have always been so opposed to P., and he knows it, and no doubt dislikes me, I live with them as much as if we were the greatest friends. Lord P. is a most remarkable-looking man for his age, which is seventy-two or seventy-three. He exhibits no signs of old age, and is extremely agreeable. His account of Turkey was very different from my ideas about the state of the country, but I fancy all he says is *sujet à caution*. He describes the Sultan to be intelligent, liberal, and independent, that is, really master, and not in the hands of any party; the Turkish public men very able, the country improving in its internal condition, especially its agriculture, and its revenue flourishing—five millions a year regularly collected, not a farthing of debt, and the whole military and civil service of the State punctually paid.

October 12th—The controversy about the American Treaty is vigorously maintained. The letter in the 'Morning Chronicle' was written by John Mill, and now Charles Buller has taken the field (in the 'Globe'). John Russell says 'it is advantageous and honorable to America, but not disadvantageous to us.' But he thinks it has been clumsily managed and that we might have got better terms; that Aberdeen and Everett might have settled it here more favorably for us. This is mere conjecture and worth nothing. The truth is, he does not disapprove, but finds Palmerston has taken such a violent part that he must, out of deference to his colleague, find as much fault as he possibly can. The account of the revenue came out yesterday, and a very sorry account it is.

October 18th, Tuesday—On Wednesday last to the Grove; on Friday to Gorhambury to meet the Bishop of London, who came there in the course of his visitation; yesterday back to London. It is always refreshing, in the midst of the cold hearts and indifferent tempers one sees in the world, to behold such a spectacle of intimate union and warm affection as the Grove presents. A mother,[1] with a tribe of Brothers and sisters, and their respective husbands and wives, all knit together in the closest union and community of affections, feelings and interests—all, too, very intelligent people, lively, cheerful and striving to contribute to each other's social enjoyment as well as their material interests. I have always thought Clarendon the least selfish, most generous, and amiable man with whom I am acquainted. I suppose this strikes me the more forcibly from the contrast which it exhibits to my own family, and the enormous difference between their mode of living together and feeling towards each other and that of my relations.

Edward Villiers, who is just come from Germany, told me nothing could exceed the disgust excited all over that country by the publication of Lord Hertford's trial, and that there was an universal impression there that the state of society in England and the character of its aristocracy was to the last degree profligate and unprincipled. We are mighty proud of our fine qualities, and plume ourselves on our morality; but it must be owned that a German public, which can know nothing of English society but from the specimens it sees of Englishmen, or what it reads in the press of English doings, may well entertain a less exalted idea of our perfections. They read a few years ago the case of De Ros. They now read that of Lord Hertford, and they have seen the ostentatious infidelities of Wm. Russell, our Minister at Berlin, besides the esclandre of F. Molyneux at Frankfurt and the well known misconduct of Abercrombie in Germany and Italy. Add to this Melbourne's trial (Prime Minister of England) and we need not wonder

[1] Mrs. George Villiers; Lord Clarendon was her eldest son.

at the impressions which we think so unfair, and which are not in fact correct.

The Bishop of London was (and is still) going about his diocese, delivering a very elaborate Charge, which has excited a good deal of notice, and parts of which have been well enough quizzed in the 'Morning Chronicle.' To the surprise of many people, his charge (like those of the Bishops of Exeter and Oxford) contained some crumbs of compliment to the Puseyites, and an endeavour to prescribe some formal observances half-way in advance towards their opinions. There is an evident desire on the part of these dignitaries to conciliate the Tractarians, probably because they are aware of, and alarmed at, their remarkable superiority in everything which relates to ecclesiastical learning. It is curious, too, to see the 'Times,' which certainly exercises no small or limited influence, become decidedly Puseyite. Its Catholic tendencies are intermingled with its Poor Law crotchets, and both are of a highly democratic character. The present object of attack is the pew system, which certainly appears obnoxious to censure. I asked the Bishop of London what the law was with regard to pews, and he owned that the whole thing was an anomaly, in some respects doubtful, but in many regulated by ancient usage, or by local Acts of Parliament. His answer indicated a consciousness of weakness. The Bishop is an agreeable man in society, good-humoured, lively, a little brusque in his manner. He sang a duet with Lady Jane Grimston on Friday evening, when there was no company. Though he is intemperate and imperious, he has always been distinguished for great liberality and a munificent disposition, and from an anecdote I heard of him at the Grove, he must be of a generous mind, and capable of forgiving an enemy, and casting aside feelings of resentment and wounded pride. Wm. Capel, Brother of the late Lord Essex, a disreputable, good-for-nothing Parson, and rector of Watford, neglected his clerical duties, and incurred the displeasure of the Bishop, who insisted on Capel's appointing a Curate, which he refused to do, on which the Bishop (who became very angry) appointed one himself, and sent him down there. Capel resisted stoutly, and on one occasion the Rector and the Curate had a race for the reading-desk in Church. He refused to receive the Curate or to pay him, and forbad him at his peril to execute any clerical function. The end of it was a trial at the Hertford Assizes, when the Parson beat the Bishop, who in his angry haste had failed to comply with all the forms or conditions which the law requires. The trial cost the Bishop near a thousand pounds, and Capel was triumphant. I don't know what happened in the interim, but a few years after, and a year or two ago, they had become such good friends that the Bishop came down to preach a charity sermon at

Watford, when he was the guest of Wm. Capel, dining and sleeping at his house. Upon that occasion such was his want of common decency, that, having the Bishop for his guest, and under circumstances which demanded more than an ordinary respect and attention, he came down to breakfast in an old grey dressing-gown and red slippers, much to the surprise and something to the discomposure of his Diocesan. Nobody would believe Capel when he told them that the Bishop was going to be his guest. 'The Bishop of London!' said Clarendon to him, when he told him, 'how on earth did you contrive to get the Bishop of London to come to your house?' 'How,' said the other, 'why I gave him a d—d good licking and that made him civil. We are very good friends now.' The only pity is, that having the quality of generosity and forgiveness of wrongs—for successful resistance is the same as a wrong—those virtues did not find a more estimable subject for their exercise.

October 23rd—To the Grove on Thursday; came back yesterday to dine with Mr. Grenville; passed the whole morning of Saturday at the British Museum, where I had not been for many years, but where I propose to go henceforward very often. The number of readers is now on an average three hundred a day; in the time of Gray (as may be seen by his letters) it was not half a dozen. I had never dined with Mr. Grenville before, though he has more than once asked me, and I was glad to go there. He is a man whom I have always looked at with respect and pleasure. It is a goodly sight to see him thus placidly and slowly going down the hill of life, with all his faculties of mind and body, not unimpaired, but still fresh and strong. One would rejoice to procure a new lease for such a man. He may well look round him, as he sits in his unrivalled library and surrounded by his friends, serene and full of enjoyment, and say, like Mazarin, 'Et il faut quitter tout cela!' but no reflections or anticipations seem to overcast the mild sunshine of his existence. I certainly never saw so graceful and enviable an old age; and though he is eighty-six, and I am forty-eight, I would willingly change lives with him. I would much rather be approaching the end of life as he is approaching it, than live any number of years that I may yet chance to have in store as I am likely to live them. Mr. Grenville is rather deaf, and he complains of loss of memory, but he hears well enough for social purposes, and he is full of recollections of former times and remarkable people. He only laments his own infirmities on account of the trouble or inconvenience they may cause to others; not that he does not hear all that is said, but he pities those who are obliged to exert their voices to make him hear. No old man was ever less selfish and querulous. He told a story of Porson, which I will put in his own words:—'When I was a young man, which is now about seventy years ago, I used to live with Cracherode and —— and other literary men of that day, who were good enough to allow me to come among them, and listen to their conversation, which I used to take great delight in doing, and I remember one day going into the room at ——, and finding Cracherode and —— in a dispute about language, and whether a certain word had ever been used by any good authority. In the middle of the dispute, one of them said, "But why do we go on talking here, when that little fellow in the corner can tell us in a moment which of us is in the right?" The little fellow was Porson, who was on his knees poring over a book. They called him up, told him what they were disputing about, and asked if he knew of the word having been used, and by whom. He at once replied, "I only know of one instance, and that is in Fisher's funeral sermon on the death of Margaret of Richmond, the mother of Henry VII, and you will find it about the third or fourth page on the right-hand side"; and there accordingly they did find it.'

October 26th—Poor Irby died on Monday last at Newmarket, the place where he had passed all the pleasantest hours of his life. He was an honorable, inoffensive man, who never made an enemy, and with whom I have passed my *racing* life. That was a sort of man who devoted himself to the turf without any misgivings of shame and regret, and he was, accordingly, happy. He strolled through life, without ambition or vanity, was what he seemed, and did not aspire to be thought better or wiser than he was. He had friends to whom he was attached, one sister whom he loved, and few or no relations to annoy or trouble him. He was affluent in circumstances, respected in character, and contented in disposition; and such a man is to be envied, living or dying.

Yesterday morning I called on Mr. Grenville, and sat with him for an hour, while he told me many old stories of bygone times, and showed me some of his books, particularly his 'Julio Clovio,' which was what I went on purpose to see. He is a remarkable man, with his mind so fresh and firm, and teeming with recollections, a sort of link between the living and the dead, having been forward enough in his youth to mix with the most distinguished characters, literary and political, more than half a century ago, and still vigorous enough to play his part with those of the present time. He had often dined with Horace Walpole at his grandmother's in Grosvenor Square (before it was planted), and he describes him as effeminate in person, trifling in conversation, and much less amusing and piquant than might be expected from his letters. He talked much of Lord North, whose speaking he thinks would not be admired now. It was of a sing-song, monotonous character. His secretary —— used to sit behind him, and take notes of the debate, writing down every point that it was necessary for him to answer, with the name of the speaker from whom it proceeded. When he got up he held this paper in his hand, and spoke from it, sometimes blundering over the sheets in a way Mr. Grenville imitated, and which would certainly be thought very strange now, but he had great good humour and much drollery. He told me a story of Lord North and his Son Frank (afterwards Lord Guildford) of whom he was very fond, though he was always in scrapes and in want of money. One day, Frank seemed very much out of spirits, and his Father asked him what was the matter. With some hesitation, real or pretended, he at last said, 'Why, Father, the truth is, I have no money, and I am so distressed that I have been obliged to sell that little mare you gave me the other day.' To which Lord North replied, 'Oh, Frank, you should never have done that; you ought to have recollected the precept of Horace, "Equam memento rebus in arduis servare."' Mr. Grenville talked of the Elder Pitt, whom he did not admire, but had never heard him except as Lord Chatham. Rigby was a very agreeable speaker, and in style not unlike Tierney.

October 29th—Melbourne has had an attack of palsy, very slight, and he is recovering, but it is of course alarming. He is not himself aware of the nature of the seizure, and asks if it was lumbago. This shows how slight it was. Macaulay's book, which he calls 'Lays of Ancient Rome,' came out yesterday, and admirable his ballads are. They were composed in India and on the voyage home. He showed them to Dr. Arnold, who advised him to publish them, but probably while he was in office he had not time to think about them, and the publication is the result of his leisure. He has long been addicted to ballad-writing, for there is one in the American edition of his works, and there is a much longer one written when he was at Cambridge (or soon after), upon the League, and one of Henry IV's battles, which is very good indeed. He is a wonderful fellow altogether.

Canadian affairs and Bagot's proceedings have lately occupied the world for want of something better. The Whigs are pleased that he has so fully admitted and acted on the principle of Parliamentary controul, and carried out practically the theory of the Constitution which they gave the provinces, while the Tories are indignant that he should have been dictated to by men whom they consider disaffected to this country, and who were looked upon as quasi-Traitors till a very short time ago, and as they have no taste for the independence and supremacy of a Canadian Parliament, there is no triumph of a principle to console them for what they consider dangerous in practice. But both parties, and everybody without exception, blame the manner in which he has acted, which was indiscreet, undignified, and gives a poor idea of his qualifications for Government. He is certainly not a strong man, and he has succeeded one who undoubtedly was. Sydenham turns out to have been a man of first-rate capacity, with great ability, discrimination, judgement, firmness, and dexterity. His whole administration in Canada fully justified the choice which John Russell made of him, and the confidence he reposed in him. It is to the credit of John Russell that he discovered and appreciated the talents of a man who was underrated here; but occasion and circumstance draw out the latent resources of vigorous minds. He was always known to be a man of extraordinary industry, but nobody knew that he had such a knowledge of human nature and such a power of acquiring influence over others as he evinced when he went to Canada. Murdoch, who was his Secretary, and himself a very clever man, gave me a remarkable account of him. He was in the habit of talking over the most inveterate opponents of his Government, so much so, that at last it became a matter of joking, and the most obstinate of his enemies used to be told that if they set foot in Government House they would be mollified and enthralled whether they would or no, and so it almost always was. Though of a weak and slender frame, and his constitution wretched, he made journeys which would have appeared hard work to the most robust men. On one occasion he travelled, without stopping, from —— to ——, and the moment he got out of his carriage he called for his papers, and went at his business as if he had only returned from a drive. This is something very like greatness; these are the materials of which greatness is made—indefatigable industry, great penetration, powers of persuasion, confidence in himself, decision, boldness, firmness, and all these jumbled up with a finikin manner, and a dangling after an Old London harridan; but, as Taylor says so well, 'The world knows nothing of its greatest men,' and half mankind know nothing of their own capacity for greatness. The mistakes made by ourselves and by each other with respect to moral qualities are incessant and innumerable.

November 2nd—At Windsor yesterday for a Council; almost all the Cabinet went together in a special train. A Whig Engineer might have produced an instantaneous and complete change of Government. The Royal consent was given to the marriage of the Princess Augusta with the Prince of Mecklenburg. The Chancellor there, looking very ill and broken, but evidently wishing to be thought strong and capable. He not only affected to be very merry, but very active, and actually began a sort of dancing movement in the drawing-room, which reminded me of Queen Elizabeth and the Scotch Ambassador; seventy years of age, ten years of idleness, and a young wife will not do for the labour of the Great Seal. The Ministers are all come to hold Cabinets, and lay their heads together, with, God knows, plenty to occupy them. Lord Wharncliffe and Kay Shuttleworth, who are both come from the North, have given me an account of the state of the country and of the people which is perfectly appalling. There is an immense and continually increasing population, deep distress and privation, no adequate demand for labour, no demand for anything, no confidence, but an universal alarm, disquietude, and discontent. Nobody can sell anything. Somebody said, speaking of some part of Yorkshire, 'This is certainly the happiest country in the world, *for nobody wants anything.*' Kay says that nobody can conceive the state of demoralisation of the people, of the masses, and that the only thing which restrains them from acts of violence against property is a sort of instinctive consciousness that, bad as things are, their own existence depends upon the security of property *in the long run.* It is in these parts that the worst symptoms are apparent, but there are indications of the same kind more or less all over the country, and certainly I have never seen, in the course of my life, so serious a state of things as that which now stares us in the face; and this, after thirty years of uninterrupted peace, and the most ample scope afforded for the development of all our resources, when we have been altering, amending, and improving, wherever we could find anything to work upon, and being, according to our own ideas, not only the most free and powerful, but the most moral and the wisest people in the world. One remarkable feature in the present condition of affairs is that nobody can account for it, and nobody pretends to be able to point out any remedy; for those who clamour for the repeal of the Corn Laws, do not (at least those who know anything of the matter) really believe that repeal would supply a cure for our distempers. It is certainly a very dismal matter for reflection, and well worthy the consideration of the profoundest political philosophers, that the possession of such a Constitution, all our wealth, industry, ingenuity, peace, and that superiority in wisdom and virtue which we so confidently claim, are not sufficient to prevent the existence of a huge mountain of human misery, of one stratum of society in the most deplorable state, both moral and physical, to which mankind can be reduced, and that all our advantages do not secure us against the occurrence of evils and mischiefs so great as to threaten a mighty social and political convulsion.

November 7th—Follett moved on Friday in the Q. Bench and got a rule to show cause why the verdict which I obtained at Guildford should not be set aside, and either a non-suit entered or a new trial granted.[1] Upon

---

[1] The *Sunday Times* had libelled Greville over his racing.

this occasion he acted with the same unfairness which he did on the trial. It is extremely disagreeable to me personally because it hangs up the final determination of this question for a year at least, and if there should be a non-suit, I shall incur heavy expences, besides which my antagonists will gain a great triumph. If there should be a new trial ordered I shall be a loser, but will submit to the loss rather than have these revolting proceedings again brought forward. In any case my character has been vindicated and cannot be damaged by any legal result, as it is entirely on technical grounds that Follett has appealed to the Court. I was extremely surprised to witness his very unscrupulous mode of conducting the case of his client at Guildford, though I had witnessed something of the same kind in the previous trials at Guildhall; but I now find that he is notorious for acting in this way. His prodigious talents make him a most powerful advocate and he takes liberties and avails himself of his pre-eminence in a manner which no inferior person or with less authority would venture to do.

Brougham, in one of his famous speeches on the Queens' trial, laid down the duty of an advocate to his Client as paramount to any other consideration by which that duty might peradventure be crossed; and on this principle Follett usually acts to the fullest extent. I have often doubted whether I should have got out of my trial as I did, if instead of the acute Abinger I had had some dull Judge who would not have detected and exposed the fallacies and misrepresentations of Follett's speech. In his application the other day he said what was totally untrue, and set before the Court a case completely at variance with the true one, which few other men would have done because, as these applications are always *ex parte*, the Bench relies on the honor of the Advocate to state nothing but what is really true.

I have been engaged these last few days in devising the means of stifling the scandalous stories which have gone all over the world about P. George of Cambridge and Lady Augusta Somerset. The story is, that He got her with child, that the D. of Beaufort wished him to marry her, that He did not object, but that the Royal Marriage Act stood in the way and the Queen was indisposed to consent; and this story with many trifling variations has been in all the newspapers and been circulated with incredible success not only all over England but over the Continent also. The whole is false from beginning to end, except that He did flirt with her and She with him last year at Kew, where she was staying while her Father was abroad—flirtation such as is continually going on without any serious result between half the youths and girls in London. As soon as the parties became aware of the universal diffusion of the scandal, they thought it necessary to take some measures for suppressing it; and after a good deal of deliberation Adolphus

FitzClarence (on the part of P. George) and I (on that of the D. of Beaufort) went together to the 'Times' office and asked them to put a formal contradiction into their paper, which they immediately consented to do, and did yesterday morning. If anything can correct the mischief which these reports have done, such a contradiction as this will do it; but the appetite for scandal is so general and insatiable, there is such a disposition to believe such stories and such reluctance to renounce a belief once entertained, that it is very improbable that what has been done can be entirely undone, and this calumny will affect the Lady more or less as long as She lives. Though it is totally false that she was ever with child, and P. George certainly never thought of marrying her, it is probably true enough that She behaved with very little prudence, delicacy or reserve, for she is a very ill-behaved girl, ready for anything that her caprice or passions excite her to do. Fortunately He is a very timid unenterprising youth, not unwilling to amuse himself but by no means inclined to incur any serious risks, as he has abundantly shown on other occasions. His vanity prompts him to make love to the Ladies whom he meets in his country quarters, and as Princes are scarce his blood royal generally finds easy access to rural and provincial Beauties. But when he finds these affairs growing serious and the objects of his admiration evince an embarrassing alacrity to meet his flame with corresponding ardour, I am told that he usually gets alarmed and backs out with much more prudence than gallantry.

November 17th—Went to Cromer on Monday week, and returned on Monday last. I am fond of that wild and bleak coast with its 'hills that encircle the sea,' the fine old tower of the Church and the lighthouse, whose revolving lights it is impossible not to watch with interest. I went one day to Felbrigg and looked into the library—a fine old-fashioned room full of Mr. Windham's books, all full of notes and comments in his own hand, but library and books equally neglected now that they have fallen into the hands of a rough, unlettered Squire.

As soon as I got to town I read the attacks in all the newspapers upon Chesterfield, on account of his appearance in the case of Batthyany in the Rolls Court—another discreditable transaction affecting high names and tending to bring the aristocracy into contempt. It serves him right, and is a just reward for his idleness and folly; but these things are to be deplored for the mischief they do and the false notions they create. Public opinion lumps all together such men (and such cases) as Lord Hertford, Lord Frankfort, Lord De Ros, Lord Huntingtower, Lord Chesterfield, and others in different degrees.

November 18th—Called on Mr. Grenville yesterday morning. He told me he was eighty-eight, and had never been ill in all his life; had colds, but never been ill enough to keep his bed a whole day since he was born. His memory (he said) failed as to dates and names. He told me a curious anecdote of Wolfe. In Pitt's administration, when Wolfe was going out to take command of the Army in America, at that time a post of the greatest importance, Mr. Pitt had him to dinner with no other person present but Lord Temple (Mr. Grenville's Uncle). After dinner Wolfe got greatly excited, drew his sword, flourished it about, and boasted of the great things he would do with it in a wonderfully braggart style. Lord Temple and Mr. Pitt were horror-struck, and when the General was gone, they lifted up their hands and eyes, and said what an awful thing it was to think that they were about to trust interests so vital to the discretion of a man who could talk and bluster in such a way. Mr. Grenville said he had never liked to repeat this anecdote, and had never done so till very lately, for he had been reluctant to say anything which might, by possibility, throw a slur on the reputation of Wolfe. But I told him it was too curious to be suppressed; curious as a peculiar trait of character, and that the heights of Abraham had secured the fame of Wolfe beyond the possibility of being injured.

November 22nd—At Hillingdon[1] from Saturday till Monday. I never go to that place without looking with envy and admiration at a scene of so much happiness. There is certainly nothing to admire but the result. There are none of the qualities which are generally desirable; but if happiness is the aim and object of life (by which I mean something active, sentient and intelligent, not the happiness of an oyster or an opium-eater) then these people have attained it, subject only to its disturbance from the ordinary and unavoidable accidents and vicissitudes of existence. I suppose that happiness depends on (as wit has been described by) negatives. They are happy because they are without avarice, or ambition, or vanity, or envy. They have no extravagant or unreasonable pretensions, and therefore are not subject to perpetual mortifications and disappointments. They lead an easy, placid semi-sensual but not vicious life, with a full flow of affection for each other, and a natural ever-springing chearfulness and content.

Dined yesterday with Lady Holland, John Russell and Charles Austin, Lady Charlotte Lindsay. John told us some things about the Reform Bill, interesting enough. The first he heard of it was by a letter from Althorp, who told him Lord Grey and He wished him (John) to bring in the Bill (he was not in the Cabinet). He wrote back that he could not agree to bring in the Bill without having a share in its concoction, which they agreed he was entitled to. He came to town and Lord Grey begged him to put himself

---

[1] The Banker, R. H. Cox, lived here.

in communication with Durham. He went to Durham and had a long conversation with him, and they agreed that a Committee should be formed which should meet constantly and settle the terms of the Bill. The first person suggested was the D. of Richmond, but John objected to him, and then they settled to have Graham and Duncannon. They used to meet at Durham's every day and discuss the details of the Bill. Among these was the question of Ballot, Graham and Durham being strongly for it, John Russell against, and Duncannon neuter. The point was, however, referred to the Cabinet, and immediately negatived. John said that the only chance they had of carrying such a Bill was the preservation of impenetrable secrecy. If once the plan got out, their own friends would be alarmed, and their success infallibly compromised. Accordingly they contrived to keep their plan secret till the last moment. So little did their opponents expect anything of the kind, that Peel, in a speech about a fortnight before, taunted them in these terms: 'You came into power avowedly to promote peace, retrench-ment, and reform. Your peace is in the greatest danger of being broken; your estimates are not less than ours were; and as to your reform, I predict that it will be some miserable measure, with all the appearance of a change in the Constitution, without the reality of any improvement.' When the measure came out, many of the friends of Government were exceedingly frightened, and thought it would not fail to be their ruin. Hardinge told Graham in the lobby that 'of course they had made up their minds to resign.' Allen said that there had always existed a strong opinion that Peel might have crushed it at first, if he had refused leave to bring in the Bill, but John denied that this was feasible. He said, let Peel do what he would, they would have got a debate of several nights, and he had always told his timorous and desponding friends, that when the plan went forth to the country it would be responded to by such great and enthusiastic approval and so supported that it would be impossible for the Opposition to resist it. And this was what happened. The date of eight nights gave time for the press to act, and the country to declare itself. Allen then said they had done wrong in giving way (as they had) on some points, particularly as to the freemen; they had gained nothing by so doing, and had injured the Bill. But John said they had got all they expected. This sacrifice was made to Lords Harrowby and Wharncliffe, who had in consequence of it carried the second reading in the H. of Lords, which could not have been done without them; and this had prevented the creation of Peers. Lord Grey was so determined to make Peers, if the second reading was not carried, that John had himself given notice to some of his Tory friends, that if they wished to prevent this evil, they had better vote for it. We then discussed the communications which afterwards took place between Lord Grey and Palmerston and Harrowby and Wharncliffe, and Lyndhurst's famous motion, which produced such momentous results. I said that Harrowby and his friends had always accused Lord Grey of acting unfairly, but that I had always said that no man could act a more straitforward and consistent part than he did. I told John he ought to write a history of the Reform Bill, which would be a very curious narrative.

November 23rd—A torrent of Indian news and successes arrived almost all at once, an important and agreeable budget of intelligence, though without much of glory in it. It is a delightful thing to finish the Chinese war anyhow. We were ashamed of our successes, and the reports of victories gained and towns taken never gave any satisfaction, or excited a particle of pride or triumph. We now see our way out of two difficult quarrels which we never ought to have got into. The only good we shall have gained will have been a very imposing exhibition of our power and resource, and it will have cost us many millions of money, and many thousand lives to make it.

November 25th—I went last night to a place called 'The Judge and Jury Court'—Bingham Baring, Charles Buller, Freddy Leveson, and myself— and there we found several others of our acquaintance who had been attracted to the same place. It is difficult to imagine anything more low and blackguard than this imitation of and parody on a Court of Justice, and if the proceedings of last night are to be taken as a fair sample of the whole, it is not very amusing. There is a long low room opposite Covent Garden Theatre (in Bow Street) lit with tallow candles and furnished along its length with Benches; opposite these benches is a railed-off space for the Bar and the Jury, and an elevated desk for the Judge. You pay one shilling entrance, which entitles you to a cigar and a glass of rum or gin and water, or beer, a privilege of which almost every man availed himself. The room was pretty well filled and in a cloud of smoke, and there was a constant circulation of these large glasses of liquid; smoking and drinking were, indeed, the order of the day. The Judge, the Counsel, and the Jury, all had their cigars and gin and water, and the latter, as a recompense for their public services, were entitled to call for what they pleased gratis. Here they try such notorious cases as have been brought in any shape, complete or incomplete, under public notice, and last night we had 'Chesterfield v. Batthyany,' the names being slightly changed, but rendered sufficiently significant to leave no doubt of who and what was meant. *Maidstone*, for example, was examined as a witness under the title of Lord *Virgin Rock*, and so of the others which, however, I don't remember. The Chief Baron is a big burly fellow, Editor of a paper (which I never heard of before) called 'the Town,' and the Jury are sworn upon *the Town*. I don't know who the Counsel were, but there was one fellow who was a caricature of Brougham, certainly like him, and he attempted an imitation of him in manner, gesture, and voice, which was not very bad, and therefore rather amusing. But though the man had some humour, there was not enough or of sufficiently good quality to support the length of his speech. He opened the case for the Plaintiff; the counsel for the Defendant seemed very dull, and we would stay no longer. They say the charge of the Judge is generally the best part of it. They deal in very gross indecencies, and this seems to amuse the audience, which is one of the most blackguard-looking I ever saw congregated, and they just restrain their ribaldry within such limits as exclude *les gros mots*. Everything short of that is allowed, and evidently the more the better. They had had Alice Low and Lord Frankfort the week before. On the whole it was a poor performance. It bore (in point of character and decency) about the same relation to a Court of Justice that Musard's balls do to Almack's.

November 27th—After looking for him for several mornings in the Park through which he walks in his way to the Courts, I fell in with Thessiger and talked to him about the rule which Follett had obtained in my case with the 'Sunday Times.' He said he had no apprehensions as to the result and that if the action had been brought in any other Court He would never have got a rule, but the Court of Q.B. is in such a lamentable state that it is impossible ever to tell what they will do there; that Denman has just law enough to lead him almost always wrong, John Williams has no law at all, Wightman is idle and Coleridge weak; and Martin told me besides that it would be a blessing to the country to give Denman 10,000 a year and let him retire from the Bench, where he does nothing but harm. This is miserable work; for till this second rate Whig adherent was promoted by his friends the Chief Justice of England has for nearly a century past been a Lawyer of great eminence and authority. Mansfield, Kenyon, Ellenborough and Tenterden (none of them without faults) were great men in their profession. Denman is as honest as any of them, but has neither learning nor decision.

The Palmerstons came through town the other day in their way to Brocket, and I met them at dinner at Lady Holland's. They are both very much provoked at the Indian and Chinese successes, as their remarks showed; She complained that it was Elliot's fault that all this was not done two years ago, as he had the same instructions and the same means of executing them that Pottinger had, and He harped again upon the old tune of Ellenborough's orders and counter-orders, and tried to make out that it was his fault that the re-occupation of Cabul had been delayed so many months; and the 'Morning Chronicle' has been labouring to make out that all the glory of these successes is due to Palmerston alone.

November 30th—Ellenborough's Proclamation, which has just appeared, has been fiercely attacked by the Whig Palmerstonian press, but the purport of it seems to be pretty generally approved. Ellenborough is certainly not happy in his measures, his manners, or his phrases. He began by his much-abused orders for retreat, he lost no time in quarrelling with his Council and making himself personally obnoxious, and his present Proclamation is very objectionable in many respects, though it appears to me perfectly clear half the world think he meant to censure the policy of his Predecessor, and though he certainly meant no such thing, he ought not to have left room for any doubt on that point. He enters into reasons for his measures, which is never advisable in such a document as this, and especially in India. In the midst of all our successes, however, the simple truth is that Akbar Khan and the Afghans have gained their object completely. We had placed a puppet King on the throne, and we kept him there and held military possession of the country by a body of our Troops. They resolved to get rid of our King and our Troops and to resume their barbarous independence; they massacred all our people civil and military, and they afterwards put to death the King. We lost all hold over the country except the fortress we continued to occupy. Our recent expedition was, in fact, undertaken merely to get back the Prisoners who had escaped with their lives from the general slaughter, and having got them we have once for all abandoned the country, leaving to the Afghans the unmolested possession of the liberty they had acquired, and not attempting to place upon their necks the yoke they so roughly shook off. There is, after all, no great cause for rejoicing and triumph in all this.

On Sunday morning I called on John Russell, and we had an argument about Lord Ashburton and his Treaty, which he abused very roundly, saying all that I had before heard of his writing to his Brother against it, but still owning that it was not very injurious. I have a great respect for John, who is very honest and very clever, but in this matter he talks great nonsense. Palmerston is much more consistent and takes a clear and broad view of it. He says, 'We are all in the right, and the Americans all in the wrong. Never give up anything, insist on having the thing settled in your own way, and if they won't consent, let it remain unsettled.' But John merely says you might have got better terms if you had held out for them, that *he thinks* Ld. Aberdeen and Mr. Everett would have arranged it here more favorably for us than Ld. Ashburton did there; that if Ld. Aberdeen had proposed such and such terms to Everett they would have been agreed to in America, and that Lord Ashburton gave up certain things for which he did not obtain a just equivalent—all of which is mere gratuitous assumption, and may be true or may be false. However, he owned that the public was disposed to be satisfied with the Treaty, and he did not deny my assertion that Palmerston had committed a blunder in attacking it with such violence.

The fifth volume of Madame d'Arblay's journal or memoirs is just come out. I have read the first three volumes, and then could read no more, it was so tiresome; but I returned to the fifth because I found everybody was amused by it. It is certainly readable, for there are scattered through it notices of people and things sufficiently interesting, but they are overlaid by an enormous quantity of trash and twaddle, and there is a continuous stream of mawkish sentimentality, loyalty, devotion, sensibility, and a display of feelings and virtues which are very provoking. The cleverest part of it is the remarkable memory with which she narrates long conversations and minute details of facts and circumstances. It is true She generally makes her people converse in a very ordinary commonplace style, and She hardly ever tells any anecdote or any event of importance or of remarkable interest. Nevertheless her rambling records are read with pleasure, for there is and ever will be an insatiable thirst for familiar details of the great world and the people who have figured in it. Anecdotes of Kings, Princes, Ministers, or any *celebrities* are always acceptable. I have often thought that my journal would have been much more entertaining if I had scribbled down all I heard and saw in society, all I could remember of passing conversations, jokes, stories, and such like, instead of recording and commenting on public events, as I have often (though irregularly) done. To have done this, however, and done it well, required a better memory and more diligence than I possess, to be more *Boswellian* than I am. I believe, however, there is and can be no general rule for journalising. Everybody who addicts him- or herself to this practice must follow the dictates of his taste and fancy or caprice. It is a matter in which character operates and shows itself, for people are open and confidential or reserved with their blank pages in the same way as their living friends. Some, indeed, will pour forth upon paper, and for the edification or amusement of posterity, what they never would have revealed to living ear; but the majority of those who indulge in this occupation probably only tell what they desire to have known. Few write of themselves only as a sort of moral exercise, or for the refreshment of their own memories, or because they feel a longing to give utterance to, and record the feelings and thoughts that are rising and working and fighting in their minds. It is curious that so many great men, as well as so many small ones, have written journals, and an essay on the subject would be interesting enough if well done. Johnson, Walter Scott, Wilberforce, Windham, Byron, Heber, Gibbon, all kept journals, and many others, no doubt, whom I don't recollect at this moment. I omit Pepys and Evelyn, as men of a different sort.

December 6th 1842—Ellenborough's Proclamation which came out a week ago has been the principal topic of conversation and has been violently attacked by the Opposition and their papers. The general and impartial opinion is, that he is quite right to have withdrawn the army . from Afghanistan, and to have announced a pacific policy for the future, but that he is much to blame in having adopted such a tone as the paper is couched in, to have cast an indirect slur on the policy of Auckland, and condemned in such unqualified terms the errors of men who are not alive to defend themselves, or of the survivors who are going to be tried by a Court of enquiry. On the whole Ellenborough has not given satisfaction to any party or set of men. Conservatives complain of him as well as Whigs. He has given personal offence in India, and political offence here, and the appointment, from which such great things were expected, has turned out ill. The Duke of Wellington, however, is perfectly satisfied with what he has done, and as the Government meant to support him before all these successes, much more will they do so now.

December 8th—I saw Emily Eden[1] yesterday, and found they were full of bitterness against Ellenborough, and no wonder. In the first place, He and Auckland had always been friends. When Ellenborough came into office, he wrote to Auckland a friendly letter, in which he said what was tantamount to an invitation to him to stay in India. On his arrival at Calcutta, He was Auckland's guest for the first three days (till he was sworn in) and then Auckland was his, and when A.'s sisters wanted to leave Government House and go and pay a visit to a friend of theirs, Ellenborough would not hear of it, and made such a point of their remaining there till their departure that they did. He lived with them morning, noon and night, on terms of the greatest cordiality and repeatedly expressed his regret that they were going away. This renders his Proclamation particularly odious, and the more because She told me that during the last months of his Government, Auckland had done everything he could not to compromise or embarrass his successor, and had taken great pains to provide for any future military operations on which he might determine, which was a

[1] Lord Auckland's sister.

matter of considerable financial difficulty. All this makes them feel very sore, and they are besides of opinion that it is a grievous fault for a Governor to proclaim to the world that errors have been committed, and that the policy of the Indian Government is going to be altered. I am not so surprised at Ellenborough's *animus* since my Brother told me the other day that he had told him when he was at the Board of Control that he never lost an opportunity of letting the Queen know his opinion as to the errors and blunders of his predecessor and his colleagues.

I have been seeing lately a great deal of Mrs. Butler,[1] whose history is a melancholy one—a domestic tragedy without any tragical events. She went to America ten years ago in the high tide of her popularity and when She was making a fortune. There Pierce Butler fell in love with her and She fell in love with him. She gave up her earnings (£6000) to her Father, left the stage, married, and settled in America. And now after wasting the best years of her life in something very like solitude near Philadelphia, with two children whom She is passionately fond of, what is her situation? She has discovered that She has married a weak, dawdling, ignorant, violent tempered man, who is utterly unsuited to her and She to him; and She is aware that She has outlived his liking, as He has outlived her esteem and respect. With all her prodigious talents, her fine feelings, noble sentiments and lively imagination, She has no tact, no judgment, no discretion. She has acted like a fool, and he is now become a Brute. The consequence is she is supremely and hopelessly wretched; She sees her husband brutal and unkind to her, ruining himself and the children by his lazy stupid mismanagement of his affairs; and She lives in perpetual terror lest their alienation should at last mount to such a height that their living together may become impossible, and that then she shall be separated from her children for whom alone she desires to exist. Among the most prominent causes of their disunion is her violent and undisguised detestation of slavery, while he is a great slave Proprietor. She has evinced this feeling (laudable enough in itself) without a particle of discretion, and it has given him deep offence. She is certainly one of the most remarkable women I ever saw, but one who never could have been happy in whatever condition of life she might have been placed. But her lot has been singularly unfortunate, and it would have been impossible to do worse for herself than She has done. She now casts many longing, lingering looks back towards the stage, the scene of her triumphs, the source of independence, and compares the condition from which she once so desired to escape with her present lot.

December 9th—Francis Baring told me yesterday a curious anecdote

[1] Fanny Kemble.

relating to a Spanish MS. which would be interesting to Bibliomaniacs. Sampayo, a half Portuguese, half English, at Paris, was a great book-collector, particularly of Spanish and Portuguese, both book and MSS. He was aware of a MS. of Antonio Perez, relating to the wars of Granada, in the public library at Seville, and he asked Cuthbert, who has been living at Seville for some time, to ask leave to have it copied, and if he could get leave to find somebody to copy it. He got leave, and it was copied in a fair round hand for some sixteen dollars. After the copy was made, the librarian said to Cuthbert, 'You may take away which you please, the copy or the original.' He jumped at the offer, and sent the original MS. to Sampayo. His library was sold the other day, and Francis Baring said he believed this MS. was bought by the Royal Library of France, and it probably fetched a great deal of money.

December 14th—At Windsor for Council on Saturday. Queen beginning to show her grossesse. Peel staying there, but nobody else invited. Ellen-borough's Proclamation is still occupying general attention. My Brother writes me word from Paris that it is generally blamed there, for the same reasons that it is here; and the D. of Bedford tells me that Lord Spencer's political apathy has been excited very highly, and that he is full of such indignation at it that he talks of coming down to the H. of Lords to attack it. They talk of it as a document deserving impeachment, which is going to very absurd lengths. The Palmerstonians are still screaming themselves hoarse in their endeavours to get the credit of the success. Lady Palmerston wrote to Madame de Lieven (dear friends, who hate one another cordially) in a rage, because the latter said to her that She was sure, setting all party feeling aside, as a good Englishwoman, she must rejoice at the successes in the East. The other Lady replied, that She did not know what she meant, and that all the merit of the success was due to Palmerston and the late Government. To this Madame de Lieven responded as follows: 'Je vous demande bien pardon de ma légèreté, mais je vous assure que moi et toutes les personnes que je vois, ont été assez niais pour croire que les grands succès de l'Orient étaient dus à Sir R. Peel et à son gouvernement. Apparem-ment nous nous sommes trompés, et je vous demande mille excuses de notre légèreté.'

I had a conversation the other day with Adelaide Kemble about her sister and her domestic unhappiness, when she told me many particulars of her behaviour for many years past, which prove how greatly She has been the artificer of her own misery. The sorrows of these creatures of genius and imagination look very grand at a distance, and when they are set forth with all the pomp of passionate tears and glowing eloquence they rouse a host of sympathies and indignant feelings; but they do not bear to be looked into more closely when their sublimity almost entirely disappears, for we then find want of taste, temper and judgment—overlooking the obvious and the natural duties of her condition, while pursuing some imaginary or unattainable object, which what she dignifies with the name of conscience sends her in pursuit of. And what is the result of the whole? Good done to any class of mankind, or to any individuals even of our species? Any great and good cause advanced and promoted? Not at all; there is no result but misery, degradation and perhaps ruin to all that belong to her. A thousand times better would it have been for her to have exchanged all her fine qualities for a few homely and useful ones; to have been unable to write journals, tragedies and poems, and have been destitute of any grand aspirations after the emancipation and amelioration of her fellow creatures, but impressed with a sense of domestic duty and have studied the character of her husband for the purpose of improving it, and corrected the faults of her own in order to make him happy.

December 20th—Went to the Grove on Friday, and came back yesterday. Nobody there but Charles Buller and Charles Villiers. Clarendon told me that when he was at Bowood there was a sort of consultation between him, Lord Lansdowne, and John Russell, about the 'Morning Chronicle' and Palmerston, the latter having been already stimulated by the report (which his Brother, the Duke, had made him) of the opinions of himself, Lord Spencer, and other Whigs, who had met or communicated together on the same subject. The consequence was that John Russell wrote a remonstrance to Palmerston, in which he told him what these various persons thought with regard to the tone that had been taken on foreign questions, especially the American, and pointed out to him the great embarrassment that must ensue as well as prejudice to the party, if their dissatisfaction was manifested in some public manner when Parliament met. To this Palmerston replied in a very angry letter, in which he said that it was useless to talk to him about the D. of Bedford, Ld. Spencer, and others, as he knew very well that Edward Ellice was the real author of this movement against him. He then contrasted his own services in the cause with those of Ellice, and ended (as I understood) with a tirade against him, and a bluster about what he would do. John wrote again, temperately, remonstrating against such a tone as he had adopted, and telling him that the persons whose sentiments he had expressed were very competent to form opinions for themselves, without the influence or aid of Ellice. This letter elicited one much more temperate from Palmerston, in which he expressed his readiness to co-operate with the party, and to consult for the common advantage, but that he must in the course of the session take an opportunity of expressing his own opinions upon the questions of foreign policy which would arise. He and Ellice, it seems, hate each other with a great intensity, and have done for many years past, since Palmerston suspected Ellice of intriguing against him; and latterly Ellice, who is very vain, busy, and meddling, has taken an active and a noisy part against Palmerston's foreign policy generally, so that he is, and has been for some time, Palmerston's *bête noire.*

We were talking at the Grove about the Bishopric of Jerusalem, when Clarendon told me that the history of our consenting to that ridiculous appointment was that it was given to Ashley as the price of his negotiating with the 'Times' their support of, or cessation of opposition to, the Syrian war.

December 28th, Wednesday—Went to Woburn on Saturday morning to breakfast (with Dundas) and returned yesterday. John Russell there, in very good spirits, more occupied with his children than with thoughts of politics and place. The Duke and he discussed the prospects of their party, when the former advised him to take a moderate course, considering what was right and nothing else, and adhere to that, whether it led him to support or oppose the measures of Government. I heard nothing particular.

We were talking about the false statements which history hands down, and how useful letters and memoirs are in elucidating obscure points and correcting false impressions. The Duke said that it was generally believed, and would be to the end of time, that the influence exercised by O'Connell over the late Government had been very great, and it never would be believed that the three great Irish measures which they adopted were opposed vehemently, instead of being dictated, by O'Connell, and yet this was the case. One of these measures everybody knows he opposed—the Poor Law—but the other two, the Appropriation Clause, and the Irish Municipal Bill, have always been supposed by the world at large to have been his own measures. I have, I think, somewhere else noticed his opposition to the first of these, and his vain attempts to induce John Russell (who was the author of this very indiscreet measure) to give it up. The truth of the matter, as regards the Corporation Bill, is rather more complicated and curious. The Lords made amendments in this Bill, and the question arose whether Government should take them or reject them. O'Connell strenuously urged their acceptance, and asked if it was not a good thing to get rid of the old corporations on any terms; but John and the Government, after much discussion, resolved to reject them, not, however, making their determination known to O'Connell or to anybody else. While matters were in this state, O'Connell had some communication with Normanby, from which he inferred that Government had resolved not to take the Bill, upon which he immediately determined to anticipate this decision, and to proclaim his own hostility to the amended Bill, in order that its rejection might appear to be attributable to him; and accordingly he published a violent letter in the newspapers, in which he said that the Bill ought to be indignantly kicked off the table, or some such words. The Duke of Bedford, who read his letter, and was aware of his previous opinion, was exceedingly disgusted at what he thought a flagrant instance of duplicity and hypocrisy, and, happening to meet him one day alone at Brooks's, he asked him how he reconciled this letter with the opinions he had previously expressed on the subject, to which appeal he had no satisfactory reply to make, but only some very lame excuses in his usual civil and fawning manner. The fact is, that it suited his purpose to have it supposed that his influence over the Government was very great, and that he could make them do what he pleased; and as he gave every colour, by his conduct, to the accusations of the Tories, it is no wonder that the reputation of the power was much greater than the reality. It was the interest of the Tories to make this out, as it was O'Connell's own, and it was vain for the Whigs to deny what facts appeared to prove, and which he himself tacitly admitted.

The Duke also gave us an account (which was not new to me) of his interview with the Duke of Wellington at the time of the Bedchamber quarrel. The day on which the Cabinet was held at which they resolved to stand by the Queen and stay in office, the D. of B. had been with the D. of W. on other business, after concluding which, the D. of W. began on that. He said there appeared to be a difference, which he regretted to find was not likely to be adjusted; that he gave no opinion upon the matter itself, and merely gave it upon the principle involved; that Lord Melbourne was now Minister, and it was for him to advise the Queen; and then he stood up, and with great energy said, 'and if he will take upon himself the responsibility, he may rely upon me, and I will put myself in the breach.' The D. of B. asked him if he might go to Lord M. and tell him this. He said he might. The D. of B. went to the Palace, but M. was in Downing Street, the Cabinet sitting. He wrote what had passed, and sent it in to him. The letter was read and a long discussion ensued on it, but they finally resolved to return to office, and a more fatal resolution for themselves never was taken.

Dundas was very agreeable. I think I have seldom seen any man more agreeable in society. He is a great talker, but his manner and voice, and general style of conversation are all attractive; he knows a great deal, his reading has been extensive and various, and his memory appears rententive of such things as contribute to the amusement and instruction of society; remarkable passages, curious anecdotes, quaint sayings, and a general familiarity with things worth hearing, and people worth knowing, render his talk very pungent and attractive.

1845

September 7th—A complete absence of events, till a few days ago, when after a very short illness Lord Spencer died at his House near Doncaster. My own acquaintance with him was not intimate, but I had a great respect and esteem for him, and no man ever died with a fairer character, or more generally regretted. In his County he was exceedingly beloved and respected, not less by those who differed from him, than by those who agreed with him in politicks, and his personal friends and former colleagues, who were warmly attached to him, highly valued his opinions upon public matters, and on all important occasions anxiously sought, and placed great reliance on his advice. The career of Lord Spencer presents few materials to the biographer, for he had neither the brilliant nor even plausible exterior which interests and captivates vulgar imaginations, but he had sterling qualities of mind and character which made him one of the most useful and valuable, as he was one of the best and most amiable men of his day. He was the very model and type of an English gentleman, filling with propriety the station in which fortune had placed him, and making the best use of the abilities which Nature had bestowed upon him. Modest without diffidence, confident without vanity, ardently desiring the good of his country, without the slightest personal ambition, he took that part in publick affairs which his station and his opinions prompted, and he marched through the mazes of politicks with that straitforward bravery, which was the result of sincerity, singleness of purpose, the absence of all selfishness, and a true, genuine, but unpretending patriotism. His tastes, habits, and turn of mind were peculiarly and essentially English; he was a high-minded, unaffected, sensible, well-educated English gentleman, addicted to all those rural pursuits and amusements which are considered national, a practical farmer and fond of field sports, but enjoying all things in moderation, and making every other occupation subordinate to the discharge of those duties to his country, whether general or local, the paramount obligation of which was ever uppermost in his mind. In his political principles he was consistent, liberal, and enlightened, but he was too much of a philosopher, and had too deeply studied the book of life, to entertain any wild notions of human perfectibility, or to countenance those extravagant theories of popular wisdom and virtue which are so dangerous to peace, order, and good government. He observed, therefore, a just proportion, and a perfect moderation in his political views and objects, firmly believing in the capacity of the Constitution to combine the utmost extent of civil and religious liberty with the predominance of law, and a safe and vigorous administration of publick affairs. His whole life, therefore, was devoted to the object of widening and strengthening the foundations of the commonwealth, of abrogating exclusive and oppressive laws, of extending political franchises, of giving freedom to commerce, and by the progress of a policy at once sound and safe, to promote the welfare and happiness of the mass of the people, and the power and prosperity of the country.

Lord Spencer came into office as Chancellor of the Exchequer and Leader of the H. of Commons with Lord Grey's Government in 1830; on the death of his Father in 1835 his elevation to the H. of Lords obliged him to relinquish that office, upon which (as is well known), King William dismissed the Whig Government, on the pretext that it was so weakened as to be unworthy of publick confidence and incapable of carrying on the business of the country. This was indeed only a pretext for getting rid of an obnoxious Ministry; but the King's venturing upon so bold a step upon such grounds affords a convincing proof of the high consideration which Lord Spencer enjoyed in the House of Commons and in the country. Nor, indeed, was it possible to exaggerate that consideration. The greatest homage that ever was rendered to character and publick virtue was exhibited in his popularity and authority during the four eventful years when he led the Whig Government and party in the H. of Commons. Without one showy accomplishment, without wit to amuse or eloquence to persuade, with a voice unmelodious and a manner ungraceful, and barely able to speak plain sense in still plainer language, he exercised in the House of Commons an influence and even a dominion greater than any Leader either after or before him. Neither Pitt the Father, nor Pitt the Son, in the plenitude of their magnificent Dictatorships, nor Canning in the days of his most brilliant displays of oratory and wit, nor Castlereagh, returning in all the glory of an ovation from the overthrow of Napoleon, could govern with the same sway the most unruly and fastidious Assembly which the world ever saw. His friends followed this plain and simple man with enthusiastic devotion, and he possessed the faculty of disarming his political Antagonists of all bitterness and animosity towards him; he was regarded in the House

of Commons with sentiments akin to those of personal affection, with a
boundless confidence and an universal esteem. Such was the irresistible
ascendency of truth, sincerity, and honor, of a probity free from every taint
of interest, of mere character unaided by the arts which captivate or sub-
jugate mankind. This is the great practical panegyrick which will consecrate the memory of Lord Spencer, and transmit it nobly to the latest
posterity; but it is a panegyrick not more honourable to the subject of it
than to the national character which is susceptible of such impressions, and
which acknowledges such influences. We may feel an honest pride and a
happy confidence in the reflection that it is by such sterling qualities, by the
simple and unostentatious practice of publick and private virtue, that men
may best recommend themselves to the reverence, the gratitude, and the
affection of their countrymen, and be remembered hereafter as the benefactors of mankind.

London, November 16th—More than two months have elapsed, and I
have not in this interval been able to muster resolution to write a line here.
I have passed the last two months in locomotion and amusement, without
anything worth noticing but a visit to the Grange, where I went purposely
to meet Thiers. He came to England in his way from Spain, and passed
about a fortnight here. He was extremely well received, invited to Bowood
and to the Grange, dined with Lady Holland in London, and had interviews with Palmerston and Aberdeen. I had met him some years ago at
Talleyrand's, in London, but he of course had forgotten me, nor do I know
whether he recollected or not my connexion with Guizot during his administration in 1838 (1840). Whether he did or not, he was extremely civil and
disposed to talk to me, though unfortunately the extraordinary rapidity
of his utterance and the thickness of his articulation, added to my deafness,
rendered half of what he said unintelligible. He was very agreeable and
very loquacious, talking with a great appearance of abandon on every subject, politicks general and particular, and his own History, which he was
ready to discuss, and to defend against all objections and criticisms, with
great good humour. On the Sunday morning he took me aside, and talked
for a long time about his position and prospects, and he then said that it
was to be regretted that Aberdeen had evinced such a preference for one
political party in France, and it was a mistake; and, for his part, he considered that he had nothing to do with Whigs or Tories here, but that it
was his business to be equally well with publick men of all parties; that
he had called on Palmerston, and he should have called on Peel and Aberdeen, if they had been in town, and he expressed a wish that I would make
his sentiments known to them. I said I certainly would, and regretted that

they were not in London to receive him. Soon after I learnt that Aberdeen was to be in town the next day in his way to the Grove (where I was to meet him) when I resolved to write to him and tell him what Thiers said, and to suggest that he should see him. We all went to town the next morning by rail, and on arriving at the station a Messenger met me with a note from Aberdeen, saying he should be very glad to see Thiers if he would call at the F.O. I told him, and he was extremely pleased. I took him there and introduced him to Aberdeen, who received him very cordially, and their interview lasted an hour and a half. When he came to the Grove he told me he was much obliged to me for bringing Thiers to him, and very glad to receive him. He thought him very agreeable, but not so fair to Guizot as Guizot was to him, for the latter always spoke handsomely of Thiers, while Thiers spoke very disparagingly of him; in fact, Thiers speaks of Guizot with the greatest contempt. He says he is great in the tribune, but good for nothing elsewhere, neither a Statesman nor a man of business, which is certainly doing his great Antagonist much less than justice. We had a great battle in the train about many points of his History, and with a self-delusion, which is marvellous if sincere, he said that nobody could accuse him of any want of candour towards our country and of not having rendered us ample justice! I am sorry now that I did not at the time write down some particulars of his conversation and opinions about men and things which would not be devoid of interest. The only thing of any consequence I recollect now is the fact, which he asserted on the evidence of letters now in existence, of Talleyrand's having advised the Spanish war, whereas it has always been supposed that he opposed it, and that his opposition to it was a principal cause of his disgrace with the Emperor. Nothing persuaded him that Our Government had not been implicated in George's[1] conspiracy and his plots of assassination, but he entertained the most vulgar and mistaken notions about us, our affairs, and our national character. I take it, however, that he was not more surprised than pleased at his reception here, so frank, cordial, and dignified, received and entertained at Whig and Tory houses with equal cordiality, with the attention due to his celebrity as a writer and a Statesman, and without the slightest appearance of resentment (or anything but the most perfect indifference) at his Anti-English prejudices and violence. All this must have struck him with no small respect as well as wonder. I have heard since that the Queen said she should have been glad to receive him if he had expressed any desire to be presented to her; that she was not in the habit of receiving foreigners (passing through) at Windsor, but would have made an exception in his favor.

[1] George Cadoudal: executed for royalist conspiracies.

It has been during the last two months that I have been too idle to write that the rage for railroad speculation reached its height, was checked by a sudden panic in full career, and is now reviving again, though not by any means promising to recover its pristine vigour. I met one day in the middle of it the Governor of the Bank at Robarts', who told me that He never remembered in all his experience anything like the present speculation; that the operations of '25, which led to the great panic, were nothing to it, and that there could not fail to be a fearful reaction. The reaction came sooner than anybody expected, but though it has blown many of the bubbles into the air, it has not been as yet so complete and so ruinous as many of the wise men of the East still expect and predict. It is incredible how people have been tempted to speculate: half the fine Ladies have been dabbling, and the men most unlikely have not been able to refrain from gambling in shares, even I myself (though in a very small degree), for the warning voice of the Governor of the Bank has never been out of my ears. Simultaneously with all this has grown up to a gigantic height the evil of the potato failure, affecting in its expected consequences the speculations, and filling with fear and doubt every interest. That the mischief in Ireland is great and increasing is beyond a doubt, and the Government are full of alarm, while every man is watching with intense anxiety the progress of events, and inquiring whether the Corn Laws will break down under this pressure or not.

There have been Cabinets held, with long and anxious consultations, and (as it is believed) debates, but as I do not know what passed with anything approaching to certainty, I shall say but little about them. It has been said that Peel was not indisposed to take this opportunity of doing away with the Corn Laws, and again that he was resolved not to abandon his sliding scale; that Aberdeen was the strongest of any against the Corn Laws; the Duke most determined to support them. I am inclined to believe the two latter suppositions to be true, and I lean to the belief that Peel is waiting for a case sufficiently strong to lay before his Agricultural friends, before he tells them that he must throw the ports open. There have not been wanting circumstances significant of Peel's disposition, especially a speech which Dr. Buckland made at Birmingham of a very Free Trade complexion; and he went there from Drayton, and has since been made Dean of Westminster. However, it is idle to speculate on intentions, which a short time must develop and explain.

All the world went last night to the St. James's Theatre to see the second representation of 'Every Man in his Humour,' by Dickens and the 'Punch' people. House crammed full. I was in a bad place, heard very ill, and was so bored that at the end of the third act I went away. Dickens acted Bobadil very well indeed, and Douglas Jerrold (the author of the Caudles) Master Stephen well also; the rest were very moderate and the play intolerably heavy. A play 250 years old, a comedy of character only, without plot or story, or interest of any sort or kind, can hardly go down. The audience were cold as ice, because (it was said) they were too fine; but I believe they were not at all amused.

I have said nothing of Newmarket. My horse 'Alarm' proved himself the best going (to all present appearance) and won the great Stake of the Houghton meeting; but I won very little on him, not daring to back him. I had the mortification of seeing it proved that he would, beyond all possibility of doubt, have won the Derby but for his accident. That would have been worth winning; it would have rendered me independent, enabled me to relinquish my office when I pleased and be my own man, and given me the power of doing many an act of kindness, and assisting those I care for. Such a chance will probably never occur again.

Worsley, November 22nd, Saturday—I came here (for the first time) on Monday last, to see the fine new house Francis Egerton has built. It is a very handsome specimen of Blore's architecture, rather spoilt by alterations made while the building was in progress; comfortable enough, but with many faults. The place is miserable; no place at all; no trees worth looking at, and a wet clay soil; no extent, and everything to make. The House stands on an eminence, and commands a very extensive prospect of a rich flat country, the canal (source of his wealth) running beneath, not a quarter of a mile off, while a little further off the railroad crosses Chat Moss, and all day long the Barges are visible on the one, and continual trains snort and smoke along the other, presenting a lively exhibition of activity and progress. But it is a miserable country to live in; so wet and deep that the roads all about are paved, and the air is eternally murky with the fire and smoke that are vomited forth from hundreds of chimneys and furnaces in every direction; no resources, such as hunting and shooting, and no society but the rare visitants from distant parts. In such a place as this they have expended £100,000 in a fine house, with all the appendages of gardens, etc., and they have done this and much more from a sense of duty, from fully recognising the authority of the maxim that 'Property has its duties as well as its rights.' The Duke of Bridgewater created this vast property, and his enterprise and perseverance were crowned with a prodigious success. He called into activity and gave employment to an immense population, and he occasionally resided at Worsley, to have the satisfaction of witnessing the astonishing results which he had obtained; but with this he was contented. He bequeathed the canal and the Collieries to his Agent Bradshaw (with unlimited power of management) in trust for the late Duke of Sutherland, and after him to Francis Egerton. During the long reign of Bradshaw and the Duke the property continued to increase in value. Bradshaw was a profligate Old dog, who feathered his own nest, and lived a dissolute life. The Duke touched the proceeds, and never troubled himself about the source from which he derived them. At length He died. The trust remained unaltered, but the new *cestuy que use* came to the enjoyment of his enormous fortune with other ideas and a more stringent sense of obligation. He and his wife thought it behoved them to inquire into the condition of the population in their employment, and to do their best to improve it. They found that it was very bad; that the mass of the people was in the lowest state of ignorance and degradation, and that there was plenty for their beneficence to do. They soon set about the task, and began by making a bargain with Bradshaw to get him out of the trust. He made it over to a man of the name of Sotherton, who had been for some time employed in the Canal office, and who was believed to be a fit and proper person. Sotherton no sooner found himself in power (for the power of the Trustee is almost unlimited) than he began to play all sorts of pranks and to quarrel with the Lord. They endeavoured to oust Sotherton, and went to law with him, but found the difficulties so great that they ended by compounding with him, and gave him £45,000 to relinquish the trust and appoint a nominee of Francis's in his room. He selected Locke, who is now Trustee. This done, they set to work in earnest. This House was erected, and they have built Churches and established schools and reading-rooms in various places; they have done all they could, sparing neither pains nor money, to civilise and improve the population, to diffuse education, and encourage habits of sobriety and order, and a taste for intellectual occupations. They have evinced a solicitude for the welfare of the people under their influence that has produced a very beneficial effect, and they are gradually improving their condition and purifying their morals, without, however, entertaining any extravagant expectations of superhuman success.

I have passed these few days in seeing this place and some of the manufacturing wonders at Manchester. On Tuesday I went over the House and place; and then to Francis's yard, a sort of small dockyard and manufactory; then on the Canal in the Trust boat—a luxurious Barge fitted up with every convenience and comfort, with a fireplace, and where one may write, read, and live just as in the house; a kitchen behind. The boat is drawn by two horses with Postilions in livery, and they trot along a merry pace, all the craft (except, by compact, 'the Swift boats,' as they are called) giving way to the Trust boat. On Wednesday I went through the subterraneous canal, about a mile and a half long, into the coalpit, saw the working in the mine, and came up by the shaft; a black and dirty expedition, scarcely worth the trouble, but which I am glad to have seen. The Colliers seem a very coarse set, but they are not hard worked, and, in fact, do no more than they chuse. There are many miles of this underground canal. On Thursday to Manchester, and saw one of the great cotton and one of the great silk manufactories; very curious even to me, who am ignorant of mechanicks, and could only stare and wonder, without being able to understand the niceties of the beautiful and complicated machinery by which all the operations of these trades are performed. The heat of the rooms in the former of them was intense, but the man who showed them to us told us it was caused by the prodigious friction, and the room might be much cooler, but the people liked the heat. Yesterday I went to the infant School, admirably managed; then to the recreation ground of the Colliers and manufacturers—a recent establishment. It is a large piece of ground, planted and levelled round about what is called the paying-House, where the men are paid their wages once a fortnight. The object is to encourage sports and occupations in the open air, and induce them not to go to the Ale-House. There are cricket, quoits, and football, and ginger-beer and coffee are sold to the people, but no beer or spirits. This has only a partial success. Afterwards to Patricroft, to see Messrs. Nasmyth's great establishment for making locomotive engines, every part of which I went over. I asked at all the places about the wages and habits of the workpeople. In Birley's (cotton) factory 1200 are employed, the majority girls, who earn from ten to fourteen shilling a week. At Nasmyth's the men make from twenty to thirty-two shillings a week. They love to change about, and seldom stay very long at one place; some will go away in a week, and some after a day. In the hot factory rooms the women look very wan, very dirty, and one should guess very miserable. They work eleven hours generally, but though it might be thought that domestic service must be preferable, there is the greatest difficulty in procuring women-servants here. All the girls go to the factory in spite of the confinement, labour, close atmosphere, dirt, and moral danger which await them. The Parents make them go, because they earn money which they bring home, and they like the independence and the hours every evening, and the days from Saturday to Monday, of which they can dispose.

Worsley, November 24th—To Manchester this morning; to the Collegiate Church; good chanting and an excellent reader; to the Athenæum (or the

Institute), and saw Dr. Dalton's statue, a good work of Chantrey's; then to Messrs. Hoyle's Calico-printing establishment; extremely well worth seeing, interesting, and the more because intelligible. People know very little how many processes the Calico they wear so cheaply goes through, and what a mighty business its preparation is. They told us 800 men were employed here, the highest wages two guineas a week. The room containing the copper cylinders has in it a capital of £100,000, the cost of these cylinders. I was surprised to hear that the price of labour (the wages) is not affected by the more or less irksome nature of the employment. The workman at the calico Printing, which is much more agreeable than the Cotton-weaving business, is as highly paid as the latter, perhaps more highly; indeed the lowest rate of wages seems to be at the Mill.

The day I came here Lady Holland died, that is, She died at two o'clock in the preceding night. She evinced during her illness a very philosophical calmness and resolution, and perfect good humour, aware that she was dying, and not afraid of death. The religious people don't know what to make of it. She never seems to have given the least sign of any religious feeling or belief. She has made a curious will, leaving the greater part of the landed property at her disposal to John Russell for his life, and her jewels to Lady Elizabeth Grey, a poor Parson's wife—bequests severely blamed, and justly. The legatees ought not to accept what She has bequeathed to them, but give all up to her daughter, who wants it. Though She was a woman for whom nobody felt any affection, and whose death therefore will have excited no grief, She will be regretted by a great many people, some from kindly, more from selfish motives, and all who had been accustomed to live at Holland House and continued to be her habitués will lament over the fall of the curtain on that long drama, and the final extinction of the flickering remnant of a social light which illuminated and adorned England and even Europe for half a century. The world never has seen and never will again see anything like Holland House, and though it was by no means the same thing as it was during Lord Holland's life, Lady Holland contrived to assemble round her to the last a great society, comprising almost everybody that was conspicuous, remarkable and agreeable. The closing of her house, therefore, will be a serious and an irreparable loss, especially to those Old friends who are too Old to look out for new places of resort and to form new social habits. She was a very strange woman, whose character it would not be easy to describe, and who can only be perfectly understood from a knowledge and consideration of her habits and peculiarities. She was certainly clever, and She had acquired a great deal of information both from books and men, having passed her whole

life amidst people remarkable for their abilities and knowledge. She cared
very little for her children, but she sometimes pretended to care for them,
and She also pretended to entertain strong feelings of friendship for many
individuals; and this was not all insincerity, for, in fact, She did entertain
them as strongly as her nature permitted. She was often capricious, tyran-
nical, and troublesome, liking to provoke, and disappoint, and thwart her
acquaintance, and she was often obliging, good-natured, and considerate
to the same people. To those who were ill and suffering, to whom she could
show any personal kindness and attention, among her intimate friends, she
never failed to do so. She was always intensely selfish, dreading solitude
above everything, and eternally working to enlarge the circle of her society,
and to retain all who ever came within it. She could not live alone for a
single minute; she never was alone, and even in her moments of greatest
grief it was not in solitude but in society that she sought for consolation.
Her love and habit of domination were both unbounded, and they made
her do strange and often unwarrantable things. None ever lived who
assumed such privileges as Lady Holland, and the docility with which the
world submitted to her vagaries was wonderful. Though she was eternally
surrounded with clever people, there was no person of any position in the
world, no matter how frivolous and foolish, whose acquaintance she was
not eager to cultivate, and especially latterly she had a rage for knowing
new people and going to fresh houses. Though often capricious and impertinent she was never out of temper, and she bore with good humour and
calmness the indignant and resentful outbreaks which she sometimes provoked in others, and though she liked to have people at her orders and
who would defer to her and obey her, she both liked and respected those
who were not afraid of her and who treated her with spirit and freedom.
Although she was known to be wholly destitute of religious opinions She
never encouraged any irreligious talk in her house. She never spoke dis-
respectfully or with levity of any of the institutions or opinions which
other people were accustomed to reverence, nor did she at any time, even
during periods of the greatest political violence, suffer any disloyal language
towards the Sovereign, nor encourage any fierce philippicks, still less any
ribaldry against political opponents. It was her great object, while her
society was naturally and inevitably of a particular political colour, to
establish in it such a tone of moderation and general toleration that no
person of any party, opinion, profession, or persuasion might feel any difficulty in coming to her house, and she took care that no one who did should
ever have reason to complain of being offended or annoyed, still less shocked
or insulted under her roof. There never was anybody more invariably kind

to her servants or so solicitous for their comfort. In this probably selfish considerations principally moved her; it was essential to her comfort to be diligently and zealously served, and She secured by her conduct to them their devoted attachment. It used often to be said in joke that they were very much better off than her guests.

London, December 5th—I came to town yesterday, and find political affairs in a state of the greatest interest and excitement. The whole town had been electrified in the morning by an article in the 'Times,' announcing, with an air of certainty and authority, that the discussions (and disputes) in the Cabinet had terminated by a resolution to call Parliament together early in January and propose a total repeal of the Corn Laws, and that the Duke had not only consented, but was to bring forward the measure in the H. of Lords. Nobody knew whether to believe this or not, though all seemed staggered, and the more so because the 'Standard,' though affecting to disbelieve the 'Times,' and treating it as a probable fiction, did not contradict it from authority, as might naturally have been expected if it had been untrue. This morning Reeve came to me when I heard the whole matter precisely as it stands, and the whole affair, including the way it comes to my knowledge, presents a curious undercurrent in politicks. I introduced Reeve to Barnes many years ago and procured him his situation of writer in the 'Times.' Barnes died, and was succeeded as Editor by Delane, who has become Reeve's intimate friend and their mutual confidence is complete. Delane has become neither more nor less than the Confidant of Aberdeen, who has been too sensible of the value of having the 'Times' as the Advocate and Defender of his foreign policy not to keep well with the paper even while it attacked all his Colleagues separately and the Government generally; and accordingly his confidential communications with Delane have not been limited to Foreign Affairs but have extended to other matters. On this question of the Corn Laws Aberdeen has taken a very strong and decided part, and He has been Peel's most strenuous supporter in the contest he has had to maintain in his Cabinet, for it now appears that Peel has all along been for repealing the Corn Laws, and has not (as I was once led to believe) been disposed to stand by his own sliding scale—but it will be better to state the substance of Reeve's information to me:—It appears that before the appearance of John Russell's letter, the Free-Trading Ministers were disposed to take the course now determined on, and Aberdeen thinks it was a great error and misfortune that they did not do so in November, and so appear to have taken the initiative, rather than to be goaded to it. John's letter, however (which was written without concert with, or the knowledge of, anybody) fell like a spark on a barrel of gunpowder. The effect it produced was far greater than he even could have expected, greater probably than he is yet aware of. It struck despair into the hearts of the protectionists, but it really was of service to Peel, though it appeared to put him in fresh difficulty. The publication of the letter was followed by an article in the 'Times,' alluding to this difficulty, and the day this article appeared Aberdeen sent for Delane, and told him that Peel considered the letter mischievous, but the article far more mischievous than the letter. In the course of this and other conversations he gave Delane to understand what his own opinions were, and told him pretty clearly what sort of a contest was going on in the Cabinet. The Duke was (at first) decidedly against repeal; and Ripon and Wharncliffe were, as far as I can make out, the most strenuous opponents besides. On Tuesday last the decisive Cabinet was held, at which it was finally to be determined which party should prevail, and if Peel could not carry his views, it was his intention to resign, and Aberdeen with him. On Wednesday, Aberdeen sent again for Delane, and after talking to him about all sorts of matters connected with Foreign policy, and many other things, and when Delane was preparing to leave him, he began upon the Corn Laws, and told him everything. He told him, in fact, the substance of what appeared in the article yesterday, together with many details which did not appear. He told him that the Duke had offered to resign, but that Peel said, if He resigned, He himself would also, for he could not undertake to carry the measure unless with the Duke's concurrence and support, and at last the Duke gave way, and agreed to stay in, and use his influence to carry it through the House of Lords. Peel was aware that without this it would have been impossible, and as it is, He expects great opposition, and several resignations in the Cabinet. These resignations will, however, materially strengthen the Government, as the men who go out will probably be replaced by Ellenborough, Dalhousie, and Gladstone, a great improvement in point of capacity.

When the article appeared yesterday morning, Wharncliffe was in a great state of agitation, and told Reeve (as he had done before) that it was not true, that the 'Times' was mystified, and had been all along. Reeve said that certainly Delane thought he had good authority for what he had put forth, and would not have risked his credit so far without strong grounds, and that He (Reeve) had received his information from Delane, but that if Lord Wharncliffe really meant to declare that to his knowledge the statement was false, he would, if he pleased, send for Delane and tell him so. He hung back on this, and said he did not wish to appear. R. said he need not appear, but if he would *authorise* the contradiction, it should be contradicted. He would not, however, but said that 'nothing was settled.' I have no doubt that though everything is virtually settled, the matter remains to be formally settled. The Chiefs are agreed, but the whole Cabinet is not yet agreed, and this is what he means, while any hopes he may have entertained of staving off the blow are defeated by this rapid publication. There can be very little doubt that it was Aberdeen's object that Delane should publish what he did, though he did not tell him to do so, and the reason is very obvious. Yesterday the American mail went off, and it took with it the morning papers, and consequently this article in the 'Times.' It was exactly what Aberdeen wanted. As Foreign Secretary, his most earnest desire is to get over the Oregon affair as well as he can, and he knows that nothing will have so great an effect in America, nothing tend so materially to the prevalence of pacifick Counsels, as an announcement that our Corn Laws are going to be repealed.

December 6th—It is impossible to describe the agitation into which all classes of persons have been thrown by the announcement about the Corn Laws—the doubts, hopes, and fears it has excited, and the burning curiosity to know the truth of it. Some deride and scout it; others believe it, partly or entirely. Yesterday morning I went to the office and saw Wharncliffe. 'His face was as a glass, where men might read strange matters'; it was easy to see his state of agitation. He soon asked me if I had seen the 'Times' and if Reeve had told me what had passed between them. I told him I had heard it, and then, assuming it was all true, I said I hoped he did not mean to resign, and that whatever his opinions might be, if the Duke did not, he surely need not either, and any break-up of the party would be an evil. He acknowledged nothing, but replied, very lugubriously, that he was seventy years old! I did my best to encourage him, and he did his best to make me doubt the accuracy of the 'Times'' statement, telling me nothing, but mysteriously saying a very short time would reveal the truth. In the afternoon he went to a Cabinet. Meanwhile the 'Standard' appeared with a contradiction of the 'Times' in large letters. Wharncliffe came into my room from the Cabinet much excited, but apparently rather hilarious. I asked him if he had seen the 'Standard.' He said no, he wanted to see it. He read it, and then said, 'What do you say to that?' I said, I laughed at it, and had not a doubt that the 'Times' was right. 'Very well,' he replied, 'it will soon be seen who is right; but I tell you the "Times" has been mystified, and neither you nor Reeve know anything of what is going on.' I was enough staggered by his manner to write to Reeve and tell him this, and he went to Delane. They went over all that had passed with Aberdeen, which was too clear, too precise, and too decisive to admit of any mistake.

After his communication to DeL., A. asked him what he meant to do with what he had told him. 'Publish it,' he answered, 'to be sure!' A pretty strong proof that He told it him for no other purpose. Palmerston hit the right nail on the head, for Wm. Cowper told me last night he had guessed that Aberdeen had got this information put into the 'Times,' that it might go over to America and influence the Oregon question; only he did not seem certain it was true, and was not without a suspicion that it was done with an intention to deceive, and not to enlighten the American public. Aberdeen's conduct was quite unaccountable, and if truly reported by Delane, was unfair by his Colleagues and unfair to the 'Times' likewise.

December 9th, Tuesday—On Saturday afternoon Wharncliffe came to the office and sent for me. I found him walking about the room, when he immediately broke out, 'Well, I must say the impudence of the "Times" exceeds all I ever knew.' 'What's the matter?' I asked, 'what have they done?' 'Why, notwithstanding the contradiction in the "Standard" last night, they have not only neither qualified nor withdrawn their assertion, but have repeated the statement more positively than before. I must say this beats every other impudence.' 'Well,' I said, 'don't you see the reason, namely, that the "Times" does not care for the denial of the "Standard," and thinks its own authority for the statement better than any the "Standard" can have for denying it?' I then told him that everybody believed the 'Times'; go where you would people canvassed which was the most credible, and all believed the 'Times.' Lord Carnarvon, whom I met in the morning, for instance, and I believed it; that is, I believed it to be substantially correct, though perhaps not so in all its details. 'Very well,' he said, 'a short time would show the truth; but I tell you again that the "Times" knows nothing about it, has been mystified, and you will soon see that you are all wrong.' On this I said, 'Am I then to understand you that the facts put forth by the "Times" are really untrue, that no resolution has been come to by the Cabinet, and that the Duke of Wellington in one House and Peel in the other are *not* going to bring forward a measure which, without quibbling or splitting of hairs, is a virtual abandonment of the principle of protection?' He said, 'Well, I do mean to say that all this is untrue, it is not the fact; I positively tell you so, and I mean it without any quibbling whatever.' 'Very well, of course you know and I cannot, and I am bound to believe you. May I then contradict it on your authority?' 'No, I will not have my name used. I tell you not to believe it, and you may say what you please as from yourself, but I will not have my authority mentioned, and events will contradict it soon enough.' We had a great deal more talk. He complained of the mischief that the report had done, the speculation it had set afloat, etc. After this contradiction so positive, specific, and peremptory, I knew not what to believe. I wrote to Reeve, and he saw DeL. the next morning (Sunday). On Monday I looked with anxiety for the article in the 'Times,' and found only a calm adhesion to its story. Yesterday morning Reeve informed me that DeL. had seen Aberdeen the evening before, who said to him that he had not said a bit too much, except that his statement the second day, that 'the Heads of the Government had agreed,' was more correct than that of the first, which said that 'the Cabinet' had. He desired him to go on in the same strain, reasoning on it as a fact. He gave him, however, to understand that the publication had created considerable agitation; seemed somewhat disturbed at the charges of violation of oath against the revealer, whoever he might be. Delane in the course of conversation said that the whole thing turned on the D. of W., whether he was consenting or not, but Aberdeen would not tell him which way the Duke was.

In the afternoon I saw Delane himself. Peel went down to the Queen on Saturday, came up yesterday afternoon, and there was a Cabinet at five o'clock. Wharncliffe told me that Peel was very angry at the article in the 'Times,' and sent a Messenger to the Queen thereupon. There is no doubt that Delane, in the excitement of the moment, said more, much more, than he ought to have said, and that Wharncliffe's statement to me was really true, for the *Cabinet*, so far from being agreed on a measure, was in a state of disagreement, amounting almost to dissolution. DeL. was very imprudent, for he might have guarded his statement and yet produced precisely the same effect. My own belief is that yesterday evening decided the fate of the Government, and that all turned on the Duke. If he consented, Peel will stay in and the dissentients retire. If he would not, Peel will resign and the Government is at an end; and I have always had a suspicion that the Duke had consented and afterwards drew back, either incensed at the publication or for other reasons. However, a very short time will clear up everything. Meanwhile the agitation, excitement, and curiosity are universal and intense. The rising wrath of the Tories and Landlords is already muttering at the bare suspicion of the intended act, and it will be awful when all the truth breaks upon them. Peel's situation is very curious, and though many will think he has done a great service, he has so played his cards from first to last that his reputation will be irretrievably damaged by it, for men of both, or indeed all, parties will unite in condemning him. He is now going to reap the fruits of the enormous error he committed in coming into office on the principle of Corn Law protection and the sliding scale, an error the more unpardonable because it was quite unnecessary.

Thursday, December 11th—On Tuesday afternoon Ld. Wharncliffe sent for me, and told me Parliament was to be prorogued, but not called for despatch of business. This was enough: it satisfied me that the Ministers were out; there was no other solution of so strange a fact. Yesterday morning we went down to the Council at Osborne; the Duke joined us at Basingstoke. Nothing was said. I never saw the Cabinet in such a state of hilarity. Peel was full of jokes and stories, and they all were as merry (apparently and probably really) as men could be. Peel and Aberdeen alone had long audiences of the Q.; nothing transpired there. When I got back to town I found the reports of resignation current, and at dinner at George Harcourt's it was treated as a thing certain, and my conversation with Jem. Wortley and then with Sir R. Gordon and Canning quite satisfied me that my conjectures the day before had been fully realised. When we returned from Osborne I had no idea the Ministers had already resigned some days before, for they none of them took leave, and Peel and Aberdeen only had audiences. Not one of them hinted to me what was going on, and the only thing said about it was a joke of Stanley's, who said to a Bishop, who was of the Party, that the Right Reverend Prelate had probably often seen as much patience, but never could have seen so much resignation.

Friday, December 12th—Yesterday all was known. Peel had resigned on Saturday, and John was sent for the same day, but the Ministers kept that secret, nor did Aberdeen tell Delane the state of the case; I suppose he was afraid to tell him any more. John was at Osborne yesterday, and has called his friends together to-day. The Whig talk at Brooks's is that the Government about to be formed cannot stand, that they will be able to do nothing with the H. of Lords, and assuming that the D. of W.'s opposition has broken up the Government (which was totally untrue) they conclude that he will head the Tories in support of the Corn Laws in his House. I met Macaulay at dinner at Milman's yesterday (for the Westminster Play), and he told me this was the tone at Brooks's. I told him I did not think they would have so much difficulty as they imagine, that Peel would support them, and the Duke, so far from leading on the Landed interest, would keep them quiet if he could and help the Government.

It is now more than ever to be regretted that John is not on better terms with Peel, and that he should have allowed himself to twit him so offensively as he did in his letter the other day, for it is essential that there should be some concert between them; and when John's Government must in fact depend for its existence on Peel's support, it would have been far more becoming and more convenient that their personal relations should be amicable, and that they should not be separated from each other by a barrier of mutual antipathy. I believe, however, that John's feelings towards Peel are not at all reciprocal. The Tories will now bitterly regret that they rejected the eight-shilling duty, and how true have been the prognosticks that they never would have again so good an opportunity of making a compromise. I doubt whether their rage and fury against Peel will be the least diminished by his resignation; on the contrary, they will think he has cast them into the Lion's mouth. Everybody asks first of all what was the crisis, what the necessity which compelled him to insist on throwing over the Corn Laws, and making it the condition of his remaining in office; and next, why, when the majority of the Cabinet would have supported him, he did not let the dissentients go and fight his battle out. These questions will be answered in time.

John gave considerable offence to some of his Colleagues by his letter; two only, however, objected (in letters to him) to what he said—Lansdowne and Palmerston. Clarendon objected to his firing off such a letter without consulting anybody, but did not write to him at all; he wrote to the D. of Bedford. However, as Palmerston's objection was grounded on an assumption that it would *strengthen* Peel, now that Peel is out, and the doors of the F.O. are thrown open to him, he will be no doubt reconciled to it; for I don't imagine he cares about corn, fixed duty, sliding scales, or anything else, except so far as they may bear upon his return to that abode of his bliss.

Saturday, December 13th—Yesterday morning I called on Wharncliffe, who was still ill in bed, and very low. He complained of the 'Times' for saying that the Duke of Wellington had broken up the Government by changing his mind, first consenting and then withdrawing his consent; and 'it was hard upon the Old man,' who had behaved admirably throughout, never having flinched or changed, but said to Peel that He (Peel) was a better judge of the question, and he would support him in whatever course he might take. I said 'the Old man' would probably not see the paper, and certainly not care a straw if He did. I told him everybody asked why they had resigned, and when the day of explanation came, that it would be difficult to give a satisfactory answer to the question. He said He thought so too; that He never could see any sufficient reason (it being now clear that the supposed deficiency of food would furnish none); but that from the beginning Peel and Graham, especially Graham, had appeared *panic-struck*, and would hear no reasons against the course they had resolved upon; that Lord Heytesbury had contributed to this panic by his representations; that the original statement in the 'Times' was the more extraordinary, because *on the very day* when it appeared, *Thursday*, the Government was virtually broken up. Peel resolved to repeal the Corn Laws, but only to attempt it provided he could do so with an unanimous Cabinet. This He found was impossible, and that very Thursday he determined to resign. They begged him not to be in a hurry. He said he would not, and would take twenty-four hours to consider it. He did so, and on Friday he announced to his Colleagues that he persisted in his resolution, and should go down the next day to Osborne to resign. All this, which I had from Wharncliffe's lips, is unquestionably true, and it makes Aberdeen's communications to Delane most unaccountable. The only solution of it I can imagine is this; that Delane at first mistook A.; that A. told him (as was true) that the Heads and majority of the Cabinet had consented. Perhaps A. himself anticipated that it would end in the whole Cabinet uniting. But at all events DeL. jumped to the conclusion that the Cabinet was agreed, and he put forth the statement without sufficient caution. It is a remarkable proof how inaccurate the 'Times' not unfrequently is, and how unsafe it is always and implicitly to rely upon it.

There is no doubt that the Ministers, Peel especially, were amazed and exasperated to the greatest degree at the appearance of this article, and it is easy to suppose they were not silent on the subject. Aberdeen in all probability did not dare say or do anything more which might have contributed to increase the suspicion that already attached to him in some degree. To have corrected the first statement and have told the story more accurately would have betrayed a knowledge of what was passing in the Cabinet dangerous to the man who gave it; and therefore A. preferred leaving the 'Times' in its error. This is the best guess I can make at what is otherwise quite incomprehensible.

At John Russell's in the morning no one was present but Palmerston, Cottenham, Clarendon, and Macaulay, who came in at the end. The letters convening his other friends had not reached them in time. Clarendon came to me afterwards, and told me what had passed. The Queen wrote to John, and summoned him to her presence. She said Sir R. Peel had resigned, and She had thought it expedient to send for him to assist her. He asked her why Peel had resigned. She said that since November last He had been satisfied that the time was arrived when the Corn Laws must be repealed, but that the difficulty he had found with his Cabinet had at length induced him to resign. John then said that, before he could undertake anything, he must know what would be Peel's course in respect to the measures he should propose, and what chance he should have of being able to carry them. The Queen told him that Peel had given her every assurance of his support. He left her without anything being settled, and He is in fact not yet Minister. At the meeting yesterday, Cottenham alone was against undertaking it; but John was pretty well determined, only they all agreed that he must feel his way and obtain some positive information as to the sort and amount of support which Peel would and could give him. Clarendon urged this very strongly, and John quite agreed. This morning, at eleven o'clock, they are all to assemble at his house, and in the afternoon John and Lord Lansdowne are to go down to Windsor together. Nothing will, I apprehend, be definitely settled till some communication, direct or indirect, has taken place between Peel and John, so that the latter may have some certain knowledge of the intentions of the former. John has, however, already had some communication with Graham, but I do not know what. The language at Brooks's is generally that of extreme despondency; but I have done my best to encourage them, and have told all those I have communicated with (and most of them come to me for information or an opinion) that the new Government will not fail. I met Lord Lansdowne last night, and I found that he meant to come back to his Old office. However, the distribution of places will be a very difficult matter, the adjustment of claims and expectations, and making these square with the exigencies of the crisis.

Clarendon just come in. Yesterday afternoon Graham met Lord Lansdowne and John; the conversation was frank and amicable. Lord John said He must ask 'what was the measure which Peel had intended to propose.' Graham said he could not tell him without Peel's consent. This morning he received a letter from Graham recapitulating what had passed, but informing him Peel declined to tell him what his intended measure was. It seems, however, that it was a measure of Repeal, or leading to ultimate Repeal, accompanied with certain other measures of relief; that in November He announced to his Cabinet that he thought this necessary; but that it was received with such opposition that *He never laid before them his measures*, and the Cabinet has actually broken up without knowing what they were. Strange and incredible as this appears, it must be true, for Graham told John so. His and Peel's motives were, that the state of Ireland is so awful (famine and complete disorganisation, a social war probable) that money and coercive laws must have been called for; and these they could not demand of Parliament, and leave the Corn Laws as they are.

There was a meeting at John's house at eleven to-day; present, the same as before, and the Duke of Bedford and Baring. John produced Graham's letter. Lord Lansdowne said that certainly he could not say there was anything in it at variance with what he had said at their interview, but that there was an appearance of drawing back in it, and something in the tone that he did not like. The feeling of the meeting was, that Peel and Graham were not going to deal fairly and frankly with them, and they would not hear of Peel's excusing himself from divulging his intentions, and giving as the excuse for his refusal that he could not tell a plan which he had not told his colleagues. They unanimously agreed that great caution and determination were necessary, and that they must see their way more clearly before they committed themselves to taking office. It was settled that Ld. L. and John should go together to Windsor and tell her My. what they proposed. This was, that Peel should be again invited to state frankly what sort of measure he contemplated and would be prepared to support; and if he refused to do this, John was to commit to paper a project, which was to be sent to Peel, desiring at the same time that he would say whether he would support it, and what amount of support he calculated on being able to bring with him. They will have no appearance of intrigue or underhand dealing, but an open, frank proceeding which may enable them to see the exact condition in which they stand. I saw the Duke of B. soon after Clarendon, who gave me precisely the same account that C. had done; that John had acted with great judgement in his communication with the Queen, not pressing her or asking for details about the differences in the late Cabinet, taking what she chose to tell. He advised her to ask the Duke of Wellington, as from herself and before the new Government was formed, to continue at the Head of the Army, as He said the Duke might not chuse to remain if invited by John, but probably would if desired by her; and she said she would. She wrote to Melbourne, and told him she had sent for John, knowing that the state of his health would not admit of his assisting her. He wrote back word that a voyage from Southampton to Cowes would be as bad for him as to cross the Atlantick.

The Queen began to John immediately about Lord Palmerston, and expressed great alarm at the idea of his returning to the F.O., and her earnest desire that he would take the Colonial Office instead, and that John would propose it to him. She had already talked to Aberdeen about it, who told her she must make up her mind to P.'s returning to the F.O., as he would certainly take nothing else. They agreed (John and those whom he told of this) that it would never do to propose any other office to him, and it was much better to avoid any appearance of reluctance or distrust, and to give it him at once. But they mean that the Queen should herself express to P. her earnest desire that nothing may be said or done to interrupt the amicable relations which subsist between her and the K. of the French, and that P. should be at once made to understand that the F.O. is to be a Department of the Government, the affairs of which are to be considered in common, and not dealt with according to his good will and pleasure. He will not like this, but (with or without a struggle) he will no doubt conform to it; and John Russell is not a man to surrender the proper functions of a Head of the Government, or to be either tricked or bullied into letting Palmerston be independent and arbitrary. Clarendon told John not to think about him in making his arrangements. John threw out a hint about Ireland; but he at once said he could not go there at the expense of the certain ruin of his health. He asked his Brother[1] if He would take office, but he said it was out of the question. I try to persuade him to be in the Cabinet without a place, and to this he seems rather inclined. There will be great difficulties about the offices, between the necessity of inviting new men (such as Cobden and C. Villiers); men once but not last in office, like Grey, Auckland, C. Wood, G. Grey, Clanricarde, etc.; and adjusting the pretensions of the men turned out by Peel. Then Minto in his own person presents an enormous difficulty, being universally considered a detriment and a disgrace to the Government, a man whom all would repudiate, but who, being John Russell's Father-in-law, will come in if he insists on it, and to whom it would be difficult for the others out of delicacy to object. There was an admirable article in the 'Times' (13th), giving the whole *rationale* of Peel's four years of office, of his conduct, motives, and the feelings and sentiments which he engendered, excellently done and perfectly true.

Tuesday, December 16th—Nothing settled; L. and J. R. went to Windsor on Saturday. The first novelty that struck them was the manner of their reception; all changed since they went out of office. Formerly the Queen received her Ministers alone; with her alone they communicated, though of course Albert knew everything; but now the Q. and Prince were together, received Lord L. and J. R. together, and both of them always said *We*— '*We* think, or wish, to do so and so; what had *we* better do, etc.' He is become so identified with her that they are one person, and as He likes and she dislikes business, it is obvious that while she has the title he is really discharging the functions of the Sovereign. He is King to all intents and purposes. I am not surprised at this, but certainly was not aware that it had taken such a definite shape. However, they told the Sovereigns that they thought it necessary to obtain a positive assurance that the dissentient section of the Cabinet was unable, and would in no case undertake, to form a Government, and suggested that they should either send for or write to Peel, and ask him the question. The Prince wrote, and last night John R. got from him Peel's answer, which was a distinct declaration that those persons could not and would not attempt to form a Government. This

[1] The Duke of Bedford.

morning there is another and more numerous meeting, for now the scattered Whigs have had time to arrive. Peel having refused to disclose his intentions in his Cabinet, it now remains for John to tell him what he is inclined to propose, and to ask him if he will support it. What this shall be will be discussed this morning. The greatest doubt prevails in the town about the formation of the Government, but I have no doubt that it will be formed. If Peel and Graham would communicate frankly with J. R., and really try to come to some understanding or fair compromise; if they would consider the difficulties together and make a joint attempt to remove them, the work would not be difficult; but there is always a great difficulty when it is necessary to deal with such men as Peel and Graham—the one cold, reserved, suspicious, and insincere, the other slippery.

Certainly the contrast between Peel's position and his reputation on his coming into office four years ago, and at this moment of his quitting it, are most remarkable and curious. Never was any Minister so triumphant as He was then. He had routed his opponents, reduced them to a miserable state of weakness, and heaped unpopularity and discredit upon them. With his own party He was like a General who had just led his troops on to victory; they looked up to him with admiration, and obeyed him implicitly; all the world was admiring and applauding him, abroad and at home. And what has been his career before the world? Successful to the uttermost of general expectation; personally he vanquished the dislike of the Queen and ingratiated himself entirely with her. He terminated dangerous contests and embarrassing disputes, he restored peace, he put the finances in good order. It would be difficult to point out any failure he suffered, and easy to show that No Minister ever had to boast of four more prosperous years, or more replete with public advantage and improvement. His majority in both Houses of Parliament has certainly not been diminished; and if He had met Parliament as Minister next Session, He would in all probability have found himself supported by majorities quite as large as when he took possession of the Government. And the end of all this triumph, popularity, prosperity, and power is a voluntary fall, a resignation of office in the midst of such a storm of rage, abuse, and hatred as No other Minister was ever exposed to. His political opponents are not disposed to give him credit for either wisdom or patriotism, while his followers (friends he has none) heap reproaches upon him, in which they exhaust the whole vocabulary of abuse, and accuse him of every sort of baseness, falsehood, and treachery. And what is the cause of this mighty change? It is because he is wiser than his people, that he knows better than they do what are the true principles of national policy and national economy; because, amidst a chaos of conflicting prejudices and interests, amidst the clashing of mighty powers, he entertains sound views and wants to give effect to them. It was well said that it was his purpose 'to *betray* the country into good measures.' The tendency of his measures has been good. If he had had time, he would have accomplished much good; but he was unfortunately 'cribbed, cabined, and confined' by his antecedent conduct, and he has been obliged to work his way by the employment of means destructive of his character, subversive of his influence, and, in the end, fatal to the objects which he had in view. The history of Peel's four years is well worth a close study. There is so much in it in connexion with the past to blame, so much in connexion with the future to praise, and all well worth pondering upon and fit to point a moral.

Afternoon—The meeting took place this morning, fourteen or fifteen present. The day before Howick[1] had arrived, and immediately began squabbling with and dissenting from everybody. He and Ellice were with John together, and John so much disagreed with Howick's violent views (for he was all for extreme measures, immediate repeal, no compensation, tramping on adversaries), that H. said pettishly, 'I see it would be useless for me to attend your meeting to-morrow.' Ellice interfered and said, 'Oh, nonsense, you had better come,' and he did. Johnny said he was very sorry Ellice had prevailed on him to come.

John had written to the Queen, and begged her to obtain a more positive answer whether the Protection part of the Cabinet would or could form a Government; and the Queen wrote to Peel accordingly. Peel's answer John received this morning; it was a long letter, four sides of paper. After stating positively that the dissentients would not make the attempt, he went on to say that he was disposed to support the measures of the new Government, but that he thought it better there should be no direct communication between them; that it would give offence to many people, and not be relished by Parliament; that he could say that there were many Peers who, whatever their opinions might be about the Corn Laws, would be anxious that any measure which passed the H. of C. should pass the H. of Lords, and would do all they could to assist it. This letter was first read separately, and then when Lord Lansdowne arrived late (from Bowood), and they all took their places, it was read aloud. After considerable discussion upon it, some thinking it was not enough, Clarendon proposed that another letter should be written to the Q., requesting that she would ask Peel whether He would be opposed to a measure of immediate and total repeal, accompanied by other measures of compensation, but entering into no details, and not saying what measures of compensation they meant. This was supported

---

[1] Greville refers to him as either Howick or Grey.

by Howick, and finally agreed to. They now know that Peel intended to propose immediate suspension and final abolition, but with a short period of revival. The Whigs think this will never do; they do not indeed see any great cause for the immediate suspension; but to say so would be inconsistent with all they have been lately urging, and would make them appear less liberal than Peel. Then they do not think the Corn Laws, once suspended, can ever be allowed to revive; so on the whole they prefer immediate and total repeal, with other measures of a compensatory nature. His letter was to be despatched to the Q. to-night, who would, of course, send it to Peel directly, and on his answer the formation of the Government depends. The Queen in sending Peel's letter expressed her concurrence with his reasoning, and her hope that it would be found satisfactory, and begged to have the letter back again directly. Clarendon, from whom I heard all this, told me the meeting went off very well, and on the whole harmoniously. I wanted C. to contrive that there should be some communication made through Graham to Peel, that he may understand how much depends on the answer he may think fit to send. He ought to be frank and candid, but it is not in his nature, and there are many people who fancy he wants to have the Government thrown back upon him, and to go on. I do not believe this.

Friday, December 19th—Yesterday morning the die was cast. John Russell accepted the Government. As I have already said, He wrote a letter to the Queen and a remarkably good one, setting forth that he did not think Sir R. Peel's plan would be sufficient, and his reasons why, and begging to know whether He would have insuperable objections to total and immediate repeal. It was certainly understood by his whole conclave that on Peel's reply to this appeal to him was to depend the question of taking or refusing the Government. The Queen sent it to Peel, and all day on Wednesday He and Graham sat in consultation upon it. On Wednesday evening He sent his reply, and yesterday morning there was another meeting at John's, where the reply was read. It was very cold, declined to enter into any discussion to give any pledges, and expressed a hope that H.M. would not consider him wanting in respect if he referred her to his former letter. On this being read there was a silence, when Clarendon first said, 'There, you now see the wisdom of having required a positive assurance from Peel. It is evident that he will not support us, and there can be no question that it will not do for us to take the Government upon it.' Howick instantly interposed that he did not see that at all, quite disagreed with him, thought Peel could not say more, and that it was quite as much as they could expect. Then ensued a quantity of conversation and discussion, all the pros and the cons, Peel's peculiar character and position, and, in short, whether they should go on or give it up. At length John, who had stood with folded arms and let this go on for some time in silence, said, 'If you wish to know my opinion, I think we ought to take the Government.' He did not enter into any argument, but thus pronounced his opinion, and at last it was put to the vote. Ten were for taking, five were for declining: Lord Lansdowne, D. of Bedford, Clarendon, and two others (whom I do not yet know) were against; all the others for. On the whole I think they did right. The only awkward part of it is that they seemed at first to announce a determination only to accept it provided they could get a certain assurance from Peel. To ask for that assurance—to be refused by him—and then to draw back from their announced resolution—to submit to his refusal—and take the Government without it as they could not have it with it—there is something in this rather mortifying and a little undignified. But though Peel would not pledge himself to any particular course, there is one very important feature in his conduct. If He has not said that he had no insuperable objection to the measure they contemplate, neither has he said that He has; and he has, after learning the extent to which they mean to go, given the same assurance of a disposition to support them which he gave before he knew it. I think, therefore, that he means to act fairly by them, to give them his support, and that he really does think that it is better for them as well as for himself that he should not say more or pledge himself more, and that he should be able to tell the H. of C. and his friends that he is unfettered, and that there is neither arrangement nor understanding between them. I should certainly have voted for accepting if I had been there. It is obviously Peel's interest to act a fair and honorable part. In no other way can he stand well with the country; and in spite of the hatred of the Tory Landlords and his political followers, and the abuse of the Press, there is a very strong impression throughout the country amongst the well-informed and business-like middle Classes that Peel is the ablest of our public men, that his intentions are good, his principles sound, and his measures wise and skilful; that on the whole, in spite of prejudice and obloquy, he has governed the country well and supplied correction and improvement in every department and direction. Peel's conduct at the present moment seems to me to be inconsistent with any design of acting unfairly by the new Government. There is such an inveterate distrust and suspicion of him that many people cannot be persuaded he is not hatching some secret and cunning plot to overthrow them in the end; but if his object had been to recover power and reconcile himself with the Tories, he had now in his hands a better opportunity than he can ever expect to find again; if he had only said one word, the Government fell back at once into his hands; if he had said he had insuperable objections to total and immediate repeal, J. R. would at once have declined, and the Q. would have sent for him again. He would have reformed and reinforced his Cabinet, and he would have told the Tories he came back to save them from the extreme measure of John Russell; he would have invited them to support his safer and more moderate measure; instead of appearing as their destroyer he would represent himself as standing between them and destruction, as their defender against ruin. That with his dexterity he might have turned this to account and have assuaged the fury of many of them can hardly be doubted. But he has done nothing of the kind; and in not taking this advantage and rejecting the Government thus placed within his grasp, I think there is far greater assurance of his fair intentions than reason to doubt them because he will not give specific and definite pledges and assurances. All this I have said to Clarendon this morning who has been all along disposed to take a different view of the case, and has been the principal Advocate for caution and non-acceptance.

December 20th, Saturday—No novel or play ever presented such vicissitudes and events as this political drama which has been for ten days acted before the public. Yesterday, when I went to dinner at Lord Foley's, Leveson whispered to me that 'everything was at an end.' I had seen nobody in the afternoon and knew nothing, but after dinner he told me Gore had told him this. I went off to Kent House[1] and there heard the whole story. Yesterday morning they met at John Russell's as usual, and first began by a discussion of the compensations, Lord Lansdowne and others thinking it advisable to come to an agreement as to the general principles on which they should proceed in this important particular. Howick as usual argued, disputed, and battled, but at last this question was settled. Then J. R. said, 'Now, if you please, I want to see you singly, and I will begin with Howick.' Accordingly the rest went into the next room. Howick remained there forty minutes, at the end of which he stalked (or rather limped) out, head in the air, and, without saying a word to anybody, took himself off. J. R. then called in one or two more and told them what had passed. He had offered Howick the Colonies. H. accepted, but begged to know the other arrangements, and particularly who was to have the F.O. He told him 'Palmerston.' Then said H., 'I will not be in the Cabinet.' He argued with him, told him all the reasons for this arrangement, said everything he could think of, but all in vain. So they parted. The Bear Ellice, whom John called into Council, said it was intolerable; and He and Sir G. Grey (who

[1] The London home of Mrs. George Villiers.

was to have the Home Office) went after him, and it was settled there should be another meeting in the evening. They could not find him for a long time, and when they did he was as obstinate as a mule and would hear of nothing. It appears that some days ago John Russell did sound P. about taking another office, hinted that people were alarmed at him, but said he would not offer him anything else, and that the F.O. was at his disposal. P. did not bite the least, but treated the alarms as fictitious or ridiculous, said he knew nothing of any other office, eulogised his own administration, and said he would take nothing else. Howick had on his side written a letter to J. R., not objecting to P., but intimating that he should expect to be informed how the offices were to be allotted: something indicative of a possible breeze, but not of the storm which has burst forth. In the middle of the day J. R. wrote to P. and told him a difficulty had arisen, and that *one* of their colleagues objected to his taking the F.O. P. very properly replied that 'this was an additional reason for his accepting no other.' In the afternoon J. R., finding Howick would come to no terms, declared that he would throw the whole thing up, that he could not do without Grey in the Lords, and that the breach with him would produce difficulties and embarrassments that would materially impair his chance of success. Peel was to go down to Windsor this morning to resign, and J. R. wrote to the Queen to inform her of what had occurred, and begged her to put Peel off till the afternoon, and meanwhile he would himself go down to Windsor, where he is, in fact, gone, to resign. I find that most of his colleagues concur in this resolution: Auckland (who was at Kent House) Clarendon and Ld. L., both of whom have always been against taking office, and I know not who besides. I think they are wrong. It may be a question whether they ought to have accepted or refused upon Peel's letter, whether they had then grounds enough; but it seems to me pusillanimous and discreditable to suffer Howick to break up the Government they had consented to form, upon a purely personal question, unmixed with any political one. So far from considering it a misfortune and his secession a loss, it ought to be considered a great gain; for with such a temper and disposition as his, it is evident that if it would be difficult to go on without him, it would be much more difficult to go on with him. There is a want of dignity and firmness in suffering such a man and such a cause to overthrow an arrangement all but completed, which will, I think, expose to censure all the parties concerned; and especial indignation will be excited against Howick. Such is the state of things this day at twelve o'clock; but from hour to hour it is impossible to say or guess how it may all be changed.

The Government is really like a halfpenny whirling in the air, with J. Russell's head on one side, and Peel's on the other.

Sunday, December 21st—J. Russell went down at eleven o'clock, resigned, and the Queen accepted his resignation. He gave her a Minute, setting forth his difficulties (but without naming Grey and Palmerston) and explanatory of his motives; exceedingly well done, I am told, terse and clear. This he left with her to show to Peel. She behaved very graciously to him, thanked him for his exertions, approved of his conduct, particularly in supporting Palmerston, on whom She pronounced a high eulogy; praised his talents and industry, and said she was sure he would have ably and faithfully discharged his duty; and She expressed her indignation at Howick's conduct in the affair; and said that She had felt sure it was Howick who had caused the difficulty the first moment she heard of it, for she had just been reading over all Melbourne's letters to her during his Administration, and she found in them repeated complaints of Howick's behaviour. While he was in office every difficulty that occurred was attributable to him. She showed J. R. a letter from Louis Philippe, very judicious and expressive of his confidence that the change in her Government would in no way affect the good understanding which existed between the two countries. Nothing could be more satisfactory than this interview.

At two Peel arrived, and upon her informing him that J. R. had resigned, giving him the Minute to read, and requesting him to re-take the Government, he immediately and without making any difficulty consented to do so, saying, however, that he would have supported John Russell if he had formed his Government. The Queen wrote to J. R. and told him what had passed, which he announced to us at dinner at Palmerston's. I never saw people so happy, as most, perhaps all of them, are to have got out of their engagement; even Lady Palmerston said She did not wish for the Foreign Office again. It was generally known yesterday that Howick was the cause of this sudden break-up, and what he had done, and there was a general disposition to blame him severely, but also to blame them for not having let him depart and gone on without him. If they had been really anxious to come in, and if they had had an entire confidence in Peel's intentions, they no doubt would have done so; but the Peers of the party, who were all of them opposed to taking office on Thursday, were still more decidedly against it when they found Howick was to leave them. They had counted upon him as their principal Speaker in the H. of Lords, and when they found that the whole burthen was to fall on them, and that they were very likely to have Howick against them instead of for them, urging impossible measures, they vehemently pressed John to give it up; and this disinclination on the part of so many members of his Cabinet to face these difficulties determined him to resign. If Peel's engagement to support them had been more definite and positive, they would probably not have cared for Howick's secession; but, already dissatisfied with Peel, they were too happy to take the opportunity which Howick afforded them to draw back altogether. Peel's reserve was really then the cause of the failure, and I have a strong suspicion that he was thus reserved and abstained from pledging himself because he thought J. R. would very likely not be able to accomplish his task, that in case of failure the Government would fall back into his hands, and that He was resolved all the time to retake it if it was offered to him again. At all events he has shown his prudence, and it is very fortunate for him that he did not pledge himself to any particular course, and that he has kept himself at liberty to do exactly what he pleases. He is not the least pledged either for or against total repeal. The conversation I had with Sidney Herbert some nights ago gave me a suspicion that they were looking forward to the possibility, if not the probability, of their immediate resumption of office. I think, on the whole, John had sufficient reason for giving it up, but that the world—that is, the Whig world—and those who desired his success, who cannot know what was passing in his green-room, will thing he ought, after going so far, to have gone on to the end. The last scene will not appear to have been well played out. It will be thought that if they saw cause enough on public grounds to undertake it, they ought not to have been deterred from proceeding because one unreasonable member of the Cabinet raised objections and difficulties of a purely personal nature, and which had no reference to the great measure which it was their mission to carry through. This is, as far as one can see, the general opinion.

1847

April 2nd—My birthday: a day of no joy to me, and which I always gladly hasten over. There is no pleasure in reaching one's fifty-third year and in a retrospect full of shame and a prospect without hope; for shameful it is to have wasted one's faculties, and have consumed in idleness and frivolous, if not mischievous, pleasures that time which, if well employed, might have produced good fruit full of honor and of real, solid, permanent satisfaction. And what is there to look forward to at my time of life? Nothing but increasing infirmities, and the privations and distress which they will occasion. I trust I shall have fortitude and resignation enough to meet them, and I pray that I may be cut off and be at rest before I am exposed to any great trials. When we have no longer the faculty and the means of enjoyment in this life, it is better to quit it. With regard to that great future, the object of all men's hopes, fears, and speculations, I reject nothing and admit nothing.

> Divines can say but what themselves believe;
> Strong proofs they have, but not demonstrative.

I believe in God, who has given us in the wonders of creation irresistible—to my mind at least irresistible—evidence of his existence. All other evidences offered by men claiming to have divine legations and authority are, to me, imperfect and inconclusive. To the will of God I submit myself with implicit resignation. I try to find out the truth, and the best conclusions at which my mind can arrive are really *truth* to me. However, I will not write an essay now and here. Sometimes I think of writing on religious subjects among the many others which it occurs to me to handle. Ever since I wrote my book,[1] I have been longing to write again, and for more than one reason: first, the hope of again writing something that the world may think worth reading; secondly, because the occupation is very interesting and agreeable inasmuch as it furnishes a constant object and something specific to do; and thirdly, because I find that nothing but having a subject in hand which renders enquiry and investigation in some particular line necessary is sufficient to conquer idleness. Mere desultory reading does not conquer it, and there is a want of satisfaction in reading without an object. Why then do I not write, when I am conscious that I have a very tolerable power of expressing myself? It is because I am also conscious that I want knowledge, familiarity with books, recollection sufficiently accurate of the little I have read, and that facility of composition which extensive information and the habit of using it alone can give. It is when this struggle is going on in my mind between the desire to write and the sense of incapacity, that I feel so bitterly the consequences of my imperfect education, and my lazy, unprofitable habits. But no more of this now. To-morrow I am going to Newmarket to begin another year of the Old pursuits.

London, October 23rd 1847—After many weeks (or months) during which from idleness or unexplainable repugnance I have never written a line, I at last resume my pen, less for the purpose of writing the history of these past weeks than to begin again to record what occurs to me. Stirring

[1] Presumably his pamphlet on Ireland which had been published two years previously.

weeks they have been, and full of interest of the most general and lively description. In the midst of all the agitation that has prevailed at home and abroad, intrigues and quarrels and wars begun or threatened in various countries, we have been absorbed by the great panic in the money market, which is still at its height, and of which no man ventures to predict, or thinks he can see, the termination. There never was a subject on which such diversified opinions prevail. Men are indeed pretty well agreed as to the cause of the present distress, and in admitting that it is the result of over-speculation, and of the Railway mania which fell upon the country two years ago. But the great contest is as to the share Peel's Bill of '44 has had in aggravating and keeping up the state of distress and difficulty in which trade and commerce are involved, and whether this Bill ought to be presently relaxed by the authority of Government or not. On these points the greatest disputes and varieties of opinion exist. Charles Wood has, however, been stout and resolute from the first, and quite determined not to consent to any interference. There have been some different opinions, and some shades of difference, some doubts, amongst the members of the Cabinet, though I do not know the particulars of them; but yesterday the Cabinet broke up, having terminated their deliberations, and resolved *as matters now stand* not to do anything. My own belief is that this will prove a sound resolution, and that they would only have aggravated the evil by interference. I shall not, however, write anything more now on this subject. I have nothing secret or curious or interesting to record, and the details of it will be found in a hundred publications.

The most remarkable circumstance is the intense interest and curiosity which are felt about Peel's opinions and intentions. Everybody asks with anxiety what he says, what he thinks, what he will do. His vanity may well be gratified by the immense importance which is attached to his opinions and to the course he may take and recommend; his power seems to be as great out of office as it ever was in office; nothing was ever so strange or anomalous as his position. Half the commercial world attributes the distress and danger to his Bill; he is liked by nobody. The Conservatives detest him with unquenched hatred, and abuse him with unmitigated virulence. The Whigs regard him with a mixture of fear, suspicion, and dislike, but treat him with great deference and respect. There is a party which is called by others and by itself, but not (publickly at least) acknowledged by him as his party; it is far from numerous, and too weak for substantive power. He has never opened his lips on the great questions of the day, and is an Oracle shrouded in mystery. It would seem as if a man thus abandoned by the majority of his former political friends and adherents, without personal attachments and following, an object of hatred to one party and of suspicion to the other, the country at large or a great proportion of it attributing to his financial measures the distress by which all are afflicted or endangered, could by no possibility occupy any great and important position in the country: nevertheless he does. All eyes are turned upon him as if by a sort of fascination. If the country could be polled to decide who should be Minister, he would be elected by an immense majority. There is a prevalent opinion that he *must* return to power; nobody knows when or how, but the notion is that the present men are weak, that the publick necessities and perils are great, and if a crisis of difficulty and danger should arrive, that Peel is the only man capable of extricating the country from it. The consequence of all this is that his prestige and his influence are enormous.

Newmarket, November 1st, Monday—I came here last Saturday week. On Friday I believed it to have been *settled* that nothing should be done by the Government to relieve the panic. On that day, however, G. Glyn and other bankers had had an interview with John Russell, and they came from it with a persuasion that He would do something. The same evening Peel came to town in his way to Windsor. Charles Wood went to him, laid before him the state of affairs, telling him all the accounts they had received from the country, all the pressure they were undergoing, and explained their views and intentions. On the next day (Saturday) still more urgent demands were made, and still more alarming representations arrived. On Sunday, a Cabinet (or half Cabinet) was held, and there it was resolved to grant the relief that has been seen. The D. of Bedford was bidden to Windsor to meet Peel, who went there on Saturday. At dinner on Sunday the Queen received John's box with the result of the deliberations of the Cabinet, which He desired H.M. to communicate to Peel. The next day the Duke of Bedford had a long conversation with Peel, very amicable and very satisfactory. He spoke in high terms of John Russell and commended the Government, expressed his acquiescence under the peculiar circumstances of the case in the resolution they had come to, and declared his intention to support them. He appears to have talked very openly, and in a very friendly and even generous spirit. The Duke happened to have with him a letter which John had written to him at the time of Peel's Bill passing through Parliament, in which he had expressed his approval of the general principle, but found fault with some of the details. This letter the Duke showed to Peel, who was exceedingly pleased, and told him his brother was quite right, and that his Bill had been faulty in the details which he had remarked upon.

London, November 8th—The Archbishop of York is dead.[1] He was in no way remarkable except for the wonderful felicity of his whole life from first to last. It would perhaps be difficult to find a greater example of uninterrupted prosperity. He was not a man of great capacity nor of profound learning, but he had peculiarly the mens sana in corpore sano. He was nobly born and highly allied. He enjoyed robust health, had a vigorous frame with a sound understanding, and he was cheerful, obliging, good-tempered, and sociable; his profession, his tastes, pursuits, and the quality of his mind cast him into the best and choicest society, where he played his part not brilliantly, but with an amiable and graceful propriety. He had many friends and no enemies, was universally esteemed and respected, and beloved by his own family. He was the most prosperous of men, full of professional dignities and emoluments, and the inheritor of a large private fortune; he was the Father of a numerous family, whom he saw flourishing around him in opulence and worldly success; he lived in the exercise of a magnificent hospitality, and surrounded with social enjoyments. No misfortunes or sorrows disturbed the placid current of his life, and his mental and bodily faculties continued unimpaired to the last; his illness, which lasted only a few hours, was without pain, and no more than the natural exhaustion of ninety-one accomplished years. Such a life and such a death so irreproachable and fortunate may well excite envy and admiration. He and Mr. Grenville so conjoined in life died at the same age, each having reached his ninety-first year, and within eighteen months of each other—men in their different ways equally prosperous, virtuous, and happy.

November 21 1847, Sunday—Parliament met on Thursday; very queer-looking people among the new members, particularly Fox. I was introduced to him many years ago, when I went to Finsbury Square to hear him preach; he was a very fine preacher; never have seen him since.

State of Ireland awful. I have written to Clarendon repeatedly, urging him to ask for great powers. He was reluctant, and wanted to try the force of the law as it is, and the Cabinet were not disposed to adopt strong coercive measures; but the public voice loudly demands coercion and repression, and Ld. Lansdowne told me yesterday he was resolved to act in accordance with the general feeling. Parliament never met in more difficult and disturbed times: complete disorganisation, famine and ruin in Ireland, financial difficulty, general alarm and insecurity here, want of capital, want of employment. It requires all one's faith in the general soundness and inherent strength of 'the thing' (as Cobbett called it) to silence one's apprehensions. Then Colonial distress is impending (by which I am likely to be

[1] Edward Harcourt. He was 91.

personally affected to the extent perhaps of half what I possess). I thank God that I regard this contingency with the utmost tranquillity or insensibility. I should not like it, but if the necessity arises I hope and believe I can make the necessary sacrifices and changes in my habits without repining outwardly or inwardly. I have not heard or known much lately that is worth recording, and I am in one of my fits of disinclination to write.

December 1st—I went to the H. of Lords the night Parliament opened, and heard Stanley's speech. It lasted above two hours, was a declaration of war, very slashing and flashing, and drew forth vehement cheers from the Lords behind him. It was a regular Stanleyan speech, just like himself, and exhibits all his unfitness for the great functions of Government and legislation: not but what there was much truth in a great deal he said, especially about Ireland. The next day G. Bentinck bellowed and gesticulated for two hours in the H. of Commons with the same violence but without the same eloquence as Stanley. Everybody looked with impatience for the Irish measures, and everybody expected (most people earnestly desiring) that they should be as strong as they could be made. In the H. of Lords I had seen the D. of Bedford for a moment, who told me they were the result of a compromise between Clarendon and the Government, the latter refusing to give all he had required, and the former having resolved not to stay with less than he eventually obtained. The night before last Grey introduced the Government measures, which appeared to almost everybody insufficient for the object. Peel, however, supported them in a very dexterous speech. He said he felt bound to support the Government in whatever they thought fit to propose, and that it was not for Parliament to force upon them greater powers than they in their discretion required; but he hinted his apprehensions lest some of the provisions of the Bill (or rather its deficiencies) would be found obstructive of the objects in view. The Irish were evidently surprised and had expected more stringent measures, and in truth it would have been just as easy to carry a really efficient measure as this, which will probably prove abortive. This morning I have a letter from Clarendon, who tells me what took place between himself and the Cabinet on the subject. He says, 'I expect the Bill will prove unsatisfactory to all parties ... nevertheless I hope it will answer not so much by its own provisions as by the evidence it will afford that Parliament and the Government are in earnest. ... In the present temper of England fancy what a figure the Government would have cut if they had opened Parliament without any repressive measure and announced that the ordinary law would prove sufficient, and that *to it* things were left! They would have been looked on as little better than accessories or instigators, and at all events I have the satisfaction of having saved them from this very serious scrape, which really would have caused an immediate increase of murder here. No one could be more desirous than myself to avoid Coercion Bills, or indeed to ask for any increased powers; but when I found that the ordinary law was insufficient to protect life and property, I sent over the head of two Bills, both of which I meant should be permanent—one for punishing districts in which crimes were committed; the other for registering arms, etc.—a sort of police regulation proper for any country and especially required for Ireland. *These Bills were ignored by the Cabinet,* for which various utterly inexplicable reasons were given, and J. Russell said he hoped at least to get through the winter without any extraordinary measures. I then wrote both to Ld. Lansdowne and J. R. to say that though I did not wish to cause them any embarrassment, and would get on here as well as I could for as long as I could, yet that nothing should induce me to remain an hour after I thought my power of usefulness was gone, as I was sure it would be unless my hands were strengthened. This produced an immediate change, and the only question then was what would be the best form of repression. A good deal of time was lost on this, and G. Grey at length proposed as a model one of the Six Acts (1819). I did not like it very much, but I had no wish obstinately to adhere to my own Bills, which perhaps might not have been stringent enough, as they were proposed before things had got so bad and the spirit of combination was so manifest, and they were moreover intended to be permanent. So, after amending the Bill a little with the law officers here, I consented to it, and hope it will not be a failure when put into operation.' So that if John and his Cabinet had been left to themselves they would have done nothing, and have let the Irish murderers do their worst with no other hindrance than the ordinary course of law! Clarendon saved the Government by insisting; for if they had met Parliament and proposed nothing, they would have been swept away in a whirlwind of indignation. Addresses would have been proposed in both Houses and carried by immense majorities, and the Government would have been at an end.

December 7th—The Irish measures were introduced, and everybody was surprised they were not stronger. Peel supported the Government, and there was hardly any opposition. The Government people tell everybody that Clarendon is satisfied with the measures, thinks they will prove effective, and his name and authority silence objections. The day after Grey's speech I met Peel in the Park. He was in high force and good humour, and looking very fresh and well. After talking of some other things, I said, 'You supported the Government very handsomely in their Irish measure.' He replied, 'Yes, and I mean to support them; but they have made a great mistake and

missed a great opportunity; Parliament and the country would have confided to the Lord-Lieutenant any powers the Government chose to ask for;
they have totally misunderstood the state of Ireland and the feeling and
opinion of this country.' In short, he entirely agreed with me that they
ought to have asked for much stronger coercive powers. There are people
nevertheless who think it of greater importance to pass a measure quickly,
and with nearly general concurrence, and therefore that this is better than
one more vigorous, but which would be more strenuously opposed.

On Friday last Peel made a great speech on Wood's statement in re the
Bank Charter. It was very able, and the Government were delighted because
he supported them so cordially; the Opposition cut a very miserable figure,
and showed how wavering and uncertain they are, without plan, object, or
tacticks. They divided on a question of adjournment, and sent their weakness forth to the country, and did not move an amendment on which they
might have united all their force and caught many stray votes. I saw
Graham two days ago; he was chuckling over their mismanagement, said
that if they had moved that it should be an instruction to the Committee
to report at once on the Bill of '44, they would have put the Government
into difficulties and might have divided a large number; but he sees how
disorganised and inefficient they are. He talked about a great many things
in an amicable strain towards the Government, and a great deal on the
defences of the country, about which the Duke of W. is in such a perturbed
state of mind.

The Duke wrote a very long and able letter to Sir John Burgoyne some
time ago on this subject; this letter Lady Burgoyne and her daughters
copied and distributed among their friends. Pigou, a meddling zealot, who
does nothing but read Blue Books and write letters to the 'Times' and
'Chronicle,' contrived to get hold of a copy, and fired off a letter to the
'Morning Chronicle,' with a part of its contents. The Duke was not pleased
at this, and John Russell was very angry; it has made a noise in the world.
The Duke always accuses his old colleagues of doing nothing about the
defences, and turning a deaf ear to his remonstrances. Graham says this is
not true, and he showed me a very elaborate paper he had drawn up for
the Cabinet, with various recommendations, which he left with G. Grey
when he left the Home Office, and the copy of a Bill for calling out the
militia, which was also left with Fox Maule. He talked about Ireland, and
said that the Master of the Rolls (Smith) had drawn up a Bill for the sale
of the entailed estates, which he recommended Clarendon to look at. He
told me that Peel thought this an excellent Parliament, promising to be
practical and business-like, serious listeners and men intent on not letting

the time of the House be wasted as it has lately been by eternal talkers, and continual early adjournments. Everybody was alarmed at the aspect of this Parliament at first, even the Speaker, who thought it would be unmanageable. I laughed at their fears from the first, and now everybody says it is an excellent Parliament.

December 15th—The Chancellor[1] is very ill and not likely ever to sit again on the Woolsack. Great speculation, of course, about his successor (which people fancy will be Campbell or Rolfe), and Brougham evidently not without hopes of clutching the Great Seal himself. He has been attending assiduously at the Judicial Committee and behaving marvellously well, so attentive, patient, and laborious, everybody is astonished; but the D. of Bedford writes me word he has had letters from him expressing the utmost anxiety to see him and talk to him *on a matter of great importance which he can speak of to nobody else,* not even to John or to Lansdowne, and signing himself, 'Yours most affectionately, H. B.'! This is very amusing.

Hampden's Bishoprick has made a great stir after all: thirteen Protesting Bishops, a stout answer from John, a long, very clever rejoinder from the B. of Exeter, and a sensible protest the other way from Bishop Stanley. There never was a greater piece of folly than John's bringing this hornet's nest about his ears, nothing could be less worth while. It is not over yet, and there will be more kicking and clamouring; but John, however foolish he was in making the appointment, must of course go through with it now, and then like everything else it will be soon forgotten.

December 22nd, Tuesday—On Sunday to the Temple Church; divine musick and a very good preacher—a Mr. Hawes. Monday night dined with Milman and went to the Westminster Play; pretty well done. The Hampden controversy flares away. H. himself has written a long, querulous, ill-composed letter to John Russell, which he had better have let alone; if he did write, he should have written a shorter, more pithy, and more dignified letter. Every day makes the fault of having appointed him more apparent.

December 24th—John R. wrote an answer to the B. of Exeter, correcting a mistake in the B.'s letter, and assuring him of his persuasion that he had conscientiously fulfilled his duty in writing, and his respect for his talents and his position in the Church. This brought a rejoinder which is a curiosity —so writes the D. of B. to me, but I had already heard of the Bishop's answer—which was written in a state of delight at the politeness of John, and abounding in suavities of the most juicy description. John persists that he has done a very wise thing, and predicts that before long everybody will admit it, and this opinion is grounded on the knowledge he has of the

[1] Lord Cottenham.

dangerous progress of Tractarianism, which this appointment is calculated to arrest.

I went yesterday to St. George's Hospital to see the chloroform tried. A boy two years and a half old was cut for a stone. He was put to sleep in a minute; the stone was so large and the bladder so contracted, the operator could not get hold of it, and the operation lasted above twenty minutes, with repeated probings by different instruments; the chloroform was applied from time to time, and the child never exhibited the slightest sign of con-sciousness, and it was exactly the same as operating on a dead body. A curious example was shown of what is called the *étiquette* of the profession. The operator (whose name I forget) could not extract the stone, so at last he handed the instrument to Keate (who is the finest operator possible) and he got hold of the stone. When he announced that he had done so, the first man begged to have the forceps back that he might draw it out, and it was transferred to him; but in taking it he let go the stone, and the whole thing had to be done over again. It was accomplished, but not of course without increasing the local inflammation, and endangering the life of the child. I asked Keate why, when he had got hold of the stone, he did not draw it out. He said the other man's 'dignity' would have been hurt if he had not been allowed to complete what he had begun! I have no words to express my admiration for this invention, which is the greatest blessing ever bestowed on mankind, and the inventor of it the greatest of benefactors, whose memory ought to be venerated by countless millions for ages yet to come. All the great discoveries of science sink into insignificance when compared with this. It is a great privilege to have lived in the times which saw the production of steam, of electricity, and now of ether—that is of the development and application of them to human purposes, to the multi-plication of enjoyments and the mitigation of pain. But wonderful as are the powers and the feats of the steam-engine and the electrick telegraph, the chloroform far transcends them all in its beneficent and consolatory opera-tions.

December 26th—Lamartine's 'Histoire des Girondins' is the most success-ful book that has been published for many years. He is the Jenny Lind of literature; his book is on every table and in every mouth; it just suits the half-informed and the idle, whom it dazzles, amuses, and interests; only his apparent partiality shocks the humanity of the age; and the generality of readers are unable to comprehend his philosophical analysis, and psycho-logical theories of Robespierre's character. One of his most striking anec-dotes is the conversation he gives between Louis Philippe and Danton, in which, according to Lamartine, Danton predicts to the young Duc de

Chartres that he will one day be King, and tells him when that happens to remember the prophecy of Danton. I last night asked the Duc de Broglie if that anecdote is true. He said it was not true: the King indeed had had a conversation with Danton, when the latter said to him, 'Young man, what do you do here? Your place is with the Army.' So much of it is true, but the rest—the essential part, the prediction—is all false. The Duke told me he had read the King's own account of the conversation in his own journal, where it is recorded as he described. He said the King had kept a copious journal (now very long) from a very early period. He afterwards talked a great deal about him, of his great industry and activity, of the quantity he read and wrote, and that he read and commented upon all the documents submitted to him for his signature. I regret not having made more acquaintance than I have done here with the Duke de Broglie, and Jarnac gives me to understand that he had rather expected me to cultivate him more than I have, and was well disposed to receive my advances. The chief reason for my not doing so was that I found the greatest difficulty in understanding what he says.

1848

January 1st—The Hampden affair is still *boring* on with prejudicial effects to everybody concerned in it. Dean Merewether, who is piqued and provoked at not having got the Bishoprick himself (which Wm. 4th once promised him), wrote a foolish, frothy letter to John R., who sent an equally foolish, because petulant, reply—only in two lines. The B. of Oxford has recanted, and He of Salisbury has apologised for their respective parts; the former in a very ridiculous letter, not calculated to do him any credit. Everybody will believe that he found his conduct unpalatable at Court, so took a protext for shuffling out of it. So much for Sly Sam!

Last week, after a few days' illness, without pain or trouble, Lord Harrowby died at Sandon, having just completed his eighty-fifth year. The three Old friends, Tom Grenville, Archbishop of York, and Ld. H., thus died all three of old age, peacefully and painlessly, within twelve months. Ld. H. survived Mr. G. exactly a year, and the A.B. three months. He was the last of his generation and of the colleagues of Mr. Pitt, the sole survivor of those stirring times and mighty contests. He had all along such bad health that half a century ago his life was considered a very bad one, and yet he reached his eighty-sixth year with his faculties very little impaired. He was at the top of the second-rate men, always honorable and strait-forward, generally liberal and enlightened, greatly esteemed and respected. No man ever passed through a long political life more entirely without blemish or suspicion. It is curious that in the biographical notices of him, which according to the custom of the present day have appeared in the newspapers, no mention (or hardly any) has been made of by far the most remarkable transaction in which he ever was engaged, that of procuring the passing of the second reading of the second Reform Bill in the H. of Lords—one of the most important services (as it turned out) that any man ever rendered to his country. In conjunction with Ld. Wharncliffe he accomplished this, his conduct being perfectly disinterested, for he had long before resolved never again to take office, and had refused to be Prime Minister on the death of Canning. I was in their confidence, and much concerned in the whole of that transaction, as fully appears in my journal of that period. His speech on the first Reform Bill was very celebrated, exceedingly able, and superior to any other he ever made. He was remark-ably well informed. Madame de Staël speaks of him somewhere as 'Lord Harrowby, qui connaît notre littérature un peu mieux que nousmêmes'; but his precise manner and tart disposition prevented his being agreeable in society. He was very religious, very generous, and a man of the strictest integrity in private and in publick life. I lived a great deal with him, but all my intimacy was with his admirable wife, whose virtues and merits I have elsewhere recorded.

Bowood, Friday, January 7th—Came here on Tuesday, D. Bedford, Chan-cellor of Exchequer, Lord Devon, Auckland, etc., etc. Wood talked to me about his scheme of taxation; he has been in great doubt how he should apportion and increase (as he must) the income-tax, whether *income* or *property*. After much consideration he appears to have nearly made up his mind to impose three per cent. on Ireland, and to raise it in England to five, or perhaps something less; to announce that the increase is to be temporary, but the *three* per cent. to be permanent; and then, on the strength of the extension to Ireland, to propose a grant to that country, without which Clarendon cannot get on. Peel will concur in this plan.

Great talk here of G. Bentinck's resignation of the Leadership of the Opposition. John Russell and his colleagues are very sorry for it; nobody can think of a successor to him, and, bad as he is, he seems the best man they have. It seems they detest D'Israeli, the only man of talent, and in fact they have nobody; so much so, that Wood thinks they will be obliged to go back to G. B.; very strange state of things! G. B. and Stanley disagree on many points, especially on taxation; nevertheless this party, thus acephalous and feeble, have really been fancying they could come into office, and their notion is that if the dissolution had been delayed they would have had a majority, and would have come in. The D. of Beaufort told Bessborough so very seriously, and Lady Jersey told me the same thing, and that G. B. had promised her Son Francis a place at the India Board! These things are hardly credible, but they are nevertheless true.

The Hampden war has been turning greatly to the advantage of the Doctor; his enemies have exposed themselves in the most flagrant manner, and Archdeacon Hare has written a very able pamphlet also exposing the rascality (for that is the proper word) of his accusers, and affording his own valuable testimony to Hampden's orthodoxy; above all things, Sly Sam of Oxford (my would-be Director and Confessor) has covered himself with ridicule and disgrace. The disgrace is the greater because everybody sees through his motives: he has got into a scrape at Court and is trying to scramble out of it; there, however, he is found out, and his favor seems to have long been waning. The D. of Bedford tells me the Q. and P. are in a state of hot zeal in this matter. The P. writes to John every day very violent, and urged him to prosecute Dean Merewether, which of course John is too wise to do. That Dean is a very paltry fellow, and has moved heaven and earth to get made a Bishop himself; besides memorialising the Queen, he wrote to Lord Lansdowne and suggested to him to put an end to the controversy by making him a Bishop now, and Hampden at the next vacancy. The whole proceeding reflects great discredit on the great mass of Clergymen who have joined in the clamour against Hampden, and on the Oxonian majority who condemned him, for it is now pretty clear that very few, if any, of them had ever read his writings. Now that they are set forth, and people see his unintelligible jargon about dogmas themselves unintelligible, there must be some dispassionate men who will be disgusted and provoked with the whole thing, and at the ferocity with which these holy disputants assault and vituperate each other about that which none of them understand, and which it is a mere mockery and delusion to say that any of them really believe; it is cant, hypocrisy, and fanaticism from beginning to end. There is that old fawning sinner, the B. of Exeter; it appears that a dozen years ago he called on Hampden at Oxford to express to him the pleasure with which he had read his Bampton Lectures, and to compliment him on them. The Archbishop of Dublin was present on this occasion; he told it to Clarendon, who wrote it to the D. of Bedford, who told it to me.

January 12th 1848—From Bowood to Middleton on Saturday, to town on Monday (10th). The morning I left Bowood, Senior showed me the correspondence (not published) between the B. of Oxford and Hampden. It is creditable to the latter; the former really very despicable. The Bishop put a parcel of questions to him as to his belief on points of faith and doctrine, some of which were the most ordinary matter of belief, others unintelligible. Hampden said he might have regarded such questions on the most elementary points of doctrine as an insult, but he would accept his assurances that they were put in a friendly spirit (though he must say much of his conduct was at variance with such professions), and would therefore say 'Yes' to all of them. To his last letter announcing his having withdrawn the charges and read his work, etc., Hampden merely sent a dry acknowledgement of having received the letter.

January 17th—Still this Hampden affair. Kelly got a rule in Queen's Bench, and it will be argued in a few days. Tractarians hope from the known Puseyism of Coleridge and Patteson that the rule may be made absolute; but the Lawyers don't expect it, and think a *strong* Court would not have given a rule. However, it shows the anomaly (not to say worse) of the whole ecclesiastical proceeding under the Act of Henry VIII. The High Churchmen, who want a separation of State from Church (though it does not seem clear what it is they contemplate), are on the qui vive, and fancy their projects are put in a fair train by all these proceedings; but though some of my friends think very seriously of these crochets, I believe they are very despicable and harmless. This morning I got a letter from the D. of B. enclosing one from William Cowper to him, informing him what took place when Hampden was made Regius Professor. William Cowper had given me some account of it at the time, which I inserted in my journal, and I copied it out for the D. of B. during our discussion. I don't find that this more detailed account varies much from the other, though it contains several more particulars, and one (the Archbishop's nominees) curious enough. His account of the transaction is this, saying he got it from Lord Melbourne, and by reference to letters which passed at the time: 'The Archbishop of Canterbury came to Ld. M. to announce the death of Dr. Burton. In the conversation that ensued my Uncle requested the Archbishop to send him the names of the persons that occurred to him as best qualified for the situation, and begged him not to confine the list to a small number. The Archbishop sent a list including Pusey, Newman, and Keble; and if it was, as I believe, the list of the Archbishop which is now before me, it contained nine names; but it is possible he may have sent only six, and that the other three were added from another quarter. Ld. M. sent the nine names to the Archbishop of Dublin without mentioning who had recommended them ... and he justified the confidence reposed in him by giving a full and impartial statement of what he conceived to be the qualifications of each. But previous to this he had been consulted by Ld. M., and asked whom he would recommend, and had written (on 22nd January, 1836) a long letter in which he said: 'The best fitted for a theological professorship that I have any knowledge of are Dr. Hampden and Dr. Hinds (afterwards Principal of Alban Hall); the qualifications I look to, and which (in combination) they both possess in a higher degree than any others I could name, are, first, sound learning; second, vigour of mind to wield that learning, without which the other is undigested food; and third, the moral and intellectual character adapted for conveying instruction. . . . Both Hinds and Hampden are what are considered of liberal sentiments, but agree with me in keeping aloof from parties political and ecclesiastical." . . . Ld. M. doubted for some time between Arnold and Hampden, but, thinking the former rather too rash and unsettled in his opinions for so responsible a post, decided in favor of the latter; and it was not till after he had made up his mind that Hampden was the fittest person that he asked Dr. Copleston to give him his opinion of him, which opinion was so favorable that it confirmed him in his choice; he did not send any list to Copleston. You may rely on the accuracy of this statement as far as it goes.' The Duke also told me in his letter that there had been a very curious correspondence between Prince Albert and the Bishop of Oxford.

January 18th—I have this morning received a copy of the Archbishop of Canterbury's letter to John about making Hampden B. of Manchester. John wrote to him for his opinion, and here is his reply:—

> My dear Lord,—During the ten years which have passed since Dr. H. was appointed Regius Professor of Divinity at Oxford, I have no reason to believe that he has taught from the Chair any doctrines at variance with the Articles of our Church; and in justice to him I must say that I have discovered nothing objectionable in the few publications of his which I have seen and which are ably written; of his discretion or talents for business I have no means of judging. These qualifications may be more than ordinarily required in the first Bishop of such a place as Manchester. I have the honor to be, etc.
>
> W. CANTAUR.

This is his letter, which certainly warranted John in saying 'he received no discouragement from the Archbishop of Canterbury.' It amounts very nearly to a sanction of the appointment; and nothing but the Archbishop's age, and the timidity, both natural to him and belonging to his age, can excuse his not having taken a more active part in allaying the irritation than he has done. So far as the Archbishop was concerned, John understated his case.

January 21st, Friday—Dined on Wednesday with Baron Rolfe—Campbell, Langdale, Wilde, and Solicitor-General (Dundas); much talk about the rule in Queen's Bench (in Hampden's case), and whether the law must be altered. Campbell against alteration, the rest thinking there must be some, and the old law of Edward VI making the Bishopricks donative restored. This is what Lushington told me must be done.[1]

Brocket, January 22nd—Came here this afternoon, Melbourne having at last invited me. I have been intimately acquainted with him for thirty-five years, and he never before (but once to dinner) asked me into his house. He expects people to come, and at dinner to-day he proclaimed his social ideas and wishes. 'I wish,' he said, 'my friends to come to me whenever they please, and I am mortified when they don't come.' I told him he ought to send out circulars to that effect. He is well and in good spirits, and ready to talk by fits and starts, very anti-Peel and anti-Free-trade, rattled away against men and things, especially against the Denisons, and the Bishop of Salisbury in particular. I asked 'Why then did you make him a Bishop?' He said 'It was the worst thing I ever did in my life.' As usual, he put forth some queer sayings, such as that 'Nobody ever did anything very foolish except from some strong principle, he had remarked that.' M. said very little about the Hampden quarrel, only that he 'thought John might have avoided it.' He told me he had wished to make Arnold a Bishop, but —— (I forget who) had told him if he did he thought the Archbishop would very likely refuse to consecrate him; so he gave up the idea without finding out what the Archbishop thought of it. Beauvale very strong against Palmerston and delighted with the articles in the 'Times' attacking his administration and his letter to the Greek Government; thought it very lucky he had not gone to Paris, where he must have quarrelled with P. for not obeying his absurd instructions, qu'il avait passé par là at Vienna. When he was there, Lady Westmorland told him She had been commissioned to give him a hint that he would not be able to remain there and oppose Palmerston as he often did. He asked her who told her this; she said *Melbourne*! This was the way

[1] On December 11th an attempt was made to arrest the confirmation of Dr. Hampden as Bishop of Hereford in the church of St. Mary-le-Bow. But this was overruled by the Commissioners. On December 24th the Attorney-General showed cause against a rule *nisi* granted on the 14th by the Court of Queen's Bench, for a mandamus against the Archbishop of Canterbury. Judgment was given on February 1st. Mr. Justice Coleridge and Mr. Justice Erle were in favour of granting the mandamus; Lord Denman, C.J., and Mr. Justice Patteson against it. The Court being equally divided, no mandamus was issued.

the Prime Minister tried to prevent a rupture between his brother and his brother-in-law, not daring to face P., though disapproving of his policy and his ways. Well might Beauvale say P. would always have his way, for he was bold, resolute and unscrupulous; would not yield to others, and would make all others yield to him; and he is unchecked by publick opinion here, nobody knowing or caring anything about foreign affairs.

Lady Beauvale told me some anecdotes of the Royal children, which may some day have an interest when time has tested and developed their characters. The Princess Royal is very clever, strong in body and in mind; the P. of Wales weaker, more timid, and the Q. says he is a stupid boy; but the hereditary and unfailing antipathy of our Sovereigns to their Heirs Apparent seems thus early to be taking root, and the Q. does not much like the child. He seems too to have an incipient propensity to that sort of romancing which distinguished his Uncle, George 4th. The child told Ly. B. that during their cruise he was very nearly thrown overboard and was proceeding to tell her how, when the Q. overheard him, sent him off with a flea in his ear, and told her it was totally untrue.

January 26th, Wednesday—Came back from Brocket on Monday. Melbourne not much inclined to talk; dined at a quarter-past seven, and he went to bed, or at least to his room, at half-past eight. He is as Anti-Palmerstonian as his brother, agreed with me that P. had all along greatly exaggerated the importance of the Spanish marriage. Much talk with Beauvale, particularly about P., told me an anecdote of him which shows the man and how difficult he is to manage. During the Spanish discussions B. was at Windsor, and one day when the Prince was in his room a despatch from P. to John Russell arrived, which he wanted to show to the Prince, and afterwards to submit to the Q. for her sanction. Finding the P. was in B.'s room, he came there and read out the despatch. There was a paragraph in it saying that the succession of the Dsse. de Montpensier's children would be inadmissible by the constitutional law of Spain (or words to this effect). John said he thought this ought to be expunged; that we might say what we pleased as to the effect of treaties, but it did not become *us* to lay down the constitutional law of Spain; the Prince and B. both concurred, and John said he would strike out this passage, and submit it so amended to the Q. He did so, and H.M. took the same view. It was returned (so altered) to Palmerston; but when the despatch was published, it was found that Palmerston had re-inserted the paragraph, and so it stood! What more may have passed I know not, but it is clear that they all *stood* it, as they always will.

Lady Beauvale gave me an account of the scene at dinner at Windsor when Melbourne broke out against Peel (about the Corn Laws). She was sitting next M., who was between her and the Q.; he said pretty much what I have somewhere else stated, and he would go on though it was evidently disagreeable to the Q., and embarrassing to everybody else. At last the Q. said to him, 'Ld. M., I must beg you not to say anything more on this subject now; I shall be very glad to discuss it with you at any other time,' and then he held his tongue. It is however an amiable trait in her, that while she is *austere* to almost everybody else, She has never varied in her attachment to him, and to him everything has always been permitted; he might say and do what he liked. Now she constantly writes to him, never forgets his birthday. She is certainly an odd woman; her devotion and submission to her husband seem to know no bounds. When first she married Melbourne told her she must not expect her domestick happiness *never* to be ruffled. She did not like this at all. But it never has. Albert never looks at her handsome Ladies and Maids of Honor. He is absorbed with other objects, is full of ambition and the desire of governing and having political influence. He has attained this object for He and the Queen are now *one* with the Ministers, with these as well as with the last. It was very different in Melbourne's time. They think her clever; some say that she is cleverer than Albert, but he is remarkably well informed and takes vast pains with himself.

I wrote a letter the other day to the D. of Bedford about Palmerston and the impression his letter had caused, for him to send to John *if he chose it*. This morning I hear that he has sent it to him. He tells me at the same time that when he was at Windsor the Q. and A. both spoke to him about P., saying that they could say only to John what they said to him,—'very confidential'; but it is quite superfluous to tell me their sentiments.

January 27th—The D. of Bedford sent my letter (about P.) to J. R., who defends him; admits the letter was too strong, but goes off on his great ability and merit as displayed in the Swiss question: which nobody denies. I am not surprised at this; John is often obstinate and often weak. Le Marchant (his âme damnée) said this of him to me. He has his grievance, thinking he ought to have been Secretary to the Treasury and believing that Palmerston was the cause of his not being appointed. He thinks P. has taken a dislike to him, because he was the organ of communication between John and the 'Times.' This enraged Easthope, who saw the Government information flow towards the 'Times' instead of the 'Chronicle'; and he made his complaints to P.

The Attorney-General[1] has got into a scrape about his Son's election, but

[1] Sir John Jervis.

248

it remains to be seen if he will not get out of it; there was a petition against Young Jervis, and they gave the Petitioners £1500 to drop it. The bargain was discovered, and other parties presented a petition just in time. Dundas would be thrown into a great embarrassment by anything that removed the Attorney-General; he *could* not succeed; the Government would not have him, nor would be undertake it; he has no briefs, a thing unheard-of for a Solicitor-General, and the Government found him so useless that they ceased to consult him, and, desirous of getting somebody more efficient, they proposed to him to be Judge-Advocate, which however he refused: he hardly could have accepted it. He has many good qualities, is agreeable, and I like him; he is honorable, high-minded, proud, charitable, generous, accomplished, well-informed, and clever; but he is weak, timid, fastidious, affected, sentimental, and very often absurd, and in no small degree *a humbug*. Altogether he is unfit for rough work and active life, either forensic or political.

February 8th, Tuesday—Fortnight arrear. On Saturday week to Burnham Beeches; the Grotes, Mrs. Butler and Prandi, a Piedmontese Patriot, and formerly refugee, now restored by the adoption of liberal principles in Piedmont. He was condemned to death above twenty years ago, and escaped with great difficulty. He has lived ever since in London.

On Monday we received news of the revolution in Sicily, of the concessions extorted from the King, and since, of the promulgation of a constitution at Naples.

On Saturday week I read in the newspapers the speech Cobden made at Manchester abusing the D. of Wellington, and scouting the national defences. On Wednesday I wrote a letter to him in the 'Times,' which has had great success. I have received innumerable compliments and expressions of approbation about it from all quarters, and the Old Duke is pleased. I had no idea of making such a *hit*, but the truth is, everybody was disgusted at Cobden's impertinence and (it may be added) folly. His head is turned by all the flattery he has received, and he has miserably exposed himself since his return to England, showing that he is a man of one idea and no Statesman.

There was a meeting yesterday at Stanley's to chuse a Leader, but they parted without doing anything. Stanley said it was not for him to point out a Leader to the Members of the H. of C., and he eulogised G. Bentinck (who has taken his place on the back benches). They are to meet again to-morrow, and it is supposed Granby will be their choice! Except his high birth he has not a single qualification for the post; he is tall, good-looking, civil and good-humoured, if these are qualifications, but he is heavy, dull and ignorant, without ability or knowledge, destitute of ideas to express and of the art of expressing them if he had any; and yet this great party can find no better man.

February 10th—The Protectionists met yesterday and elected Granby, all the world laughing at their choice. It appears that the reports of G. Bentinck's easy and good-humoured retirement are not true. There was an angry correspondence, much heat, and considerable doubt about the sucsuccess, some being for Stafford, the majority for Granby, in the proportions of 60 to 40.

February 13th, Sunday—On Friday was with Graham for a long time, who talked of everything, affairs at home and abroad, Peel, J. R., Government prospects, etc., etc.; expressed a doubt if the Ministers were up to their work and capable of coping with all their difficulties, said Peel was 'more *sullen* than he had seen him,' and had the same doubts, but nevertheless was more than ever resolved to take office; hoped, however, that John might bring forward the state of the nation on Friday, and by making a great speech upon it show he was up to his situation; talked a good deal of colonial matters, and said the change in our commercial policy brought about the necessity of a great one in our Colonial policy, that we ought to limit instead of extending our colonial Empire, that Canada must soon be independent. He condemned the Caffre war, and extension of the Cape Colony, that we ought only to have a *Gibraltar* there, a house of call; condemned New Zealand and Labuan and Hong Kong; considered the West Indies interest as gone, and dilated at great length (and very well) on these points. Then on foreign affairs, which he thinks very critical, especially estranged as we are from France; wants Beauvale to be sent to Paris and Vienna to concert measures, and try to avert the dangers he apprehends. He is all for 'defence,' but says the only way is to draw our troops home which are scattered over our useless and expensive dependencies; entirely against the squadron on the African coast and keeping up that humbug, which he says costs directly and indirectly a million a year. I told him Auckland said it only cost £300,000; he replied, it was not so, and that including indirect expenses it cost a million. Caffre war another million, and now that we were going to add to the income-tax, it would only be endured by showing that we had made or would make every practicable reduction, and that we maintained no establishments that were not really necessary. He highly approved of my letter.

February 18th—Sumner appointed Archbishop, a great mortification to the Tractarians, and great joy to Low Church; but he is so excellent a man, and has done so well in his diocese, that the appointment will be generally approved. Went last night to the Lords to hear Lord Lansdowne bring in the Diplomatick Bill (with Rome); he made a very good speech.

I could not stay out the debate, being engaged to dine with Chief Justice Wilde, where he had a great party, almost all Lawyers, Parke, Alderson, Lushington, Talfourd. I sat next to Alderson, and found him a very agreeable man, Senior Wrangler, Senior Medallist, a Judge (and really a Lawyer), a Wit; a life all of law and letters, such as I might have led if I had chosen the good instead of the bad path. I always think of this when I meet such men who have 'scorned delights, and lived laborious days,' and now enjoy the benefit thereof. He told me he had been writing an exercise in the morning for one of his Sons at Oxford, a dialogue between Erasmus and More, on the preference of the Latin to the Greek as an universal language. There is a good saying going about of the Court of Exchequer and its Barons; it runs thus—Parke settles the law, Rolfe settles the fact, Alderson settles the bar, Platt settles nothing, Pollock unsettles everything. Campbell is anxious to write again, and talked to me of writing the history of the Reform Bill. I told him I could give valuable materials, but that it is not yet time. He wants me to write memoirs of the last twenty years, and was pleased to say no man was so well qualified to do it. That is not true, but I have some qualifications from personal acquaintance with the actors and knowledge of the events of that period, and I might have had, and ought to have had, much more, but my horrible life, habits and pursuits have prevented me, and only left me mere snatches of such real knowledge as could be turned to account.

September 28th—I was about to record my own proceedings and such other scraps as occurred to me, when my mind was diverted from all other topics by the intelligence of the death of George Bentinck. This event was so strange and so sudden, that it could not fail to make a very great sensation in the world, and so it did. It would be false and hypocritical were I to pretend that it affected me personally with any feeling of affliction, but I can say with truth that I was much shocked, and that I was sincerely sorry for it. I was sorry for the heavy blow thus inflicted on his Father and his family, and it was impossible not to regard with compassion and something of regret the sudden termination of a career which promised to be one of no small prosperity and success. He was in truth a very remarkable man, of a very singular character and disposition, and his history is one very much out of the common way. I am in one respect better, and in another worse, fitted to describe him than any other person, for nobody knew him so intimately and so well as I once did, nobody is so well acquainted with his most private thoughts and feelings as well as with his most secret practices; but, on the other hand, I should never be deemed an impartial biographer of a man from whom I have been so long and completely estranged, and between whom and myself there existed such strong feelings of alienation and dislike. Nevertheless, I will try to describe him as I think he really was, nothing extenuating, and nothing setting down in malice. The world will and must form a very incorrect estimate of his character; more of what was good than of what was bad in it was known to the publick; he had the credit of virtues which he did not possess, or which were so mixed with vices that if all had been known he would have been most severely reproached in reference to the matters in which he has been the most loudly and generally bepraised; but his was one of those composite characters, in which opposite qualities, motives, and feelings were so strangely intermingled that nothing but a nice analysis, a very close and impartial inspection of it, can do him justice. His memory has been kindly and generously dealt with; he was on the whole high in favor with the world; he had been recently rising in publick estimation; and his sudden and untimely end has stifled all feelings but those of sympathy and regret, and silenced all voices but those of eulogy and lamentation. He has long been held up as the type and model of all that is most honorable and high-minded; 'iracundus, inexorabilis, acer,' indeed, but the lofty and incorruptible scorner of everything mean and dishonorable, and the stern exposer and scourger of every species of delinquency and fraud, publick or private. Oh for the inconsistency of human nature, the strange compound and medley of human motives and impulses, when the same man who crusaded against the tricks and villainies of others did not scruple to do things quite as bad as the worst of the misdeeds which he so vigorously and unrelentingly attacked! But it is only possible to make his character intelligible by a reference to certain passages of his life, especially to his transactions and connexions with myself.

He was brought up at home under a Private Tutor, was not studious in early life, and very soon entered the army. I do not remember whether he went to a publick school. He soon distinguished himself in the army by his great spirit and courage, and by that arrogance which was his peculiar characteristic, and which never deserted him in any situation or circumstance in which he was placed. I well remember his getting into a quarrel which would have led to a duel, if his Father had not got me to go to the Duke of York, by whose interposition the hostile collision was prevented. I have, however, forgotten both the name of his antagonist and the merits of the case. He very soon quitted the Army, and when Mr. Canning became Prime Minister he made George his Private Secretary. It has been said that

Canning predicted great things of him if he would apply himself seriously to politicks, but I do not know whether this is true. It is certain that after Canning's death, although by no means indifferent to publick affairs, he took no active or prominent part in them, and the first development of his great natural energy took place in a very different field. He fell desperately in love with the Duchess of Richmond, and he addicted himself with extraordinary vivacity to the turf. At this time and for a great many years we were most intimate friends, and I was the depository of his most secret thoughts and feelings. This passion, the only one he ever felt for any woman, betrayed him into great imprudence of manner and behaviour, so much so, that I ventured to put him on his guard. I cannot now say when this occurred, it is so long ago, but I well recollect that as I was leaving Goodwood after the races I took him aside, told him that it was not possible to be blind to his sentiments, that he was exposing himself and her likewise; that I did not mean to thrust myself into his confidence in so delicate a matter, but besought him to remember that all eyes were on him, all tongues ready to talk, and that it behoved him to be more guarded and reserved for her sake as well as his own. He made no reply, and I departed. I think I repeated the same thing to him in a letter; but whether I did or no, I received from him a very long one in which he confessed his sentiments without disguise, went at great length into his own case, declared his inability to sacrifice feelings which made the whole interest of his existence, but affirmed with the utmost solemnity that he had no reason to believe his feelings were reciprocated by her, and that not only did he not aspire to *success*, but that if it were in his power to obtain it (which he knew it was not), he would not purchase his own gratification at the expense of her honor and happiness; in short, his letter amounted to this—

> Let me but visit her, I'll ask no more;
> Guiltless I'll gaze, and innocent adore.

At the time it was much believed that a liaison existed between them, and there were persons who pretended that they knew it. Stradbroke spoke to Richmond about it, and articles appeared in some of the low weekly papers, dealers in scandal, which he traced (as he believed) to George Lennox, Richmond's brother. Once and once only he spoke to me on this subject. He then poured forth all his feelings, but he gave me to understand that something had occurred of a painful nature. I did not ask and never knew what it was, and we neither of us ever recurred to the subject again. His intimacy with the whole family continued the same in appearance, but it was not without disagreeable drawbacks and occasional clouds.

I allude to this to show the terms of intimacy on which he and I were, and likewise to do justice to the purity and unselfishness of his devotion, for I am certain that all he said to me was true. He was, however, not of a very warm temperament, and this may perhaps materially diminish the virtue and the value of his high-flown and self-immolating sentiments; but let them pass for what they are worth.

The first time I ever knew him much occupied with politicks was during the great Reform battles in 1831 and 1832, when he was member for Lynn. He took much the same views that I did, and was very anxious to modify the Reform Bill and render it a less Radical measure. The people of Lynn wanted a member and commissioned him to find one, and he exerted himself greatly for that purpose. By his desire I applied to Kindersley, then a man of some eminence at the Chancery bar, but he declined. I remember that He and his Father did not coincide in their opinions. The Duke was frightened out of his wits, dreaded the loss of his vast property, and thought that the only safe policy was unconditional submission to the roar for Reform. Hating the measure in his heart, he was against any endeavour to arrest its progress; and he was not at all pleased with George for the part which he took. The latter, however, to do him justice, was never afraid of anybody or anything; and he sturdily but deferentially adhered to his own opinion in opposition to the Duke's. Meanwhile, he constantly attended Newmarket, and it was not long before he began to have horses of his own, running them, however, in my name. The first good racehorse he possessed was 'Preserve,' whom I bought for him in 1833, and She, alas! was the cause of our first quarrel, that which was made up in appearance, but in reality never. Of course in this quarrel (which took place in August 1835) we both thought ourselves in the right. Till then not an unkind word had ever passed between us, nor had a single cloud darkened our habitual intercourse; but on this occasion I opposed and thwarted him, and his resentment broke out against me with a vehemence and ferocity that perfectly astounded me, and displayed in perfection the domineering insolence of his character. I knew he was out of humour, but had no idea that he meant to quarrel with me, and thought his serenity would speedily return. I wrote to him as usual, and to my astonishment received one of his most elaborate epistles, couched in terms so savage and so virulently abusive, imputing to me conduct the most selfish and dishonorable, that I knew not on reading it whether I stood on my head or my heels. I was conscious that his charges and insinuations were utterly groundless, but what was I to do? I could not tamely endure such gross and unwarrantable insults, and I could not challenge my Uncle's Son. In this dilemma I consulted a friend, and placed the letter in his hands; he went to him, and (not I believe without great difficulty) he persuaded him to *ask* to withdraw it. It was agreed that the letter should be destroyed, and that there should be no ostensible quarrel between us; but it was evident that our turf connexion could no longer subsist, and accordingly it was instantly dissolved, and other arrangements were made for his stud. He sold some of his horses and got Lord Lichfield to take the others.

Then commenced his astonishing career of success on the turf; he soon enlarged the sphere of his speculations, increased his establishment, and ultimately transferred it all to John Day at Danebury, where he trained under all sorts of different names, it being a great object with him to keep his Father in ignorance of his proceedings. He and I met upon civil but cool terms, according to the agreement; but in about two years we began to jumble into intimacy again, and at length an incident happened which in great measure replaced our relations on their former footing. My horse 'Mango' was in the St. Leger, and I wanted to try him. John Day told me he was sure Lord George would gladly try him for me. I proposed it to him, and he instantly assented. We went down together and tried him. He won his trial, won the St. Leger, and George won £14,000 on the race.[1]— All this contributed to efface the recollection of past differences, and we became mutually cordial (and 'Yours affectionately') again.[2] With me the reconciliation was sincere. I had forgiven his behaviour to me, and desired no better than to live in amity with him for the rest of my life; whether it was equally sincere on his part he alone knew, but I very much doubt it. We continued, however, to live very well together up to the time when he brought out the famous 'Crucifix,'[3] when, without any fresh quarrel, our

[1] In 1837.

[2] It was not long after this that a very important incident in his *turf life* occurred. The Duke, his Father (the most innocent of men), had his curiosity awakened by seeing a great number of horses running in the names of men whom he never saw or heard of. These were all his Son's aliases. He asked a great many questions about these invisible personages, to the great amusement of all the Newmarket world. At last it was evident he must find out the truth, and I urged George to tell it him at once. With great reluctance and no small apprehension he assented, and mustering up courage he told the Duke that all those horses were his. The intimation was very ill received; the Duke was indignant. He accused him of having violated his word; and he was so angry that he instantly quitted Newmarket and returned to Welbeck. For a long time he would not see George at all; at last the Duchess contrived to pacify him; he resumed his usual habits with his Son, and in the end he took an interest in the horses, tacitly acquiesced in the whole thing, and used to take pleasure in seeing them and hearing about them—*G.*

[3] 'Crucifix' won the Two Thousand Guineas and the Oaks in 1840.

intimacy became somewhat less close in consequence of my perceiving a manifest intention on his part to keep all the advantage of her merits to himself without allowing me to participate in them. Still we went on, till the occurrence of the notorious 'Gurney affair,' on which he and I took opposite sides, and in which he played a very conspicuous and violent part.[1] While this was going on we were brought into personal collision at Newmarket in a matter relating to the revision of the rules of the Jockey Club, when his arrogance and personal animosity to me broke out with extraordinary asperity. There was still no regular and avowed quarrel till the Spring following (184–), when at a meeting of the Jockey Club I made a speech in opposition to him which he chose to construe into an intentional insult, and the next time he met me he cut me dead. I made several attempts, as did our mutual friends, to do away with this impression and to effect a reconciliation, but he refused to listen to any explanation or overture, and announced his resolution not to make it up with me at all. From that time our estrangement was complete and irreparable. He was now become the Leviathan of the turf; his success had been brilliant, his stud was enormous, and his authority and reputation were prodigiously great.

In 1844 he became still more famous by his exertions in detecting the 'Running Rein' fraud, and in conducting the 'Orlando' trial. There can be no doubt that the success of that affair was in great measure attributable to his indefatigable activity, ingenuity, and perseverance. The Attorney in the cause was amazed at the ability and dexterity he displayed, and said there was no sum he would not give to secure the professional assistance of such a coadjutor. He gained the greatest credit in all quarters by his

[1] A full meeting of the Jockey Club was held on February 5th, 1842, to consider the betting transactions of Richard Gurney at the Derby of 1841. Gurney had been a heavy winner but a still heavier loser over the account; and the Jockey Club had appointed three managers to collect the debts and pay the creditors, and until their certificate had been received Gurney was to be considered a defaulter. The required certificate that all the creditors had been paid in full was presented by the managers in the previous December, but Lord George Bentinck protested that some of the creditors had accepted a composition, which he held to be unfair to those who had paid their debts in full. After four hours' discussion Lord George was outvoted and the Jockey Club sanctioned the settlement arrived at. Thereupon a Mr. Thornton, who had paid £1250 into the pool under guarantee that the creditors were to be paid in full, sued the managers in the Exchequer Court and recovered the money, which he handed over to Christ's Hospital. The Stewards retaliated by advertising Thornton a defaulter; and they called upon the Duke of Portland, the lessee of Newmarket Heath, to warn him off. This the Duke refused to do, and published a letter in support of his son's view of the matter; while Thornton sued the Stewards for libel and was given £200 damages.

The Coalition Ministry, 1854

Left to right: Sir Charles Wood, Sir James Graham, Sir William Molesworth, W. E. Gladstone, The Duke of Argyll, Lord Clarendon, Lord Lansdowne, Lord John Russell, Lord Granville, Lord Aberdeen, Lord Cranworth, Lord Palmerston, Sir George Grey, Sidney Herbert, The Duke of Newcastle

From a pencil-and-wash drawing by Sir John Gilbert, 1855

Lord Palmerston

*From the portrait by
John Partridge, 1846*

Charles Spurge[

*Detail of the portra[
Alexander Melvi[*

conduct throughout this affair, which was afterwards increased by his manner of receiving a valuable testimonial, subscribed for the purpose of honouring and rewarding his exertions: he refused to accept anything for himself, but desired the money might be applied towards the establishment of a fund to reward decayed and distressed Servants of the turf, which was eventually denominated 'The Bentinck Fund.'

It was in the course of this transaction that an incident occurred which had in the end, though indirectly, an important influence upon his Character and his career. The Baron de Teissier, who was a Steward of Epsom races, had refused to entertain the protest which (before the Derby) was tendered to him against 'Running Rein.' His conduct was discussed at a meeting of the Jockey Club, when G. Bentinck openly and with his usual vehemence accused him of corrupt motives. The Baron demanded an enquiry; and one took place before the whole Jockey Club, at which G. Bentinck brought forward his charges in a very elaborate speech of two hours long. It will be seen hereafter what important consequences flowed from this speech. The following year (1845) there was a great explosion in consequence of certain malpractices (and suspicions of others) on the turf, and here again George B. took a very leading part, both in the Committees in Parliament and in the Jockey Club. He had now proclaimed himself to the world as the stern and indignant vindicator of turf honor and integrity, and he announced his determination to hunt out all delinquencies and punish inexorably the delinquents in whatever station of life they might move. Accordingly a great enquiry took place in October 1845 into the conduct of certain Jockies and others, as well as into that of two gentlemen (Messrs. Crommelin and Ives), against whom he displayed the most determined and bitter hostility. These men were frightened out of their wits, well knowing the vigilance, perseverance and virulence of their enemy; and they came to me to help them out of their dilemma. Their conduct had been very questionable, but there was enough that was doubtful in it, and it was in fact so very little worse (if proved) than that of many who carried their heads high in the air, that I could without any violent breach of conscience lend them my aid to extricate them from his clutches. I had been now so long pitted against him, and we had had so many encounters, that I will not deny that I took a personal pleasure and interest in baffling him; and I did so before I became acquainted with the disclosures which were elicited in the progress of this case.

About two years before this time his connexion with John Day had ceased. Differences had arisen between them and he had transferred his horses to Goodwood. The consequence was that He and the Days regarded each other with sentiments of mutual dislike; and they were exceedingly well acquainted with the characters of each other. Crommelin had long been connected with the Days, and in the hour of his danger they came in a very extraordinary manner but very effectively to his assistance. They told him they could furnish him with weapons which in case of necessity he could wield against Lord George with terrible effect; and that if the latter persisted in pursuing him to his ruin, he might overwhelm his accuser in a destruction not less complete. They had preserved all his correspondence during the whole period of their connexion, and the whole of it they now abandoned to Crommelin. He selected from the vast mass a number of important letters, which he brought to me. They were damning in their import, for they disclosed a systematick course of treachery, falsehood and fraud, which would have been far more than sufficient to destroy any reputation, but which would have fallen with tenfold force upon the great Purist, the supposed type and model of integrity and honor. (While I am writing this, I read in 'The Economist' as follows:—'He was the open and avowed enemy of the tricks by which horse racing is contaminated, and had acquired reputation by exposing and putting some of them down.')

I have now only a faint recollection of many of these revolting details, but some of them are indelibly impressed on my memory. The case of 'Crucifix' is at once the strongest and the most personal to myself. She was an extraordinary animal and great was his anxiety to turn her to the best account. In October, just before She ran for the Criterion stake at Newmarket, She hit her leg while turning round in the stable and after the race it was very much swelled. When he went to the stable and saw this he took fright, came down to the rooms, and availing himself of the favor She was then in he laid a great sum of money against her for the Oaks by way of hedging. This was quite fair, but the important part is what follows. He sent for the Veterinary Surgeon, Barrow by name, who, not knowing the cause of the swollen leg, gave an opinion that it was a very bad case, that She probably would not stand sound, and at all events must be blistered, fired, and thrown up for a long time. As soon, however, as She got home to Danebury young John Day, who was himself a Veterinary Surgeon, ascertained that no mischief was done and informed G. B. that She required none of the treatment Barrow had prescribed, but would be well again in ten days. On this he formed his scheme, his object being to get back all he had laid against 'Crucifix' and as much more as he could; and in order to do this, to make everybody believe she was lame and would never run again. He began by writing to Barrow and desiring him to send him in writing his opinion of the case; and having obtained this, he had a copy made of the letter which he sent to John Day, retaining the original in his own hands. Day was ordered to show this letter to everybody to whom he could find any pretext for showing it, while he did the same with the other, amongst other people to *me*, with whom he was then living on terms of amity and ostensibly of confidence. He knew that I had backed 'Crucifix,' and he showed me this letter by way of friendly advice that I might take an opportunity of hedging my money, while he took care to plant somebody to take the odds of me, when I laid them, as I afterwards did. This game he played with others who had backed 'Crucifix,' showing them (as if by accident and while talking of other matters, and complaining of his ill luck) Barrow's letter and advising them to hedge. He spared nobody. One letter to John Day which I saw was to this effect:—He told him that *George Byng* and *Mr. Greville* were going down to Mr. B. Wall's and would probably go over to Danebury to see the horses; that he would naturally show them, and he must take care to make 'Crucifix' look as bad and as 'bedevilled' as he could; that at any rate *I* should go over, and that if I did he was to take care to show me Barrow's letter. In a subsequent letter he said that he need not show me Barrow's letter, as he had already shown it me himself. The burthen of all his letters to John Day was to show Barrow's letter to as many people as he could. It completely answered, for he got a great sum of money upon her, both for the 2000 Guineas stake and the Oaks, both of which she won.

Besides this unparalleled issue of fraud, falsehood and selfishness, the secret correspondence divulged many other things, plans and schemes of all sorts; horses who were to be made favourites in order to be betted against—not intended to win; then horses who were to run repeatedly in specified races and get beat, till they were well handicapped in some great race which they were to run to win. There was a horse called 'Meunier,' against whom a great sum of money was laid, which was divided between *the Duke of Richmond* and himself.

One of his letters distinctly alluded to the bribery of Jockies who were to ride against him. He tells John Day he shall want to back some horse for so much for himself, so much for certain other people, and so much 'for the Jockies who were to ride against him in the race.' It would be unfair, however, to accuse him on this of direct bribery to the other Jockies not to win if they could. It was not this, but he thought it advisable as one of the means of success that the other Jockies should have some interest in his winning if they could not. However such a letter, if it had appeared, would have had a very *ugly* and suspicious look; and one can easily imagine what he would have said of it in anybody else's case.

All these things were concocted with infinite care and explained in elaborate detail, the whole forming such a mass of roguery that any attempt at explanation, extenuation, or palliation would have been vain. I will acknowledge that when this black budget was put before me, and I saw the man who had pursued me with the most unrelenting hatred thus delivered into my hands and his honor and position in the world placed at my mercy, a feeling of satisfaction was mixed with that of disgust and resentment. Not that I ever contemplated for a minute conniving at his exposure; I hope and believe that I should not have done so under any circumstances. But on his Father's account and for the credit and the peace of his family I would have done anything to prevent these letters being made publick. I therefore advised Crommelin to keep them for his own security and to deter G. B. from driving him to the wall, but neither then or at any other time to make use of them. Crommelin scrambled out of his difficulty, and the letters remain in his possession to this hour. The contents of them were made known to a few persons—I think to 4 or 5, amongst others to George Anson, who was one of the Court of enquiry (on Crommelin and the others), and who was put in possession of these documents that he might slur the matter over and, by saving Crommelin, be the means of saving G. Bentinck also; for if the former had been condemned and disgraced he was determined to publish the whole correspondence and drag his accuser down with him, and most assuredly he would have done so.

An intimation was conveyed to G. B. that he was threatened with a retaliation of some sort, and that the Days had put Crommelin in possession of certain letters of his. He affected great indifference, but the notification had a very evident effect on his conduct during the remainder of the enquiry and from that time he never molested Crommelin any more. As we were already not on speaking terms, I had no opportunity of evincing the feeling produced on my mind by these disclosures; but I rejoiced that the quarrel had never been made up, and of course resolved that it never should be, for I must have been the greatest of hypocrites if I could have ever met him again on terms of cordiality, knowing what I knew of his baseness to me. But the only revenge which I ever desired to take was this: I wished the day might come when he should know that I had been fully acquainted with his conduct in all its details, and that I had used my best endeavours (and that successfully) to prevent a publick exposure of it. This satisfaction was never given to me and he died in ignorance of all that had passed, and no doubt with the same sentiment of enmity and dislike, which when once kindled in his bosom was rarely if ever extinguished.

And now, after having laid bare his conduct, I will endeavour to do justice to his character, which, paradoxical as it may appear, I do not believe to have been nearly so bad as such facts would warrant its being pronounced. It was in truth a strange compound of inconsistent qualities and opposite impulses, which sometimes drove him into evil, but often urged him into good courses. Undoubtedly the man who *could* act thus must have had much that was sordid and selfish in his disposition and could not have been animated with those high and unerring principles which shrink instinctively from flagrant breaches of integrity, good faith and good feeling. His mind was disturbed and debased, and bad habits and evil desires had for a time at least silenced the voice of conscience and honor and made him no better than a rogue. But this was not his natural disposition; I believe that all the time he hated and was ready to wage war with every kind of villainy which he could detect in others, and had no indulgence for any misdeeds but his own. He had made for himself however a certain system of right and wrong, in which he allowed himself a very strange and enormous latitude. He would never have done anything which he thought wrong and which was not consistent with his own ideas; but he had taught himself to believe that such practices as I have described were permissible and all fair at the game he was playing.

He was exceedingly self-willed and arrogant, and never could endure contradiction; and whatever he undertook he entered into with an ardour and determination which amounted to a passion. As he plunged into gaming on the turf, he desired to win money, not so much for the money, as because it was the test and the trophy of success; he counted the thousands he won after a great race as a General would count his prisoners and his cannon after a great victory; and his tricks and stratagems he regarded as the tactics and manœuvres by which the success was achieved. Not probably that the money itself was altogether a matter of indifference to him: he had the blood of General Scott in his veins, who won half a million at hazard, and the grandson most likely chassait un peu de sa race.

But to do him justice, if he was 'alieni appetens,' he was 'sui profusus.' Nobody was more liberal to all his people, nor more generous and obliging in money matters to his friends, and I am inclined to think that while he was taking to himself the mission of purifying the turf, and punishing or expelling wrongdoers of all sorts, his own mind became purified, and (though I do not know it) I should not wonder if he looked back with shame and contrition to all the schemes, plots, and machinations which, in the ardour of his racing pursuit, he had so cunningly devised. What makes me think that it was less the base desire of pecuniary gain than the passionate eagerness of immense success which urged him on, is the alacrity

261

with which he cast away his whole stud (at a moment when it promised him the most brilliant results and most considerable profits) as soon as another passion and another pursuit had taken possession of his mind; one in which there was not only no pecuniary benefit in view, but the entire occupation of which obliged him to neglect his turf concerns so entirely that he lost a great deal of money in consequence.

This brings me to his very extraordinary political career. There was a paper published in 'John Bull' on Sunday last with a sketch of it, which is so true and accurate that I will insert it here. 'I well remember, in the winter of '45 (when Peel's intentions began to be known or suspected) what indignation he expressed and what violent language he used about him. As soon as Parliament met he began to take an active part amongst the Protectionist malcontents, and he devoted much time to getting up the pro Corn Law case. He had never studied political economy, and knew very little on the subject, but he was imbued with the notions common to his party that the repeal of the Corn Laws would be the ruin of the landed interest; he therefore hated the Anti-Corn Law League, and—considering that the first and most paramount of duties was to keep up the value of the Estates of the order to which he belonged, and that Peel had been made Minister and held office mainly for this purpose—he considered Peel's abandonment of Protection, and adoption, or rather extension, of Free Trade, as not only an act of treachery, but of treason to the party which claimed his allegiance, and he accordingly flung himself into opposition to him with all his characteristic vehemence and rancour. Still neither He himself nor any one else anticipated the part he was about to play, and the figure he was destined to make. One of the men whom he was in the habit of talking to, was Martin, Q.C.' and he told him that he had a great mind to speak on the Corn Law debate, but that he did not think he could; he had had no experience and could not trust himself. Martin told me this. I said I thought he could; that I had been struck with a speech he had made against the Baron de Teissier, when he had spoken for two hours, and in a way which satisfied me he had *speaking in him*. Martin went and told him this, which struck him very much, and it decided him (so Martin told me) to make the attempt. It was a remarkable exhibition, and made a great impression at the time: not that it was a very good, still less an agreeable speech; quite the reverse. He chose the worst moment he possibly could have done to rise; the House was exhausted by several nights of debate and had no mind to hear more. He rose very late on the last night, and he spoke for above three hours; his speech was ill-delivered, marked with all those peculiar faults which he never got rid of; it was very tiresome; it contained much that was in very bad taste; but in spite of all defects it was listened to, and it was considered a very extraordinary performance, giving indications of great ability and powers which nobody had any idea that he possessed.

The rest of his career is well known. He brought into politicks the same ardour, activity, industry, and cleverness which he had displayed on the turf, and some of the same cunning and contrivances too. He never was and never would have been anything like a Statesman; he was utterly devoid of large and comprehensive views, and he was no pursuer and worshipper of truth. He brought the mind, the habits, and the arts of an Attorney to the discussion of political questions; having once espoused a cause, and embraced a party, from whatever motive, he worked with all the force of his intellect and a superhuman power of application in what he conceived to be the interest of that party and that cause. No scruples, moral or personal, stood for a moment in his way; he went into evidence, historical or statistical, not to inform himself and to accept with a candid and unbiassed mind the conclusions to which reason and testimony, facts and figures, might conduct him, but to pick out whatever might fortify his foregone conclusions, casting aside everything inimical to the cause he was advocating, and seizing all that could be turned to account by any amount of misrepresentation and suppression he might find it convenient to employ. It was thus he acted in the West India Committee; his labour and application were something miraculous; he conducted the enquiry very ably, but anything but impartially; having had no political education, and being therefore unimbued with sound principles on fiscal and commercial questions, he had everything to learn; and having flung himself headlong into the Protectionist cause, he got up their case just as he did that of 'Orlando' and 'Running Rein,' and ran amuck against everything and everybody on the opposite side.

Against Peel he soon broke out with indescribable fury and rancour. Nothing could be more characteristic than the attack he made upon him about his conduct to Canning, which has been since ascribed to his attachment to the latter, and a long-cherished but suppressed resentment at Peel's behaviour to him. Nothing could be more ridiculously untrue; he did not care one straw for Canning, alive or dead, and he did not himself believe one word of the accusations he brought against Peel; but he thought he had found materials for a damaging attack on the man he detested, and he availed himself of it with all the virulence of the most vindictive hatred. It was a total failure, and he only afforded Peel an opportunity of vindicating himself once for all from an imputation which had been very generally circulated and believed, but which he proved to be altogether false. The

House of Commons gave Peel a complete triumph, and G. B. was generally condemned; nevertheless, with more courage and bulldog perseverance than good taste and judgement, He returned to the charge, and instead of withdrawing his accusations, renewed and insisted on them in his reply. This was just like him; but though his conduct was very ill advised, I well remember thinking his reply (made too against the sense and feeling of the House) was very clever.

I have always thought that his conduct in selling his stud all at one swoop, and at once giving up the turf, to which he had just before seemed so devoted, was never sufficiently appreciated and praised. It was a great sacrifice both of pleasure and profit, and it was made to what he had persuaded himself was a great publick duty. It is true that he had taken up his new vocation with an ardour and a zeal which absorbed his old one, but still it was a very fine act, and excessively creditable to him. He never did anything by halves, and having accepted the responsible post of Leader of his party, he resolved to devote himself to their service, and he did so without stint or reserve; and when he had ceased to be nominally their Leader (a transaction in which his behaviour was honorable and manly), and took up particular questions and the interests of particular parties, he voluntarily and gratuitously imposed upon himself an amount of labour and anxiety, which beyond all doubt contributed to the accident which terminated his life. Notwithstanding his arrogance and his violence, his constant quarrels and the intolerable language he indulged in, he was popular in the House of Commons, and liked more or less wherever he went. He was extremely good-looking and particularly distinguished and high-bred; then he was gay, agreeable, obliging, and good-natured, charming with those he liked, and by whom he was not thwarted and opposed. His undaunted courage and the confident and haughty audacity with which he attacked or stood up against all opponents, being afraid of no man, inspired a general sentiment of admiration and respect, and his lofty assumption of superior integrity and his resolute determination to expose and punish every breach of publick honor and morality were quietly acquiesced in, and treated with great deference by the multitude who knew no better, and were imposed on by his specious pretensions. The sensation caused by his death, the encomiums pronounced on his character, and the honors paid to his memory, have been unexampled in a man whose career has been so short, and who did not do greater things than he had it in his power to accomplish. He made himself, however, the Advocate of powerful interests, and of vast numbers of people whose united voices make a great noise in the world, and there is something in the appalling suddenness of the catastrophe which excites general sympathy and pity, and makes people more inclined to think of his virtues, his powers, and his promise, than of his defects. Of the latter perhaps the greatest was his constant disposition to ascribe the worst motives to all those to whom he found himself opposed;

Suspicion always haunts the guilty mind;

and when he invariably fancied that he saw intentional fraud and the utmost baseness in the conduct of his antagonists, it is impossible not to ascribe such false and erroneous views of human nature to the moral consciousness which was the result of his own former courses, constantly suspecting others of the same sort of practices with which he was once so familiar. I have not the least doubt that, for his own reputation and celebrity, he died at the most opportune period; his fame had probably reached its zenith, and credit was given him for greater abilities than he possessed, and for a futurity of fame, influence, and power which it is not probable he ever would have realised. As it is, the world will never know anything of those serious blemishes which could not fail to dim the lustre of his character; he will long be remembered and regretted as a very remarkable man, and will occupy a conspicuous place in the history of his own time.

1851

December 3rd—At twelve o'clock yesterday morning the wonderful Electric telegraph brought us word that two hours before the President had accomplished his Coup d'État at Paris with success. Everybody expected it would happen, nobody that it would happen so soon. Madame de Lieven wrote to Beauvale on Sunday, giving him an account of the efforts that were making by the Moderates, Guizot at the head of them, to bring about a reconciliation and compromise with the President and auguring success. She says, 'Beaucoup de personnes prétendent que, tout en ayant l'air de s'y prêter, le Président n'a pas grande envie de ce moyen; un coup d'état le ferait mieux arriver: il s'y est tout préparé, la troupe est à lui, le pays aussi.' She little thought that in twenty-four hours the coup d'état allait éclater, and that all was in preparation for it, while he was amusing the 'Bourgeois and Moderates' with negotiations and pourparlers, in which he was never serious.

Panshanger, December 14th—Naturally the French Revolution has absorbed all interest. The success of L. N.'s coup d'état has been complete, and his audacity and unscrupulousness marvellous. The French are indeed a strange people, so restless, fierce, and excitable that they are ready to upset Governments with the smallest possible show of reason or necessity—with cause as in 1830, or without cause as in 1848—and they acquiesce without a struggle, and tamely endure the impudent and vulgar democratic rule of the blackguards and mountebanks of the Provisional Government at the latter period, and now the unlimited and severe military despotism of Louis Napoleon. The Press in this country has generally inveighed with great indignation against him, and the 'Times' particularly, very much overdoing the case. Society in general is in a rather neutral state. Few can approve of the very violent measures and arbitrary acts, but on the other hand there was such a general feeling of contempt for the Constitution, and of disgust at the conduct of the Assembly and the parties which divided it, that nobody lamented their overthrow, or regarded with the slightest interest or compassion the leaders who have been so brutally and ignominiously treated. Everybody rejoices at the misfortunes of Thiers, who is universally regarded as the evil genius of France and the greatest maker of mischief who ever played a part on the stage of politics. Flahault, who has been the Agent and confidant of the President, writes word that He has saved France, and it is the object of his adherents to make the world believe that his measures were rendered necessary by a Socialist plot, which he has saved the country by putting down; and besides this we hear of an Orleanist plot, and of the violence of the Assembly was about to have recourse to against him, if he had not anticipated them. These seem to be, and probably are, mere pretences, got up to cover his violence with something plausible, and which the world may swallow; the truth being that He prepared all that he has done with singular boldness, secrecy, adroitness, and success, amusing his enemies with the semblance of negotiations which he never meant seriously to carry out to an end, and relying (as it has turned out that he could do) upon the Army, by whose aid he has taken all power into his own hands. Having done so, he resolved to do nothing by halves, and certainly by the prompt, peremptory, and arbitrary measures he adopted he has secured present success, given confidence as to the stability of his Government, raised his own reputation for energy and ability, and in all probability prevented a great amount of disorder and bloodshed, which would have taken place if his success had been less complete than it was.

December 19th—Disraeli sent me his book,[1] which, though principally recording very dry Parliamentary debates, he has managed to make very readable. He does ample justice to his Hero, but I think without exag-

---

[1] The biography of Lord George Bentinck, published at this time.

geration; and he certainly makes him out to have been a very remarkable man, with great ability and a superhuman power of work. It is the more extraordinary because for above forty years he was indolent, and addicted to none but frivolous pursuits, though he always pursued his pleasurable occupations in a business-like and laborious manner. The character of Peel in this book is curious, but I do not think it is unfair, and it is in a becoming spirit of seriousness and even respect, fully acknowledging his great qualities, but freely criticising his character and his career. The Jewish episode is amusing, and I like it for its courage.

Something, but I know not what, has happened about Palmerston. The D. of Bedford, who is by turns confidential and mysterious, and who delights in raising my curiosity and then not satisfying it, has written to me thus. After a good deal about John's defending P. and his not approving (in one strain one day and another the next), he said there had been a correspondence between them on the subject, which he was to see. He never said more about it, and to a question I put to him thereon he sent no answer. In another letter I alluded to this, but added that it did not now much signify, on which he writes: 'You attach no importance to the correspondence I told you of, and do not now care to know about it, but if I am not mistaken you will ere long change your opinion.'

December 22nd—A Cabinet has been suddenly called to-day, which is about the matter the Duke alluded to—foreign matters.

December 23rd—Palmerston is out!—actually, really, and irretrievably out. I nearly dropt off my chair yesterday afternoon, when at five o'clock, a few moments after the Cabinet had broken up, Granville rushed into my room and said, 'It is none of the things we talked over; Pam is out, the offer of the F. Office goes to Clarendon to-night, and if he refuses (which of course he will not) it is to be offered to me!!' Well might the Duke of Bedford say I should 'change my opinion,' and soon think this correspondence did signify, for it was on the matter which led to the fall of Palmerston. Granville came to town on Saturday, not knowing (as none of the Ministers did) what the Cabinet was about. On Sunday he received a note from J. Russell, begging him not to come to it, and telling him he would afterwards inform him why. This of course surprised him, but after going about amongst such of his colleagues as were here, he arrived at the conclusion that the matter related to foreign affairs, that Normanby was to be recalled, and the Paris Embassy offered to him, or that he was to be sent to Paris on a special mission. We discussed these contingencies together with all others (changes of office) which occurred to us, but we neither of us dreamt of the truth. It now appears that the cause of Palmerston's dismissal (for dismissed he is) is his having committed the Government to a full and unqualified approval of N.'s coup d'état, which he did *in conversation* with Walewski, but so formally and officially, that Walewski wrote word to his own Government that ours approved entirely of all that L. N. had done. Upon this piece of indiscretion, to which it is probable that P. attached no importance, being so used to act off his own bat, and never dreamt of any danger from it, Johnny determined to act. I do not know the details of the correspondence, only that He signified to Palmerston his displeasure at his having thus committed the Government to an approbation he did not feel, and it ended in his turning Palmerston out, for this was in fact what he did. But though this was the pretext, the *causa causans* was without any doubt the Islington speech and deputations, and his whole conduct in that affair.[1] The Queen had deeply resented it, and had had a quarrel with John about it, for he rather defended Palmerston, and accepted his excuses and denials. It is evident that he did this, because he did not dare to quarrel with him on grounds which would have enabled him to cast himself on the Radicals, to appeal to all the Kossuthian sympathies of the country, and to represent himself as the victim of our disgraceful subserviency to Austria. But having thus passed over what would have been a sufficient cause of quarrel, he at once seized upon one much less sufficient, but which was not liable to the same difficulties and objections. In fully approving L. N.'s coup d'état, P. has taken a part against the feelings of the Radicals, and if the cause of the quarrel is made public, their approval will ad hoc be rather with John R. than with him.

December 24th—To my unspeakable astonishment Granville informed me yesterday that Clarendon had refused the Foreign Office, and that he had accepted it. John must have given notice to Clarendon the day before the Cabinet that he was going to propose him, or they could not have heard yesterday. Clarendon declined, and advised John to offer it to Granville, which he instantly did, and the things was settled at once. I have not yet heard from C., and am curious to know his motives for refusing an appointment which I should have thought would be not only peculiarly agreeable to him, but which would have enabled him to quit Ireland in so honorable a manner. In no other way could he have left his present post, just after the recent trial of Birch *v.* Somerville,[2] and this trial with its disclosures must render it particularly irksome with him to stay there. Granville, albeit conscious of the weight, accepted the office without a moment's hesitation.

Brocket, Christmas Day—I received a letter from Clarendon yesterday

[1] Welcoming the exiled Hungarian patriot Kossuth.
[2] The claim by a newspaper for money for supporting the English government.

afternoon with his reasons for declining. They are very poor ones, and amount to little more than his being afraid of Palmerston, first of his suspecting it was an intrigue to get rid of him, and secondly, of the difficulties Pam would throw in his way at the F.O. He had advised John to take Granville, but he said if it was absolutely necessary, he would accept. I can't help thinking he will be mortified at his refusal and his advice being so immediately taken. His conduct has been to my mind very pusillanimous and unworthy of him.

Beauvale has had a long letter from Lady Palmerston with her version of the whole affair, which is true in the main, but as favorably coloured towards Pam as the case will admit of. She is in a high state of indignation and resentment, and bitter against John and the colleagues who did not support P. They evidently expected when the Cabinet met the other day that the Colleagues would have pronounced John's ground of quarrel insufficient, and protested against his dismissal, and they are extremely mortified that nothing of the kind was done. She complained that Pam's best friends were absent. Not one person at the Cabinet said a word for him or made an effort to keep him, but this she does not know. Her account is as follows. On December 3rd Palmerston told Walewski *in conversation* that he thought the President was fully justified in his coup d'état, as *plots were hatching* against him. He *says* that he expressed his approbation in this conditional form. Walewski wrote to Turgot what Palmerston had said, and at the same time P. wrote a very strong letter to Normanby, finding fault with his conduct, and advising him to hold language calculated to satisfy the President that he was not unfriendly to him, as he had reason to believe that the President did regard him as so inimical, that he was meditating an application to the British Government to recall him. (Whatever P. really did say to Walewski, we may safely assume that W. made the most of it to Turgot, and that he did convey to him the unqualified approbation of the English Government, and Turgot probably communicated Walewski's despatch to Normanby.) Normanby was exceedingly annoyed at this communication, and wrote to John Russell, conveying to him what had passed, and complaining of the ill-usage he had received. (John upon this must have gone to the Queen, and settled with her what was to be done.) John shortly after wrote to Palmerston, sent him a Minute of the Queen's, in which H.M. expressed her displeasure at Palmerston's having committed her Government by an unqualified approbation of the President's measures, and he added from himself that he agreed with her, and thought Palmerston had acted with great indiscretion, that he was tired of these repeated difficulties and disputes, and he had to inform him that it was the wish of the Queen to transfer the Foreign Office to other hands. Palmerston wrote a reply, stating his readiness to give up the seals whenever his successor should be appointed. He defended his own conduct, denied that he had committed the Government, and said he had only expressed his own individual opinion, and that a qualified one, and then set forth the inconvenience there would be if a Minister could not hold friendly communication with an Ambassador in his own person, without being supposed to commit the whole Cabinet, in mere conversation. It did not appear to me that the excuses he made, according to her (Lady Palmerston's) own account of them, were very good ones, and they were not likely to produce any effect upon John, who had evidently already determined to get rid of him. What more passed I do not know, but from her letter they clearly entertained some hopes that Palmerston's position was still retrievable; that when the Cabinet met, his colleagues would make an effort to retain him; and that in spite of what John had written to him he would have kept his post if he could. It seems incredible that any man of high spirit and with a spark of pride should consent to stay in office after being told by the Prime Minister that he had been indiscreet, that the P.M. was tired of his repeated misconduct, and that the Q. wished to get rid of him. But it seems by what Lady P. says, that he would have swallowed all this if he could have made it up. She writes in a spirit of great bitterness and resentment, hints at conspiracies, and intimates her belief that the ground taken by John was merely a pretext, and not the real cause of what had been done. In this She is quite right. The case is cumulative, and the Islington deputations is the causa causans, though the Paris communication is made the pretext of John's coup d'état. Beauvale thinks the last and ostensible cause is insufficient, and that John would have done better to act at once on the matter of the deputations. I am inclined to think it is sufficient, though far less strong than the other, and it would have been more straitforward as well as bold to have acted on the first, and I believe it would have been quite as safe. Labouchere (a very honorable man) told me, when all was known, he thought John's conduct would come out in a very favorable light. So probably there are circumstances which Lady P. suppresses, which would not improve P.'s case. The most striking circumstance in all this affair is the conduct of John Russell. He took it up, and without imparting what he was about to any one of his colleagues, leaving them all completely in the dark, He and the Queen settled the whole thing between them. For nearly three weeks a correspondence was going on between the Q., J., and P., of which not one word transpired, and which was known to nobody but the D. of Bedford. None of the Ministers had the least idea why they were summoned. Lords Grey and Lansdowne and Sir F. Baring all came up together from the Grange, asking each what it was about; nor was it till they were all assembled in the Cabinet room in Downing Street that they were apprised of the astounding fact that Palmerston had ceased to be their colleague. The secret was as well kept as Louis Napoleon's, and the coup d'état nearly as important and extraordinary.

December 27th—Council at Windsor. Palmerston did not come, but desired Stanley (Lord Eddisbury) to send the seals to Ld. John. Nevertheless he was expected, and the Queen would wait for him above an hour. It now turns out that the F.O. was not offered to Clarendon at all. In his letter to me he says, it cannot be said that I refused what was never offered me. John wrote him word on Sunday that it would be offered him; but the offer, which Granville told me on Monday afternoon was gone, never did go. All along the Q. and J. Wished to have Granville instead of Clarendon. He tells me when I know all that has passed between J. R. and himself, I shall see he could not possibly accept it. Ld. Lansdowne was evidently put out by what he heard yesterday. He said to me, 'You know it was offered to Clarendon.' I said, 'He does not so consider it.' 'Oh! it certainly was. It was clearly so understood in the Cabinet, when I left on Monday, and I wrote to him myself.' I said he had better enquire, and he would find no offer was sent. He then talked to J. R. and Grey, and I asked him afterwards, when he shrugged his shoulders and said I was right; but he did not understand it. The truth is oozing out by degrees. Grey and I had some talk about it, when I told him that I thought the former ground (the deputations) the stronger of the two, and I should have turned him out then, and he said he agreed with me. Madame de Lieven writes in transports of joy, and on the whole the satisfaction seems very general. Granville is very popular at Manchester and with the Free Traders, which is a great thing; and as he is more of a Reformer than Palmerston, he will not be attacked in that quarter. Brooks's and the ultra Whigs and Radicals are sulky, but don't quite know what to make of it. It seems John struck the blow at last with great reluctance; but having made up his mind, he did it boldly.

Bunsen told Reeve a version of the story, which he got from Stockmar, and which came direct from the Court. Normanby wrote home for instructions. At a Cabinet (on the 8th) it was determined that he should be instructed to abstain from expressing any opinion, but to act with perfect civility and every expression of international amity towards the President, but with reserve. John went down to Osborne on the 9th, and informed the Q. of the resolution of the Cabinet. If, as Ly. P. says, the conversation with Walewski had taken place before, he did not tell the Cabinet what he had said to him; but, be this as it may, they say he did not act in the spirit of the Cabinet resolution, but in that of his own communication, which was very different. I expect that it will not be easy to make a good case out of this, especially as the Queen's name must not be brought in. Pam, who is so adroit and unscrupulous, will deny half that he said, and find plausible excuses for the other half, and will probably make it appear that the ostensible casus querelæ was not the real one. However, in matters of this sort, John is tolerably dexterous too, and he may have better materials than I am aware of to employ.

Flahault arrived last night, and came here this morning to talk to Granville. He said that Palmerston's dismissal and the cause of it, as hinted at in the newspapers, had produced a disagreeable impression at the Elysée, especially after all the violence of the press. He said he had told the President that what he had done could not fail to shock English feelings and prejudices, and the Press was sure to hold such language. He received from Granville assurances as pacific as he could desire, and he will probably have little difficulty in satisfying the President and his Government that they will lose nothing by the change. I have seen to-day an admirable letter of Guizot's, full of a melancholy and dignified resignation to a state of things he abhors, commiserating and ashamed of the condition of his country. He says if he was disposed to triumph over his enemies il a bien de quoi. Where, he asks, is Thiers, where is the Republic, where is Palmerston? France is now so frightened at Socialism, and so bent on averting the peril of anarchy, that she will submit to anything. But this panic will one day pass away, and Government cannot be carried on for ever by Soldiers and Peasants, and in spite of all the intellect and all the elevated classes in the country.

Sunday—Yesterday Granville was with Palmerston for three hours. He received him with the greatest cordiality and good humour. 'Ah, how are you, Granville? Well, you have got a very interesting office, but you will find it very laborious; seven or eight hours' work every day will be necessary for the current business, besides the extraordinary and Parliamentary, and with less than that you will fall into arrears.' He then entered into a complete history of our diplomacy, gave him every sort of information, and even advice; spoke of the Court without bitterness, and in strong terms of the Queen's 'sagacity'; ended by desiring G. would apply to him when he pleased for any information or assistance he could give him. This is very creditable, and (whatever may come after it) very wise, gentlemanlike, becoming, and dignified. Meanwhile his family are furious and open-

Lord John Russell
*From a pencil-and-water-
colour drawing by
G. F. Watts*

Lord Clarendon
*Detail of the drawing by
George Richmond*

Charles Greville
From a portrait, about 1855, in the Goodwood Collection

mouthed. Ly. P. says She can neither eat nor sleep, and they raise already the cry of 'foreign influence.' Nobody can yet make out what the real cause of it all is.

1854

*Lord Aberdeen's Coalition Government had been formed in January 1854.
Its conduct of the Crimean War, which began in March 1854, destroyed
its popularity, and it fell at the beginning of 1855.*

Monday, August 14th—The Session closed on Saturday, and, all things considered, the Government wound it up tolerably well. Clanricarde, true to the last to his spiteful opposition, gave Clarendon an opportunity of making a parting speech on foreign affairs, of which he acquitted himself very successfully, and placed himself and the Government in a very good position as respects our diplomacy and the conduct of the war. But though all immediate danger is removed from the Government, and, unless they fall to pieces during the recess by any internal dissensions, they will probably go on unscathed, the state of affairs is very unsatisfactory, and pregnant with future troubles and difficulties. The condition of the Government in its relations with the H. of Commons throughout the past session has been extraordinary, and I believe unprecedented. From the Revolution to the time of the Reform Bill, that is during 150 years, the system of Parliamentary government had been consolidating itself and was practically established; the Sovereign nominally, the House of Commons really, appointed the Ministers of the Crown, and it was settled as an axiom that when the Government was unable to carry its measures, and was subjected to defeats in the H. of Commons, its resignation was indispensable—not indeed that any and every defeat was necessarily fatal, because Governments have often been beat on very important questions without being ruined or even materially weakened, but it was supposed that repeated defeats and Government measures repeatedly rejected implied the withdrawal of the confidence and support of Parliament so clearly that in the aggregate such defeats were equivalent to an absolute vote of want of confidence, which is in itself a sentence of political death. In former times the Crown was a Power, and the H. of C. was a Power, generally blended and acting harmoniously together, but sometimes resolving themselves into their separate elements, and acting independently, perhaps antagonistically, towards each other.

In modern times, and more entirely in our own, this separate and independent action ceased, the Crown became identified with the majority of the H. of Commons, and no Minister, when he could no longer command that majority so as to be certain of carrying out all, or nearly all, his measures of Government and legislation, could continue to be Minister, and was obliged as a matter of course to surrender office to those who were in possession of, or could count upon, that command. The Ministers were taken from the ranks of the Parliamentary majority, and when once appointed it was considered indispensable and certain that the same majority would place confidence in them, accept at their hands all the measures they should concert and propose, and support them against all hostile attacks, the spirit of party and combination suppressing all individual prejudices, crotchets, fancies, and partial or local influences. The Government and the Party were bound by a sort of mutual allegiance to each other, and supposed to be, and usually were, animated by the same spirit and a community of opinion and interest. Such were the general relations and such the normal state of things, liable to occasional variations and disturbances, bringing about various political changes according to circumstances. But the system was complete, and practically it worked well, and conduced to the prosperity and progress of the country.

When the great measure of Reform in Parliament was introduced in 1831, apart from all question of party struggles there was the still greater question considered by many reflecting People, whether the new Parliamentary and electoral system would be found compatible with the old practice of Government by means of party and steady Parliamentary majorities. The Duke of Wellington in particular expressed his apprehension that it would not, and he put the question which has so often been quoted and referred to, 'How is the King's Government to be carried on?' He did not (so far as I remember) develope his thoughts at the time, and argue the matter in detail, but it is very evident that what he anticipated was some such state of things as that at which we now appeared to have arrived. For a long time his apprehensions appeared to be groundless, and certainly they were not realised by the course of events. In consequence of political circumstances I shall not stop to specify and explain, notwithstanding all the changes which were effected, the Governments contrived to go on without any insuperable difficulties, and without any striking difference from the way in which Governments had been previously conducted. The popularity of the Reform Bill Government supported them for a few years, and the Tory reaction, together with the great abilities of Sir Robert Peel, supported the Conservative Government for a few years more. Matters went on better or worse, as might be, till the great Conservative schism in 1846, which completely broke up that party, and produced a final separation between the able few and the numerous mediocrity of the Party. Ever since that time the House of Commons has been in a state of disorganisation and confusion: the great party ties had been severed. After the repeal of the Corn Laws and the establishment of Free Trade it was difficult to find any great party principles which could be converted into bonds of union, and every day it became obviously more and more difficult to form any Government that could hope to be strong or permanent. John Russell succeeded on the fall of Peel, but the Peelites warmly resented the conduct of the Whigs in Peel's last struggle, and, though they hated Derby and his crew much more, never gave John's Government a cordial support.

Next came the quarrel between Palmerston and John and the fall of the Whig Government. Many people, and Graham especially, were of opinion that a Derby Government *for a time* was a necessary but indispensable evil, and after one abortive attempt at length a Derby Government was formed. From the beginning nobody thought it could last; the wretched composition of it, its false position, and the mixture of inconsistency and insincerity which characterised it, deprived it of all respect, authority, and influence, and it was the more weak because divided and dissatisfied within, and that all the more honest and truthful of the party were disgusted and ashamed of the part they were playing. Thus feeble and powerless, despised by the public and detested by the Court, the first moment that the different parties and scattered sections of parties combined to overthrow them, their destruction was inevitable, and after enjoying office for one year they fell.

It was easier to turn them out than to find a good and strong Government to replace them. It was obvious that neither the Whigs nor the Peelites could form a government, still less Palmerston or the Radicals, and it became a matter of absolute necessity to attempt a coalition, which, whatever objections there might be to coalitions, would at least have the advantage of filling the several offices with able men.

When the Queen had a short time before (in anticipation of the event) consulted the Duke of Bedford as to whom she should send for when Derby resigned, he had advised her to send for Lansdowne and Aberdeen, being himself conscious that John could not again form a Government, at least not at that time. She did send for them, and each of them very sincerely and earnestly endeavoured to persuade the other to accept the post of Prime Minister, and the task of forming a Government. Lansdowne was ill at the time, and while it is very doubtful if anything would have induced him to come forward, his attack of gout was enough to ensure his peremptory refusal, and nothing remained but that Aberdeen should make the attempt. The task was difficult and unpleasant, for it was impossible not to make many people discontented and mortified, inasmuch as places could not be found for all who had previously been in office, or who aspired to it, and it was no easy matter to decide who should be taken in, and who left out. Aberdeen resolved to make the coalition very comprehensive, and as much as possible to form a Government which should represent the Opposition which had turned Derby out, but he put almost all the Peelite leaders into good offices, and the exclusions were principally on the Whig side. For a long time it was very doubtful whether John Russell would join the Government at all, but Aberdeen was so well aware that he could not do without him that he announced his determination to throw up the Government unless John consented to join. After much hesitation, and a struggle between his family and some malcontent hangers-on who wished him to keep aloof, on one side, and the wisest of his political friends and colleagues who urged that it was his duty to come forward on the other, John consented to lead the H. of Commons, but without an office. He proposed indeed to take the Presidency of the Council, to which Aberdeen objected, but gave him the choice of every other office. He said if he could not be President of the C. he would be nothing at all, and so it was settled. Next came the negotiation about Palmerston, who first refused, and afterwards, at the pressing solicitations of Lansdowne, agreed to join. Molesworth came in to represent the Radicals; Monsell and Keogh (not in the Cabinet) represented the Irish, and so the Coalition Government was completed.

Very strongly composed, it never, however, was so strong as it looked. The Ministers, Aberdeen, John Russell, Palmerston, having consented to act together, were too sensible, too gentlemanlike and well-bred, not to live in outward good fellowship with each other, but their respective and relative antecedents could not be forgotten. There could be no real cordiality between Palmerston and Aberdeen, or between Palmerston and John Russell, and both the latter all along felt uncomfortable and dissatisfied with their respective positions. John fancied he was degraded, and his wife and her flatterers endeavoured to persuade him he was so, by joining a Government of which he was not the Head, and by serving under Aberdeen. Palmerston could not forget the long and bitter hostility which had been carried on between himself and Aberdeen upon foreign policy, and still less his having been turned out of the Foreign Office by John Russell. The Whigs were dissatisfied that the Peelites, who had no party to bring to the support of the Government, should have so large a share of the offices, and above all the great bulk of the Whig party could not endure that a

Peelite should be at the Head of the Government, and of all the Peelites they most particularly disliked Aberdeen, so that they yielded a reluctant allegiance, and gave a grudging and capricious support to the Coalition.

Nevertheless, the first Session of Parliament was pretty well got through, principally owing to Gladstone's successful Budget, the great ability he displayed in the H. of C., and the efficient way in which the public business was done, while the numerous measures of improvement which were accomplished raised the reputation of the Government, and gave them security if not strength. The Session of 1853 closed in quiet, prosperity, and sunshine, but during the recess clouds began to gather round the Government; they were beset with internal and external difficulties. John Russell became more and more discontented, and at last he announced to Aberdeen that he was resolved not to meet Parliament again in his present position, and intimated his intention to be once more Prime Minister, or to quit the concern. In the meantime the Turco-Russian quarrel had begun, the hostile correspondence with Russia was in full activity, the public mind in a high state of excitement, the Press bellowed for war and poured forth incessant volleys of abuse against the Government, but more particularly against Aberdeen, who was singled out as the object of attack, and the persevering attempts to render him unpopular produced a certain amount of effect. The Cabinet became divided as to the mode of carrying on the dispute and the negotiations, some being for what were called vigorous measures, that is, for threats and demonstrations of force which could only lead to immediate war, while others were for exhausting every attempt to bring about an accommodation and preserve peace. Something was known or suspected of these divisions, they were published and commented on with enormous exaggerations and the most unscrupulous violations of truth, and the Tory and Radical newspapers vied with each other in the violence of their denunciations of Aberdeen, and (in a less degree) of Clarendon.

When this fury was at its height, the world was startled and astounded by the news of Palmerston's resignation. It is needless to state here the history of that affair, which I have already recorded in ample detail. It was in vain that the 'Times' proclaimed that it was the Reform Bill and not the Eastern question which was the cause of it. The statement was scouted with the utmost scorn, and the public incredulity was confirmed when the 'Morning Post' (which was notoriously devoted to P.) asserted the direct contrary. Everybody imagined that the Government would go to pieces, that when Parliament met there would be prodigious revelations, and that the Eastern question with its supposed mismanagement would prove fatal to the Coalition Cabinet. The Derbyites were in raptures, and already counted on

Palmerston as their own. Great as has been the public surprise and the exultation of the Carlton Club at Palmerston's resignation, greater still was that surprise and the mortification and disappointment of the Carlton, when a few days afterwards it was announced that Palmerston had changed his mind and was not going to resign. Nobody could comprehend what it all meant, and ample scope was afforded to every sort of conjecture, and to all the statements and inventions that anybody chose to circulate. But as about the same time the Eastern affair progressed a step or two, and some energetic measures were adopted, the most plausible explanation was, that Palmerston had resigned because enough was not done, that the Government had been frightened into doing what he had before advised, and that, on their adopting his suggestion, he had consented to remain. In process of time the truth began to ooze out, but it never was completely known till Parliament met, and even then many people continued to believe that though the Reform Bill was the pretext, the Eastern question was the real cause of Palmerston's conduct.

These threatening clouds cleared away. Aberdeen told John nothing should induce him to resign after all the attacks that had been made on him, and he would meet Parliament and defend himself. John gave up his demands, and consented to go on leading the House of Commons. Palmerston agreed to swallow the Reform Bill, and at length Parliament met. Everybody was ravenous for the Blue Books, which as soon as possible were produced. Their production was eminently serviceable to the Government, and though some criticisms were made, and there were some desultory attacks in both Houses, and the Press continued to be as scurrilous and abusive as ever, the general impression was extremely favorable. Clarendon's despatches were highly approved of, and all fair and candid observers, including many who had found fault with the Government before, declared that they were perfectly satisfied that our policy had been wise and proper, and the whole of the negotiations very creditable to all who had been concerned in carrying them on. So little did the event correspond with the general expectation, that the Eastern question, which had been considered to be the weak part of the Government, turned out to be its great strength; and the war which eventually broke out has been the principal cause of their being able to maintain themselves in power. It is now the fashion to say that if it were not for the war, they would have been turned out long ago. It is certainly true that their power in the H. of Commons has been limited to all that concerns the war, in respect to which they have had no difficulty to contend with. The estimates have been granted without a semblance of opposition, and they have received hearty and unanimous support in every measure and every demand requisite for carrying on the war, nor, though exposed to some adverse criticism, have they been seriously assailed with regard to their diplomacy or their warlike preparations.

But while this, which is the most essential, has also been their strongest point, on everything else, without exception, they have been almost powerless, and the House of Commons has run riot with an independence, a waywardness and a caprice of which it would be impossible to find an example. The Government has had no majority on which it could depend, and it has never brought forward any measure which it could count upon carrying through; it has been repeatedly defeated. Obliged to withdraw many measures altogether, and to submit to the alteration of others till they became totally different from what they originally proposed, their defeats have been innumerable, and nobody seemed to have the smallest scruple in putting them in a minority upon any occasion; at the same time it was very evident that the House of Commons was determined that they should continue in office, for whenever any vital question arose, or any vote which could be construed into a question of confidence, and therefore involved the existence of the Government, they were always sure of a majority, and the Derbyite opposition, while they were able to worry and insult them by partial defeats and by exposing their general weakness, found themselves miserably baffled whenever they attempted anything which had a tendency to place the Government in serious embarrassment. The whole conduct of the session, and the relations of the Government with the H. of Commons, presented certainly something very different from what had ever been seen before in the memory of the Oldest Statesman, implied a total dissolution of party ties and obligations, and exhibited the Queen's Government and the H. of Commons as resolved into their separate elements, and acting towards each other in independent and often antagonistic capacities. Disraeli was always reproaching the Government with holding office on what he termed the unconstitutional principle of not being supported by a majority of the H. of C., and of living from hand to mouth; but though this was a plausible topic, he knew very well that no other Government could be formed which could exist otherwise, and that the H. of Commons, while it buffeted the Government about au gré de ses caprices, was quite determined to keep it alive, and not to allow any other to be substituted for it. At present it is difficult to see how this state of things is to be altered, and time alone can show whether great parties will again be formed, and Governments be enabled to go on as in times past, powerful in a consistent and continual Parliamentary support, or whether a great change must be submitted to, and Governments be content to drag on a precarious existence, taking what they can get from the House of Commons, and endeavouring to strengthen themselves by enlisting public opinion on their side.

With regard to the prospects of this Government, much depends on the progress of the war; for though they have done their part and are not responsible for failure or success, they are sure to be strengthened by success by weakened by failure. But much depends also upon what passes in the Cabinet. John Russell, whose mind is in a state of chronic discontent which was suspended for a time, is again becoming uneasy and restless, and will soon begin making fresh difficulties. Then his Reform Bill, which he gave up so reluctantly, is still in his thoughts, and he will most likely insist upon bringing it forward again, a proposition which is sure to produce dissension in the Cabinet.

August 29th—Out of town since the above was written; at Grimston for York races, where Derby was in high force and spirits, carrying everything before him at the races, and not a word was ever uttered on politics. There is no news, but dreadful accounts of the health of both armies and of the prevalence of cholera both abroad and at home. The French particularly, who have lost the most, are said to be completely demoralised and disheartened, and to abhor the war, which they always disliked from the beginning. My present impression is that we shall come to grief in this contest; not that we shall be beaten in the field by the Russians, but that between the unhealthy climate, the inaccessibility of the country, and the distance of our resources, Russia will be able to keep us at bay, and baffle our attempts to reduce her to submission.

1857

January 28, Wednesday—Two remarkable deaths, one of which touches me nearly, that of Madame de Lieven; the other is the D. of Rutland. Madame de L. died, after a short illness, of a severe attack of bronchitis, the Duke having lingered for many months. Very different characters. Madame de Lieven came to this country at the end of 1812 or beginning of 1813 on the war breaking out between Russia and France. Pozzo di Borgo had preceded the Lievens to renew diplomatic relations and make arrangements with us. She was at that time young, at least in the prime of life, and though without any pretensions to beauty, and indeed with some personal defeats. She had so fine an air and manner, and a countenance rather pretty and so full of intelligence, as to be on the whole a very striking and attractive person, quite enough so to have Lovers, several of whom she engaged in succession without seriously attaching herself to any. Those who were most notoriously her Slaves at different times were the present Lord Willoughby, the Duke of Sutherland (then Lord Gower), the Duke of Cannizzaro (then Count St. Antonio), and the Duke of Palmella, who was particularly clever and agreeable. Madame de Lieven was a très grande dame, with abilities of a very high order, great tact and finesse, and taking a boundless pleasure in the society of the great world and in political affairs of every sort. People here were not slow to acknowledge her merits and social excellence, and she almost immediately took her place in the cream of the cream of English society, forming close intimacies with the most conspicuous women in it, and assiduously cultivating relations with the most remarkable men of all parties. These personal liaisons sometimes led her into political partisanship not always prudent and rather inconsistent with her position, character, and functions here. But I do not believe she was ever mixed up in any intrigues, nor even, at a later period, that she was justly obnoxious to the charge of caballing and mischief-making which has been so lavishly cast upon her. She had an insatiable curiosity for political information, and a not unnatural desire to make herself useful and agreeable to her own Court by imparting to her Imperial Masters and Mistresses all the information she acquired and the anecdotes she picked up. Accordingly while she was in England, which was from 1812 to 1834, she devoted herself to society, not without selection, but without exclusion, except that she sought and habitually confined herself to the highest and the best. The Regent, afterwards George IV, delighted much in her company, and she was a frequent guest at the Pavilion, and on very intimate terms with Lady Conyngham, for although Madame de Lieven was not very tolerant of mediocrity, and social and colloquial superiority was necessary to her existence, She always made great allowance for Royalty and those immediately connected with it. She used to be a great deal at Oatlands, and was one of the few intimate friends of the Duchess of York, herself very intelligent, and who therefore had in the eyes of Madame de L. the double charm of her position and her agreeableness. It was her duty as well as her inclination to cultivate the members of all the successive Cabinets which passed before her, and She became the friend of Lord Castlereagh, of Canning, the Duke of Wellington, Lord Grey, Lord Palmerston, John Russell, Aberdeen, and many others of inferior note, and she was likewise one of the habitués of Holland House, which was always more or less neutral ground, even when Lord Holland was himself a member of the Government. When

Talleyrand came over here as Ambassador, there was for some time a sort of antagonism between the two Embassies, and particularly between the Ladies of each, but Madame de Dino (now Duchesse de Sagan) was so clever, and old Talleyrand himself so remarkable and so agreeable, that Madame de Lieven was irresistibly drawn towards them, and for the last year or two of their being in England they became extremely intimate; but her greatest friend in England was Lady Cowper, afterwards Lady Palmerston, and through her She was also the friend of Palmerston, who was also well affected towards Russia, till his jealous and suspicious mind was inflamed by his absurd notion of her intention to attack us in India, a crochet which led us into the folly and disaster of the Afghan war. In 1834 the Lievens were recalled, and she was established at Petersburg in high office about the Empress, but her séjour there was odious to her, and she was inconsolable at leaving England, where after a residence of above twenty years she had become rooted in habits and affections, although she had never really and completely understood the country. She remained at Petersburg for several months, until her two youngest children were taken ill, and died almost at the same time. This dreadful blow, and the danger of the severe climate to her own health, gave her a valid excuse for desiring leave of absence, and She left Russia never to return. She went to Italy, where M. de Lieven died about the year 1836 or 1837, after which she established herself in Paris, where her salon became the rendezvous of the best society, and particularly the neutral ground on which eminent men and politicians of all colours could meet, and where her tact and adroitness made them congregate in a sort of social truce.

I do not know at what exact period it was that She made the acquaintance of M. Guizot, but their intimacy no doubt was established after he had begun to play a great political part, for his literary and philosophical celebrity would not alone have had much charm for her. They were, however, already great friends at the time of his Embassy to England, and she took that opportunity of coming here to pay a visit to her old friends. The fall of Thiers' Government and Guizot's becoming Minister for Foreign Affairs, of course drew Madame de Lieven still more closely to him, and during the whole of his Administration their alliance continued to be of the closest and most intimate character. It was an immense object to her to possess the entire confidence of the French Minister for Foreign Affairs, who kept her au courant of all that was going on in the political world, while it is not surprising that he should be irresistibly attracted by a woman immensely superior to any other of his acquaintance, who was fully able to comprehend and willing to interest herself about all the grave and impor-

tant subjects which he had to handle and manage, and who associated herself with a complete sympathy in all his political interests. Their liaison,
which some people consider mysterious, but which I believe to have been
entirely social and political, grew constantly more close, and every moment
that Guizot could snatch from the Foreign Office and the Chamber he
devoted to Madame de Lieven. He used to go there regularly three times
a day in his way to and his way from the Chamber (when it was sitting)
and in the evening; but while He was by far her first object, she cultivated
the society of all the most conspicuous and remarkable people whom she
could collect about her, and she was at one time very intimate with Thiers,
though his rivalry with Guizot and their intense hatred of each other eventually produced a complete estrangement between her and Thiers.

The revolution of 1848 dispersed her friends, broke up her salon, and
terrified her into making a rather ludicrous, but as it turned out wholly
unnecessary, escape, She came to England, where she remained till affairs
apeared to be settled in France and all danger of disturbance at an end.
She then returned to Paris, where she remained, not without fear and
trembling, during the period of peril and vicissitude which at length ended,
much to her satisfaction, with the coup d'état and the Empire. Guizot had
returned to Paris, but constantly refused to take any part in political affairs,
either under the Republic or with the new Government of Louis Napoleon.
This, however, did not prevent Madame de Lieven (though their friendship
continued the same) from showing her sympathy and goodwill to the
Imperial régime, and her salon (which had been decimated by previous
events) was soon replenished by some of the Ministers or adherents of the
Empire, who, though they did not amalgamate very well with her old
habitués, supplied her with interesting information, and subsequently, when
the war broke out, rendered her very essential service. When the rupture
took place all the Russian subjects were ordered to quit Paris. She was
advised by some of her friends to disobey the order, for as she was equally
precluded from going to England, the circumstances in which this order
placed her were indescribably painful and even dangerous, but she said
that however great the sacrifice, and though she was entirely independent,
she was under so many obligations and felt so much attachment to the
Imperial Family that, cost her what it might, she would obey the order,
and accordingly she repaired to Bruxelles, where for a year and a half or
two years she took up her melancholy and uncomfortable abode. At last
this banishment from her home and her friends, with all the privations it
entailed, became insupportable, and She endeavoured through the inter-
vention of some of her Imperialist Friends, to obtain leave of the French

Government to return to Paris, either with or without (for it is not clear which) the consent of her own Court. The Emperor Napoleon seems to have been easily moved to compassion, and signified his consent to her return. No sooner did this become known to Cowley and the English Government, than they resolved to interpose for the purpose of preventing her return to Paris, and Cowley went to Walewski and insisted that the Emperor's permission should be revoked. The entente cordiale was then in full force, nothing could be refused to the English Ambassador, and Madame de Lieven was informed that She must not come back to Paris. She bore this sad disappointment with resignation, made no complaints, and resolved to bide her time. Some months later She caused a representation to be made to the French Government that the state of her health made it impossible for her to pass another winter at Brussels, and that she was going to Nice, but as it was of vital importance to her to consult her medical adviser at Paris, she craved permission to proceed to Nice viâ Paris, where she would only stay long enough for that purpose. The permission was granted. She wrote me word that She was going to Paris to remain there a few days. I replied that I was much mistaken in her if once there she ever quitted it again. She arrived and was told by her Doctor that it would be dangerous in her state to continue her journey. She never did proceed further, and never did quit Paris again. The Government winked at her stay, and never molested or interfered with her. She resumed her social habits, but with great caution and reserve, and did all she could to avoid giving umbrage or exciting suspicion. It was a proof of the greatness of her mind, as well as of her prudence and good temper, that She not only testified no resentment at the conduct of Cowley towards her, but did all she could to renew amicable relations with him, and few things annoyed her more than his perseverance in keeping aloof from her. From the time of her last departure from England up to the death of F. Lamb (Lord Beauvale and Melbourne) She maintained a constant correspondence with him. After his death She proposed to me to succeed him as her correspondent, and for the last two or three years our epistolary commerce was intimate and unbroken. She knew a vast deal of the world and its history during the half century she had lived and played a part in it, but she was not a woman of much reading, and probably at no time had been very highly or extensively educated, but her excessive cleverness and her finesse d'esprit supplied the want of education, and there was one book with which her mind was perpetually nourished by reading it over and over again. This was the 'Letters of Madame de Sévigné,' and to the constant study of those unrivalled letters she was no doubt considerably indebted for her own epistolary eminence, and for her admirable style of writing, not, however, that her style and Madame de Sévigné's were at all alike. She had not (in her letters at least) either the variety, the abundance, or the abandon of the great Frenchwoman, but she was more terse and epigrammatic, and She had the same graphic power and faculty of conveying much matter in few words.

Nothing could exceed the charm of her conversation or her grace, ease, and tact in society. She had a nice and accurate judgement, and an exquisite taste in the choice of her associates and friends; but though taking an ardent pleasure in agreeableness, and peculiarly susceptible of being bored, she was not fastidious, full of politeness and good breeding, and possessed the faculty of turning every one to account, and eliciting something either of entertainment or information from the least important of her acquaintance. It has been the fashion here, and the habit of the vulgar and ignorant Press, to stigmatise Madame de Lieven as a mischievous intriguer, who was constantly occupied in schemes and designs hostile to the interests of our Country. I firmly believe such charges to be utterly unfounded. She had resided for above twenty years (the happiest of her life) in England, and had imbibed a deep attachment to the country, where she had formed many more intimacies and friendships than she possessed anywhere else, and to the last day of her life she continued to cherish the remembrance of her past connexion, to cultivate the society of English people, and to evince without disguise her predilection for their country. She had never lived much in Russia, her connexion with it had been completely dissolved, and all she retained of it was a respectful attachment to the Imperial family, together with certain sympathies and feelings of loyalty for her native Country and her Sovereign which it would have been unnatural and discreditable to disavow. But her notorious correspondence with the Imperial Court was only caused by the natural anxiety of those Great Persons to be kept au courant of social and political affairs by such an accomplished correspondent, but I do not believe she was ever employed by them in any business or any political design;[1] but on the contrary, that she was rather distrusted and out of favor, on account of her being so denaturalised and for her ardent affection for England and the English. Russia was the country of her birth, France the country of her adopted abode, but England was the country of her predilection. With this cosmopolite character she dreaded everything which might produce hostile collision between any two of these

[1] 'She owned she always sent all the letters you write her to the Emperor of Russia, who is perfectly familiar with your handwriting, though it sometimes bothers his Imperial eyes.' (Letter of Reeve to Greville of December 23rd, 1845. *Letters*, p. 131.)

countries. She was greatly annoyed when the question of the Spanish marriages embittered the relations between France and England, but infinitely more so at the Turkish quarrel, and the war which it produced. Those who fulminated against her intrigues were, as I believe, provoked at the efforts she made (so far as she had any power or influence) to bring about the restoration of peace, an unpardonable offence in the eyes of all who were bent on the continuation of the war. She lived to see peace restored, and closed her eyes almost at the moment that the last seal was put to it by the Conference of Paris. Her last illness was sudden and short. Her health had always been delicate, and she was very nervous about herself; an attack of bronchitis brought on fever, which rapidly consumed her strength, and brought her, fully conscious, within sight of death; that consummation, which at a distance she had always dreaded, she saw arrive with perfect calmness and resignation, and all the virtues and qualities for which the smallest credit was given her seem to have shone forth with unexpected lustre on her deathbed. Her faculties were bright and unclouded to the last, her courage and presence of mind were unshaken, she evinced a tender consideration for the feelings of those who were lamenting around her bed, and she complied with the religious obligations prescribed by the Church of which she was a member with a devotion the sincerity of which we have no right to question. She made her Son Paul and Guizot leave her room a few hours before she died, that they might be spared the agony of witnessing her actual dissolution, and only three or four hours before the supreme moment, she mustered strength to write a note in pencil to Guizot with these words: 'Merci pour vingt années d'amitié et de bonheur. Ne m'oubliez pas, adieu, adieu.' It was given to him after her death.

February 8th, Sunday—I am just come from hearing the celebrated Mr. Sturgeon (Spurgeon) preach in the Music Hall of the Surrey Gardens. It was quite full; he told us from the pulpit that 9000 people were present. The service was like the Presbyterian: Psalms, prayers, expounding a Psalm and a sermon. He is certainly very remarkable, and undeniably a very fine preacher: not remarkable in person, in face rather resembling a smaller Macaulay, a very fine and powerful voice, which was heard through the whole hall; a manner natural, impassioned, and without affectation or extravagance; wonderful fluency and command of language, abounding in illustration, and very often of a very familiar kind, but without anything either ridiculous or irreverent. He gave me an impression of his earnestness and his sincerity, without book or notes, yet his discourse was evidently very carefully prepared. The text was 'Cleanse me from my secret sins,' and he divided it into heads, the misery, the folly, the danger (and a fourth which

I have forgotten) of secret sins, on all of which he was very eloquent and impressive. He preached for about three-quarters of an hour, and, to judge of the handkerchiefs and the audible sobs, with great effect.

1860

London, November 13th—At the end of three months since I last wrote anything in this book I take my pen in hand to record my determination to bring this journal (which is no journal at all) to an end. I have long seen that it is useless to attempt to carry it on, for I am entirely out of the way of hearing anything of the slightest interest beyond what is known to all the world. I therefore close this record without any intention or expectation of renewing it, with a full consciousness of the smallness of its value or interest, and with great regret that I did not make better use of the opportunities I have had of recording something more worth reading.

Index

Abercrombie, J., later 1st Lord Dunfermline, 162, 182

Aberdeen, 4th Lord, Prime Minister, 1852–5, 34, 39, 51, 138, 142, 282, 195, 196, 205–7, 213–20

Coalition Government, 273–81

Adair (George III's solicitor), 18

Adélaïde, Madame, 103

Adelaide, Queen, 30, 31, 34, 44, 69, 73, 76, 113, 121, 127, 130, 133

Afghanistan, 179, 195, 196, 282

Agar-Ellis, G. J. W., *see* Dover

Agricultural labourers, 102

Akbar Khan, son of Dost Mohammed, 195

"Alarm" (race-horse), ii, 208

Alban Hall, 245

Alava, Spanish patriot, 21

Albemarle, 4th Lord, Master of the Horse, 113, 120

Albert, Prince, 180, 181, 223, 243–8

Aldborough, Lady, 55

Alderson, Sir Edward, High Court Judge, 1830–57, 251

Alexander, Grand Duke, afterwards Emperor, 162

Algiers, 2

Allen, William, scientist and philanthropist, 38, 79, 192

Almack's, 194

Alten, General Victor, 140

Althorp, Lord, afterwards 3rd Lord Spencer, Whig statesman, 59, 61, 64, 71–5, 81, 82, 89, 94, 101, 158, 159, 191, 199, 200, 203, 205

Alvanley, 2nd Lord, wit, 48, 51, 107–110

Amelia, Princess, daughter of George II, 164

America, 216

American Boundary Treaty, 177–81, 191, 195

Amherst, 1st Lord, Governor-General of India, 14, 15

Ancient Concert, the, 69, 73

Anglesey, 1st Marquess, soldier and statesman, 5, 51, 95, 148

Angoulême, Duc and Duchesse d', 30

Anson, George, C-in-C, India, during Mutiny, 5, 56, 76, 260

Anstey, Christopher, 170

Anti-Corn Law League, 262

Appropriation Clause, 201

Apsley House, 24, 36, 38, 80, 95–7, 111, 153–5, 165

Arblay, Madame d', diarist, 1, 196

Arbuthnot, Tory politician, 10, 68, 155

Arguelles, Augusto, Spanish politician, 21

Arnold, Dr., Headmaster of Rugby, 186, 245, 246

Arundel, 46

Ascot Races, 76, 113, 166

Ashburton, 1st Lord, banker, *see* Alexander Baring

Ashley, Lord, afterwards 7th Lord Shaftesbury, philanthropist, 83, 150, 151, 201

Aston, Arthur, diplomat, 103

Athenaeum Club, 68

Attwood, Thomas, banker and Chartist, 65

Auckland, 1st Earl, Whig politician, 78, 119, 196, 229, 242, 250

Augereau, Pierre, Marshal of France, 53

Augusta, H.R.H. Princess, 31, 34

Augusta of Cambridge, Princess, 187

Austin, Charles, lawyer and conversationalist, 125, 191

Austria, 13, 19, 46, 50, 53, 246, 268

Badajoz, Fall of, 140

Bagot, Sir Charles, 186
Ball, Mr., 2
Ballot Question, 162-5, 192
Bampton Lectures, 243
Bank Charter, 238
Bankes, William, M.P., 75, 85
Bankhead, Charles, M.D., 11
Bank of England, Governor of, 207
Baring, Alexander, 41, 60, 93, 96, 97, 221
Baring, Bingham, 2nd Lord Ashburton, 177, 193, 195-6
Baring, Sir Francis, afterwards 1st Lord Northbrook, 198, 199, 271
Barnes, Thomas, Editor of The Times, 213
Barrington, Bishop, 171
Barrington, 6th Lord, 58
Barrow (veterinary surgeon), 258
Basingstoke, 171, 218
Batchelor, Page to George IV, 49, 50, 133
Bath, 130, 169
Bath, Lady, wife of 2nd Lord, 4
Bathurst, Lady, 12
Bathurst, 3rd Lord, Tory politician, 9, 11, 31-3, 38, 39, 57, 80, 120, 170
Batthyany, 190, 193
Baudrand, General, 51, 54
Beaudesert, 147, 148
Beaufort, Duchess of, 166
Beaufort, 1st Duke of, 167
Beaufort, 7th Duke of, 33, 58, 74, 172, 190, 243
Beauvale, Lady, 247
Beauvale, Lord, later 3rd Lord Melbourne, diplomat, 246, 247, 250, 265, 269, 270
Bedchamber Question, the, 151 ff., 202
Bedford, Duchess of, 33, 79
Bedford, 7th Duke of, 181, 199-202, 219-23, 227, 234, 236, 239, 242, 248, 267, 270, 275
Belfast, Lord, later 3rd Lord Donegal, 32, 76
Belgium, 46, 79, 99, 102
Belvoir Castle, 142-5
Bentinck Fund, 257

Bentinck, Lady Charlotte, i
Bentinck, Lord George, sportsman and M.P., i, ii, 12, 15, 134, 236, 242, 249
his life and character, 251-65
Bentinck, Lord Henry, 110
Bentinck, Lord William, 14
Bentley (publisher), 145
Berlin, 182
Bessborough, Lady, wife of 3rd Lord, 1, 2
Bessborough, 4th Lord, 243
Birch v. Somerville, 268
Birley's cotton factory, 210
Birmingham, 128, 129, 207
    Railroad, 128, 129
    riots, 172-4
    Union, 93
Bishops, 84, 89, 117, 120, 121, 239 ff.
Black Book, the, 60
Blandford, Lord, afterwards 6th Duke of Marlborough, 89
Bloomfield, Benjamin, 1st Lord, 6, 11
Blore, Edward, Architect, 52, 168, 208
Blue Books, 278
Blues, the (Horse Guards), 42, 43
Blücher, Field-Marshal, 23
Board of Control, 75
Board of Health, 78
Bonham, F. R., Tory Whip, 130
Bordeaux, Duc de, de jure King of France, 41, 48
Borgo, Count Pozzo di, Russian diplomat, born in Corsica, 39, 280
Bourmont, Comte de, Marshal of France, 40
Bowood, 200, 205, 225, 243
Brabazon, Lord, afterwards 11th Lord Meath, 89
Bradshaw (agent to D. of Bridgewater), 209
Breadalbane, Lady, 172
Bridgnorth, 164
Bridgewater Canal, 208-10
Bridgewater, Duke of, 208
Bridgewater House, 35
Brighton, 6, 7, 10, 13, 32, 47, 112, 130, 281

Bristol, 169
British Museum, 184
Broadlands, 177
Brockett, 246, 247, 268
Broglie, Duc de, French Ambassador in London, 104, 105, 241
Brooke, Major, 22
Brooks's Club, 161, 202, 218, 221, 271
Brougham, Lord, Whig politician: Lord Chancellor, 13, 40, 50, 51, 59, 60, 63–7, 72, 79, 89, 92, 110, 120, 145, 148, 158–60, 165, 174, 175, 239
Brownlow, 1st Lord, 35
Brussels, 283, 284
Buckhurst, 113
Buckingham, 1st Duke of, 101, 142
Buckingham House or Palace, 17, 18, 36, 154, 157, 166
Buckland, Dr., geologist, Dean of Westminster, 207
Buckstone, the, 168
Buller, Charles, Radical M.P., 182, 193, 200
Buller, James, Clerk of the Council, 28, 61, 115
Bülow, Baron Henry von, 40
Bunsen, C. K., Prussian politician, 271
Burdett, Sir F., Radical M.P., 2, 71
Burghley House, 5
Burgoyne, Sir John, General, and Lady, 238
Burke, Edmund (qu.), 81
Burney, Fanny, see Madame d'Arblay
Burnham Beeches, 249
Burton, Dr., Regius Professor at Oxford, 244
Bury, Lady Charlotte, 147
Bushey, 29, 30
Butler, Mrs. (Fanny Kemble), 198, 249
Butler, Pierce, husband of above, 198
Byng, George, later 2nd Lord Strafford, 259
Byron, Lord, 138, 147, 197

Cabul, retreat from, 179
re-occupation of, 195
Caffre War, 250

Calcraft, John, M.P., 62, 68
Calico printing, 211
Calvert, John, M.P., 69, 75
Cambridge, 31, 125, 186
Cambridge, Duchess of, 175
Cambridge, Prince George of, afterwards 2nd Duke, 189
Cambridgeshire, 74, 83
Canada, 139, 142, 144, 173, 186
Canada Bill, 174, 186, 187, 191, 250
Canals, 208–10
Canning, George, statesman, 3, 7, 9, 11–14, 26, 122, 204, 218, 242, 252, 263, 281
Canning, Mrs., wife of above, 15
Cannizzaro, Duchess of, daughter of Governor Johnstone, 118
Cannizzaro, Duke of, a Sicilian, 281
Canterbury, 41
Canterbury, William Howley, Archbishop of, 59, 116, 117, 118, 132, 244, 245
Cape Colony, 250
Capel, Reverend William, 183, 184
Caradoc, later 2nd Lord Hobart, 116
Carlton Club, 161
Carlton House, 2, 55, 149, 278
Carnarvon, Lord, 91, 99, 216
Caroline, Lady, see Wortley
Caroline, Queen, 2, 13, 18, 55, 171
Carrier (de Nantes), 44
Cartwright, John, Reformer, 74
Cassilis, Lord, 69, 118
Cathcart, 12th Lord, 43
Catholic Emancipation, 7, 57, 74, 86, 95, 145
Cavendish, Lord, 89
Caversham, Berks, 5
Cayla, Comtesse du, 22
Census (1831), 73
Chantrey, Sir Francis, sculptor, 170, 211
Charles X, King of France, 20, 22, 39, 44, 47, 50, 51
Charlotte, Princess, 5, 122
Charlotte, Queen, 17, 18
Charlton, 38
Chartism, 173, 174
Chartres, Duc de, see Louis-Philippe

Châteaubriand, Vicomte de, 48
Chatham, Lord, statesman, 17, 170, 186, 191, 204, 241
Chat Moss, 208
Chatsworth, 167
Chepstow Castle, 169
Chesterfield, 6th Lord, 30, 190, 193
Chetwynd, 5th Lord, Clerk to the Privy Council, 2
China, 193, 194
Chloroform, early use of in surgery, 240
Choiseul, Duc de, French politician, 41
Cholera, 77, 78, 84, 280
Christ's Hospital, 256
Cirencester, 8
Civil List, 62
Clanricarde, 3rd Lord, Whig politician, 56, 223, 273
Clarence, Duke of, see William IV
Clarendon, 9th Lord, statesman, 72, 159, 172, 174, 178, 182, 184, 200, 201, 219–29, 235–7, 242, 267, 268, 271, 273, 277
Clarke, Rev. Dr., Canon of Windsor, 3
Cleveland, Lord, later 3rd Duke of, 46
Clifton, 169
Cliver, Robert, 38, 166
Clogher, Percy Jocelyn, Bishop of, 8
Coal mine, 210
Cobbett, William, Radical writer, 101, 235
Cobden, Richard, Radical M.P., 233, 249
Coercion Bill, 237
Colborne, Sir John, afterwards Lord Seaton, 139
Colburn, Henry, publisher, 147
Coleridge, Mr. Justice, 194, 244
College of Physicians, 78
Colonial Office, 222, 228, 250
Combermere, 1st Lord, 32, 43
Congress of Verona, 18, 19
Conroy, Sir John, Comptroller to Duchess of Kent, 113, 116, 126, 130, 132, 162, 163
Conservatives, 197, 233, 275
Constantinople, 117
Conyngham, Lord Francis, 6

Conyngham, Lady, 3, 5, 6, 11, 12, 31, 43, 49, 77, 281
Conyngham, Lady Elizabeth, 3
Conyngham, Lord, 1st Marquess, 27, 113, 121, 132
Coplestone, Edward, Dean of St. Paul's, 245
Cormorants, 170
Corn Laws, 188, 207, 248, 262, 275, Repeal of, 213 ff.
Cornwallis, 2nd Marquess, 24
Cottenham, 1st Earl and Lord Chancellor, 220, 239
Cotton Industry, 210, 211
Council, Meetings of the, 179, 187, 199, 271
Covent Garden Theatre, 1, 193
Cowes, 52
Cowley, 1st Earl, diplomat, 284
Cowper, Lady, later Lady Palmerston, 67, 163, 175, 282
Cowper, William, M.P., later Lord Mount-Temple, 216, 244
Cracherode, C. M., 185
Cradock, J. H., 2nd Lord Howden, diplomat, 54
Cranworth, see Rolfe
Craon, 23
Craven, 2nd Lord, 58
Craven Race Meeting, 176
Cray, 9, 10
Crimean War, 273, 280
Criterion Stakes, 258
Crockfords, 36
Croker, J. W., 79, 86, 96
Cromer, 190
Crommelin, a racing-man, 257–60
"Crucifix" (race-horse), 255
Cumberland, 75, 127
Cumberland, Duke of, 24, 29, 30, 31, 38, 42, 43, 52, 80, 115, 119, 142, 179
Cumberland, Prince George of, 31
Cumming, John, 105
Cuthbert, 199

Dalhousie, James, 10th Lord, 214
Dalton, John, statue of, 211

Danebury, 255, 259
Danton, 240, 241
Davout, Marshal, 52
Dawson, G., Irish M.P., 41, 62
Day, John, racing-man, 255, 257, 258
Delane (Editor of *The Times*), 213, 218, 220
Delbury, 166
Denison, John Evelyn, Speaker, 59, 246
Denison, *see* Salisbury
Denman, Lord, Lord Chief Justice, 68, 110, 114, 194, 246
Denmark, "Old Treaty" with, 179
Derby, *see* Stanley
Derby Races, ii, 7, 23, 256
Devon, 20th Lord, 242
Devonshire, 6th Duke of, 60
Dickens, Charles, 207, 208
Digby, Admiral, 55
Dino, Duchesse de, 88
Diplomatic Bill, 251
Disraeli, Benjamin, Prime Minister, 242, 266
Doncaster Races, 13, 134
Dorsetshire Elections, 83
Douro, Lord, 2nd Duke of Wellington, 36, 37, 129, 148
Dover, 1st Lord, 13, 35, 55
Downing Street, 202, 271
Downton Castle, 166
Drayton, 207
Dresden, Battle of, 53
Drury Lane Theatre, 1
Dryden (qu.), 146
Dublin, 41
Dublin, Archbishop of, 243, 244
Dudley, 1st Lord, Canningite, 54, 55, 80
Duncannon, Lord, later 4th Lord Bessborough, Viceroy of Ireland, 65, 127, 165, 191
Duncombe, Tom, M.P., 96
Dundas, Sir David, Q.C., M.P., 201, 202, 246, 249
Durazzo, Madame, 104
Durham, 1st Lord, statesman, 2, 58, 72, 91, 116, 126, 127, 192

Eastern Question, 277
Easthope, Sir John, M.P., owner of *Morning Chronicle*, 248
East India Bill, 101
East India Company, 14, 15
Eastnor Castle, 167
Ebrington, Lord, later 2nd Lord Fortescue, 79, 81, 89
Economist, The, 258
Eddisbury, Lord, afterwards 2nd Lord Stanley of Alderley, 271
Eden, Emily, author, 197
Edinburgh Review, 139
Education, 159, 175, 176
Edward VI, 246
Egerton, Francis, Lord, afterwards 1st Lord Ellesmere, 208, 209
his industrial welfare scheme, 210
Egremont, 3rd Lord, 32, 135–7
Eldon, 1st Lord, Lord Chancellor, 63, 80, 148
Elections, General, 74, 129
Electric Telegraph, 240, 265
Ellenborough, 1st Earl, Governor-General of India, 87, 91, 92, 165, 179, 194, 198, 214
his Proclamation, 194, 197, 199
Ellesmere, Lady, i, 7
Ellesmere, 1st Lord, i
Ellice, Edward, "Bear", Whig politician, 58, 59, 65, 200, 201, 225, 228
Elliot, Capt., Secretary to Admiralty, 78, 194
Elveden, Norfolk, 5
Emily, Princess, *see* Amelia
England, conditions in Northern, 188
Epsom, 113
Erle, Mr. Justice, 246
Ernest Augustus, King of Hanover, *see* Hanover
Erroll, 18th Lord, Master of the Horse, 29, 31, 114, 166
Essex, 74
Essex, Lord, 183
Esterhazy, Prince, Austrian Ambassador, 37

Eton College, ii
Eugène, Prince, Beauharnais, 53
Euston, Norfolk, 1, 5, 13, 25, 135
Evelyn, John, 197
Everett, Edward, United States Minister in London, 182, 195, 196
Every Man In His Humour, 207
Ewart, William, M.P., 130
Ewart family, 59
Examiner, The, 178, 180
Exchequer Court, 256
Exeter, Bishop of, Henry Phillpotts, 89, 91, 183, 239, 243
Exeter, 2nd Marquess of, 138, 139

Falck, Baron, Dutch diplomat, 37, 39
"Family Compact, the", 23
Felbrigg, 190
Fern Hill, 76
Fife, 4th Lord, 2
Finsbury Square, 235
Fisher, John, Bishop of Rochester, 185
Fitzclarence, Adolphus, Lord, Rear-Admiral, son of William IV, 113, 124, 131, 180, 189
Fitzclarence, Augustus, 76
Fitzclarence, George, Lord, later Lord Munster, son of William IV, 28, 31, 33
Fitzgerald, Vesey, President of Board of Trade, afterwards 1st Lord, 34, 38, 44, 96, 142, 145, 146, 179
Fitzharris, Lord, afterwards 3rd Lord Malmesbury, 40
Fitzherbert, Mrs., 30, 112, 164
Fitzjames, Duke of, French Royalist, 48
Flahaut, Comte de, son of Talleyrand, 266, 272
Fleetwood, Sir Peter Hesketh, M.P., 162
Foley, 1st Lord, 164
Foley, 4th Lord, 95, 228
Follett, Sir William, M.P., lawyer, 188, 194
Fordwich, later 6th Lord Cowper, 41
Foreign Office, 178, 219, 222, 228, 268, 269, 271

Fox, Charles James, statesman, 89, 145, 164
Fox, William Johnson, Unitarian and M.P., 235
France, 19, 39 ff., 47, 65, 102, 250, 272, 285
   Coup d'Etat (1851), 265 ff.
   Royal Library of, 199
Frankfort, 2nd Lord, 190, 193
Frankfurt, 182
Freemasons, 35
Free Trade, 207, 213, 246, 271, 275
French armies, 140, 280
Freyre, Manoel, Spanish General, 21
Frogmore, 29, 45
Fuentes d'Onoro, battle of, 141

Galway Bill, 51
Gascoyne, Isaac, General, M.P., 70
George II, King, 164
George III, 56, 179
   his Will, 17
George IV, i, iii, 1, 3–6, 10, 11, 27, 49, 77, 112, 116, 121, 133, 149, 155, 164, 179, 247, 281
George, Prince, see Cumberland *and* Cambridge
Germany, 182
Gibbon, Edward, 197
Gibbs and Howard, moneylenders, 2
Gibraltar, 77
Gilbert, Davies, M.P., 97
Gladstone, W. E., statesman, 214, 277
Glengall, Lady, 7, 52, 55
Glengall, 2nd Lord, 48
Gloucester, Duchess of, 24, 31, 69
Gloucester, 2nd Duke of, 31, 38, 52
Gloucestershire, 74
Glyn, G., banker and M.P., 234
Goderich, Lord, afterwards Lord Ripon, Prime Minister, 63, 91
Gold Stick, 29, 42, 56
Goodrich Castle, 168, 169
Goodrich Court, 168
Gordon, Jane, Duchess of, 16
Gordon, Sir Robert, diplomat, 218
Gordon, Sir James Willoughby, 56
Gore, Charles, Commissioner of Woods and Forests, 228

Gore, Sir John, Admiral, 30

Gore, Lady, 30

Gorhambury, 18, 182

Goulburn, Henry, Chancellor of the Exchequer, 34, 60, 79, 96

Gower, Lord, later 2nd Duke of Sutherland, 44, 281

Graham, Sir Bellingham and Lady, 23

Graham, Sir James, statesman, 58, 60, 62, 65, 72, 75, 78, 92, 125, 127, 153, 165, 192, 219, 221–3, 226, 238, 250, 275

Graham, Sir Thomas, later 1st Lord Lynedoch, 139

Granby, Marquess of, later 6th Duke of, 249, 250

Grange, the, 205

Grant, Charles, afterwards 1st Lord Glenelg, 62, 63

Grant, Sir Robert, brother of above, 62

Granville, 1st Lord, 5, 8, 13, 103, 105

Granville, 2nd Lord, statesman with whom Greville latterly lodged, 193, 228, 267–71

Great Seal, the, 188

Greece, 246

Greenwich, 34, 35, 175

Gregory, G. de L., 142

Grenfell, Charles, 59

Grenville, Thomas, 184, 185, 190, 235, 241

Greville, Algernon, brother of Charles, 1, 198, 199

Greville, Brooke, first cousin of Charles, 76, 108, 109

Greville, Charles Cavendish Fulke, early education and government appointments, ii
character, ii, iii
horse-racing, ii, 7, 11, 13, 23, 31, 72, 76, 113, 128, 134, 135, 176, 208, 255, 280

Greville, Fulke, grandfather of Charles, i

Greville, Harry, uncle of Charles, 170

Greville, Richard, first cousin of Charles, 106

Grey, Lady Elizabeth, 211

Grey, 2nd Lord, Prime Minister, 50, 51, 55–8, 67, 72, 76–9, 81, 84–100, 117, 121, 123, 127, 128, 156, 169, 191–3, 204, 229, 236, 281

Grey, Sir Charles, 56

Grey, Sir G., Home Secretary, 223, 228, 230, 238

Grimston, 280

Grimston, Lady Jane, 183

Grosvenor, 2nd Lord, later Lord Westminster, 32

Grosvenor Square, 185

Grote, George, historian and M.P., 129, 162, 249

Grove, the, 182, 200, 206

Guards, Brigade of, 29, 30, 36, 127

Guildford, 188, 189

Guilford, 4th Lord, 185

Guizot, François, French politician, 205, 206, 265, 272, 282, 283, 286

Gunton, 135

Gurney, Richard, 256

Gwydir, 2nd Lord, 6

Gwynne, Nell, 49

Haddington, 9th Lord, 91, 99

Halford, Sir Henry, doctor to the King, 77

Hampden, R. D., Bishop of Hereford, 239 ff.

Hampshire, disorders in, 56, 58

Hampton Court (near Malvern), 167

Hanover, 17, 99, 115, 142, 177, 179

Harcourt, Edward, Archbishop of York, 235, 241

Harcourt, George, M.P., 218

Harding, Henry, 1st Lord, Commander-in-Chief, 57, 62, 192

Hardy, Lady, 79

Hardy, Sir Thomas, Admiral, 78

Hare, Archdeacon, 243

Harris, 1st Lord, soldier, 16

Harrowby, Lady, 3, 4, 115

Harrowby, Lord, leader of the Waverers over Reform Bill, 82, 84, 86–91, 99, 115, 192, 193, 241

Hastings, Lady Flora, 165, 171

Hastings, 1st Lord, 155

Hastings, 2nd Lord, 34, 72

Hawes, Rev. Mr., 239
Hay, R. W., Permanent Under-Secretary at War Office, 34
Heber, Bishop, 197
Henry V, 168
Henry VII, 185
Henry VIII, 244
Hereford, 2nd Lord, 38
Herries, J. C., Chancellor of the Exchequer, 76
Hertford Assizes, 183
Hertford, 3rd Lord, 1
dispute over his Will, 182, 190
Heytesbury, 1st Lord, 219
Heythrop, 58
Hill, Rowland, 1st Lord, Commander-in-Chief, 56, 125, 140, 142, 145
Hillingdon, 191
Hinds, Samuel, Bishop of Norwich, 245
Hobart, Henry, Dean of Windsor, 127
Hobhouse, John Cam, later 1st Lord Broughton, 3, 64, 86, 151
Hodgson, Francis, 147
Holland House, 80, 163, 211, 281
Holland, Lady, the celebrated hostess, 178, 191, 194, 205, 212
Holland 3rd Lord, 55, 89, 90, 145, 163, 177, 178, 211, 281
Holmes, William, Tory Whip, 50, 130, 142
Home Office, 229
Hong Kong, 250
Hope, William, 104
Hope, General, later 3rd Lord Hopetoun, 140
Horse-racing, ii, 7, 11, 13, 23, 31, 72, 76, 113, 128, 134, 135, 176, 208, 254, 255, 280
Horton, Sir R. Wilmot, 5, 11
Houghton Race Meeting, 13, 208
Hounslow, 8
House of Commons, 273 ff.
Howe, 1st Earl, 30, 81, 156
Howick, Lord, afterwards 3rd Earl Grey, 58, 67, 163–5, 225, 226–31
Hoyle's Calico Printing Works, 211
Hume, John Robert, M.D., 4
Hume, Joseph, M.P., 101

Hunt, Henry, M.P., 70
Huntingtower, Lord, eldest son of Lord Dysart, 190
Huskisson, William, M.P., 15, 50, 55
Hyde Park, 36

IncomeTax, 242
India, 9, 14, 193, 194, 197, 243
Ingestre, Lady Sarah, 166
Inglis, Sir Robert, Bart., M.P., 63, 97
Invalides (Paris), 103
Irby, W. H. R., 185
Ireland, 57, 70, 75, 101, 102, 127, 146, 174, 207, 232, 235, 237, 238, 242
Irish Municipal Corporation Bill, 79, 114, 201
Irun, 21
Italy, 53, 182, 282
Ives, racing enemy of Lord George Bentinck, 257

Jamaica Bill, 159
Jeffrey, Francis, founder of the Edinburgh Review, 64
Jerrold, Douglas, 208
Jersey, Lady, 12, 41, 65, 175, 243
Jersey, 5th Lord, 29, 36
Jerusalem, Bishopric of, 201
Jervis, Sir John, Attorney-General, 248, 249
Jervis, John, son of above, 249
Jockey Club, ii, 98, 162, 256, 257
Jockeys, Bribery of, 259
John Bull, 262
Johnson, Samuel, 197
Jordan, Mrs., 122
"Judge and Jury Court", 193
Judicial Committee, 239
Julio Clovio, 185

Kay-Shuttleworth, Sir James; his school, 175
Keate, Dr., 89, 240
Keble, John, 244
Kelly, Sir Fitzroy, Solicitor-General, 244
Kemble, Adelaide, 199
Kemble, Fanny, 198, 249

Kempt, Sir James, 178
Kenilworth, 129
Kennedy, Lord, M.P. for Evesham, 89
Kensington Palace, 113, 116, 122, 125, 132
Kent, Duchess of, 113, 115, 120, 123, 125, 126, 130 ff., 162
Kent, Edward, Duke of, 17, 18
Kent House, 228, 229
Kenyon, 2nd Lord, 80, 194
Keogh, W. N., M.P., 276
Keppel, Sir William, 4
Kindersley, Sir Richard, 254
Knaresborough, 60
Knatchbull, Sir Edward, Tory M.P., 68
Knight, Richard Payne, 166
Knighton, Sir William, 11, 12, 24, 49, 112
Knowsley, 128, 129
Kossuth, Louis, Hungarian patriot, 268

Labouchere, Henry, M.P., 153, 270
Labuan, 250
Lafitte, Jacques, 41
Lamartine's *Histoire des Girondins*, 240
Lamb, F., *see* Melbourne, Lord
Lambeth Palace, 52
Lambton, *see* Lord Durham
Landed Interests, 102, 217, 227
Langdale, H. B., 1st Lord, Master of the Rolls, 246
Lansdowne, 3rd Lord, Whig states-man, 68, 78, 79, 115, 120, 127, 128, 200, 219, 221, 225–9, 235, 237, 239, 243, 251, 275, 276
Laon, 23
Lauderdale, 8th Lord, 8
Laval, Duc de, 37, 40
Lawley, Sir Francis, 7th Bt., 79, 89
Ledbury, 167
Leeds, 6th Duke of, 30, 33
Lehzen, Baroness, Queen Victoria's Governess, 116, 132, 133, 156, 181
Leicestershire, 74
Le Marchant, Sir Denis, 1st Bt., 149, 248

Lennox, Charles, Colonel, afterwards 4th Duke of Richmond, 16
Lennox, Lord George, 253
Lennox, Lady Charlotte, later Duchess of Richmond, 16
Lennox, Lady Georgiana, later Lady de Ros, 7
Leopold, Prince, afterwards King of the Belgians, 24, 79, 116
Leveson-Gower, Lord Francis, 63
Leveson, *see* Granville
Lewis's *Italian Journal*, 145
Lichfield, Lady, 160
Lichfield, 1st Earl, 255
Lieven, Madame de, wife of Russian diplomat, iii, 3, 6, 7, 12, 104, 131, 199, 265, 271, 280 ff.
Lieven, Paul de, son of above, 286
Life Guards, 29, 42
Lindsay, Lady Charlotte, 191
Littleton, E. C., M.P., later 1st Lord Hatherton, 79, 89
Liverpool Election, 59, 130
Liverpool, 2nd Lord, Prime Minister, 3, 9, 11, 13, 14, 18, 25, 122, 153
Liverpool Races, 128
Locke (Bridgewater Trustee), 209
Lollards' Tower, 52
London, C. J. Blomfield, Bishop of, 116, 117, 159, 182, 183, 184
London Elections, 129
London, Lord Mayor of, 73
Londonderry, 3rd Lord, previously Castlereagh, 8, 9, 10, 13, 16, 204, 281
Londonderry, 4th Lord, 71, 72, 87, 174
Longmans, Messrs., v
Lonsdale, 2nd Lord, 46
Louis-Napoleon, *see* Napoleon III
Louis-Philippe, King of the French, 28, 41, 42, 45, 46, 48, 50, 51, 103, 222, 240, 241
Lovaine, Lord, later 5th Duke of Northumberland, 2
Lowe, Alice, 194
Ludford, 167
Ludlow, 164
Ludlow Castle, 166
Lushington, Mr. Justice, 245, 246, 251

Luttrell, Henry, the wit, 79
Lygon, Henry, later 4th Lord Beauchamp, 74
Lyndhurst, Lady, 79, 80, 81
Lyndhurst, Lord, Lord Chancellor, 33, 57, 71, 76, 79, 80, 81, 91–3, 97, 99, 100, 114, 115, 142, 175
Lynn, 254
Lyttelton, 3rd Lord, 74

Macaulay, Thomas, historian, 63, 79, 81, 86, 101, 162, 165, 218, 220
Lays of Ancient Rome, 186
McFlecknoe, 31
Macmillan (publishers), iv
Madeleine, the (Paris), 103
Magistrates, 173
Maidstone, Lord, later 11th Lord Winchilsea, 193
Malmesbury, 1st Lord, diplomatist, 170
Malt Tax, 101
Malta, 118
Malvern, 167
Manchester, 209, 210, 249, 271
Athenaeum, 210
Collegiate Church, 210
"Mango" (race-horse), 74, 134, 255
Manners, Lord Charles, 74
Manners, Lord Robert, 74
Manners-Sutton, Charles, afterwards 1st Lord Canterbury, 15, 96, 97, 125
Mansfield, 1st Lord, 194
Mansfield, 3rd Lord, 71, 73, 78, 99
Marescalchi, Madame de, 104
Margaret, Countess of Richmond, 185
Marion, 6
Marlborough, 1st Duke of, 172
Marmont, Marshal, 23, 41, 52, 53, 55, 140
Martin, Sir Samuel, Q.C., 194, 262
Martin, Sir Thomas Byam, 78
Maryborough, Lord, later 3rd Lord Mornington, 24
Marylebone, 88
Mash, Thomas, 71
Masséna, Marshal, 22

Matuscewitz, Count André, Russian diplomat, 36, 37, 39, 40, 48
Maule, Fox, M.P., later 11th Lord Dalhousie, 61, 174, 238
Mauritius, 170
Mazarin (qu.), 184
Mecklenburg-Strelitz, Prince of, 187
Medical etiquette, strange case of, 240
Melbourne, 2nd Lord, Prime Minister, 58, 86, 88, 92, 114–19, 122–5, 132, 145, 149–61, 165, 166, 172, 175, 181, 182, 202, 222, 230, 244, 246–8
Melton, 146
Melville, 2nd Lord, 9
Merewether, Dean of Hereford, 243
"Meunier" (race-horse), 259
Meynell, Henry, M.P., 69
Meyrick, Sir Samuel, 169
Mickleham, 159
Middlesex, 88
Middleton, 243
Miguel, Dom of Portugal, 43
Milan Commission, 12
Milman, H. H., author, 218
Milton, Lord, afterwards 3rd Lord Fitzwilliam, 74, 75, 82
Minto, 2nd Lord, 223
Moira, Lord, see 1st Lord Hastings
Molé, M. de, 51
Molesworth, Sir W., M.P., Radical, 276
Molyneux, F., 182
Molyneux, Lord, later 3rd Lord Sefton, 89
Monarchy, the, 160, 161, 174, 273
Monmouth, 74, 167
Monmouth, Geoffrey of, 167
Monrose, C. B. (actor), 103
Monsell, William, M.P., later 1st Lord Emly, 276
Montagu, Edward, later 5th Lord Rokeby, 5
Montagu, Henry, later 2nd Lord Montagu, 76
Montpensier, Duchesse de, 247
Montreal, 139
Montrond, Comte de, French diplomat and friend of Talleyrand, 45, 51

Montrose, Duchess of, 166
Montrose, 3rd Duke of 27, 166
Moore, General Sir John, 16
Mornay, Charles, French diplomat, 48
Morning Chronicle, 144, 178, 180, 182, 195, 200, 238, 248
Morning Herald, 85
Morning Post, 165, 171, 172, 277
Morpeth, Lord, later 7th Lord Carlisle, 151
Mortemart, duc de, 54
Moscow, 52, 77
Moss, Mr., 34
Mount Charles, Lord, later 2nd Lord Conyngham, 12, 29, 30, 33, 49
Münster, Count, Hanoverian diplomat, 8
Muntz, George, M.P., 173, 174
Murdoch, Sir Thomas, Civil Servant in Colonial Office, 187
Murray, Sir George, Secretary of State for Colonies, 34, 44, 139
Musard, Philippe, founder of a dance-hall in Paris, 104, 194

Naples, 19, 117
Napoleon I, 22, 52, 53, 140, 204
Napoleon III, 265 ff., 283, 284
Nasmyth Locomotive Works, 210
Nelson Memorial, 162
Newcastle, cholera at, 185
Newcastle, 4th Duke of, 32, 98, 144
New Forest, 178
Newman, Cardinal, 244
Newmarket, 5, 13, 31, 70, 72, 92, 134, 135, 146, 176, 185, 208, 234, 254, 256
New Zealand, 250
Nice, 284
Nollekens, Joseph, sculptor, 170
Norbury, 1st Lord, 2
Normanby, Lady, 151
Normanby, 1st Lord, 174, 175, 201, 269, 271
North, social conditions in the, 188
North, Lord, Prime Minister, 71, 185, 186
Northamptonshire, 74, 75

Northumberland, Duchess of, 114, 116
Northumberland, 4th Duke of, 38
Norwich, 129
Norwood, Poor Law School at, 175
Nun Appleton, 5

Oakley Park, 166
Oaks, The (horse-race), 23, 255, 259
Oatlands, 5, 17, 281
O'Connell, Daniel, M.P., Irish Patriot, 57, 65, 73, 82, 127, 128, 201
Odier, Antoine, French banker, 4
O'Donnell, Joseph Henry, commanded Spanish forces in Peninsula, 141
Ompteda, Baron, Hanoverian Minister, 179
Oregon, 215, 216
"Orlando" (race-horse), ii, 256, 263
Orléans, Duc d', *see* Louis-Philippe Ferdinand-Philippe, eldest son of Louis-Philippe, 103
Osborne, I. o. Wight, 218, 220, 271
Osnaburg, Bishopric of, 17
Osterley, 45
Oxford, 31
    Bishop of, Samuel Wilberforce, 183, 241, 243–5
    Christ Church, ii

Pall Mall, 32
Palmella, Duke of, Portuguese Ambassador in London, 21, 281
Palmer, J. H., M.P. for the City, 129
Palmer, Charles, M.P., 130
Palmerston, Lady, 178, 194, 199, 230, 269–73
Palmerston, 3rd Lord, statesman and Prime Minister, 50, 55, 62, 76, 91, 92, 105, 117, 118, 177–80, 193, 194, 200, 205, 216, 219, 220, 228, 230, 246, 247, 267, 269, 271, 272, 275, 277, 278, 281, 282
Panshanger, 6
Panthéon (Paris), 103
Paris, 102, 250
    Conference of, 286
    Revolt in, 40–2, 267, 282, 283

Parke, Mr. Justice, later Lord Wensleydale, 251
Partridge, Mr. and Mrs. Ralph, iv
Patricroft, 210
Patteson, Mr. Justice, 244
Payne, George, partner of Greville's on the Turf, 110
Peel, Sir Robert, statesman and Prime Minister, 2, 9, 11, 12, 38, 43, 57, 62–5, 69, 71, 79, 81, 86, 92, 95–101, 114–6, 119–22, 125, 146–53, 157, 162, 165, 179–82, 192, 195, 213, 214, 217
  resigns, 218 ff.
  accepts government, 230–7, 242, 248, 263–7, 274
Peers, creation of, 84, 87, 89, 90, 97, 100, 192
Pembroke, 12th Lord, 104
Peninsular War, 16, 139, 146
Pensions, 60, 62
Pepys, Samuel, iii, 197
Perez, Antonio, 199
Perier, Casimir, President, *Chambre des Députés*, 41
Petersham, Lord, later 4th Lord Harrington, 2
Petersburg, 282
Petworth, Sussex, 136
Pew system (in churches), 183
Phillpotts, Henry, *see* Exeter
Picton, Sir Thomas, General, killed at Waterloo, 8
Piedmont, 249
Pigou, 238
Pitt, *see* Chatham
Planta, Joseph, Tory Whip, 130
Platt, Mr. Justice, 251
Poix, Duc de, French diplomat, 104
Poland, 53, 65
Pole, Sir C., Admiral, 30
Polignac, Prince de, French Royalist leader, 28, 39, 41, 47, 51, 54
Pollock, Mr. Justice, 251
Ponsonby, Lord, later 1st Viscount, diplomat, 117, 118, 181
Poor Law, 173, 183, 201
Poor Law School, 175
Porson, Richard, 185

Portland, William Henry, 3rd Duke of, i, ii
Portland, William Henry, 4th Duke of, 15, 254, 255
Portman, Edward, M.P., later 1st Viscount, 89
Portugal, 16, 21
Potocki, Stanislas, 48
Pottinger, Sir Henry, first Governor of Hong Kong, 194
Poulett-Thomson, C. E., *see* Lord Sydenham
Praed, W. M., poet and M.P., 165
Prandi, Piedmontese patriot, 249
"Preserve" (race-horse), 254
President S. S., 177
Press, the, 83, 85
Preston, 70
Princess Royal, Victoria, 247
Prussia, 53
Prussia, Frederick William Louis, Prince of, 31
Punch, 207
Pusey, E. B., leader of Oxford Movement, 244
Puseyites, 183, 244

Quakers, 38
Quarantine, 77, 78
Queen's Bench, 188, 194, 244, 246

Radford, Jack, stud-groom to the King, 50
Radicals, 66, 84, 124, 129, 130, 144, 149, 152, 154, 160, 163, 271, 276
Radnor, 7th Lord, 60
Radnorshire, 166
Raglan Castle, 168, 169
Railway speculation, 207
Railway travel, 128, 129, 206
Ramozet, de Ros' servant, 106
Ravensworth, Lady, 38
Reeve, Henry, leader-writer on *The Times*, iii, 213–15, 217, 271, 285
Reform, 3, 59 ff., 83–100, 123, 274
Reform Bill, 61, 62, 79, 83, 123, 156, 191, 251, 277, 278, 280
Reform Club, 152
Regency Bill, 115

Rendlesham, 13

Richmond, Duchess of, 253

Richmond, 4th Duke of, 16

Richmond, 5th Duke of, 56, 71, 72, 76, 87, 94, 127, 128, 177, 192, 259

Riddlesworth, 5, 13

Riga, 77

Rigby, Richard, M.P., 186

Roberts, A. W., banker, 207

Robespierre, 240

Ripon, 2nd Lord, 214

Roebuck, J. A., M.P., 101, 114, 130

Rogers, Samuel, 79, 177

Rolfe, Baron, later Lord Cranworth and Lord Chancellor, 177, 239, 246, 251

Rolls Court, 190

Romilly, Sir Samuel, 61

Romsey, 177

Ros, Lady Georgiana de, 106, 109

Ros, 19th Lord de, 105–11, 152, 190

Ros, William de, 106, 109

Ross (Monmouth), 167

Ross, Charles, M.P., 70, 130

Ross, "Man of", 167

Rosslyn, 2nd Lord, 35, 44

Rothschild, Jacob, 40, 41

Rotten Boroughs, 88

Roubiliac, 170

Royal Marriages Act, 189

"Running Rein" (race-horse), 256, 263

Russell, Lord John, afterwards 1st Earl, statesman, 15, 61, 62, 67, 70, 79, 85, 96, 114, 124, 127, 149–52, 159, 162–5, 180, 182, 187, 191, 195, 200, 211, 213, 218 ff., 225

accepts government, 226

resigns, 230, 234, 237–39, 242, 245–8, 267–71, 276–81

Russell, William (Ambassador to Berlin), 182

Russia, 19, 39, 52, 53, 77, 117, 277, 280, 282, 285

Rutland, 5th Duke of, 44, 46, 144, 145

St. Antonio, Count, see Cannizzaro

St. George's Hall, 52, 76

St. George's Hospital, 240

St. James's Theatre, 207

St. Leger, 11, 23, 134, 255

St. Petersburg, 77, 282

Salamanca, Battle of, 52

Salisbury, Bishop of, E. Denison, 241, 246

Cathedral, 170

Salisbury, Lady, 36, 138

Salisbury, 2nd Lord, 138

Salmon, crimped, 168

Sampaye, 199

Sandon, Lord, afterwards 2nd Lord Harrowby, 56, 75, 148, 241

Sandwich, Lady, 172

San Sebastian, 21

Saxe-Weimar, Princess Ida of, 76

Scarlett, James, later Lord Abinger, 129

Schedule "A" (Reform Bill), 90

Scott, General, 261

Scott, Sir Walter, 138, 147, 197

Scribe, Eugène, French playwright, 2

Sébastiani, Comte, French Ambassador, 105

Sefton, 2nd Lord, 8, 36, 45, 62, 67

Selwyn, George, 163, 164

Senior, Nassau, political economist, 61, 243

Seringapatam, Siege of, 16

Sévigné, Madame de, 284

Seville, 199

Seymour, Horace, 69

Seymour, Lord, later 2nd Duke of, 54

Shaftesbury, 6th Lord, 72

Sheridan, R. B., 145

Shiel, Richard, M.P., 82

Shrewsbury, 162

Shuttleworth, see Kay-Shuttleworth

Sidmouth, Henry, 1st Lord, Home Secretary, 9

Sidney, Sir Philip, 31

Simmons Rock, 168

Six Acts, the (1819), 237

Smith, Thomas Cusack, Master of the Irish Rolls, 238

Smith, Sydney, 79

Socialism, 272

Somers, 1st Lord, 44

Somerset, 11th Duke of, 64

Somerset, Lady Augusta, 189
Somerset, Lady Fitzroy, 33
Somerset, Lord Fitzroy, later Lord Raglan, 48, 74, 85, 139
Sotherton (agent to Bridgewater Trust), 209
Soult, Marshal, 21
Späeth, Baroness, Lady-in-Waiting to Duchess of Kent, 132
Spain, 19, 139, 140, 174, 205, 247
Spanish Marriage Question, 247
Spectator, The, 180
Spencer, Captain, afterwards 4th Lord 74
Spencer, 3rd Lord, *see* Althorp
Sporting Magazine, 135
Spring Rice, T., later 1st Lord Mounteagle, 125
Sprotborough, 5, 11
Spurgeon, Charles, preacher, 286
Stade Treaty, 179
Staël, Madame de, 242
Stafford, S. A. O., M.P., 250
Standard, The, 180, 215
Stanhope, 4th Lord, 60
Stanley, Bishop of Norwich, 239
Stanley, Lord, later 15th Lord Derby, Prime Minister, 62, 64, 65, 86, 92, 101, 125, 218, 236, 242, 249, 275, 276, 280
Stanley, Edward John, M.P., later 2nd Lord Stanley of Alderley, 152, 271
Stapylton, Martin, 51
Steam engine, 240
Stephenson, Sir Benjamin, Surveyor-General of Works, 25
Stewart, Lady Dudley, daughter of Lucien Bonaparte, 53
Stockmar, Baron, adviser to the royal family of Coburg, 271
Stoke, 48, 50
Stonehenge, 170
Stradbroke, 2nd Lord, 76, 253
Strathaven, Lord, later 10th Lord Huntly, 29
Stuart, Sir Charles, later Lord Stuart de Rothesay, 39, 40, 54, 84
Sudely, 1st Lord, 167

Sumner, Charles, Bishop of Winchester, 3, 250
Sunday Times, 188, 194
Sunderland, 84
Surgery, 240
Surrey Gardens, 286
Sussex, 135
Sussex, H.R.H. Duke of, 29–31, 35, 36, 119
Sutherland, Duchess of, wife of 2nd Duke, 144
Sutherland, Duke of, *see* Gower
Sutton, 147
Swift, Jonathan (qu.), 82
Swiss Question, the, 248
Sydenham, 1st Lord, Governor-General Canada, 59, 61, 67, 78, 187
Syria, 177, 178, 201

Talavera, Battle of, 141
Talfourd, Mr. Justice, 251
Talleyrand, Prince de, 23, 104, 105, 205, 206, 282
Tankerville, Lady, 40, 41
Tapps, Mr., 143
Tascher de la Pagerie, Louis, 53
Tavistock, Lady, 76
Tavistock, Lord, afterwards 7th Duke of Bedford, q.v., 76, 82, 96, 127, 153, 154, 157, 159, 164, 172
Teissier, Baron de, 257, 262
Temple Church, 239
Temple, Richard Grenville, Lord, 191
Tennyson, Alfred, 71
Test Acts, Repeal of the, 57
Thames Tunnel, 36
Théâtre Français, 103
Thesiger, Frederick, later Lord Chancellor and 1st Lord Chelmsford, 194
Thiers, Louis-Adolphe, French statesman, 205, 206, 266, 272, 282
Thornton, John, 256
Tierney, George, M.P., 186
Times, The, 85, 144, 148, 158, 161, 174 178, 180, 183, 190, 201, 213, 214–19, 223, 238, 248, 266
Tintern Abbey, 169

Titchfield, Lord, eldest son of 4th Duke of Portland, 13, 14, 15, 26,

Torreno, 21

Tory Party, 66, 74, 78, 82, 84, 87, 90, 92, 94, 97, 98, 102, 116, 124, 127–30, 136, 148–52, 161, 172, 175, 186, 197, 202, 217, 227

Toulouse, Battle of, 146

Town, The (Periodical), 194

Tractarianism, 183, 240, 244, 250

Troy House (near Malvern), 167

Tuileries, 103

Turgot, Marquis de, French politician, 269

Turkey, 117, 181, 277, 286

Turner, Mr. (Keeper), 49

Two Thousand Guineas Race, 255, 259

Tyrrell, Sir John, Bt., M.P., 74, 75

Urquhart, David, M.P., 117

Usk, River, 168

Uxbridge, Lord, later 2nd Marquess of Anglesey, 2, 166

Vandamme, General, 53

Vansittart, Nicholas, Chancellor of Exchequer, 9

Vaudreuil, Vicomte de, 40, 44

Vaughan, Sir Charles, 117, 118

Vellore Mutiny, 15

Verulam, 1st Lord, 100

Victoria, Queen,
    as Princess, 113–18
    accession, 118, 119, 132
    as Queen, 198, 217, 234, 243, 247, 269
    character and early tendencies, 125, 127, 130
    disregards late King's family, 131
    receives Address of the Commons 137
    receives Melbourne's resignation, 149
    sends for Peel, 150
    refuses to change her Ladies of the Bedchamber, 151 ff.
    her feelings towards Melbourne, 156
    insulted by the Duchess of Montrose, 166
    appoints new Lady of the Bedchamber, 172
    her Scottich tour, 180
    pregnancy, 199
    willingness to receive Thiers, 206
    sees Peel with regard to Repeal of Corn Laws, 217
    sends for Russell, 220, 222, 223
    appoints him Prime Minister, 225
    accepts Russell's resignation and asks Peel to form Government, 230
    her devotion to Prince Albert and Melbourne, 248

Vienna, 246, 252

Villèle, M. de, 20, 22, 46

Villiers family, 61, 65, 182

Villiers, C. P., M.P., 200, 223

Villiers, Edward, 110, 182

Villiers, George, see Lord Clarendon

Villiers, Thomas Hyde, 75

Villiers, Mrs. George, 182, 228

Virginia Water, 45, 48

Vivian, Sir R. R., M.P., 163

Volnys, Madame, French actress, 103

Vyvyan, Sir R., M.P., 71

Wages, industrial, 210, 211

Wales, Prince of, 246

Walewski, Comte, French Foreign Minister, 268–71, 284

Walker, Dr., 77

Wall, C. B., M.P., 259

Walpole, Horace 185

Warren Hill, 138

Warrender, Sir George, 34

Warwick Castle, 129

Watford, 183, 184

Watson-Taylor, George, 30–2, 61, 187

Welbeck, 5, 13, 14, 255

Wellesley, Richard, Marquess, 6, 74, 75, 148

Wellington, Duke of, i, iii, 5, 7, 11, 16–18, 24, 27, 34–43, 50–7, 60–5, 68, 69, 73, 79–84, 89–100, 111, 113, 118–23, 138 ff., 144–53, 156, 160–3, 172, 174, 197, 202, 213, 216, 218, 238, 249, 274, 281

Wellington Memorial, 162

West India Committee, 263

West Indies, 25, 101, 250

Western, Charles, M.P., 1st Lord, 74, 89

Westminster, Dean of, *see* Buckland

Westminster Play, 239

Westmorland, Lady, 246

Wetherell, Sir Charles, M.P., 63

Wharncliffe, 1st Lord, leader of Waverers, 70, 71, 84, 87–93, 98, 152, 153, 188, 192, 193, 214–19, 242

Whersted, 5

Whig Party, 9, 66, 84, 95–8, 102, 116, 124, 127, 128, 150, 155, 158, 160, 172, 179, 186, 197, 202, 218, 233, 271, 275

White's Club, 106, 161

Whiting, John, 133

Wightman, Mr. Justice, 194

Wilberforce, William, 197

Wilde, 1st Lord, Lord Chancellor, 246, 251

William IV, i, iii,
    as Duke of Clarence, 1, 17, 18, 27, 122
    as King, 27 ff., 69, 70, 74, 81, 89, 92, 93, 97–100, 113–18, 133, 179
    his character, 121 ff.
    funeral, 126

Williams, Mr. Justice, 194

Willoughby de Eresby, 22nd Lord, 281

Wilton, 170

Wilton, 2nd Lord, 138, 146, 151

Winchilsea, 10th Lord, ii, iv, 99, 160

Winchester Racecourse, 134

Windcliffe, 169

Windham, William, M.P., statesman, 190, 197

Windsor, 25, 29, 36, 45, 116, 133, 179, 181, 187, 199, 220, 234, 271

Windsor, Dean of, *see* Hobart

Woburn, 58, 181, 201

Wolfe, General, 191

Wolverhampton, 164

Wood, Charles, M.P., later 1st Lord Halifax, 58, 88, 93, 223, 233, 234, 238, 242

Woolwich, 39

Worcester, Lady, death of, 4

Worcester, 2nd Marquess, 168

Worcester, Lord, *see* 7th Duke of Beaufort

Worcestershire, 74

Wortley, Lady Caroline, afterwards Lady Wharncliffe, 5

Württemberg, King of, 33, 34

Württemberg, Queen of, 36

Wyatt, Mr., 168, 169

Wye, River, 167–9

Wykeham, Sophia Elizabeth, later Baroness Wenman, 122

Wynn, C. W. Williams, 15, 38, 64, 68

Yarmouth, 129

Yellow Fever, 77

York, Archbishop of, *see* Harcourt

York, Duchess of, 281

York, Duke of, H.R.H., ii, 1, 2, 5, 8, 10, 13, 16, 18, 24, 27, 31, 49, 50, 122, 252

York Races, 280

Yorke, Sir J., 65

Young, probably T. or "Ubiquity", 61